ZERO SUM

'A magnificent book. A tour de force exploration of the rollercoaster story of Western capitalists and their misadventures in post-communist Russia, chronicling the hope, the naivety, the idealism, and the greed, arrogance and folly in glorious, highly readable detail. There has been no more thorough, moving or better-researched study of the epic cycle of the opening of Russia's economy in a blaze of ill-founded optimism in the early 90s to its closing in bitter recrimination and conflict in the wake of Putin's invasion of Ukraine. Tight and acutely observed with an expert reporter's eye, this book explains in forensic detail Russia's path, made of equal parts of hope and venality, from what could have become a prosperous, peaceful European nation to its descent into bandit capitalism and totalitarian kleptocracy.'

— Owen Matthews, author of
Overreach: the Inside Story of Putin's war on Ukraine

'Hecker captures all the adventure, greed and profound mismatch of business cultures that first enriched and then burned Western investors in post-Cold War Russia, a "Las Vegas with snow." *Zero Sum* opens a new window onto how the West's brief love affair with Russia could have gone so wrong, so fast.'

— Marc Champion, international affairs columnist and
former editor-in-chief of *The Moscow Times*

'A masterful guide to Russia's 1990s peaks and troughs, its 2000s apex and its contemporary valley between sanctions and Putin's steadily tightening economic grip. *Zero Sum* lifts the veil on the thinking behind Western investment in Russia, with invaluable lessons for designing future approaches to economic security.'

— Maximilian Hess, author of *Economic War:*
Ukraine and the Global Conflict between Russia and the West

'A gripping and fresh account of the geopolitics of Western economic engagement and extrication from Russia. Hecker expertly reveals why globalisation failed to transform the country and how so many Western observers misread the Kremlin's true calculus behind its 2022 invasion of Ukraine.'

— Alexander Cooley, Barnard College, Columbia University

'A detailed and lively chronicle of the challenges faced by Western businesses trying to pursue trade and investment in Russia.'

— Craig Kennedy, Center Associate, Davis Center for
Eurasian and Russian Studies, Harvard University

'Charles Hecker has written a rollicking, readable account of a more than 30-year era in global history, marked by heady risk taking and now a heavy reckoning on Russia. As the collective bet on Russia's future comes in for rethinking, Hecker's *Zero Sum* offers hard-earned and well-written lessons to business, government, and other institutional leaders.'

— John Gans, author of *White House Warriors: How the National Security*
Council Transformed the American Way of War

 NEW PERSPECTIVES ON EASTERN EUROPE
AND EURASIA

The states of Eastern Europe and Eurasia are once again at the centre of global attention, particularly following Russia's 2022 full-scale invasion of Ukraine. But media coverage can only do so much in providing the necessary context to make sense of fast-moving developments. The books in this series provide original, engaging and timely perspectives on Eastern Europe and Eurasia for a general readership. Written by experts on—and from—these states, the books in the series cover an eclectic range of cutting-edge topics relating to politics, history, culture, economics and society. The series is originated by Hurst, with titles co-published or distributed in North America by Oxford University Press, New York.

Series editor: Dr Ben Noble—Associate Professor of Russian Politics at University College London and Associate Fellow at Chatham House

CHARLES HECKER

Zero Sum

*The Arc of International Business
in Russia*

OXFORD

UNIVERSITY PRESS

Oxford University Press is a department of the
University of Oxford. It furthers the University's objective
of excellence in research, scholarship, and education
by publishing worldwide.

Oxford New York

Auckland Cape Town Dar es Salaam Hong Kong Karachi
Kuala Lumpur Madrid Melbourne Mexico City Nairobi
New Delhi Shanghai Taipei Toronto

With offices in

Argentina Austria Brazil Chile Czech Republic France Greece
Guatemala Hungary Italy Japan Poland Portugal Singapore
South Korea Switzerland Thailand Turkey Ukraine Vietnam

Oxford is a registered trade mark of Oxford University Press
in the UK and certain other countries.

Published in the United States of America by
Oxford University Press
198 Madison Avenue, New York, NY 10016

Library of Congress Cataloging-in-Publication Data is available

ISBN: 9780197807187

Printed in the USA

To the memory of my parents,
and to Judy.

CONTENTS

A NOTE ON SOURCES

The individuals interviewed for this book are speaking entirely in a personal capacity. Their comments do not reflect or represent the views or opinions of current or former employers.

A NOTE ON TRANSLITERATION AND TRANSLATION

In transliterating Russian words into English, I have opted for readability over the strictest of accuracy and have also used generally accepted transliterations where relevant. For example, Boris Yeltsin, not Boris El'tsin, was Russia's first president; glasnost, not glasnost', was the Soviet openness policy.

In directly quoted written texts, I have not changed spellings such as "Kiev" to "Kyiv". Elsewhere, I use modern Ukrainian spellings.

Some of the interviews in this book were conducted in Russian. Any translations are mine.

LIST OF INDIVIDUALS

(The following is a list of individuals interviewed for the book, in alphabetical order)

Rawi Abdelal – Former director of Harvard University's Davis Center for Russian and Eurasian Studies and the Herbert F. Johnson Professor of International Management at the Harvard Business School.

Nabi Abdullaev – Political journalist, newspaper editor and consultant who headed Control Risks' Moscow office until it closed following the start of the full-scale invasion of Ukraine.

Tom Adshead – Head of research at a strategic advisory consultancy who left Russia when the full-scale war in Ukraine broke out.

Oksana Antonenko – Former senior political counsellor at the European Bank for Reconstruction and Development (EBRD), think tank associate and consultant at Control Risks in London. Currently an independent geopolitical risk consultant.

Patti Baral – Former senior manager at a Russian brokerage firm.

Vladimir Borodin – Former editor-in-chief of *Izvestia*, one of Russia's largest daily newspapers, and co-founder of a popular group of steakhouses in Moscow and the Burger & Lobster restaurant chain. Now a serial entrepreneur and ESG advocate in New York.[1]

Maxim Boycko – Former deputy chief of staff to Boris Yeltsin, former deputy prime minister and an architect of privatisation, now a visiting lecturer in economics at Harvard.

William Burke-White – Founding director of Perry World House at the University of Pennsylvania and professor of law at Penn's law school.

Michael Calvey – Founding partner of Baring Vostok Capital Partners, also formerly of the EBRD. Arrested on politically motivated fraud charges in February 2019 and held for two months in pre-trial detention. Baring Vostok and Calvey have since exited Russia.

Roger Canton – Former banker with Credit Suisse First Boston.

Oliver Cescotti – Former senior executive with the German engineering company GEA Group and board member of the German–Russian Chamber of Commerce.

Robert Courtney – Founding board member of the American Chamber of Commerce in Russia, came to Russia in 1992 to open the American Medical Center clinic in Moscow.

Eric Crabtree – Former Russia country head and chief investment officer for the International Finance Corporation, a member of the World Bank Group.

Alexei Evgenev – Former head of the Moscow office of Alvarez & Marsal.

Tom Firestone – Former resident legal advisor at the US embassy in Moscow and attorney with an international law firm in Moscow. In 2013, the Russian government expelled Firestone from the country for allegedly refusing to cooperate with Russia's domestic intelligence agency.

Laurie Fry – Former senior finance executive in Russia at one of the world's largest brewing companies.

Tony Gambrill – Former director of training and development at the Metropol Hotel in Moscow, later worked in the Russian brokerage sector.

Andrew Glass – Former executive with a major US commodities trader in Russia.

Nigel Gould-Davies – Author and former UK ambassador to Belarus, now a senior fellow at the International Institute for Strategic Studies.

David Grant – Former hotel development executive, later a financial services executive.

Alexander Gubsky – Former deputy editor-in-chief of *Vedomosti*, Russia's leading business newspaper, and reporter for *The Moscow Times*' sister publication *Kapital*. Now publisher of *The Moscow Times* in Amsterdam.

Seva Gunitsky – Associate Professor of Political Science at the University of Toronto.

Hugh Hallard – Former director of sales and marketing at the Metropol Hotel in Moscow and the Grand Hotel Europe in St Petersburg.

Robyn Holt – Former president of Condé Nast's Russian operations and founder of Moscow's Vogue Café.

Harry Itameri – Former head of Russia, and most of the former Soviet republics, for Novo Nordisk, one of the world's leading manufacturers of insulin.

Jeff Kaye – Former trustee at the UK chapter of Transparency International.

Elizabeth Krasnoff – Former membership director at the American Chamber of Commerce in Russia, later the spokesperson for Dermajetics, the skin care division of Herbalife.

Stuart Lawson – Former CEO of HSBC in Russia and a long-serving senior executive in Russia's financial services community.

Hassan Malik – Financial historian now in investment management at Loomis, Sayles & Company, previously worked in Russia at the investment firm Troika Dialog.

Heidi McCormack – Former executive director for new ventures, Russia and CIS, at General Motors.

Paul Melling – Former partner at Baker McKenzie's Moscow office; now a senior partner at Melling, Voitishkin & Partners in Moscow.

Cameron Mitchell – Former head of geopolitical risk for HSBC in London.

Paul Moxness – Former global head of security for Radisson Hotels.

Philip Nichols – Joseph Kolodny Professor of Social Responsibility in Business and Professor of Legal Studies and Business Ethics at the University of Pennsylvania's Wharton School and a specialist on law, ethics and Russia.

Holly Nielsen – Former Moscow attorney, securities sector advisor and director on the Funds' Board at Baring Vostok Capital Partners.

Nicolas Ollivant – Former senior banker at the EBRD, later an executive in business intelligence consultancy and in commercial real estate services.

Mitchell Orenstein – Professor of Russian and East European Studies at the University of Pennsylvania.

Paul Ostling – Early executive in EY's Russia business, later the firm's global COO.

Brian O'Toole – Former US Treasury Department officer and now a non-resident fellow at the Atlantic Council.

Richard Prior – Executive with Kroll's Russia business and later the founder of a London-based business intelligence consultancy.

William Reichert – Former Moscow-based lawyer who relocated to Dubai in 2015 following the invasion of Crimea.

Alexis Rodzianko – Former president of the American Chamber of Commerce in Russia, also formerly of JP Morgan, Deutsche Bank, Credit Suisse and a Russian investment bank.

Robert Sasson – Former entrepreneur, EBRD official, private equity executive.

Derk Sauer – Owner and founder of *The Moscow Times*, also launched *Vedomosti*, the national business newspaper, in a tripartite joint venture with his company Independent Media, Pearson and Dow Jones.

Anton Shingarev – Former vice president at Yandex and Kaspersky, now serving as an adjunct professor at the University of Texas.

Robert Starr – Former partner at law firm Salans and of counsel at Dentons.

Timothy Stubbs – Partner at Dentons who started in Russia at a predecessor firm in 1991.

Bernie Sucher – Leading figure in Russian investment banking, helped found Troika Dialog and worked at Goldman Sachs, Alfa

Capital and Merrill Lynch. Now a cannabis industry advisor; also active in US electoral reform.

Joshua Tulgan – Investor relations and corporate finance executive with two decades of experience in Russia, now living in Dubai.

Alexandra Vacroux – Executive director of the Davis Center for Russian and Eurasian Studies at Harvard University, first went to Russia in the 1990s and joined Professor Graham Allison's team supporting Russian democratisation.[2]

Regina von Flemming – Former head of Axel Springer's Russian publishing business. Headed the Russian edition of Forbes following the 2004 murder of Paul Klebnikov, the magazine's then-chief editor. Former board member of the German Chamber of Commerce in Russia.

Sergey Vorobyev – Former Moscow head of the executive search consultancy Ward Howell in Russia and member of Club 2015, a group of senior Russian executives.

Christine Wootliff – Organised medical visits to Germany for Russians in the 1990s, later supported companies with complex pre-IPO road shows across the world's financial capitals.

Roman Zilber – Member of the management committee at Raiffeisen Bank in Russia until 2022.

PREFACE

What were we thinking?

A country had just angrily fractured into its constituent pieces. Its monolithic politics had dissolved into a riotous carnival. Its rigid, hyper-centralised economy crumpled and struggled to put food on the table. A polarised geopolitical world became demagnetised and turned enemies into, well, no one really knew what. Criminals roamed the streets and strolled the corridors of power.

Opportunity was everywhere.

The unravelling of the Soviet Union ended more than seventy years of revolution, isolation, rivalry, détente and desperation. The emergence of a fragile, feverish Russian Federation as its most prominent successor was one of the most dramatic and traumatic events of the twentieth century. The USSR was dead; Russia was something new, maybe something promising, brought forth from the cathartic combination of perestroika's economic restructuring, the political openness of glasnost and an enticing law on joint ventures.

The events of 1991—Boris Yeltsin standing on a tank, the Soviet flag slowly coming down over the Kremlin—shimmered across cable TV screens in front of a globalising audience. By then, companies were going places they had never been to before. Markets once considered too far, too dangerous or too primitive were becoming hot spots.

It was time to go to Russia. Executives around the world bought heavy boots and overcoats and got on planes. They were met by a country curious about and suspicious of foreigners but starved of investment and eager to get as rich as everyone everywhere else.

Over the course of thirty years, three presidents, eleven prime ministers, two financial crashes, two cross-border wars and millions of shots of vodka, Russia went from a mysterious, opaque frontier to a complex-but-manageable place to do deals. It was exhilarating, it was scary; it was never, ever boring. Roughly during a single generation, companies and the people who ran them created, and sometimes destroyed, enormous wealth.

And then it was all over, even more brutally than it began.

Maybe the end came gradually and then suddenly, along the famous line from Hemingway. Few people in business or politics predicted that in 2022 Vladimir Putin would send the Russian army over the border toward Kyiv. When he did, it was as if the world had suddenly started to speak an unfamiliar, new language. All our reference points about how countries and companies interact were suddenly unrecognisable. It was a disorienting shock to the system, corporate and corporal. All the assumptions the international business community made about Russia, even as they had evolved and matured over the past thirty or so years, came under crushing pressure.

In the wake of the full-scale invasion of Ukraine, some companies fled Russia, incurring enormous financial costs. Other companies chose to stay in Russia, attracting enormous reputational costs. Companies in limbo between staying and leaving say they are trapped—wanting to get out but not knowing how best to do it or whether it's worth it. None of these decisions are simple or straightforward. They all involve compromise and sacrifice. Each of them is taken under a global microscope.

No other market of this magnitude has opened and closed in the space of a generation. The debut of the Russian market was a global sensation. The events that sparked its closing generated a global debacle.

What signals did we miss? What signals did we ignore? How much did we really know about Russia? How much did we really want to know about Russia, as long as the annual reports were upbeat?

This is the story of what the international business community was thinking about Russia from the moment the country opened its doors to foreign investment in the early 1990s to the moment the market painfully and imperfectly shut. It is a story about careful planning and incautious adventure in equal amounts. It is a story about diligent, deliberate choices and staggering simplification. It is a story about professional dilemmas without easy answers.

Russia is a place that provokes strong opinions. To some, it is an evil empire, an enemy to be defeated or at least isolated. To others, it is a vast place with a complex history that demands understanding and engagement. These views are not mutually exclusive—they sometimes gain or lose weight in response to events. Anyone who thought the Russia story was going away— as has been suggested from time to time—is and will be gravely mistaken. Anyone seeking black and white in this story will be disappointed. This is a dissection of uncertainty.

Most companies, like most people, do not thrive in conditions of uncertainty. Making money out of chaos, as discussed later in this book, requires a voracious risk appetite and the ability to make difficult decisions, sometimes in extreme circumstances. Throughout this book, you will read about organisations that made difficult decisions driven by countless considerations.

Some of those decisions bred spectacular success. Others, less so.

This is a story made possible by dozens of interviews with the pioneering men and women who did business in or with Russia, who studied and analysed Russia, and who helped Russia transition from its Soviet past. There are fewer women in this book than men; that is a reflection, broadly speaking, of the gender balance of the international executive community in Russia.

This story is also made possible by my own experience, initially as a student, then as a reporter at *The Moscow Times* and later in the London and Moscow offices of an international risk consultancy. An education to master's level in Russian and Soviet studies gave me the academic preparation I needed for those jobs; continuing education came courtesy of the boulevards and boardrooms of Moscow.

This is also a story told in hindsight, a book about things that have already happened. With a few exceptions, the book roughly follows the calendar as capital and capitalists flowed into and out of Russia. There are brief detours to the tsarist and Soviet periods, and side excursions into globalisation, Moscow's torrid night life, Putinism and the almost-sexy world of compliance. Wherever possible, the voices in this book have acknowledged the luxury of reflection and used it sparingly and wisely. The book ends with a look to the future.

Could the Russia story have evolved differently? Possibly, but be careful what you ask for. Endings can be better, or they can be worse. Could Russia have traced a different trajectory, and settled in comfortably as an equal at the G8 and the G20? On balance, probably not. And now, given Russia's ongoing brutalisation of Ukraine, probably not for a long time to come.

It is safe to say that just about everyone, including international companies, wanted Russia's story to follow a different course.

But the ingredients were never there at the right time or in the right quantities. Global history and its intricate geopolitical rivalries; business, competition and cooperation; foreign and domestic politics; local and distant personalities; and political institutions—or lack thereof—never lined up properly.

Going forward, as international companies urgently seek stability in a period of unending and intersecting disruption, what is the chance of any of these elements ever being present in the right place at the right time, in Russia or elsewhere?

If this book addresses any of those questions adequately, then please thank the vast generosity of the individuals who lived and worked in Russia and then shared their stories. (And please read the acknowledgements.) Some of these people are friends, some of them are strangers and some of them are people I've worked with or met along the way during forty years of personal and professional engagement with Russia.

If this book falls short of adequately discussing any of the questions it raises—or indeed fails to raise the right questions—then those shortcomings are all my own.

1

THE PHONE RINGS

Look what it took to get business out of Russia. It took a war.[1]

None of us, no one, would have imagined this. As bad as things ever got in Russia, no one would have expected this.[2]

Business class, in reverse

Paul Melling was sitting in a Frankfurt-bound Aeroflot Airbus. The usual pre-departure procedures were under way; boarding was complete, the door closed, and he was reminded to fasten his seatbelt. Melling, an international lawyer and decades-long Moscow resident, was enjoying a complimentary, business-class glass of orange juice as the plane started to push back.

And then it stopped. A few metres from the gate. And sat there. After a while, the pilot announced the flight was cancelled.

There was no technical fault. It was 27 February 2022, and EU airspace had just closed to Russian airlines. Three days earlier, Russia unleashed its full-scale invasion of Ukraine; the Western retaliation had begun. Melling had already been blocked from going to London directly—UK airspace had closed to Russian aircraft two days earlier.

Like most travellers, Melling had never gone through Russian airport procedures in reverse—he had to deplane and replicate the arrivals routine, never having left. The process, including a new trip through passport control, took hours.

"I remember walking back through Terminal C, the new terminal at Sheremetyevo Airport, watching the lights go out on the departures board, one by one, as one flight after another was cancelled, realising that my professional life as I had known it was well and truly over," Melling said. He managed to leave for Dubai the following day. "Thirty-three years living and working in Moscow, opening and building one of Russia's premier law firms—all over in four days."[3]

A few days later, international legal giant Baker McKenzie—in line with dozens of accountancies, consulting firms and law firms across Moscow—announced it was leaving Russia. The Moscow office had been Melling's professional home since the firm opened for business in the Soviet Union in 1989.

"I had become personally convinced that we would never leave," said Melling, "but the politicians and the pressure groups were demanding swift action, and my firm had little choice."

Heading for the exits

For weeks after the start of the full-scale invasion, Moscow's main airports were scenes of pandemonium. Russians and expats barrelled toward the exits; the fastest way out was by plane. Business-class tickets were wiped out instantly, even as prices added extra digits. Whole families came to the airport with more suitcases than they had hands and feet, wanting to take their entire lives with them and spending exorbitant sums of money on excess baggage.

Once EU (and UK and US) airspace closed, if you wanted to get from Russia to almost anywhere else in Europe, you needed to depart primarily from Moscow and from there fly mostly through Dubai on Emirates or through Istanbul on Turkish Airlines. Onward connections from Dubai and Istanbul's megahubs would take you to the West, or anywhere else. Emirates and Turkish Airlines laid on extra flights to respond to hurtling demand. In the days and weeks immediately following the full-scale invasion, and in September 2022, after Russia announced a partial mobilisation of citizens registered for the draft, flights sold out in minutes.

If you couldn't get to Dubai or Istanbul, you went through Tbilisi, Yerevan, Tel Aviv or Almaty, cities that still had open routes. Those places also had relatively more straightforward immigration rules compared with Western Europe. This was important to the Russians leaving Russia. Russian citizens desperate to leave bought tickets to wherever they could. Some stayed wherever they landed. Some expats left for home; others took transfers to offices outside Russia. Some stayed.

Planes, trains and automobiles. And buses

"The day before the invasion, I was out in Moscow. I was wandering around with a mate, you know, had brunch or coffee or something. And it's February, so it's dark and it's grey. But there was a mood. I remember we were walking around in the centre of Moscow, and I was thinking 'I do not like this. I don't like the mood,'" David Grant said. Grant, a Londoner, had been in Moscow for almost two decades, working in hotel development and later in financial services. He spoke Russian. He wasn't an expat: Moscow was home.

Grant, like so many others, repeated the logic of the day: "Nothing's going to happen. They surely wouldn't be so extreme to do something crazy like that."

And then:

"I woke up on the morning of the 24th and, as I do when I wake up, grabbed my phone and looked at the news and shot up in bed and thought 'They've done what?,'" Grant said. "I just could not believe what I was reading."

"It's just one of those moments that you know life is changed irreversibly," he said:

> I'd been there over nineteen years. All my suitcases were up on the top of the wardrobe. I got showered and I looked at them, got the stepladder and got them all down. And I looked at them throughout the day, thought about it for a while and the next day started packing to leave.

"And then all the banks stopped working as they had done because of capital controls, and you couldn't transfer money out and the currency was sliding and I had rouble deposits," Grant said.

Beyond that, he had two dominant thoughts in his head: he would either be forced to leave Russia or unable to leave Russia. He felt like he had to make a choice while he still could. He thought about his Moscow apartment. The furniture was all his. The closets were full of his clothes. He had equipped a kitchen that, like every kitchen in Moscow, was the centre of his home.

He gave his landlady the keys to the apartment where he had lived for twelve years. He spent two nights at a Moscow Hilton tying up loose ends, including such banalities as cancelling his internet service:

> Within two and a half weeks, I'd packed up, thrown away, sold or shipped back to London twenty years of life and belongings. I was working eighty hours a week while trying to tie up as many loose ends as I could before leaving my life in Moscow. I didn't sleep more than an hour or two a night because of the anxiety of it all. I also didn't manage to say goodbye in person to almost anyone I knew. There just wasn't time.

European airspace had closed before Grant would have headed to the airport. He left Russia on a train from Moscow to St Petersburg, a bus from St Petersburg to Helsinki and a plane from Helsinki to London.

"People were hanging from the rafters on the train," he said. Similarly suspended were his thoughts about his job, though early conversations with his boss suggested a work-from-home solution, wherever home finally made itself.

He spent two nights at a hotel in St Petersburg and caught a bus at what he recalls being 4 a.m. He was searched thoroughly at Russian customs—he had exactly the legal limit in cash, but more important was his collection of watches, a personal hobby. To his relief, the customs officers overlooked the bag stuffed with keepsakes.

He got on the coach and fell asleep. Before it left, he was awakened by pounding on the bus door.

"A couple of young people were trying to board the coach without a ticket and without a visa to get into Finland," he said.

"We refuse to live in this country, we don't want to be a part of this," were their sole credentials for trying to leave Russia, Grant said. They were refused boarding, and the bus pulled out.

"I got to Helsinki Airport, and I mean I was just physically and emotionally done by that point. I checked in my suitcase, had the most expensive cheeseburger I've ever had in my life and I FaceTimed a friend from university who is a Finn," Grant said.

"They [the Finns] have got a very unique relationship with Russia, so he was glad to see I was out and that I was in his hometown on the way home to the UK." Grant boarded the plane for London.

"We landed at Heathrow, I got my suitcase, sat down in arrivals waiting for my mate to come and pick me up in the car. And I cried my eyes out."

Upon his return, London was freshly unfamiliar to Grant, despite his periodic visits. This is a phenomenon many long-term overseas residents notice. When you leave somewhere for a long time, even a place you know well, it moves on without you. And while you're away, your experiences start to diverge from those of the people you've left behind. The meeting in Russia that Grant had over a bear-skin rug, and the time he was offered a Kalashnikov as a token of appreciation, set him apart from peers in London, where those sorts of practices are, well, less likely.

Most foreign residents who wanted to leave eventually did. Family circumstances or other considerations made that choice and that process difficult, and more, much more, than a handful of international residents stayed. Life for foreign residents in Russia—particularly getting in and out in the early days—became uncertain and unfamiliar. The full-scale war that exploded following years of fighting in the Donbas and the illegal annexation of Crimea was a shock to the international business community in Russia.

(Almost) no one saw it coming

The build-up of Russian troops on the border with Ukraine prior to the invasion triggered enormous apprehension among international companies in Russia. But the analytical community assured them the likelihood of invasion was low. Putin appeared to be scoring significant foreign policy and security concessions just by looking ready to invade. Foreign leaders shuttled back and forth to Moscow offering a menu of strategic reassurances.[4]

Only the US intelligence community, supported by its UK counterparts, suggested that an invasion was likely.[5] But after the fiasco of the US withdrawal from Afghanistan in 2021, no one was lending much credence to what the Defense Department and CIA were saying.

It later emerged that Putin had included only his closest, most hard-line confidants in planning the invasion.[6] Launching a full-scale ground war in Europe not only rocked international business and diplomatic circles; it shook Russia's political and economic elite to its core.

Assaults on the elite

The grainy images of the brutal purges of the Stalin era are now faded archival material. They show how Russia's most violent dictator and his henchmen corralled their own elite into corrupt courtrooms, charged them ludicrously with treason and sent them to rapid death by execution or slow death in prison camps.

The high-definition broadcast of the 21 February 2022 Russian Security Council meeting borrows some of the more subtle touches of the purges. That day, Putin assembled the apex of Russia's political elite, and one by one, from his pandemic-era distance across a grand, colonnaded hall, asked whether they supported independence for Donetsk and Luhansk, the regions of Eastern Ukraine in conflict since 2014. This was one of the technical pretexts for the full-scale invasion.

Putin was fidgety and impatient but had the clenched appearance of someone boiling with rage. His audience, arrayed in a semi-circle around the chamber, looked as if they might be trembling. Their faces were ashen and sullen; their eyes focused downward on their nervously shifting feet. Each of them, in front of a leader planning to unfurl deadly force on a sovereign nation, said they supported recognising Donetsk and Luhansk.

This is what terror looks like. This is what forced confessions look like. It was a show trial, but the entire nation wound up with the rigged sentence.

Around that time but before the full-scale invasion, the Harvard Club of Russia asked Alexandra Vacroux to give a talk. Vacroux first went to Russia in the early 1990s and is now the executive director of the Davis Center for Russian and Eurasian Studies at Harvard University. The Davis Center, previously known as the Russian Research Center, was one of the first academic departments in the US for the study of the Soviet Union. It is more than seventy-five years old.

As the threat of war grew louder, the Harvard Club retitled Vacroux's session to "Why Does the West Think That Russia Will Invade Ukraine?"—wording with a hint of embedded scepticism.

"They did not believe that Putin would be so stupid to try and invade," Vacroux said.[7] "I don't think the Russians saw the war coming the week before the war."

The global stupor of disbelief following the start of the war on 24 February reminded Vacroux of a Tintin postcard, where the Belgian comic hero accidentally walks into a lamppost and is sent reeling with stars circling around his head.

"We are so stupid. We totally did not see this," Vacroux said. "And we kind of got it wrong because we were making these assumptions about what's possible. And we neglected that he might try to do something impossible."

"Fundamentally, a lot of people try and understand Russia with their Western eyes and sensibilities," Vacroux said.

First looks

The story of trying to understand modern Russia with Western eyes and sensibilities lasted thirty years.

In the beginning, foreign governments pushed their companies and financiers to invest in newly open Russia. Business needed little encouragement. It became impossible—no, irresponsible— to ignore Russia as the world's latest, and one of its biggest, emerging markets. Companies saw every development—a new McDonald's here, a Snickers billboard there—as a sign the country was reforming. And not just reforming but becoming more like ... us. Communist Party General Secretary and Soviet President Mikhail Gorbachev brought perestroika and glasnost. Yeltsin in 1991 stared a communist coup into submission. Privatisation was moving companies from state control to a nascent, stumbling private sector. Russians started travelling abroad, and travellers started coming to Russia.

In 1993, Daniel Yergin and Thane Gustafson, two of the most learned observers of the Soviet Union and Russia, wrote a book called *Russia 2010 and What It Means for the World*. The book describes a series of scenarios depicting how Russia might develop. It also acknowledged the cavernous political, economic, ideological and even "identity" hole in which Russia had found itself following the Soviet collapse.

Yergin and Gustafson envisioned a set of scenarios for Russia's future over a time horizon to 2010. It's unfair to hold them up to scrutiny with the benefit of hindsight. But that is the beauty of scenarios—they are emphatically not predictions. Instead, they are possible versions of the future specifically designed to be neither right nor wrong, but to make us think. That said, anyone who has ever written a scenario is secretly pleased when real-world developments ultimately match their assumptions.

It is also unfair to summarise an influential and carefully written book from two powerhouse authors in a few paragraphs. But here goes.

Yergin and Gustafson asked us to think whether Russia could ever develop into a democracy; they were pessimistic. They also asked whether the country could develop a market economy. When they were writing *Russia 2010*, the picture was about as grim as it could get. A "bazaar," they point out, is not always a market.[8]

Their first scenario, "Muddling Down," tells a story of ongoing and chaotic decline. This pessimistic scenario nevertheless harbours the seeds of its redemption: the decline is taking place in emerging market conditions, from which Russia could emerge, as the writers put it, by "muddling up."[9]

Another scenario, "The Two-Headed Eagle," a reference to Russia's national symbol, envisions the return of the "central government," supported by "an alliance of private finance and industrial managers, with the army and the police."[10] Not too far off, really, for 2010.

The "Time of Troubles" is the next scenario; Yergin and Gustafson call this a "family of scenarios," and none of them is good.[11] The Time of Troubles label is in homage to the traumatic interregnum after the death of Ivan the Terrible's son and successor, Fyodor I, in the sixteenth century, before the establishment of the Romanov dynasty.

Finally, there is "Chudo," the Russian economic "miracle," where the name—*chudo* means miracle in Russian—sort of says it all. This miracle depended on a lot of things happening in the right way at the right time, starting with the politics and ending with the business environment.[12]

Whether they predicted Russia to 2010 correctly, Yergin and Gustafson called one thing on the nose, if you're slightly generous on timing, considering Russia illegally annexed Crimea in 2014: "The biggest danger of all is conflict between Russia and Ukraine," they wrote, citing the "many contentious issues" between the two nations.[13] Crimea was a tense flashpoint in the early 1990s as its status remained uncertain following the collapse of the Soviet Union; the territory remained with the new Ukrainian state via a political, not military, solution.[14]

Yergin and Gustafson's most important reminder, however, is how complex the ingredients of a country's future can be. They asked us, among many other things, to think about the balance between the centre and the regions in Russia; the balance between the state and the private sector; the funds to propel Russia's transition; the scope of Russia's political and social environment; and, as is the case in so many countries around the world, the ability to build stable political and economic institutions.[15]

They also threw down a major question on the relationship between international investors and Russia:

> What role will there be, in a new Russia, for Western business and investment? Foreign companies are trying to decide whether investment in Russia will be a prudent bet on the future, or money thrown down a black hole. What strategies are available for the foreign investor, and what kind of risks will an investor encounter? The answers depend on how quickly Russia can create the legal, financial, and institutional bases for foreign investment. Foreign investors will certainly encounter one fundamental obstacle: Russians themselves are unsure whether they really want Western investment, and are struggling among themselves over this question.[16]

Their description of the partly practical, partly philosophical thought process at work in the international business community was borderline clairvoyant. Western business was already on the ground when the Soviet Union collapsed, and although the country's pieces lay in total disarray, opportunity was in the air.

In the late 1990s, Sergey Vorobyev was the head of the Ward Howell executive search consultancy in Russia and a member of Club 2015. The club brought together senior Russian executives, many from inside international companies, who were seeking to transform the Russian business environment, promote Russia globally and develop a new social contract domestically. Founded in 1999, the club devised three scenarios for how its members saw Russia evolving to 2015 and worked to bring the best-case scenario to life.

The club's best-case scenario, "The New Social Contract," envisioned Russia acknowledging the flaws in its current social contract, reforming its power structures and entering into a new agreement with Russian society. The second was called "The Tale of Lost Time," in which Russia rises along with global economic growth but falls short of entering "the big leagues." The worst-case scenario was called "The Final Imperial Leap," and "MegaSerbia," which looked at the trauma of the collapse of empire, using as an analogy the downfall of Yugoslavia and the chaos, hostility and violent nationalism that rose in its wake. Russia never escaped the economic and psychological "national depression" of the 1990s and found itself in "the trap of imperial nationalism."

Vorobyev takes very little consolation in having the club's worst-case scenario come true.

"We tried to influence Russia as best we could," he said.[17]

Irrational actors, 2022

The theory of the rational political actor—someone who predictably acts in their nation's best interests—argued against the idea that Putin would pull the trigger. No one thought it was in Russia's best interest to invade Ukraine.

It was especially against Russia's interests from a business perspective, reflecting the view in commercial circles that Russia was more a market than a political or military entity. This is the line of thinking based on, among other things, *New York Times* columnist Thomas Friedman's 1996 suggestion that two countries with McDonald's have never declared war on each other.[18] More broadly, electoral democracies are not supposed to wage war on each other, an idea first hinted at by German philosopher Immanuel Kant at the end of the eighteenth century. More recently, in executive offices across Europe, in the US and in Asia, Russia was a component in the EMEA acronym linking markets in Europe, the Middle East and Africa. And markets don't declare war—a notion that only added to the shock of what was happening.

Surely the cost to Putin and Russia of an invasion would be astronomical; surely, Putin knew it. If he did invade, perhaps he would venture only a minor border incursion into the Donbas and test the international community's reaction. A handful of hawks had been predicting worst-case scenarios including a full-scale invasion; the end of 2021 and the beginning of 2022 brought moments of vein-popping tension. But a ground war in Europe? Decades of relative peace on the continent—the Balkans as the standout exception—had gradually crowded the thought from our collective minds.

"The fact that he would do something that would in essence damage enormously Russia's economic and political prospects with the West now and for many years to come, made no sense to those people that thought of him as a rational actor," said Stuart Lawson, former CEO of HSBC in Russia and a long-serving senior executive in the financial services community there. "So the fundamental misunderstanding was he's going to act rationally. And if he was acting rationally, he wouldn't have done what he did."[19]

If Putin wasn't a rational actor, perhaps he was more of a pragmatic actor.

"There was a tendency to treat him, not necessarily as a rational actor, but as a pragmatic actor," said Seva Gunitsky, associate professor of political science at the University of Toronto. "That perception disappeared almost immediately after the invasion." Gunitsky himself said he did not see something like the full-scale invasion coming, though he had thought that if it did, "it would be a disaster."

No single factor drove the decision to invade, Gunitsky said, in a view widely shared among academics and analysts. "We're all speculating here. When you read the actual account, from what little we've been able to see ... historical grievance, indignation at Western influence, what might have happened is that he isolated with COVID and was reading too much Russian history."

"It's never a good idea for an isolated ruler to read about a country's history. They start getting some very bad ideas," Gunitsky said, adding that Putin was probably also developing errant ideas about Russia's military capability.

"He was, and is, in an informational bubble," Gunitsky said. "It was the historical grievances about Russia and Ukraine not being two separate countries. It's not a calculus that we understand, but there is some calculus." As the full-scale invasion got under way, Putin delivered a speech to the nation espousing the view that Ukraine had no claim to nationhood separate from Russia.[20]

Others suggested that NATO expansion—including the possibility of one day including Ukraine—provoked Russia and left Putin with little choice but to attack. These views were espoused by a wide range of academic and other analysts and gained traction among international businesspeople who had lived and worked in Russia and knew the country well.[21] One of them was Alexis Rodzianko, a former president of the American Chamber of Commerce in Russia. Rodzianko said that if the US were in Russia's position, it would have behaved similarly.

"Imagine Mexico doing a military alliance with Russia, and putting missiles on the border with the US, and just for good measure, Canada joins in," Rodzianko said. "You know the US. It wouldn't last a week."[22]

"A low likelihood event"

Think tanks, governments, consultancies, journalists and geopolitical analysts all over the world frantically tried to grasp what might happen as Russian troops in the spring of 2021 began to assemble near the border with Ukraine. The business community wanted to hear how bad things could get, and whether they should be packing their bags.

In a chorus, the geopolitical risk business was saying "nothing to see here." The business community remained nervous but reassured that the worst-case scenario—a full-on invasion and a war—was a "low likelihood event."

At the Moscow offices of Alvarez & Marsal, an international consultancy, Alexei Evgenev and his colleagues put together a few scenarios—they were more like predictions, as they had likelihoods attached to them—to help the firm's clients evaluate the likelihood of war.

"We're paranoid by nature because of what we do,"[23] Evgenev said. "We started contingency planning in November, four months before the war."

The most likely scenario, one that Evgenev gave 50 per cent probability, was "it will just blow over." Their second most likely scenario, at 40 per cent probability, was that Russia would invade the Donbas, where Russian proxies had been fighting Ukrainian forces since 2014.

"We put 10 per cent for an all-out war," he said.

Crisis management

And then Russian troops trampled the Ukrainian border, reminding a globalised world that the thin black lines between countries once again mattered. Companies with crisis management plans enacted them.

There were very few of these companies.

Phones started to ring at headquarters and in security response centres. Executives in Ukraine, in Russia and around the world wanted to know whether or how they or their companies could or should get out.

From there, the questions multiplied. What do we do with expats? What do we do with local employees? Where should they go, and how would they get there? What will happen to our customers, our suppliers, our factories, our offices?

What would happen to our reputations?

The expats who wanted to go headed for the border, by land, sea or air. Initially, the companies stayed. On the mind of many companies was the Russian invasion of Georgia in 2008, which lasted a few days.

"About six weeks after the start of the war, it became clear that this was no Blitzkrieg and that Ukraine wasn't going to surrender and that this was possibly going long term," said Nabi Abdullaev, the head of Control Risks' Moscow office until it closed following the war. "And we started getting requests for help in leaving Russia."

After the first year of the full-scale invasion, more Finnish companies fully exited Russia—as a proportion of a nation's overall business presence—than businesses from any other country.[24] Decades of trading with the Soviet Union and Russia taught them how to monitor a crisis and when to say it was time to go. Abdullaev and his team helped Finnish and other Nordic companies track triggers that would mark the moment to leave. Many of the biggest investors and the bold-faced brands left early, before there were any restrictions on market exit.

That turned out to be a smart move: companies that stayed soon found themselves facing rapidly worsening terms and conditions for remaining. Putin nationalised the Russian operations of some of the world's most famous brands. Companies that stayed in Russia but weren't nationalised could no longer send profits back to headquarters.

"The earlier you left, the better," Abdullaev said. "Everyone has lost, except for the companies who got out first. Even the companies that stayed and are making some sort of profit have lost, because they can't get them out."

As the war ground on, and as NATO countries and the G7 started to send Ukraine financial and military aid, Russia's attitude toward its international investors grew increasingly sour. In August 2022, the Russian government formed a state commission to set the terms and conditions for leaving Russia. When the commission first began examining company exits, it granted permission without too much difficulty, Abdullaev said. That more or less benign environment did not last.

Putin blocks the exits

As the conflict worsened, so did the government's terms. The Kremlin was especially eager to lock in companies that supplied Russian strategic industries or provided critical support to the Russian population, such as pharmaceutical manufacturers, Abdullaev said.

The commission's terms bordered on corporate sadism: companies exiting the market would be sold at 50 per cent of their value, after an assessment from an appraiser on an approved government list. Companies exiting Russia would also have to give 10 per cent—later raised to 15 per cent—of the transaction to the Russian treasury. That was painful—transferring money to the Russian government sounded a lot like funding the war.

Once a company signalled its intent to leave, buyers would start to line up. That was the next problem. It was bad enough that the government was shaking down some of its biggest investors on the way out. Finding a buyer was another thing. The entire endeavour of leaving Russia was starting to resemble a massive redistribution of wealth, and that's using the polite expression. It was, in part, the privatisation process of the 1990s held up to a carnival mirror.

Putin was keen to cut his loyalists into this redistribution, but that presented a problem. If you were a true friend of Putin, you were likely under sanctions. Western companies would not be able to transact with anyone under sanctions, even if it was solely to exit Russia.

Putin could also re-distribute foreign-owned assets via nationalisation. The Russian Duma, the lower house of parliament, gave him the power to impose "temporary administration" on companies starting 1 January 2024.[25] There is legal debate about whether this amounts to nationalisation, but if you're in that kind of debate already, it's probably too late.

Beyond Putin's favoured circle, though, there was no shortage of phenomenally rich Russians who weren't sanctioned.

"Take for example the Russian Forbes list," Abdullaev said, naming the Russian equivalent of the famous Forbes list of wealthy business titans. "Many in the first fifty surnames are toxic from sanctions and reputational points of view, but there are 110 names in the Russian Forbes list with more than a billion dollars, so there are still at least sixty people" with enough money to buy foreign companies. "There's still a huge group of people with a pile of money."[26]

Oliver Cescotti was a senior executive with Germany's GEA Group, an engineering company, for more than fifteen years in Russia, until 2021. Once the war started, he acted as a consultant to another German company and assisted with its exit from Russia. This work brought him directly into the economic and political blast furnace that is the inner workings of the state commission adjudicating the sale of Western assets. He said the process was full of "vultures" competing against each other.[27]

The process Cescotti described sounded like a mosh pit of government officials and private investors pillaging some of Russia's best international companies to "get a piece of the cake of foreign assets being sold off with gigantic discounts." The process, he said, was full of artificial obstacles designed to direct the outcome toward one or another interested group.

Somebody's watching you

The Russian government started monitoring certain companies' behaviour on the market; any dramatic changes in company profile—production volume or product assortment, for example—triggered a crackdown. Market insiders told Abdullaev that Danone's problems started when state monitors noticed the French dairy giant had cut the variety of products it was putting on grocery shelves. In some cases, simply declaring an intention to leave was enough to trigger the government.

No matter what the industry, if the Kremlin began to suspect that critical supply chains—far beyond yoghurt—were at risk and jeopardising powerful Russian partners like Gazprom, the government put these companies under "temporary administration," Abdullaev explained. De facto, the companies were nationalised.

"This is like Venezuela," a source in the Moscow business community told the *Financial Times*. "They're giving the best to their cronies ... and then everything will go to shit."[28]

The nuclear panic button

At the outset of the full-scale invasion, few people anticipated retaliatory military strikes from Kyiv—returning fire onto Russian territory threatened an escalation bordering on suicidal. But as hostilities progressed, talk of a different escalation, between Russia and NATO, grew. Speculation surrounded the likelihood of an East–West war between Russia and NATO and the possibility that it could rampage out of control into a nuclear confrontation. Putin was already hinting he was ready to use a tactical nuclear weapon in the conflict.[29]

A rational view suggested that US President Joe Biden would keep his finger off the nuclear button and seek de-escalation. No one thought he would swap Chicago for Kyiv. But rational thinking at the outset of the war was surprisingly sparse. Nuclear hysterics were rife. In the eyes of the international business community, Russia was starting to look and feel as unsafe as Ukraine.

It was easy enough for companies to declare that the personal safety of their employees was their most important consideration. After that, it got messy.

Now what do we do?

International companies in Moscow, St Petersburg and in some of Russia's other major cities and industrial sites were reaching a critical decision. The safety and security of their people, both expats and locals, were the main issues, but the safety and security of assets and other tangibles were a close second.

Local employees of Western companies who didn't, or couldn't, leave in the early days waited to hear what their companies might do for them. Some of them even asked their employers for evacuation assistance or expected it would come without asking.[30] Russian businesspeople often went to work in international companies with the specific expectation that they would be treated better than in a Russian company, not only in terms of career development but precisely in crisis moments like this.

Certain Russian companies—the ones under Kremlin pressure to prevent brain drain—told their employees to stay put.[31] Russia's most agile employees are its young IT workers, the software engineers who need little more than a laptop and a pair of Converse All Stars to do their job. They grabbed their passports and their charger packs and legged it. Russia's more digitised domestic companies and more than a few IT departments started to hollow out.

Working from home is one thing, but when home becomes Kazakhstan, it becomes a problem for the Russian economy. The security departments inside Russian companies were easily able to detect who was logging in from abroad and sent out a message: come back to work in Russia or resign.[32] This employee-retention strategy turned out to be less successful than the government and its national champions had hoped. People still left. Since then, the Russian government's treatment of its exiles has grown exponentially harsher and more punitive. In February 2024, the Russian parliament passed a law designed to punish people who discredit the Russian army via the use of "fakes" or are deemed to have made statements that threaten national security. There is no specific crime in leaving the country. Individuals who discredit the army via the use of fakes, or who threaten national security and leave the country, are liable to seizure by the state of property used in the defamatory or threatening statements. So, if you leave Russia and keep quiet, nothing happens. You can even come back, no problem. But if you leave Russia and make illegal statements—even before leaving—the state can take your property.[33]

What is to be done?

After the first few days of the war, the Russian army began to comically underperform, but even so, bombs were falling on Ukraine. Companies needed to make critical judgement calls, but the decision-making process in large organisations, even in times of acute crisis, is usually far too slow and complicated. And even in the dire situation unfolding between Russia and Ukraine, companies had to consider multiple, and sometimes conflicting, obligations and stakeholders.

Obligations to whom? And for what? Were international companies most indebted to their employees in Ukraine and Russia, or were they more obligated to their customers, their regulators and their shareholders? At stake were decisions that had potentially high-profile and high-impact financial, operational, reputational and humanitarian dimensions. Each company established a hierarchy.

And then the West began to howl in protest at the war, and the pressure piled up. Employees in more progressive companies around the world, but especially in the US, clamoured for a rapid exit from a country run by a president bent on industrial-scale murder. For years, companies were being told with increasing fervour and frequency that they needed to have humane and compassionate values. They were now being told that an ongoing presence in Russia violated those values.

The annexation of Crimea in 2014, another inflection point for the international business community in Russia, paled in comparison to what was happening now. It was time to go. Attendance at the June 2022 St Petersburg International Economic Forum, a glitzy fixture on the international business calendar nicknamed the "Russian Davos," plummeted. For almost all the forum's years prior to the war, it was one of the most glamorous venues for international investors to shake hands with the Russian political and economic elite, as paparazzi flashbulbs popped around them.[34]

Being told what to do

Russia hawks in business and political circles, including pressure groups at the Yale School of Management[35] and the Kyiv School of Economics,[36] started to name and shame the companies that did not immediately drop everything and leave. Maintaining a presence in Russia, where taxes on your company's profits would fund the Russian government, was compared to collusion or complicity, loaded words deployed for maximum impact. War made everything black and white.

Except it didn't, in a way that inverted everything that a company's values were meant to dictate. If treating people— including employees—to increasingly high standards was the imperative *du jour* among international companies, surely that applied to employees in Russia, too?

Maybe not.

McDonald's, the company that made the golden arches a modern icon in a country with a 1,000-year history of icons, eventually understood it had to leave Russia. But McDonald's is a company that supports its people, including the people at its restaurants across Russia.[37] While McDonald's was trying to decide what to do in Russia, it furloughed its employees and paid their salaries for up to six months.

This is what stakeholder capitalism was supposed to be all about: seeing your employees as a constituency as important as your customers. But stakeholder capitalism passes through a variety of prisms. One of those prisms made it look like McDonald's, and its furloughed workers, were supporting Putin and the war.

"Make it hurt"

In an appearance on influential US business journalist Kara Swisher's podcast "Sway," Jeffrey Sonnenfeld, a professor at the Yale University School of Management, likened McDonald's to Germans who were complicit with the Nazi regime. Sonnenfeld and his team at Yale are the authors of a widely viewed "report card" of companies' reactions to the war. Companies that exited quickly and completely got an A. Companies whose exit from Russia was slow, tentative or incomplete got progressively lower grades.

It is worth reproducing an excerpt from Sonnenfeld's conversation with Swisher on the podcast:

Sonnenfeld: McDonald's, even though they were late, I think they deserve at least a B. So they're in our second category.

Swisher: And their restaurants, Russia could take over. And then they have a logo that looks like McDonald's, correct? Uncle Vanya's [after the renowned Chekhov play], is that correct?

Sonnenfeld: Yeah, and see, that's why we don't give them an A. And they're also paying their people to do nothing, their original employees, over 50,000 people. That doesn't quite do what we all would have needed for a top, you know, A categorization or a complete withdrawal because that's still pumping cash into the economy. The well-intended perhaps explanation for that is we don't want to cut off loyal, long service employees who are innocent, not a part of all this. I don't buy that.

There's a famous book called "Hitler's Willing Executioners," which is that the Second World War, the Holocaust, the Third Reich, is not all attributed to Hitler. It was the complicity of the everyday German at that time, and the complicity here of Russians. To want to support these people by paying them salaries is not what needs to be done. We need to stop civil society. Make it hurt.[38]

Sonnenfeld was far from alone. Chess Grandmaster Garry Kasparov, a virulent Putin critic, slammed Western investors, and not only for their position on Ukraine.

"Companies that were doing business in Russia decided it was worth the risk and were happy supporting a police state when the profits were good," he wrote on Twitter in 2023. "Staying after 2014 [when Russia invaded and annexed Crimea] and even after 2022 should result in sanctions, not pity. It's not 'engagement,' it's collusion."[39]

The reverse was true, too. Private companies that aren't covered by stock market analysts, and hundreds of small and medium-sized foreign companies, remain in Russia to this day because no one has ever heard of them. Some large companies have stayed, too. Figures differ on just how many companies have left and how many have stayed. Still, the Western business community is severely depleted; those still there describe Moscow as a changed city.

This was the noisy, contradictory and hostile operating environment that international companies in Russia were suddenly wading through. Biting, caustic commentary came from all quarters. Customers talked about boycotting companies doing business in Russia. Employees thousands of miles from Russia were saying they wouldn't work for a company that paid taxes to the Russian government. The bigger the brand, the louder the noise.

Companies were drowning in an ocean of grey. Yes, they wanted to protect their people. No, they didn't want to support the war. But once the state commission started dictating terms, neither did they want to deliver to Putin and his cronies a windfall made of the Russian operations of some of the world's best companies, Abdullaev said.

Companies in Russia are now genuinely trapped. If they stay, they're accused of supporting the wartime economy and paying taxes to a government bent on destroying Ukraine. "If they leave, they're criticised for gifting their companies to Putin," Abdullaev said. "It's a double-edged sword."

The worst of all circumstances, one company said, would be a television image of Putin using—and enjoying—a product from a Western brand.

"That company's share price would fall lower than the value of all its assets in Russia," Abdullaev said.

In fact, that almost happened when Putin appeared at a March 2022 pro-war rally in a puffer jacket immediately identified as coming from the Italian luxury brand Loro Piana.

The UK's muckraking *Daily Mail* got the story between its teeth and bit down hard. The paper quoted a Russia commentator as saying: "While Putin commits genocide, in Ukraine he lies about stopping genocide. While in an Italian Loro Piana coat worth more than most Russians' yearly salary."

The *Daily Mail* noted that Loro Piana, part of the LVMH luxury conglomerate, had closed its stores in Moscow and St Petersburg in response to the invasion and quoted comments from Pier Luigi Loro Piana, the brand's deputy chairman, in an Italian newspaper. The incident, Loro Piana said, "creates some embarrassment from a human point of view." But he went on to say: "It is clear which side we're on … The Ukrainians will have all our moral and practical support."[40]

Sanctions

The US, the UK, the EU and the rest of the G7 hammered Russia with a series of embargoes, bans and sanctions almost immediately following the start of the full-scale war. Russian individuals and Russian companies associated with the war were frozen out of the global economy and ejected from polite society. Russia is now more sanctioned than North Korea.[41]

Sanctions are meant to do one or both of two things: punish and modify behaviour. Sanctions on Russia have only done a little bit of both, though views on the relative success or failure of sanctions are highly politicised. Depending on your perspective, sanctions have either crippled the Russian economy or have had no impact at all—in 2023, Russian GDP grew faster than the UK's.[42]

Also in 2023, exports of cars and car parts from Germany to Kyrgyzstan leapt by 5,500 per cent, according to data compiled by Robin Brooks, former chief economist of the Institute of International Finance.[43] It is highly unlikely that the Kyrgyz economy suddenly shifted into overdrive and awarded its citizens with a new fleet of wheels. Goods from Kyrgyzstan can travel relatively easily across neighbouring Kazakhstan and into Russia. Russia has demonstrated considerable adaptability in establishing workarounds that even provide access to technology for military use.

"A ban on high-tech exports to Russia was one of the pillars of Western sanctions imposed on Moscow last year as a result of its invasion of Ukraine. Sanctions on such high-tech goods were intended not only to harm the Russian economy, but to limit the Kremlin's capacity to wage war. Russia was to be deprived of things like aviation parts, lenses, and electronic components—which are crucial in modern warfare," wrote Denis Kasyanchuk in The Bell, a source of independent, Russian economic news founded by editors sacked from a popular Russian business news site under Kremlin pressure:[44]

> But there was no defence sector collapse. Russian companies quickly set-up new supply chains and started importing high-tech goods via third countries. Dozens of cases of Western goods finding their way to Russia have been reported in the media, along with evidence including names and documents. For example, Lithuanian firms sell aviation parts to Russia via the Central Asian state of Kyrgyzstan, U.S. microchips reach Russian military factories via Kazakhstan, and components used in the manufacture of cruise missiles are transported to Russia via Armenia in the South Caucasus.[45]

Dubai, one of the world's great commercial crossroads, became a refuge for Russians and for Russian companies, but it also became a hub of alleged sanctions evasion. "Seeing how companies here are trying to bust the sanctions, you see how integrated the world economy is. You just can't put up a wall anymore," said William Reichert, another of Moscow's long-serving lawyers, who relocated to Dubai in 2015 after the Crimea invasion.

"At the start of the war, I was getting five or six calls a day from [Russian] companies who said they wanted to set up business in Dubai, and then the sanctions came and I couldn't touch any of it. If it hadn't been for the sanctions, my Russian business would have gone like this," Reichert said, pointing his finger upward.

Western exporters have responded by trying to curtail re-export of their products to Russia via third countries. Importers in those countries have to sign an agreement against forwarding goods to Russia, including via sales on electronic platforms, according to *Kommersant*, the Russian business newspaper. Concerns among Western manufacturers have arisen, though, that when they block re-routed imports, Chinese and Turkish manufacturers gladly take their place.[46]

The G7, the EU and Australia slapped a USD 60 price cap on Russian oil—any ship carrying oil sold above that price would be denied access to Western maritime services and insurance. The EU sanctioned Russian oil shipped on tankers and chased Russian gas out of European pipelines. The sanctions brought mixed results. Global energy prices initially skyrocketed as fears of shortages gripped the markets. Russia was able to work around the price cap: China and India gladly mopped up excess supply at a bargain price, and Russia launched a "shadow fleet" of ships to circumvent the insurance and services embargo. China has also become an important supplier of goods to Russia that are sanctioned for export from the West.[47] The amount of diesel Brazil imported from Russia in 2023 increased by 4,600 per cent.[48]

This is not to say that Russia's economy is thriving. The arrangements mentioned earlier make economic activity slower and more expensive, and that has a real cost to the Russian economy. The country's finances have not entirely been reconfigured to a wartime footing, but military spending is up sharply. The labour market is tight—hundreds of thousands of young Russians were sent to fight; similarly large numbers left the country. Social benefits designed to support veterans and military families, as well as broader social spending, have risen to dampen public discontent. The Bell, citing figures from the Russian Central Bank, suggests that "there is a limit to how far this growth can go."[49]

Who left, and how

Companies left Russia variously. Some left completely. These companies no longer have any economic activity connected with Russia and fit into roughly three categories. The first were the megabrands that fell under internal or external pressure to go, like McDonald's and Starbucks. Both companies were sold to local individuals.[50]

The second were the companies in strategic sectors, like the energy companies, or Boeing and Airbus. These were the companies most exposed to sanctions in Russia because their activities touched on industries important to the Russian state. They left because their home jurisdictions made it illegal to stay. Aviation sector sanctions have been high profile and sweeping, a tightening of sanctions placed on the Russian aviation sector since the downing of Malaysian Airlines flight 370 in 2014 and the illegal annexation of Crimea. Sanctions now ban the supply of components and aircraft to Russia. International leasing companies have called for the return of hundreds of aircraft leased to Russian airlines, and, as mentioned previously, Russia's access to international airspace is now severely restricted.

The third group that left Russia included companies that could afford to—Russia was a small part of their global turnover and leaving wouldn't cost that much. Doing business in Russia was becoming increasingly expensive—companies had to restructure their supply chains or their banking arrangements to avoid sanctions. They also had to try to forecast the trajectory of sanctions and anticipate where their next problem would arise.

There were companies that left because doing business in Russia simply became too complicated. Maybe your Russian business partners were not sanctioned. But they might be some day. Or perhaps there was a sanctioned entity or individual embedded deep in your Russian supply chain. Figuring that out became time-consuming and expensive.

Abdullaev points out that while the situation in Ukraine came as a surprise, the companies and executives he worked with approached the problem of what to do with their businesses methodically, once the anxiety of the expat exodus subsided. These were people who had seen crises all around the world over the course of their careers. And they had the advantage of a relatively calm first couple of months after the invasion to think things through. There was no immediate pressure—not from the Kremlin at least—for companies to go, and Russia seemed safe from the point of view of military conflict. Abdullaev said that most of the companies he advised about exits held those discussions outside of Russia.

Finally, some companies left by selling to their local colleagues. Professional services firms, including all the Big Four accounting firms, did something like that, and withdrew their brands from the market. EY is now called "Center of Audit Technologies and Solutions—Audit Services LLC (CATS Audit Services)."[51] The name doesn't exactly trip off the tongue or lend itself to an easy logo. Many of these transactions included buy-back clauses, allowing the reversal of the sale if market conditions improve.

The cleaner, faster and cheaper the sale, the lower the likelihood of attracting state scrutiny, Abdullaev said. Selling a firm without, say, a ten-year buy-back option was easier than embedding a buy-back clause in the sale agreement.

It's about the math

Mostly, companies left when the numbers stopped working.

"The 1990s were the time of a lot of adventures. The more adventurous came earlier than the less adventurous. They were absolutely happy with the high-risk, high-reward thing," said Vladimir Borodin, former editor-in-chief of *Izvestia*, one of Russia's largest daily newspapers, and now a US resident, serial entrepreneur and advocate for ethics and accountability in business.[52] Borodin is also a co-founder of the Burger & Lobster restaurant group. "I think the simplest equation and the key to understanding what was happening in Russia at the time was, if your profits were thousands—not hundreds, but thousands—of per cents, you can be interested in something like the Russian market."

And then something happens, and the bottom falls out.

"The end of this market story is not the invasion of Ukraine. It's the fact that these equations didn't work anymore. The end of the risk–reward equation," Borodin said:

> The risk is very high, but the reward is very little. In the '90s, it was one set of risks, but now it's others, right? It's Putin, it's the FSB, it's … you name it. It's a very risky market, but there are no longer the 1,000 per cent profits.

Who stayed, and how

Other companies remained in Russia but have vowed, to varying degrees, that they will make no further investment in Russia, they will stop advertising in Russia or they will divert the profits they make in Russia to supporting Ukrainian charities. All these moves carry a heightened level of risk. Mars, the pet food and confectionery giant, came under investigation by the Russian tax authorities for donating millions of dollars to international charitable organisations that were supporting Ukraine.[53]

Austria's Raiffeisen Bank stayed in Russia and, as one of the few remaining international banks there, has been a primary conduit for transferring funds out of the country. Raiffeisen's position in Russia since the full-scale invasion has made the company a critical player, and an extremely profitable one. In 2023, Raiffeisen's activities in Russia accounted for half of the parent company's profits.[54] The bank's headquarters in Vienna has been under severe and escalating pressure from banking regulators in the US, where Raiffeisen is active, to leave Russia. In June 2024, Raiffeisen said it would stop making dollar transfers out of Russia.[55]

Some companies stayed to maintain a critical humanitarian purpose: pharmaceutical companies, companies that made baby food, and others. Danone said it would stay in Russia and maintain its dairy and baby food operations. Russia then seized Danone.[56] Danone's ultimate disposition is discussed below.

"I think it depends on the business, and there are some businesses that still do really well in Russia, US businesses. Now, they've gone way, way, way below the radar, but they're there," Rodzianko said. "I mean, look: there are household product companies, food companies, candy companies that are doing just fine, thank you," he said. "They've stopped advertising, which lowers their costs, but their sales have not suffered at all, because their brands are well known, and they're on the shelves."

Products from Mondelez, maker of Oreo cookies, are still on the shelves in Russia. CEO Dirk Van de Put told the *Financial Times* that his shareholders don't "morally care" whether the company stays in Russia. Russia's contribution to Mondelez's global revenue is 2.8 per cent for 2023, down from 4 per cent the year before, according to the *FT*. Mondelez is sanctions compliant and is not investing in its business in Russia.[57]

Companies that want to leave feel as if they are stuck on flypaper. The very announcement of the intention to leave triggers a public flogging inside and outside Russia. Mondelez's Van de Put described the dilemma succinctly: "I wonder what happened with the companies that were sold, who got them and what are they doing with the cash that those companies generate? They all went to friends of Putin," Van de Put told the *FT*. "And you can bet that the cash they generate [that] goes to the war is much bigger than the taxes we could pay."[58]

In a parallel campaign aimed at Russian companies, Putin is undertaking a process known as "deprivatisation," though he has publicly rejected the suggestion that the state seizure of Russian companies is by design. Instead, state investigators are discovering alleged violations in how large Russian enterprises were privatised in the 1990s, reversing those decisions and returning companies to state ownership. In other cases, known as "soft-deprivatisation," Putin is leaving the status of private companies untouched but replacing their senior management with cronies.[59] The privatisation of former Soviet enterprises thirty years ago is discussed later in this book; deprivatisation is undermining the very foundation of the private sector in Russia.

US companies were believed to be the largest taxpayers in Russia in 2022, according to a report from B4Ukraine, a civil society group, and the Kyiv School of Economics. German companies, the report says, are the second largest taxpayers in Russia.[60]

Putin has had warm words for companies that stayed:

Many foreign organizations, regardless of the pressure from their governments, decided that they wanted to continue working in our country. We only welcome this. Many changed names and maintained their presence on the market, or simply transferred their assets to the existing management—to be honest, with a buy-back option. God give them strength, let them work.[61]

Maybe there are no good decisions in the stay-or-go dilemma. The difficulty of exiting Russia provides a convenient excuse for companies that are otherwise happy to stay. And the outcry around companies that did stay has subsided since the start of the war. Inevitably, global outrage moves on.

It gets personal

As the prospect of war loomed, Evgenev was running Alvarez & Marsal's Moscow office. Once the full-scale invasion began, he decided he had had enough. He left full-time work at Alvarez & Marsal and now lives in Dubai.

"What's happening in Russia is getting uglier and uglier with the Western companies, so I didn't really want any part of that," he said. He thinks about companies that can't make up their minds about what to do in Russia. For the companies still in Russia, decision-making has been pushed down to middle management, where decisions go to die.

"You know, those companies [that] are still there most likely missed the boat, typically because there was a slow, low-priority process being run by middle-level managers who have no authority to make quick decisions. People are trying to avoid responsibility, and try to avoid decision-making," he said. "European companies also have a very complex decision-making process. Many of them don't really want to exit, they want to drag it on as long as possible. So everything has to go back and forth 10,000 times."

Things fall apart

In April 2023, the Kremlin seized the Russian operations of Fortum of Finland and Uniper of Germany, both major players in the European energy sector. The move against Uniper was a revenge play: Germany nationalised Gazprom Germania, a Russian asset, in 2022. Russia seized Fortum's Russian assets as the company tried to sell them.[62]

A few months later, in July, Russia took Danone's Russian operations and grabbed control of Carlsberg's Baltika Breweries. France's Danone was the largest dairy company in Russia; Baltika is one of Russia's most famous brewers, and Russia was Danish Carlsberg's second largest market.[63] Russia said the confiscations came in response to Western seizure of Russian assets abroad.[64]

On 22 March 2024, Danone announced in a company statement that it had secured regulatory approval to sell its assets to a company reportedly owned by a twenty-nine-year-old businessman linked to the nephew of the strongman head of Chechnya, Ramzan Kadyrov.[65] Danone had at one point forecast that the sale could incur a write-down of EUR 1 billion.[66]

In a retaliatory move, the Danish brewing giant announced in October 2023 that it was cancelling the agreement that allowed Baltika to make and sell beers from Carlsberg's brand portfolio.[67] Carlsberg had more than 8,000 employees across eight sites in Russia; CEO Jacob Aarup-Andersen told the BBC the business had been "stolen," and "we are not going to help them make that look legitimate."[68] Russian authorities arrested two local Baltika executives during the back-and-forth over the licensing.[69]

Carlsberg is now under the control of Taimuraz Bolloev, a Putin friend who was head of Baltika when Carlsberg acquired it in the 1990s. The unexpected twist in the sale process has put other businesses trying to exit Russia on a nervous edge.[70]

The business and asset confiscations continue. In May 2024, a court in St Petersburg seized more than EUR 700 million in assets belonging to three European banks in response to claims filed by a Russian subsidiary of Gazprom. As part of the ruling, the court banned Deutsche Bank from selling its business in Russia.[71]

Preliminary totals

A summary of the losses European companies accumulated as they exited Russia about a year and a half after the full-scale invasion showed that the total hit to revenue was more than EUR 100 billion, according to a report in the *Financial Times*. This is on top of the indirect hit to all companies as a result of, among other things, increased energy prices following the war, the *FT* said.

"A survey of 600 European groups' annual reports and 2023 financial statements shows that 176 companies have recorded asset impairments, foreign exchange-related charges and other one-off expenses as a result of the sale, closure or reduction of Russian businesses," the *FT* reported. "The aggregate figure does not include the war's indirect macroeconomic impacts such as higher energy and commodities costs. The war has also delivered a profit boost for oil and gas groups and defence companies."[72]

The newspaper, citing statistics from the Kyiv School of Economics, said there were 1,871 European-owned companies in Russia at the start of the full-scale invasion, and that "more than fifty per cent" of those companies were still doing business in Russia at the time of the article. A small number of the companies that left, the *FT* said, quoting research from the University of St Gallen in Switzerland, took enormous write-downs on exiting Russia. The rest of the companies likely saw smaller losses, in keeping with their more modest footprint there.[73]

Vedomosti, one of Russia's leading business newspapers, said in November 2023 that only "nine of the world's 100 most valuable brands are staying in Russia," and that the highest-ranking remaining brand was only fifty-fifth in Best Global Brands' 2023 list. Some of these brands, the article noted, are from countries that are not sanctioning Russia. China's Xiaomi and Huawei are both in the list of top 100 brands.[74]

Kyiv School of Economics' figures for all international businesses, published in the *Financial Times* on 28 May 2024, showed that 387 companies had "exited" Russia, 1,223 businesses had "curtailed" their activities in Russia and 2,173 companies had "remained" in Russia. The same article said that some companies had changed their minds about leaving the country, as consumer demand strengthened. Avon, the cosmetics company, received offers for its Russian operations but decided not to accept them. "For over 135 years, Avon has stood for women wherever they are in the world, regardless of ethnicity, nationality, age or religion," the company told the *FT*.[75]

Back to the future

The ingenuity behind the sanctions workarounds—facilitated with a high level of Western complicity—brings back memories of the uncanny ability of Soviet enterprise managers to put patches on their deeply dysfunctional command economy to keep the entire construct from total collapse. The sanctions-busting sleights of hand also bear a strong resemblance to some of the (very) sharp practices of the 1990s.

"They are able to go back to the Soviet mentality," said Regina von Flemming, who during her decades-long career in Russia was at the top of Germany's Axel Springer publishing business in the country.[76]

Back to the past

Modern Russia is no longer the trophy business destination it once was. For international business, it is a place of regret, second-guessing and missed (and mixed) messages. The history of international business in modern Russia is full of examples of foreign companies enjoying great success and suffering punishing failure, in the Soviet period and even in tsarist Russia before then.

In her remark on sanctions workarounds, von Flemming spotted a thread of continuity between the Soviet past and current Russian reality. Many such threads connect the Soviet Union to today's Russia. A look even further back, in fact, finds common themes alive today that stretch back to the Russian Empire.

2

LOOKING BACK, WAS IT EVER THUS?

*A lot of the things we talk about in Russia today that are seen
as vestiges of the Soviet past were—before the Soviet Union
ever existed—being described in almost the exact same terms
using almost the exact same phrases by Anglophone journalists.*[1]

Plus ça change

We tend to think of globalisation only in terms of its late
twentieth-century incarnation. Capital has, however, been
crossing borders since borders existed.

So have capitalists. Businessmen visiting or living in Russia
during the country's nineteenth-century industrialisation faced
many of the same challenges as the adventurous investors who
came to the Soviet Union and Russia starting in the 1990s.
They felt isolated. Learning Russian was a challenge. They faced
corrupt government officials. They "went native" by falling for
local charms. They drank. They faced strong political, geopolitical
and competitive forces. Some of them made money.

And they had to overcome a commercial tradition that, prior to the mid-1800s, was in some respects designed to keep foreign business out.

Historian Walther Kirchner wrote:

> [T]he Western entrepreneur was, as a rule, induced to engage in business in Russia by expectation of profit, rather than by records of profit. In view of the uncertainties facing him, he then tried to get rich quickly—if possible within a few years—rather than build up solid lasting contacts. ... Few Western firms dealing exclusively with or in Russia stayed operational for more than one generation; no such firm is on record for the eighteenth century.[2]

Russia's integration into the global economy became more prominent as industrialisation started in the mid-1800s and accelerated as the century progressed. The end in 1861 of serfdom, Russia's economically and socially debilitating system of agricultural bondage, removed one of the main obstacles to Russia's industrialisation.[3]

In both the nineteenth and the twentieth centuries, Russia's industrialisation lagged behind the same process in the countries of Western Europe. But once Russia started to borrow money, pay for expertise and import technology from other countries— Germany, France and Britain figured prominently, as did Belgium for a while—its industrialisation began to look more like industrial revolutions in other countries. By the end of the nineteenth century, Russia was woven into the fabric of the international economy.[4]

The use of the textile metaphor is not accidental. The cloth industry was a prominent area of Russian industrialisation; its greatest partner in that sector was Britain. The *Manchester Examiner and Times* was feeling boosterish about Britain's chances in Russia:

> We are enabled, by private correspondence received this day, to announce the opening of negotiations by her majesty's representative

at St. Petersburgh, with the view of increasing the commercial relations between this country and Russia. A considerable change is contemplated in the import duties of articles of English manufacture, and in cotton especially, a great, though gradual *ad valorem* reduction will be made. ... Should the contemplated changes in the Russian tariff take place, we shall, no doubt, see a rapid increase in our export trade to that country, and of this increase Lancashire may reasonably hope to obtain a full share.[5]

Early globalisation: the end of the nineteenth and the start of the twentieth centuries

Long before globalisation became the modern term for an economically interconnected world, the world was probably its most intertwined during the 1800s and the beginning of the 1900s, until the outbreak of the First World War. Jeffry A. Frieden, formerly of Harvard and currently a professor of international and public affairs and political science at Columbia University, writes that the capitalism that linked countries around the world at that time was "close to the classical ideal." This system, he adds, was not exclusive to Great Britain, the US and a few Western European states. Global commerce was an open, growing and increasingly connected club.

A few figures help elucidate the scope of the earliest forms of globalisation. Over the course of the 1800s, the cost of sending a ton of cargo across the Atlantic dropped from USD 10 to USD 3; the cost of overland transit dropped even more dramatically. These changes increased global shipping capacity by a factor of 20. At the end of the 1800s, Russia had fewer miles of railroad than Britain. By 1913, it had ten times more.[6] These advances in cargo transportation were one of global commerce's greatest accelerants.

Russia was a member of the globalising club, if a slightly atypical one. Its agricultural sector, unable to reform and reorganise following the end of serfdom, remained underdeveloped relative to other large agricultural countries. Instead, non-agricultural sectors boomed as inexpensive foreign inputs leapt easily over low import tariffs. Other parts of the Russian Empire's economy were exclusively home-fed. Steel production in the part of the Russian Empire that is now Ukraine took off internally, protected by high tariffs that kept out competitors' goods.[7]

Where Russia instituted high tariffs, international investors hurdled them by opening businesses inside Russia. Russian industry was, in fact, characterised by a relatively high level of foreign ownership. Toward the end of the nineteenth century, the presence of foreign capital in Russia was significant and in some sectors approached 90 per cent, according to economic historian Malcolm Falkus.[8] Frieden contrasts this with lower-tariff Japan, which seemed more content to become interdependent with global trading partners. An unusually high concentration of Russia's workers in large enterprises became the breeding ground for revolutionary groups that organised the Russian working class, Frieden says, citing Falkus.[9]

The tsarist railroads

Tsar Nicholas I has been described as "the most peripatetic ruler Russia ever had," and as a result, "Russia had to have railroads. Nicholas, at any rate, had to have them."[10] The Americans were ready to help.

In the 1840s, renowned American railroad engineer George Washington Whistler built Russia's first large railway, the St Petersburg–Moscow line, under Nicholas I's supervision.[11] Rolling stock came from the US-based Harrison, Winans & Eastwick company.[12]

Whistler, father of famed US painter James McNeil Whistler, died of cholera in 1849 in St Petersburg;[13] Joseph Harrison Jr stepped in to take over. Whistler was paid USD 12,000 a year for his efforts, a sum equivalent to just under USD 500,000 today.

Biographical information of the time shows that Whistler, professionally and socially, was an exotic species in Russia. His local peers weren't quite sure what to do with him:

> While in Russia, Major Whistler was sometimes placed in positions most trying to him. It is said that some of the corps of the native engineers, many of whom were nobles, while compelled to look up to him officially were inclined to look down on him socially, and exercised their supposed privileges in this respect so as to annoy him exceedingly.[14]

Tsar Nicholas I was having none of it. He intentionally joined an engineer corps' tour of a St Petersburg art gallery when he knew Whistler would be in attendance. As the nobles looked on, the tsar took Whistler by the arm and escorted him personally around the gallery. The nobility's behaviour was subsequently and permanently amended.[15]

Whistler stood out for his scrupulous honesty when surrounded by corrupt entrepreneurs, at least some of whom appeared to be compatriots:

> He was not subject to corruption either for gain or for patriotic reasons, holding that the recommendation of persons or inventions merely because they were American was of no service either to the United States or to Russia, an "unpatriotic" attitude that often led to bitterness on the part of Americans interested in exploiting Russia.[16]

As it happens, the opening of the railroad, among other developments at the time, spurred a "small number" of Moscow merchant families to try to meet foreign investors halfway, the historian Alfred J. Rieber wrote. "In exceptional cases, when the family firm engaged in the export trade, the sons were sent abroad to perfect their training, acquire a veneer of European manners, and make business contacts." Daughters were trained in music and French.[17]

In 1860, Alexander II annulled an 1807 decree highly prejudicial against foreign merchants; the move resolutely placed international businesses on the same legal footing as their Russian peers. By 1895–6, Russia was the world's sixth largest country in terms of foreign trade and was responsible for more than 25 per cent of global economic activity. Russia produced 15 per cent of the world's gold and was growing into one of the largest issuers of debt placed abroad. The rouble by this time was convertible, making the country attractive to foreign capital.[18]

Early Siemens in early Russia

In its earliest days, the modern German engineering behemoth Siemens was one of the largest international players in the Russian Empire. Siemens built the Russian telegraph system and its elaborate network of cross-country overground, underground and even underwater cables.

Tsarist Russia was so important to Siemens that three brothers of company founder Werner Siemens moved there. The most prominent of those brothers, Carl Siemens, established residence in St Petersburg in 1853 and began to run the firm's business when he was twenty-three years old.[19] Carl Siemens' son was born in Russia and spoke the language. He mastered the Russian market and returned to Berlin to become the head of the firm when his namesake uncle died.

When it came to sending expats to Russia, German or otherwise, younger men were very much the order of the day. The young men sent to Russia in the 1800s in one respect bear strong resemblance to those that followed them two centuries later. Young European men were known to fall "readily under the spell" of Russia, slightly flowery language for something that today we might call "going native."[20]

Siemens' business in Russia did not consistently or uniformly thrive. Some of the company's ventures became international landmarks; others failed. Some businesses were lucrative; others turned modest profits. Across its activities, though, Siemens in imperial Russia touched on several interesting topics. They are described painstakingly—balance sheets and all—in Kirchner's "The Industrialisation of Russia and the Siemens Firm, 1853–1890."

Altogether, Kirchner writes, Siemens installed more than "9,000 verst" (about 9,600 km) of telegraph cable that variously connected Gatchina, site of an imperial palace outside St Petersburg, with Warsaw, St Petersburg and Oranienbaum, and several points in what is now Ukraine.[21] This is an early example, perhaps, of foreign capital and know-how being deployed extensively across the Russian Empire, and in a sector that was crucial to the empire's ability to engage in international economic and political relations. No one would have phrased it this way at the time, but here was an example of foreign capital in a Russian strategic sector—communications.

Siemens acquired a glass factory and converted it into a porcelain factory to make isolators for its telegraph wires and tableware, Kirchner wrote. This venture failed. Siemens purchased a copper mine in what was then called Kedabeg, now Gadabay in today's Azerbaijan. That venture prospered. Siemens built an Anglo-Indian telegraph that crossed the Russian Empire.

After this flurry of activity in the 1850s and 1860s, Siemens' business slowed in the 1870s; it remained solvent, if "quiet, rather uninteresting."[22] Business returned to robust health in the 1880s with the advent of a highly popular electric train that Tsar Alexander III rode at an exposition, triggering a flood of orders.

Siemens also began to electrify St Petersburg. Siemens bulbs lit the shops of Nevsky Prospekt and the street itself, the imperial capital's most important thoroughfare. The Winter Palace—one of the world's most elegant royal residences and now home to the renowned Hermitage Museum—glowed from within courtesy of Siemens.[23]

St Petersburg was an important focal point for foreign capital. In a review of foreign investment at the end of the 1800s and the early 1900s, Rieber wrote that "[t]he extraordinary influence exerted by foreign capital in the northwest may be gauged from the fact that this region absorbed 20 percent of all foreign investment in Russia." Areas with particularly heavy foreign investment in the region included metals and machinery factories, textiles and chemicals.[24]

Siemens' business in tsarist Russia performed under pressures that would be immediately familiar to the modern businessperson. Foreign competition was an irritant; pressure from the English in the electrical appliance business pushed Siemens to establish local production in Russia. Local players pushed back; supporters of horse-drawn carriages and gas street-lanterns sought to limit Siemens' expansion into electric carriages and electrical street lighting. Political risk came from on high; interference from the tsar and the pressure of the looming Crimean War meant that installing the telegraph line to Sevastopol happened in a hurry, and at a loss.[25]

The "Russian specific"—nineteenth-century style

Competitive and government pressures aside, what was it like to do business in tsarist Russia? International companies were present, and in some cases even prominent. What happened when they got there?

Seldom did Russians visit Western countries; generally, it was the Western businessman who had to travel East—to Novgorod, Archangel, Moscow, Caffa, later to St Petersburg, Leningrad, Cherson, or Odessa. As he was far from home and moving in a foreign atmosphere, he had to adapt himself to unfamiliar surroundings and to alien ways. Again and again, an underestimation of the special character of the conduct of business in Russia has led—aside from financial loss and, upon occasion, personal injury to the merchant himself—to an incorrect historical picture.[26]

The blending of business and public interests was a major concern for businessmen (back then it was always men), as happened via the shunting of some commercial trade to businesses connected to government officials and the injection of political considerations into business deals.[27]

Kirchner delivered an observation loaded with foresight and more than a little criticism of Russia's foreign visitors:

[The Western businessman] was not aware of, or concerned with, historical events or historical laws; he operated at a given time and was faced by concrete problems. He had to battle with a given situation and this situation meant that he often found himself ... in a "strange land." His adjustment to it, his successes and failures, and those of his Russian partner stand in need of much further investigation.[28]

The "Russian specific"—twenty-first-century style

The entire notion of "the special character of the conduct of business in Russia" is at once true and a cliché: every country has idiosyncratic business customs. But phrases describing just how different Russia was for international executives rang out loudly and repeatedly in the 1990s. Watchwords for doing business in Russia were peppered liberally throughout conversations between Russian and foreign business partners and featured prominently in sometimes tense conference calls between the Moscow offices of international companies and their distant headquarters.

The Russian-language phrase was *russkaya spetsifika*—"the Russian specific," meant to encapsulate and describe an entire universe of dystopian, Russian exceptionalism.

When Russians in the 1990s used this phrase in negotiations with their international counterparts, it was a banal statement of fact—"things are done differently here"—but it was also a warning. Sometimes, it was even an inducement to become an accomplice. The not-so-subtle subtext was: If you want to do business here, you'll have to learn to make potentially uncomfortable compromises, or you're going to have to stand on your head to avoid them.

When expats in Moscow used this phrase in conversations with their faraway bosses, it was to tell them there were certain aspects to doing business in Russia that they would never understand but grudgingly had to accept. Most of the time, these were not easy or welcome discussions. The smarter folks at the headquarters saw these sorts of statements as red flags about their business in the hinterland. Others failed to comprehend how or why things were so different in Russia. Still more saw the red flags embedded in these conversations but chose not to dwell on them.

Cescotti, formerly of publicly listed GEA Group, was also on the board of the German–Russian Chamber of Commerce. Cescotti said he relished the phone calls back to headquarters to help his bosses understand Russia.

"I loved doing that, I enjoyed that," Cescotti said. "Because I was always debating a lot with my bosses at HQ, making them understand what the specifics of Russian business are."[29]

Cescotti said he sent his bosses a well-known YouTube video ridiculing what it was like to do business in Russia. "They were laughing their heads off. They were saying 'That is actually the reality?'"

Passport and visa, please

Anyone who has ever applied for a Russian visa in the past thirty years is on well-worn ground. Foreign residents' movements could be severely restricted in imperial Russia—a capricious police force even disrupted the movements of two of the Siemens brothers. International visitors sometimes met aggressive resistance: "Upon reaching the border of the country, the foreigner was subjected to close inspection and passport control. ... Frequently, he was locked up in his quarters during the night."[30]

In the face of all this and even more hardship and suffering— we haven't touched on Kirchner's reports of skin diseases "owing to uncleanliness"[31]—foreign workers in Russia had to overcome both personal and professional obstacles.

"It is no pleasure to do business here," Carl Siemens reportedly said in the 1890s.[32] The broader business community shared his sentiments.

"Whether American railroad builder, English or French merchant, or German industrialist (including the Siemens and their co-workers)," Kirchner wrote, "they all had to face the fact that life in Russia brought dangers to their health and to that of their families, that it demanded changes in their habits, and that it isolated them from many of the things they cherished."[33]

It also immersed foreign businessmen in an environment that was not uniformly hospitable to outside capital. There is some debate about how welcome foreign investment was in Russia: the West was more technologically advanced and had lower production costs, making their arrival on the market a potentially disruptive event.

"These industrialists quite simply wanted no intruders to the golden table of Russian protectionism," historian John McKay wrote in *Pioneers for Profit: Foreign Entrepreneurship and Russian Industrialization, 1885–1913*. Ultimately, the decision about whether to cooperate with foreign investors was largely one of cost and benefit: "[T]he views of Russian big business depended mainly on whether foreign enterprise meant increased competition or increased opportunity."[34]

And for all the Russian-language students out there, your pain is centuries old. "Learning the language caused the foreigners considerable difficulties; Carl Siemens knew some Russian but never became proficient in it; most English and Americans did not even try to learn to speak it and consequently had to live as in a ghetto," Kirchner observed.[35]

Here, too, were the earliest roots of the most modern theme. In the Soviet period, foreign residents not living in embassies were required to live in official, Soviet-government-managed housing—the apartment blocks controlled by the dreaded housing bureaucracy known by its initials as the UpDK. Later, in a Russia with a more liberalised housing market, many expats lived in self-imposed, internal exile, either by huddling within suburban townhouse villas, or by never venturing beyond the limits of Moscow's tightly drawn and prosperous Garden Ring, other than to head to the airport.

In the modern period, some expats understandably chose to live close to where their children went to school, or in places that made the commute bearable. In other cases, the security of a purpose-built, gated community offered the greatest appeal. More than a few expats in Russia craved the "this could be anywhere" comfort of 100 channels of cable TV and clubhouse dining rooms.

Seriously, what sort of person would go to a place like this, whether it was fifteen years ago or 150 years ago? "[O]nly a specific type of entrepreneur was attracted to the Russian market. If he was not an outright gambler, he was often at least an adventurer," Kirchner wrote.[36]

The history of doing business in Russia then and now is carpeted with riskophiles, a phenomenon that needed a word, and in Russian is *riskofil*. Riskophiles not only had robust appetites for risk but maybe even sought the rush of high-risk, high-reward transactions.

Parallels that never fade

Political risk abounded in tsarist Russia. When Sergei Witte was Russia's finance minister in the 1890s, he was said to have favoured AEG, a German rival to Siemens, and switched Russia's allegiance in the lighting business from the incumbent to the newcomer. Siemens' business ultimately proved too big to fail, but a company's position in the tsarist economy changed every time a new tsar sat on the throne. In a separate development, Carl Siemens, through a combination of luck and carefully cultivated personal connections, established what appeared to be a solid relationship with Russia's minister of transport, only to see him and all his political connections wiped out shortly after the death of Nicholas I.[37]

Bribery and collusion were rampant.

"These decisions of Russian officials were not based primarily upon cost or quality considerations. Everyone understood this," McKay wrote. Quoting a note by a French diplomat from the late 1800s in his work *Pioneers for Profit*, McKay highlights the pointed use of euphemism: "As you know, state contracts are bid upon only as a matter of form. To obtain a contract, it is necessary to ask, to solicit, and to make certain types of sacrifices on the spot."[38]

The English were reportedly lavish bribe-givers at the time, firm in their belief that, "[a]s one Englishman once warned, 'nothing' in Russia is achieved except through money."[39] Siemens was said to have placed orders with a company partly owned by a grand duke, once Siemens executives learned he had a financial interest at stake. Siemens also paid the travel expenses when the director of the Moscow railway visited Berlin.[40]

McKay wrote that French locomotive builders were told by the French naval attaché at St Petersburg to expect "bitter competition from German industrialists who have superior sources of action, information, and of course corruption."[41]

The Americans building Russia's railroads were outright cheats, at least according to the English. The losers of the rivalry to build Russia's railroad accused the winners of placing distance markers too close together, making it look as if they had built more railroad than they had.[42]

Early HR headaches

Management, or, more precisely, finding qualified managers, was problematic. Russians of the right social status and with an appropriate education were expected to go into government service, leaving few capable candidates for the Russian offices of foreign companies. As ever, a workaround turned out to be better than the original proposition. "Interestingly, men with little training and modest background often worked out best," Kirchner wrote.[43] After spending a generation importing managers from abroad at great expense and difficulty, companies began to Russify.

If finding bosses was a problem, finding workers wasn't. Labourers were drawn to roles in foreign enterprises—working in a German, French, English or American company was preferable to working in a Russian business. Workers were paid more and treated better; Siemens even devised a pension scheme for its Russian employees. This was in part because Western European employers were more progressive than their Russian equivalents—the bar, admittedly, was low—but also because international companies were careful to avoid accusations of abusing their workforces, which could be read to mean treating them like a Russian employer.[44]

Here, too, is a strong parallel with modern-day Russia. Getting a job with an international company was a hard-won source of bragging rights among Russia's new white- and blue-collar workers. The overwhelming assumption when foreign companies came to Russia in the 1990s was that they treated their people better and were automatically better at what they did than their Russian analogues. To Russians, foreign companies had funny cultures—a bit of *Dilbert*, the business satire comic strip, came to Russia with every international company. But when compared to their Russian peers, foreign companies paid better and were more pleasant places to work, at least in the early 1990s.

At the very end of the 1800s, a number of companies entered the Russian electrification business. The market—and Siemens' place in it—remained sufficiently politicised, expensive, competitive and subject to nationalist impulses for Siemens briefly to consider leaving Russia altogether. Siemens' ongoing struggle with the complexity of the Russian market tempted other companies, including, most notably, AEG, to enter the market. AEG started its relationship with Russia via agents—some of whom proved problematic—but a successful streetcar business brought AEG founder Emil Rathenau to call Russia "a country of the future."[45]

The pre-war boom

By 1900, the Russian Empire was the world's largest oil producer; railroad construction continued at breakneck pace. Russia now had the world's largest railway network, behind only the United States.[46] Foreign capital cascaded across the border: in 1900, 269 foreign companies were doing business in Russia, most of which had come into existence since 1888. Between 1906 and 1914, the volume of foreign investment in Russia doubled. By the outbreak of the First World War, there were two trillion roubles of foreign capital invested in Russia.[47] "By 1914 foreigners ... held almost half the shares of Russian joint stock companies,"[48] not to mention their investment in Russian debt.

This presence came at a cost. Company formation was difficult; the distances involved in shipping raw materials were enormous; the costs of production were higher; and the administrative burden was backbreaking. Finally, Russian labour was less productive and often required extensive training and education.[49]

In the twentieth century, Siemens thrived in Russia—sales in Russia in 1908 equalled 6.8 million roubles (around GBP 716,845 at the time); that figure grew to 7.25 million in 1909 (around GBP 774,407 at the time) and 9.1 million roubles (around GBP 967,776) in 1910.[50] Subsequent orders surged at least partly on purchases from the Russian War Department and private companies.[51] By 1914, Siemens had 3,244 employees in St Petersburg and 855 in other locations across Russia.[52]

There is some debate about the drivers behind the boom in Russian industry: the state, the market, consumer demand and industrial consumption—including Russia's bulking up its military—were all potential sources of growth.[53] But there is little disagreement that in the run-up to 1914, Russia's economy was expanding rapidly.

"In Tsarist Russia, despite some institutional shortcomings, foreign companies found the stable environment of a market economy based on private enterprise and the support of the state."[54] The phrase "institutional shortcomings" comes across as a bit euphemistic at this point, but this would not be the first or only example of oblique language used to describe the Russian or Soviet investment environment.

Government action lured French investment to Russia, though there were also push factors. French companies were among those vaulting over Russia's punitive import tariffs of 1891 to open businesses in Russia, sometimes even after obtaining

Russian citizenship for one of their executives. In other cases, the French invested directly into existing Russian businesses. These factors came at the same time as a French industrial boom, but according to historian Olga Crisp, the French experienced a "temporary disillusionment" with the returns on customary investments in French government securities, making the move toward investments in Russia more attractive.[55]

The British presence in Russia was strong. It came in surges broken by periods of caution and stasis, but some estimates show that by 1917, British capital, invested either directly or indirectly, was almost 25 per cent of all international investment in Russia. The investment at this stage was primarily in the oil, textiles and copper sectors and was said to have amounted to GBP 110 million in 1913.[56]

Masking foreign identity was a critical survival tool for international companies in Russia: the government looked askance at foreign ownership in strategic industries, including France's investments in mining and minerals. The tsarist Russian government, in fact, reserved the authority to withdraw the rights of any foreign company to operate in Russia. Moreover, registering a new company in Russia was "lengthy, cumbersome and frequently costly," so investing into an existing Russian company was more efficient.[57] In the early 1900s, Belgian and British companies even more than the French were said to have taken special measures for doing business in Russia.[58]

Russia, like many countries, has an elaborate history of protecting strategic sectors. It also has a rich history of expropriation.

Siemens was put under local, Russian management to avoid being labelled an "enemy enterprise" during the First World War; by all accounts, Russian managers ran the business successfully. In the end, it all came to naught. Siemens in Russia was nationalised by the Bolsheviks in June 1918. Its plants in Russia became known as "Soviet state enterprises" Elektrosila, PO Sevkabel and NPO Kositzki Works, and the entire investment was lost, though not irreversibly.[59]

Back to that in a moment.

High finance

Russia was the last of the world's larger economies to join the gold standard; the impact of the move was to harmonise the Russian economy with its peer nations but also to provide a level of security and assurance that the Russian market was now easier for outside investors to understand.

"In 1914, on the eve of the First World War, Russia was the largest net international debtor in the world," borrowing more than Brazil and Argentina, among other groups of net debtor nations, writes Hassan Malik in his volume of economic history, *Bankers and Bolsheviks*.[60]

Russia arrived at this position almost entirely thanks to government policies inside and outside Russia. Germany's Chancellor Otto von Bismarck "promoted the flow of German capital to Russia during the late 1870s and early 1880s"[61] as part of his efforts to solidify the League of the Three Emperors, an alliance among Germany and the Russian and Austro-Hungarian Empires. France used its own capital to invest against Germany's influence in Russia, and ten years after Germany's dominance of Russian debt markets, France used bond purchases to bring Russia in line against Germany in 1894. War drove borrowing; interest rates made keeping money in Russia relatively attractive. Russia's joining the gold standard (in 1897) bolstered confidence in the Russian economy.[62]

The early 1890s to the 1900s saw a massive influx of financial investment into Russian securities. French foreign direct investment (FDI)—the money that built factories and created companies—similarly soared, most prominently in mining and metallurgy.[63] Investment from France and growth in foreign capital inflows to Russia coincided with a sharp increase in railroad traffic, oil production, pig iron production and cotton consumption.[64]

The French were not the only nation interested in mining and metallurgy. The Russian imperial city of Yuzovka, in what is now Ukraine's Donbas, is modern-day Donetsk. Yuzovka was founded in the late 1860s and early 1870s by Welsh businessman John Hughes and his New Russia Company. Say the word Yuzovka out loud and listen for its resonance with its founder's surname.

The growth of Russia's debt to foreign creditors is critically important and speaks to the role of the financial investment that took place in parallel to direct investment. The Paris Bourse, the capital's financial marketplace and "one of the most active and liquid exchanges in the world," was one of the main forums for the trading of Russian government debt toward the end of the nineteenth century.[65]

The French bond market, where a large amount of Russian government debt was traded, was a brutal financial arena and home to a widespread practice known as "badmouthing." Badmouthing was like blackmail, with an important difference. Blackmail is an extortion against the threat of revealing detrimental information that at least in theory is true.

Badmouthing is a form of extortion against the threat of revealing detrimental information that is entirely made up. Arthur Raffalovich, a Russian émigré living in Paris who served as commercial attaché at the Russian embassy in France, spent a small fortune to prevent badmouthing from destroying Russia's reputation as a creditworthy nation on French financial markets.[66]

Did a Western loan save or upset history?

The period following Russia's defeat in the Russo-Japanese War, a calamitous conflict that shut down Russian expansion in East Asia, and the Revolution of 1905 brought devastating political violence to Russia. Vast sums of capital—and the people who owned it—left the country.

"Cannes was allegedly full of grand dukes and their friends, and there was talk there of 'the arrival of a train full of gold sent from Russia with the proceeds of the sales of property there,'" Crisp wrote.[67]

The government, and maybe even the monarchy itself, were in deep distress politically and financially. The 1905 Revolution brought Russia its first legislative assembly, the Duma, a blow to the authority of the tsar. It was also one of the opening shots that ended in the tsar's abdication in the February Revolution of 1917.

Witte, by then prime minister, arranged for a monumental loan from France's Banque de Paris et des Pays-Bas—later known as Paribas—to keep the Russian government and the country's entire financial structure afloat. The loan syndicate included French, Dutch, British, Austrian and Russian banks. France had stopped providing credit to Russia as part of its efforts to urge the government to negotiate a peace in the Russo-Japanese War. When the war was over, loan negotiations began.

The talks were troubled from the start: the electricity was cut off at St Petersburg's Hotel d'Europe, where the participating bankers were staying. They were instead shuttled to the home of then Finance Minister Vladimir Kokovtsov, where a "double patrol of police" protected them from unrest associated with a general strike in the city.[68] These 1905 negotiations were a false start to an even more tense, but ultimately successful, set of negotiations the next year, following a change of government in France and the resolution of a fraught geopolitical triangle involving Russia, France and Britain (at the expense of Germany).[69]

A transaction of this magnitude attracted considerable controversy at the time and in its subsequent interpretation. Supporters of the loan inside and outside Russia believed the funds would not only stabilise the government but also maintain Russia's ties to the European economy and bolster its reputation as a reliable partner. Opposition liberals at the time decried the loan, saying it was pushed through without the Duma's approval and would only serve to prop up an autocratic regime that was viciously repressive and resolutely undemocratic. Malik, a financial historian now working in investment management at Loomis, Sayles & Company, writes that France's support of continuity in the Russian government was a missed opportunity to "change the course of Russian policy and indeed history."[70]

Beyond 1906

Within Russia and beyond its borders, the period between 1906 and the start of the First World War was enormously unstable, but it didn't seem to deter investors. "In 1913, Russia saw the largest capital inflow in at least 28 years," Malik wrote.[71] Relations between Britain and Russia were improving; this rapport brought increased financial and direct investment into Russia as bilateral rivalries in Central Asia and elsewhere cooled. Franco-Russian relations remained strong, as they had been in the lead-up to and aftermath of the 1906 loan.[72]

Geopolitics, however, was never very far from the financial markets, most acutely in connection with French behaviour in Russia: in 1913, "the French and Russian governments agreed on an arrangement explicitly linking bond listings in Paris to Russian actions in the military sphere." The deal stipulated that Russian railway construction include the preferences of the French General Staff.[73]

Russia's increasing integration into international financial markets made it look as if the geopolitical environment was broadly stable across Europe. As a result, participants in the financial markets almost completely failed to forecast the outbreak of the First World War.

Surely, countries whose financial and industrial sectors were interdependent would never go to war.[74]

Forecasting's fattest failure (so far)

It's easy to forget there were two 1917 revolutions in Russia—the February Revolution that brought down the royal family, and the October Revolution that brought down the entire country.

First National City Bank of New York—now known globally as Citibank—opened its first office in Moscow in January 1917.[75] After extensively studying the Russian market, First National's executives decided this was the time to commit. First National was not alone. Western investors at the height of the First World War piled into Russia. Malik identifies a group of drivers behind this phenomenon:

> First, in contrast to later observers, many contemporary foreign investors did not perceive Russia as suffering from an economic crisis— even as late as 1917. Second, a remarkably high degree of risk appetite shaped investor decision making and was in turn the product of moral hazard from government guarantees and competitive pressures. Third, geopolitics and feelings of patriotism with the context of the First World War pushed investors to engage in the Russian market in the hopes of advancing home-country interests. Finally, contemporary investors felt that by investing in Russia, they were investing in the transformation of a society—a belief that would enable them to overlook much of the political instability and violence of the revolutionary events of 1917.[76]

More than 100 years ago, investors were thinking that by investing in Russia, they could change Russia. More than 100 years ago, competitive pressures pushed investors into a country that was party to a world war and on the eve of a revolution. And finally, more than 100 years ago, risk appetite was fed by government support.

No one saw it coming

Russia may have been the world's largest net debtor nation, but it was also the world's best payor. On time, and to the kopek.

Depending on your perspective, the First World War was either (1) a death blow or (2) a gift to the Russian economy. One argument focused on the economically destructive forces the war visited on Russia. The other emphasised the boom of a wartime production economy.[77]

The banking world very much supported the glass-half-full point of view. First National City Bank of New York was ready to make its move.

In 1916, Malik writes, First National began offering its bankers Russian-language lessons, joining Spanish, Portuguese and French as the newest financial *lingua franca*. The bank identified a boarding house for its unmarried bankers, across the River Neva from its opulent St Petersburg headquarters. First National's Russia head, Henry Fessenden Meserve, was effusive about Russia's future, both in communications to clients and to the bank's headquarters in New York City.

The following is an excerpt from his communications to New York after the February Revolution toppled the tsar and brought to Russia something descriptively labelled the Provisional Government:

> I am very proud of the Russians for their wonderful self-restraint, and although matters here are still, of course, nervous for the individual, I

feel more certain than ever that Russia itself will come out in the end stronger than ever. I still consider all foreign investment here advisable and safe, and I sincerely hope that the United States will now be willing to help Russia more in every way.[78]

There is likely an element of self-promotion as Meserve promotes Russia, Malik said, but the enthusiasm is genuine, and Meserve was not alone in his excited outlook. So here he is, sending an "all OK" signal to headquarters regarding the health of the market about seven months before the October Revolution brought the Russian Empire to an end.

In June 1917, First National dispatched a thirty-two-year-old banker to Russia to open the company's second office, this time in Moscow.[79] First National's move into Russia was not considered speculative or adventuresome. To a certain degree, the bank was following its clients into Russia. That same trend was true of Russia in the 1990s.

First National in Russia was essentially telling its US executives: "Look, our Western or global relationship clients are doing direct business in Russia. They have cash management needs; we should be following them. Or we should be there because they're coming. The Singer building in St Petersburg is a symbol of this," Malik said.[80] One of those clients was called the General Electric Co. of America. As in nearly every other sector, competition in the financial services business also played a role. First National was not the only international bank eyeing Russia; other banks, including from the US, were contemplating market entry.[81] More to the point, that communiqué from a branch office to a headquarters is another in the chain of distorted signals between Russia and a distant HQ.

John Frederick Bunker, London City and Midland's man in Russia, took a relatively dim view of Harvard-educated Meserve at First National: "[T]he [National City] Bank and Corporation appear to have no manager really experienced in Russian affairs, and will therefore probably have to pay for inevitable mistakes." In several dispatches to the head office, Bunker said that company executives with "little to no knowledge of Russia and its language or culture" were forming corporate policy, Malik wrote.[82]

Malik adds, though, that even a relative Russia expert like Bunker fluctuated in his country assessments. It didn't seem to matter how intensely a company studied Russia before entering the market. International banks went into Russia because they had to. Woe unto the banker who let another bank—especially one from a rival nation—conquer the Russian market.[83]

Politics, geopolitics, commerce and personalities all combined to deliver a risk appetite—even among people who thought they understood Russia—that overlooked the advent of one of the twentieth century's most traumatic political events: the Bolshevik Revolution. Meserve told his superiors at First National that "there is a tremendous future in Russia for the National City Bank." American newspaper accounts at the time urged a long-term perspective on Russia.[84]

In February 1918, the Bolsheviks renounced all the debts of the Russian government in the largest default in history and nationalised everything that belonged to foreign investors. First National opened its Moscow office three weeks after the Bolshevik Revolution, staging an office opposite Red Square at the National Hotel, simultaneously a temporary home to Lenin and Stalin.[85]

Malik writes that staff from First National's offices in Moscow and Petrograd (as St Petersburg was known at the time) remained in Russia for a period, but that the expatriate staff left via Finland in September 1918. Ever the optimist, First National opened another office in Russia in 1919. By March 1920, First National City Bank was gone from Russia.[86]

In 1974, Citibank re-established a presence in what was then the Soviet Union, with a representative office on Karl Marx Avenue in Moscow. The office closed six years later.[87]

Citibank "cautiously" opened a representative office in the Russian Federation, again in Moscow, in 1992.[88]

3

THE "UNBREAKABLE UNION"

What was the easiest job in the world? The head of a rep office
in the Soviet Union.[1]

The aftertaste

Following the revolution, the default on tsarist loans and the nationalisation of foreign property, commercial relations with Russia turned unsurprisingly and brutally sour. Over the ensuing decades, the mood would fluctuate with the freezing and thawing of the Cold War and the expansion and contraction of the global economy. Only in 1987, in the waning years of the Soviet Union, did a desperation move throw open the doors to foreign business.

But first ...

In the 1920s—during the period of economic experimentation known as the NEP, or New Economic Policy—a trickle of international companies came to the Soviet Union under concessions, or government permission to operate, "to encourage investment in Soviet industry." Siemens was among them, back into the electrification business and in support of the construction of the Moscow metro, among other projects. These activities reportedly together amounted to less than half of 1 per cent of officially reported industrial output by 1926–7.[2]

During the Great Depression, the isolated Soviet Union became one of the United States' primary export customers: "[B]y 1931, sales to the Soviet Union constituted two-thirds of all US exports of agricultural equipment and power-driven metal-working machinery," Marshall Goldman, the late expert on the Soviet economy, writes in *Détente and Dollars*. This was, however, an early peak. The Soviet Union over-extended itself, couldn't pay for everything it ordered and began cancelling contracts. Goldman writes that Western engineers "were stranded inside the Soviet Union without funds to pay their way home."[3]

The rise of the Nazi party in Germany and the outbreak of the Second World War essentially froze Siemens' activity in the Soviet Union. Siemens factories in German-occupied Soviet territories worked for the German military, powered by forced labour from prisoners of war and civilians. In the post-war era, Siemens' business in the Soviet Union grew and diversified steadily; by 1971, the company had a representative office in Moscow. Siemens helped the Soviets build their half of the Apollo-Soyuz space project, and in 1989 the company founded a German–Soviet joint venture in medical technology.[4]

The tortured US–Soviet trade trajectory

The US under President Franklin D. Roosevelt recognised the Soviet Union in 1933 and in 1934 created the Export–Import Bank of the United States (Eximbank) almost entirely to underwrite export credits for American capital goods to the USSR.

It took almost forty years for Eximbank to close its first deal.[5]

That first loan extended USD 202.4 million to finance Soviet purchases of US-made industrial equipment.[6] The following year, US industrialist and Occidental Petroleum magnate Armand Hammer helped arrange a USD 180 million Eximbank loan to the Soviet Union as part of a larger deal to fund construction in the Soviet fertiliser industry.[7]

A 1966 bill to extend Most Favoured Nation (MFN) trading status to all the countries in the Soviet-dominated COMECON economic bloc failed, aside from Poland, which received MFN status separately in 1956. The MFN marker essentially provides for equal and non-discriminatory trade relations between countries granting each other this status.

The mood against aiding communist countries was relatively robust; US politics at the time blocked Eximbank from lending money to Eastern Europe, among other places. Congress also banned lending money to third parties doing business with communist bloc nations. This move had the perhaps unintended consequences of the United States having to unwind a USD 50 million credit to Italy's Fiat for its pioneering plant in the Russian city of Tolyatti.[8]

President Richard M. Nixon's "New Economic Policy"—the similarity to the 1920s Russian policy must be coincidental—turned the US toward promoting economic ties with the Soviet Union and led to the 1972 US–Soviet trade agreement and summit with General Secretary Leonid Brezhnev in Washington, DC. Eximbank subsequently started promoting billions of dollars of exports to the USSR, with the explicit aim "to see how to fit the non-market Communist countries into the multilateral framework of economic exchange among the Western economies."[9] On the other side of the trade agreement, the Soviets reportedly had a robust appetite for American capital to underwrite projects at home.[10]

Two years later, the Jackson–Vanik Amendment to the Trade Act of 1974 ended government support for US trade to the Soviet Union, stipulating that the US could not do business with countries that restricted their citizens' right to emigrate. This amendment was targeted at the repression of the Soviet Union's Jewish population and its *refuseniks*, individuals whose applications to emigrate from the Soviet Union were refused, rendering them internal outcasts. The 1974 act also included provisions to monitor large transactions on national security grounds.[11]

This did not, however, mean that economic relations between the US and the USSR were entirely severed. It only meant that government money was out of the game. The private sector picked up the slack.

Hammer House

In the Soviet Union's infancy, US private sector investment came in part from Hammer, who started in Russia via trade concessions granted by none other than Vladimir Lenin during the NEP period. Hammer's father Julius, a Russian émigré, was a founding member of the American Communist Party.

Depending on your perspective, Hammer has been credited with, or accused of, some of the most outrageous behaviour in the Soviet Union. He opened a pencil factory in Russia in the 1920s. He is said to have traded in luxury Russian imperial loot expropriated by the Soviets.[12] He and his Russian wife were under perennial suspicion; he was rumoured to have cooperated with Soviet intelligence.[13]

Stalin eventually threw Hammer out of the Soviet Union, but he returned in 1961, at the request of President John F. Kennedy, to negotiate the deal that built the chemical plant for fertiliser production. In 1972, during the period of détente, a relaxation of Cold War tensions between the US and the USSR, Hammer negotiated a twenty-year agreement with Brezhnev to export phosphate to the USSR; the Soviets exported natural gas for conversion into ammonia and urea through Hammer's companies. This trade was estimated to be worth USD 20 billion and involved the construction of port facilities in Soviet Odessa (now Odesa, in Ukraine) financed by Eximbank.[14]

Each of these achievements is a landmark event. To the naked eye, however, they are largely invisible. Hammer's most visible mark on the Soviet Union, and even on modern-day Russia, is on Moscow's skyline: the International Trade Center.[15] Moscow oldsters will refer to the building complex as *Khamerovsky Dom* or "Hammer House." The two-tower assembly is one of Moscow's least attractive buildings, but when it opened, it was home to some of the city's only bearable hotels and restaurants. One of the towers offered B-Class—on a good day—office space that was usually one of the first offices for companies when they arrived in Moscow.

General Electric

Other early starters in the Soviet Union include General Electric (GE), which has a long and elaborate history in the country, beginning with tsarist Russia. In 1908, Thomas Alva Edison, a founder of GE, sent one of the earliest phonographs to Leo Tolstoy, after Tolstoy participated in an 1895 project to record famous voices from around the world on the new device. Tolstoy was said to have been "enamoured" with the gift.[16] Following the revolution and in the aftermath of the First World War, GE's economic relations with the Soviet Union focused primarily on heavy industrial trade, including efforts in electrification, railways and hydroelectric and gas turbines.

During construction in the late 1920s and early 1930s, GE supplied the hydroelectric turbines to what was then called the Dnieper Hydroelectric Station in Soviet Ukraine, at the time Europe's largest hydroelectric power plant. Stalin ordered the plant destroyed to prevent it falling into German hands during the Second World War; GE also helped with its reconstruction.[17] This is the Dnipro Dam that was attacked in a Russian missile strike in March 2024.[18]

In 1930, GE opened an office in Moscow, a move reciprocated with the opening of a Soviet engineering office at GE's campus in Schenectady, New York.[19]

According to *The New York Times*, during the Second World War GE provided the Red Army with "an entire generating plant built on railroad cars that could move as military operations required."[20]

Geopolitics intervened in 1946. The US Department of State blocked the export of twenty GE electric locomotives—they were later nicknamed "Little Joes," after the Soviet dictator—that were sold instead to the former Milwaukee Road railroad; the South Shore and South Bend railroad from Chicago to South Bend, Indiana; and the Paulista Railway in Brazil.[21]

Cancelling the deal damaged the bilateral relationship between the US and the Soviets and put most activities on hold. GE and the Soviet government re-established ties in 1968, when talks began on a deal signed in 1973 to provide electric-power generating technology. The deal was anticipated to generate hundreds of millions of dollars in business for GE.[22] GE reportedly opened an office in Moscow in 1974.[23]

Geopolitics interrupted again when the Soviet Union invaded Afghanistan in 1979, and GE's presence and activities in Russia were scaled back dramatically. Only three or four people remained in GE's Moscow office; most of their focus was on the delivery of plastic to Russia's auto industry.[24]

GE as a company has evolved substantially over its history, acquiring and disposing of companies that swelled and shrank its business in Russia. In 1986, GE bought NBC, the US broadcaster that later became NBC Universal. GE divested from NBC Universal in 2013, but while a part of the GE group of companies, NBC shows like *Law and Order* were being shown on Russian TV as *Zakon i poryadok*. Russian commercial aircraft are fitted with GE engines. As a result of sanctions on the Russian economy, GE no longer services those aircraft engines.

In 2012, GE employed 3,400 people in thirty-five Russian cities. In Russia and the Commonwealth of Independent States (CIS)—a regional association of some, but not all, post-Soviet states—the company's revenues exceeded USD 2.5 billion.[25] In 2013, the company signed a strategic agreement with Rosneft that foresaw investments of USD 1 billion in oil and gas technology in Russia. Company material accompanying that announcement said that GE had been present in Russia since the early twentieth century and had participated in the earliest Soviet electrification plans, and that by 2013 all of GE's business units were present in Russia. The company's portfolio of activities in Russia included everything from healthcare to lighting and finance.

In 2018, generally thought to be the apex of GE's presence in Russia and the CIS, the company had more than 5,500 employees and offices in fifteen cities across seven time zones, according to company material. There were more than 850 aircraft in the region powered by GE and partner engines, more than 1,000 turbines and compressors across the region and more than 900 new and modernised locomotives powered by GE engines.[26]

Stalin's autarky

These examples and a few others aside, the period between Stalin's command of the Soviet Politburo in the 1930s and the end of the

Second World War was one of almost complete autarky. Foreign investment in Stalinist Russia was rare. Stalin was hostile to the West: he considered it an ideological enemy hell-bent on his and his country's destruction.

"The Soviet industrialization process took place in a totally different environment from that in any other area of the world," wrote John Slater, a former member of the Secretariat of the United Nations Economic Commission for Europe. And the differences weren't only in industry. "Although many banking and legal institutions and codes existed in the Soviet era, their functions diverged at an early stage so widely from their nominal counterparts in capitalist countries that the similarity of nomenclature was in effect without significance."[27]

This is a slightly complex way of saying that foreign and Soviet business would never understand each other.

"If you think you and your Russian business partner are going to see eye to eye, ponder this," a contemporary account of doing business in the Soviet Union reflected: "You may find the Soviet Union a strange place to do business, but for him the world of the Western businessman is even stranger."[28]

No matter how far back you can cast your mind, it is still difficult today to recall how divorced Soviet economic development was from what was happening almost everywhere else. The Soviet Union was a nuclear superpower and one of the world's largest industrialised nations on the eve of its collapse, but it had reached that status almost entirely on its own.

The Soviet economy was orchestrated from an imposing, Stalinist building in central Moscow that is now the lower house of the Russian parliament. In the Soviet period, it was the home to Gosplan, the state economic planning agency. Gosplan's primary task was to produce the five-year plans that told every factory, store and assembly line what to do, when to do it and what it would cost. Every enterprise was owned by the state.

Every employee from the tool maker to the bread baker was a government employee.

The Soviet Union had diplomatic and commercial outposts including and beyond its global network of embassies, trade offices and overseas banks. But there was little travel. There was little in the way of educational exchange. The USSR sat at the top of an Eastern European political and economic ecosystem, but none of these structures aided Soviet integration with the rest of the world—for decades, that was not even remotely a priority.

Quite the opposite: the Soviet Union's networks fed its isolationist stance and fuelled the country's opposition to a set of Western economic, social and political principles the country's hard-line Kremlin leadership found anathema. When Soviet ideology—including its dysfunctional, centralised economy—collapsed, there was nothing there to take its place, and very little homegrown capacity to absorb the changes that had taken place in the world around it.

"Soviet managers, though often dedicated and competent in ministering to outdated production systems, have virtually no usable concepts of marketing, business strategy, or commercial accounting," the attorney Jeffrey Hertzfeld wrote in the *Harvard Business Review* of 1991. "The sad truth is that there probably aren't 300 people out of 300 million in the Soviet Union who know how to read a P&L [profit and loss] statement."[29]

That was the state of play for business-oriented intellectual capital. The condition of physical assets on the ground was no better.

"The dwindling capital assets of the last decades of Soviet rule have left a legacy of useless and obsolete technology; after decades of a monolithic command system, the economies of successor states lack the managerial skills and techniques to administer changes of the transitory period," according to Alexandra

Swetzer, who worked in the United Nations Secretariat at the time of writing these words.[30]

What was referred to as "East–West trade" was, relatively speaking, fairly robust, and grew substantially, from the mid-1960s to 1980. Most of it was import–export activity. Very little of it was the sort of industrial cooperation that saw the installation of major internationally backed projects on Soviet territory. Many such cooperation agreements were discussed and even signed; very few of them ever came to fruition.[31]

In the UK

In May 1965, Aeroflot, the Soviet airline, installed an illuminated sign at the West London Air Terminal on Cromwell Road, a place where travellers could check in prior to heading out to Heathrow Airport west of London. According to the *Financial Times*, the sign was "the size of the side of a bus" and was mounted to encourage freight and business travel to the Soviet Union.[32]

In 1975, the British government allocated USD 2 billion in credits for British exporters to sell equipment to the Soviets—a sum that far outpaced any lending done by the US but, *The New York Times* noted, was slightly smaller than loans France offered.[33] Still, the vast majority of it remained untouched. The UK and the USSR exchanged political accusations over the slow uptake of credit, but the explanation lay elsewhere: private sector money was cheaper.[34]

Carbonated beverages, vodka and warships

Observers with more than a casual interest in the Soviet Union may recall how Pepsi entered the Soviet market. After a massive economic and diplomatic campaign involving both then-US Vice President Nixon and a thirsty Politburo Chairman Nikita

Khrushchev, Pepsi came to the Soviet Union in exchange for the rights to sell Stolichnaya vodka in the US.

It all started with a photo of Khrushchev sipping Pepsi from a branded paper cup at an international expo in Moscow in 1959; Pepsi executives were believed to have approached Nixon and asked the vice president to offer a drink to Khrushchev in front of the cameras—label facing out.[35] Both deals, formalised in 1972, were enormously popular: Soviet citizens swallowed carbonated cola with great enthusiasm; Stolichnaya quickly became a leading vodka brand in the US.

In 1990, when the deal was renewed, Pepsi was selling a billion servings a year in the Soviet Union and was getting about a million cases of Stoli per year into the US via an American importer. The ten-year extension saw the mutual trade in vodka and cola expanding to about USD 3 billion by 2000.[36]

According to *The New York Times*,

> Anatoly M. Belichenko, first deputy chief of the Soviet government's food and procurement commission, said that after the expansion, "all big Soviet cities will have a Pepsi bottler." He added: "I would like to give a commitment for everyone in the Soviet Union to be able to buy a bottle of Pepsi within 10 minutes of his home by the year 2000."

Belichenko admitted that the caffeinated soda was no panacea for the ills of the Soviet economy, but he and Gorbachev were said to be in search of solutions to shortages in the Soviet consumer goods market, and Pepsi was a small step in that direction.[37]

The vodka-based barter deal came about because the Soviet rouble was not a convertible currency. If the Soviet Union had paid Pepsi cash for the cola syrup (it was carbonated on arrival in the Soviet market), the roubles would be useless. The 1990 extension had a most unconventional twist: Pepsi accepted payment for the cola in ships—Russia transferred to Pepsi ownership "ten Soviet-built freighters and tankers of 25,000 to 65,000 tons, which will then be leased via a Norwegian partner."[38]

The *Los Angeles Times* reported that income from the leasing project would be re-invested into the opening of two Pizza Hut restaurants in Moscow, and that PepsiCo, owner of the Pizza Hut brand, would be the first US fast-food restaurant owner in Russia. McDonald's, which opened in January 1990, actually won that title just a few months prior.[39] Pizza Hut later made an almost equally large splash in Moscow because TV commercials released in 1997 controversially featured none other than Gorbachev. (He appeared decades later in a Louis Vuitton print ad that drew similar howls of shock and embarrassment.)

Even as these landmark transactions moved forward, the idea of doing business in the Soviet Union still chafed in some quarters. The Pepsi deal apparently provoked the ire of the US national security establishment; PepsiCo chairman Donald Kendall reportedly snapped back at National Security Advisor Brent Scowcroft and said that Pepsi was "disarming the Soviet Union faster than you are," *The New York Times* reported. US commentator William F. Buckley reportedly wondered out loud whether Pepsi was being sold in Russia's infamous gulags.[40] War History Online claims that the deal, for a while, gave Pepsi "the 6th largest navy in the world."[41]

Coca-Cola came comparatively late to the Soviet Union. The company withdrew its presence from the 1980 Moscow Summer Olympic Games in response to the Soviet invasion of Afghanistan, but the drink was still available in some of Russia's hard-currency shops.[42]

The beginning and the end—on paper

The first Soviet law on joint ventures, a transformative piece of legislation without precedent in the history of East–West trade, came into effect in January 1987. The earliest version of the law allowed foreign companies to hold a minority stake in a Soviet enterprise. This dramatic move was born primarily of desperation: the Soviet economy was in a period of deep stagnation, and across a wide range of metrics—quality of life, level of technology, life expectancy, among others—it was increasingly falling behind the West.

"In theory, everything changed in 1987, with the introduction of laws allowing joint ventures with foreign participation," Baker McKenzie's Paul Melling said. From an international business perspective, the moment was transformational. "January 7, 1987—the first period of business in the Soviet Union ends exactly on that date."[43]

The Soviet Union had ambitious goals for the programme. It wanted access to high tech. It wanted to boost exports with the help of Western manufacturing prowess. It wanted to reduce its reliance on imports. Joint ventures were designed to be a source of hard currency. And finally, Soviet leaders thought the creation of joint ventures with Western companies would be educational and create a new cadre of modern, Soviet managers.

The joint venture law came as part of Gorbachev's perestroika (rebuilding) and glasnost (openness) campaigns, a combination of cultural, political and economic broadsides at the decrepit Soviet construct, designed to reform the country's economy and extract its political and social discourse from the straitjacket of one-party rule.

A "liberal-market revolution"

Perestroika and glasnost attracted laser-like focus from Soviet watchers around the world. With Gorbachev's ascent to the Kremlin, one of the most notoriously closed countries was seeking to open from within. Politically, geopolitically and economically,

Gorbachev's work riveted attention on the Kremlin and bolted to it the hope that the Soviet Union was beginning to examine the depths of its totalitarian past and evolve away from it. More than anything else, though, Gorbachev's reforms were meant to save an economy on the verge of collapse. Allowing Western business a much firmer grip on the Soviet market might be the only thing that would save it.

Business, not for the first time, sensed an intoxicating combination of opportunity and risk.

"Companies moving into the Soviet economy must accept that they are betting on the eventual success of what perestroika has unleashed, a liberal-market revolution that will span a generation," Hertzfeld's *Harvard Business Review* article said.[44]

So here was one of the first assumptions about Gorbachev's reforms: they would follow a trajectory toward a market economy, and the politics might follow along. Hertzfeld wrote his piece around the same time as the opening of McDonald's smack in the middle of Moscow on Pushkin Square, an event that has been written about elaborately and eloquently elsewhere. Thousands of Muscovites queued for hours in the Moscow winter for a taste not only of a Big Mac but of American culture as served by one of the country's most famous commercial ambassadors. McDonald's in Moscow—the store at the time was the world's biggest—was everything the Russian restaurant scene wasn't. It was clean, its well-trained, young servers smiled, and the food included exoticisms like lettuce and sesame-seed buns. Negotiations to open the restaurant took more than a decade; as opening day approached, the restaurant received 27,000 applications for 630 jobs.[45] The trademark scent of sizzling hot and generously salted French fries led politicians, economists and executives around the world by their noses toward a euphoric optimism about the future of the Soviet economy.

Hertzfeld, a legal pioneer in Eastern Europe who was no idiot when it came to the Soviet Union, beseeched investors to go long, to shun the temptation for a quick buck and to invest for growth from the inside out:

> [A] New York garment company could still go into Leningrad with truckloads of blue jeans just written off its books and make a great many dollars. But this is no way for a global corporation to think about the future. McDonald's could eventually have more restaurants in the Soviet Union than in Germany or Japan. Procter & Gamble could sell more toothpaste in Moscow than in Cincinnati. Companies simply have to think through what McDonald's has thought through—operations that allow for expansion in the Soviet economy without dependence on periodic, massive infusions of new investment from abroad.[46]

The tone of this article is nothing short of messianic, with an overlay of economic eugenics: "Markets are made, not born. The same is true of the people who sustain them."[47]

> Planning a joint venture is therefore like planning an experiment in genetic engineering. New enterprises, like transplanted strands of DNA, will become the organizing matter of new commercial life, in this case, new forces of production that sustain wealth. The Soviets have a chance of avoiding a social disaster only if many joint ventures insinuate themselves into their civil life. By the force of their action or example, joint ventures will engender a new population of managers: marketing managers, process-technology and information-technology specialists, financial analysts, quality engineers, and business strategists who will lead the Soviet economy into the next century.[48]

The idea here is not to discredit Hertzfeld or to have a retrospective giggle at his expense. It is intended, instead, to portray what he and many other people were thinking at the time and the logic underpinning those thoughts. Hertzfeld and plenty of other professionals were entirely sober about the obstacles to investing in perestroika. He spends a lot of time in his *Harvard Business Review* article explaining many of the contradictions of the Soviet economic system, offering advice on how to unpick them and work within, or perhaps despite them. But he and others were high on the potential opportunities, too. The "flood of proposals" sent into his firm, Hertzfeld wrote, justified his enthusiasm.

The Soviets intended most of their joint ventures to focus on heavy industry, consumer-oriented sectors and high-tech activities.[49] These goals did not always align with the international companies that invested in Soviet joint ventures. Most of them primarily wanted to sell stuff to the Soviet Union's massively underserved consumer market. From Moscow to far-eastern Magadan, the Soviet consumer class had millions of roubles stashed under its mattresses.[50] At the time, this was where the Western business lens focused most easily.

The Soviet Union of the 1980s was the sort of place where international tourists were told to bring bubble gum, stockings or copies of celebrity magazines to distribute as small tokens of appreciation to workers like hotel staff, tour guides and drivers. Can you imagine giving a pack of bubble gum as a gesture of thanks to a New York taxi driver in the 1980s? You'd be pushed out of the vehicle at speed. In the Soviet Union, that bubble gum would become a birthday present for a beloved child. The truly adventurous brought extra pairs of blue jeans to trade or, better yet, sell on the emerging street market for Western talismans.

A more in-depth, and business-oriented, description of the investment climate in the Soviet Union from another close observer sets the scene in grim relief. Vesa Turtiainen was the vice president of ABB Project and Export Finance, Finland, when he wrote the following in a chapter of the aptly named collection *Trading with Uncertainty: Foreign Investment Trends in the Soviet Union*:

A potential foreign investor, exporter or importer, faces a jungle of complexities in the USSR today. There is almost daily change in the political, national, and economic life of the country. The partner you dealt with yesterday may not be there tomorrow, the license for your exports or imports may or may not be granted by a different authority tomorrow. The legal framework you counted on when planning an investment may be entirely amended the day after next and control passed to new and different powers. Finally, payments from your Soviet trading partner can run months (and possibly years) late. In short, the business outlook with the USSR for the immediate future years appears to be bleak to say the least.[51]

Once again, 100 years after some of the earliest merchants went to Russia, the question of risk appetite was newly fresh. What sort of investor saw opportunity here?

Still, the finances and the financiers flowed:

But look at the potential. Here is a network of republics and nationalities, a vast combination of natural and human resources, all undergoing the biggest transformation since 1917. The Union and the individual republics are starting the long march toward a modern market economy. There must be short, medium and long-term opportunities in such a vast and rich country. The pitfalls are enormous, but they have not stopped the flow of businessmen into the Soviet Union, and there is still tremendous enthusiasm among Western companies to find the right opportunities.[52]

Once again, investors in Russia wove a breathy expression of spectacular opportunity into cautionary language about potentially phenomenal risk.

It is astonishing to think that in 1990 and 1991, supermarkets and stores in Moscow, including in some of its most prestigious neighbourhoods, were virtually bare. Department stores at the time had the inexplainable and incongruous availability of rubber boots and fishing rods, but little else. This desperation, bordering on blight, was even more shocking because Soviet five-year plans usually ensured Moscow, the capital, always had a rich assortment of goods on store shelves.

Those central economic plans were, of course, at the heart of Soviet economic malaise. But there was more at play. While the stench of empty fish counters choked Moscow's supermarkets, Muscovites in a position of privilege could periodically deliver a dinner of roast goose with all the trimmings and a virtually bottomless supply of mood-enhancing beverages. This was not a daily occurrence, but it was an example of the luxuries available to individuals and families with connections.

Such was the scene in the home of a senior academic officer at Moscow State University, whose patriarch was a member of the Communist Party.[53] These are the sorts of individuals for whom the inaccessible was always accessible, but only via special channels. In 1991, even that level of privilege was under extreme stress. The goose that served as the centrepiece of a heaving kitchen table was most likely snatched from a supermarket display case (if it made it that far), stashed away out-of-reach and offered, most likely, in exchange for a yet-to-be-extended academic favour in return. This was just one of the manifestations of the informal economy, one that was critical in the atmosphere of shortage that dominated the end of the Soviet period.

Seeing the light

More than one of the executives interviewed for this book told the story of the widely known Soviet lightbulb market, held on a street outside the centre of Moscow every weekend. There was only one product for sale at this street market—lightbulbs that didn't work.

"It was a very popular market. People would go out there every weekend and buy broken lightbulbs," Baker McKenzie's Melling said.

Why would anyone buy a lightbulb that didn't work?

Here's why: the Soviet economy was one of constant shortage—*defitsit* in Russian, or deficit, in English. Goods of any description in short supply were often simply referred to as *defitsit*, just to emphasise their scarcity.

Shortages hit hardest on domestic and consumer items, so the workaround went something like this. On the weekend, shoppers would purchase dead lightbulbs and bring them into their workplace on Monday. Once at their office, factory or almost anywhere else, they would unscrew a working lightbulb from the ceiling or a lamp—they were almost always uniform and standard—and take it home. In its place, they'd install the dead lightbulb they picked up over the weekend and inform factory management that the bulb needed replacing.

"Everything is sort of upside down," Melling said. "That was the Soviet Union in a nutshell."

The Soviet economic system was designed to be short-circuited—five-year planning only worked through extensive patching and workarounds. It happened at the grocery store, it happened on the factory floor and it happened at the national, macro-economic level. Entire enterprises got their inputs and produced their outputs thanks to side deals among factory directors. Everyone did it, and everyone knew it. These deals were done carefully—no one could openly flout the rules under a totalitarian political and economic regime. But the informal economy in the Soviet Union was central to putting food on the table and keeping the lights on in homes and factories across the country.

The later days

The Soviet Union's last months and days brought disorienting change. Between 1982 and 1985, leadership passed from the sclerotic Brezhnev to the chronically ill Yuri Andropov and then to the wavering Konstantin Chernenko—each one of them an ailing gerontocrat. Gorbachev emerged from within the elite to become General Secretary of the Communist Party when the Soviet economy was in extremis, rotting from internal, structural failures and external political and military stressors. Gorbachev's status was telegraphed in traditional Soviet style— he planned Chernenko's funeral, the sign that he had bested the succession process.

Gorbachev did much to liberalise the Soviet Union through the one-two punch of perestroika and glasnost. The ossified Soviet edifice began to show the earliest signs of life. Gorbachev the social reformer gradually returned the country's long-suppressed memory to the status of public possession. Benefit of hindsight aside, he began a process that could not be reversed.

A small phone call

Perhaps the most symbolic gesture of that process was the 1986 release from internal exile of the dissident Andrei Sakharov and restoration of the physicist's role as the embodiment of public conscience. Sakharov was among the founders of the Soviet nuclear weapons programme but later decried the lethality of nuclear war and the horrors of the Soviet invasion of Afghanistan. It was his stance on Afghanistan that in 1980 earned him six years of inhumane treatment, including psychological abuse and physical torture during a hunger strike, within a small apartment in what is now Nizhny Novgorod, the former Gorky, about 440 kilometres to the east of Moscow.

The story of his liberation is famous. After more than six years of house arrest, workmen appeared at Sakharov's apartment to install a phone. The next day, it rang with Gorbachev's voice beckoning the Nobel Peace Prize laureate back to Moscow.[54] He briefly occupied a place of international acclaim and a prominent, if short, official role in Soviet political life. Sakharov died in 1989.

Rehabilitated dissidents aside, Gorbachev's defining gesture in the eyes of the business community was the joint venture law. The final four-ish years of the Soviet Union under the joint venture law were formative and enduring. Melling said that if you look at a standard Russian legal contract even today, you will see language in the template that traces its origins to the Soviet period of the late 1980s and the very early 1990s, down to the letter.

"Even now, I promise you if some Russian company sends you a sales contract, you can see the Soviet origins," he said.

Don't miss your flight

The Soviet state controlled all foreign trade—every purchase, every sale into or out of the Soviet Union went via some sixty-five companies called "foreign trade organisations," (FTOs). Each FTO was in charge of a carefully defined list of products. Melling was able to describe the process from memory.

A manufacturer who wanted to export to the Soviet Union might start with the Soviet Trade Delegation office in London or the British–Soviet Chamber of Commerce (BSCC). Those organisations could help organise a trip to Moscow to attend one of the hundreds of trade exhibitions held each year, each dedicated to one or more specific industrial sectors. Sellers met potential buyers and discussions would begin.

"The importance of the BSCC and other such chambers of commerce to the conduct of business in the USSR thus cannot be overestimated," Melling said. "For the last AGM of the BSCC held in Moscow, a Boeing 737 had to be chartered from BA to fly out all the British delegates."

Once it was time to discuss a purchase or sales contract, Melling said, the FTO took over the talks and an invitation to visit Russia would come from the USSR Ministry of Foreign Trade, accompanied by a purchase contract in Russian and English.

The FTO negotiators knew what they were doing, Melling said,

> particularly when it came to the dark arts of negotiation. They saved the most intense negotiation for the afternoon, their foreign counterparts by then being severely alcohol impaired as a result of all the toasts offered to business success, world peace etc.—in vodka and/ or cognac—over lunch. ... To this day there are few things a Russian enjoys more than getting a foreigner drunk on cognac while he sips his apple juice.

"Random pages of the contract would then start to emerge from the Russian side's 'computer,' a mysterious piece of machinery never actually seen by anyone from the foreign delegation," Melling said.

And then time started running out. Most international visitors came for a week of negotiations, and their visas would expire on a Friday. As those visas neared the end of their validity and the prospect of being stranded in Moscow approached, the contract pages started pouring off the printer.

"I lost track over the years of the number of contracts signed by senior executives and non-Russian speakers, contracts which provided for Russian as the dominant language in the event of conflict between the two texts, all for fear of being left behind in Moscow by British Airways," Melling said:

It was only when safely on the plane home, somewhere over Poland, that the unfortunate executive would discover one or more agreed amendments that had somehow not made it into the final text or—worse still—that he had signed a binding contract not having a clue what it said.

The how-to guides

In June 1991, the Economist Intelligence Unit ("the EIU") published a book called *Investing in Eastern Europe and the USSR: Financial Strategies and Practices for Successful Operations*. It is easy now to take pot-shots at a guide on investing in a country that ceased to exist six months later. In fairness to the EIU and all the other "how-to" publishers, the guide made frequent and specific reference to the political turmoil and economic difficulties roiling the Soviet Union in the early 1990s. Much of its basic advice was sound:

> Many companies weigh the risks against the prospects of tapping into a 280 million-strong market, starved of consumer products with reportedly huge amounts of cash, albeit roubles, stashed away. The country's extensive store of mineral wealth is, for some, worth the high degree of frustration and risk inevitable in a country where the balance of power between the federal government and republics is shifting daily.[55]

By the time the EIU guide was published, anti-Soviet, nationalist rebellions in Latvia and Lithuania had been put down by deadly force. But the guide was still forecasting the upcoming 1994 presidential elections, suggesting that Gorbachev would "face challengers from the left and right."[56] In 1994, of course, Gorbachev had long since been ousted; Yeltsin was president of an independent Russia and faced re-election in 1996.

The EIU's investment guide presented a litany of reasons not to invest in the Soviet Union. Gorbachev was weak. The republics were restive. The Soviet army was frail and riven with discord. Yeltsin was an up-and-coming threat to Soviet unity. Civil unrest was increasingly likely. The economy was nearly in tatters, ripped to pieces in part by the mid-1980s crash in the price of oil, the Soviet Union's leading export and primary hard-currency earner.[57]

And yet: "Its huge population and vast natural resources still make the Soviet Union a great long-term prospect for Western companies, but anyone looking to invest must take the short-to-medium-term political risks into account," the EIU wrote. At the time the EIU guide was written, PepsiCo had been in the Soviet Union for twenty years, ABB Combustion Engineering was "firmly entrenched" and "industry leaders like Fiat, Polaroid, Exxon, Chevron, Samsung, Hoffman LaRoche, Volvo and Olivetti are on their way in."[58]

The EIU was in good company within elite foreign policy analytical circles in its assumption that the Soviet Union was in trouble but not on the verge of collapse. The country was, in fact, in the midst of a 500-day plan designed to dislodge the planned economy and replace it with a market economy.

Very few people, including Western government officials with vast intelligence resources at their disposal, predicted the collapse of the Soviet Union. The EIU and everyone else writing and talking about the Soviet Union all saw the ongoing juxtaposition of risk and opportunity and described both ends of that equation in extreme terms. Again, from the EIU:

> Those who are there believe that if you do your homework, are creative, flexible, have nerves of steel and, above all, can keep your sense of humour, the potential pay-off is limitless. They are convinced that the Soviet Union will emerge from the turmoil of the next few years either intact, or as a group of thriving republics. Unsurprisingly, the believers

want to be a part of the change and be in position for the take-off when it comes.[59]

Nerves of steel. Sense of humour. Limitless. Thriving. These are not words you often hear in the same breath about the same place. And this doesn't even get into the issue of how the rouble was still not a convertible currency, among other important details. Joint ventures took anywhere from six months to two years to establish. Soviet ministers could, with the stroke of a pen, eliminate text the two parties had agreed after painstaking and painful negotiations.[60]

Increasingly international

Between 1987 and the end of 1991, the Soviet law on joint ventures became more flexible and favourable toward foreign participants, up to and including allowing 99 or more per cent foreign ownership of the joint venture. Gorbachev himself declared that the more foreign companies got involved, the better for Russia.

"Foreign investment would give Western firms a direct stake in the success of the reform process. They could thus become influential advocates of perestroika within Western societies," one observer wrote.[61] This sounds a little bit like Gorbachev outsourcing the hard work of economic reform—and its evangelising—to international companies.

Relaxing the joint venture laws made the prospect of investing in the Soviet Union even more appealing, and the attraction was mutual. "Foreigners in general, visiting the Soviet Union in the late 1980s, found themselves besieged by Soviet counterparts to enter into joint ventures."[62]

International companies already in Russia were encouraged to update their presence to formats in keeping with the new joint venture law. So many businesses—primarily from North America and Western Europe, and most of them in Moscow and St Petersburg—were registered in the final years of the Soviet Union that the Ministry of Finance could not keep up.[63]

Then came Combustion Engineering:

> The size of joint ventures in the Soviet Union took a quantum leap yesterday when Combustion Engineering Inc. of Stamford, Conn., agreed to participate in building and operating a $2 billion petrochemical complex in western Siberia. Announcement of the Combustion deal came as Italy's Fiat Auto company announced on the eve of a visit to Rome by Soviet President Mikhail Gorbachev that it would participate in a venture to build three plants 600 miles southeast of Moscow that will use Fiat technology to turn out 900,000 cars a year. The two new projects are by far the largest of the more than 1,000 joint ventures planned so far under Gorbachev's perestroika program, which for the first time in decades opened the doors of the Soviet Union to foreign ownership of businesses there.[64]

When it was all over, though, the number of registered businesses engaged in commercial activity was low. Despite the country's size and the scope of its resource wealth, Carl H. McMillan, then professor of economics at Carleton University in Canada, wrote that "[b]y the end of 1991, official registration data reported a stock of foreign capital committed in the neighbourhood of USD 6 billion."[65]

For comparison, China brought in USD 30 billion of foreign capital of a total of USD 60 billion committed.[66] "The Soviet experience ... cannot be regarded as constituting a rich legacy. The Soviet leaders apparently felt they could open the door to foreign investment, and it would come flooding in on their terms." By the end of the Soviet period, there were about 2,000 active foreign investment projects, most of them in Russia and most involving only a "handful" of foreign companies.[67]

The Washington Post noted that of the more than 1,000 joint ventures registered in the Soviet Union, most were formed in the few months prior to August 1989. Sixty-five of them were with American companies. Most were European companies, with West Germany (at the time) in the lead.

In 1990, the BSCC had a list of sixty-five Anglo-Soviet joint ventures.[68] Academic research into those ventures showed some of them to be dormant, idle, liquidated or registered to offshore addresses. Of the active enterprises, most were in the service sector, followed by research and development, and production.[69]

The experience of most British–Soviet joint ventures, as reported by the British side, was largely unimpressive. A couple of the joint ventures had experienced success and were happy with their activities in the Soviet Union. Another, however, complained bitterly about an ineffective banking system and "pilfering," "low morale" and "letters arriving between three and six months late, or getting lost altogether."[70]

"Our joint venture was the first operative joint venture between the United Kingdom and the USSR," said one joint venture operator, who chose to remain anonymous in a research project on the topic. "I was encouraged initially, but now I wish to pull out. Maybe I'll get over the disillusionment."

If the joint venture law became increasingly flexible and attractive on paper, reality had other plans: 1991 brought separate Soviet and sub-national Russian Republic laws on international investment. These rival laws were a symptom of a widening chasm and growing rivalry between central and more peripheral Soviet authority; the investment climate was caught in the middle of a "war of laws" between the federal level and the independence-minded republic level.[71] Beyond that and within republics, the rules were almost impossible to follow. Ministries contradicted each other: if you were obeying one ministry's rules, chances are you were breaking another's.

The push-me, pull-you nature of investment law in the Soviet Union left investors unsure where authority over business activity resided, a fog that only added to already increasing levels of uncertainty.

Important as it was, the "war of laws" was a technical manifestation of what was happening on a far wider, and even deeper, scale. A country was slowly falling apart, turning a malfunctioning society into something that was truly dystopian.

In a perverse twist, the Soviet – and later the Russian— government used this legal and economic melee to extract advantage from their foreign partners. When the harbour is difficult to negotiate, only the local pilots know how to steer. The only local individuals who really knew anything about international commerce at the time of the Soviet collapse were people who worked in the FTOs charged with shepherding foreign companies on to the Soviet market. Again, the two worlds could hardly see eye to eye.

"You can imagine. All of a sudden, throw in joint ventures with international companies and their business plans and their marketing plans and their hiring policies and of course they're all bemused. There was no understanding of commerce, of what we understand as a commercial business, at all. It was all totally new," Melling said.

The first ending

The collapse of the Soviet Union unleashed volcanic transformational forces in every direction. Gorbachev, who in February 1990 lifted the Soviet Communist Party's political monopoly and authorised multi-party elections, was placed under house arrest at his holiday villa on 19 August 1991 by a group of coup plotters known as the GKChP, the State Committee on the State of Emergency. Shortly before that, Yeltsin had been elected president of Russia while it was still one of the fifteen Soviet republics; relations between Moscow and all the Soviet republics, including Russia, were tense.

The GKChP summoned tanks into the centre of Moscow. This is where Yeltsin famously took his stance atop one of them and essentially glowered the coup into failure three days later. Gorbachev returned to Moscow ruinously undermined.

The rest of the Soviet republics broke from the Kremlin's grasp and declared independence. By 25 December, Gorbachev was out as Communist Party chief and head of the Politburo and as president of the Soviet Union. That evening, the hammer and sickle came down from above the Kremlin, and on 26 December, the Soviet Union was formally dissolved.

Watching it happen, live

As the events of August 1991 developed, the corps of foreign correspondents burst on to the streets of central Moscow at the first news of the coup to witness the tanks rolling toward the White House—then the home of the parliament of the Russian Soviet Republic—and to watch history unspool. They were joined by a smaller contingent of expats resident in Moscow, who also rushed on to the streets. Moscow is normally calm in August—it's hot, and everyone leaves town.

Witnessing history is easier with a full fridge.

"My first instinct was, 'I had better get to the grocery store. If there's going to be chaos, I want food,'" said Eric Crabtree.[72]

In 1991, Crabtree was working in Moscow with a US-based construction consultancy. He later became Russia country head and, ultimately, chief investment officer for the International Finance Corporation (IFC), an investment arm of the World Bank.

On 19 August, Crabtree felt compelled toward the standoff at the White House: "It was like 9:30 in the morning, and I thought I had better do something."

He wove his way into the swarm as it pushed through central Moscow, from the White House, past the central Moscow offices of the Ministry of Defence and toward the open expanse of Red Square and the walls of the Kremlin, where he recalled seeing policemen, arm-in-arm, surrounding Lenin's marble-and-granite mausoleum.

Crabtree said he and the approaching crowd were ultimately deflected by the entreaties of a group of elderly women who asked them to leave the policemen alone, "[s]o Lenin didn't get burned down," he said.

The mob then moved toward KGB headquarters on Lubyanka Square and likewise did not burn down the monstrous building that produced decades of repression and terror. On the night of 22 August 1991, a crane came to the front of the Lubyanka, as the KGB headquarters were referred to, draped a noose around the neck of "Iron Felix" and uprooted the towering statue of the founder of the dreaded secret police.

For the Soviet republics, the end of a brittle federal bond meant a return to sovereignty for the Baltic republics and a new, fraught and tense experiment with modern sovereignty for Ukraine and the republics of Central Asia and the Caucasus. The Russian Federation now had neighbours it called the "near abroad" or the CIS.

Set adrift

For Western Europe and the United States, the fragmentation of a nuclear superpower brought bracing, new concerns about security, alliances and geopolitics. The US and Europe, and the countries released from COMECON and the Warsaw Pact, the

Soviet-dominated economic and military blocs, experienced a sort of existential disorientation, set adrift by the collapse of the bipolar world that had anchored geopolitics since the end of the Second World War.

For almost everyone in the new Russia, the Soviet self-immolation incinerated the few remaining shreds of order, structure and logic that underpinned the system. Moscow in 1991 became a rambling, street-level bazaar of political disarray and economic chaos. A raucous, ramshackle tent city of protest and rebellion against Soviet power—people came from all over the country with handmade signs promoting their grudges—rose at the edge of Red Square in front of the hulking Rossiya Hotel. This sort of ugly, inchoate protest a few metres from the Kremlin walls was unfathomable at any time during the Soviet period. Participants in this sort of demonstration—if it had even materialised—would have immediately been arrested and imprisoned, or worse. But here, in the very centre of Moscow, was a squalid patch of rag-tag protesters, periodically using the toilets inside a hotel once considered the exclusive domain of Russia's political elite.

The economy imploded; millions of citizens of the new Russian Federation could no longer afford the basics for survival. Their daily routines were upended, they were trampled by hyperinflation and they had friends and relatives suddenly living in different countries across new national borders that rose out of nowhere.

It is difficult to overstate how fragile the ruins of the Soviet Union were. Politically, economically and geopolitically, the collapse of Soviet power could have sent a bloc of just under 300 million people spinning uncontrollably in any number of hazardous directions.

"For a considerable number of years in the 1990s, it was very unclear whether Russia was going to be a criminal state going forward, or whether the apparatus of the state was going to be able to seize control from criminal elements," said Richard Prior, an investigations executive with decades of experience in and around Russia. "I really think that was the critical question in Russia until the late 1990s. It was entirely possible that control over the entire Russian economy was going to be lost to strong criminal figures."[73]

Careful what you ask for

If the collapse of the Soviet Union came as a surprise, in some quarters it set pulses racing.

"In the early 1990s, no one in the world was prepared for the fall of the Soviet Union, and the emergence of what became known as emerging markets," said Bernie Sucher, who was to become one of the leading figures in Russian investment banking. "Nobody had that in their business plan."[74]

It was time to update the plans. For international companies, the collapse of the Soviet Union and the emergence of an independent Russia looked like opportunity. There were millions of roubles waiting to be liberated from beneath the nation's mattresses and straining to be spent on German washing machines and French shampoo. Beyond that, Russia's industries wanted—no, desperately needed—billions of dollars of investment from sector-leading companies around the world. Oil fields needed new drills, pumps and pipes. Telephone networks needed new switching stations. Roads needed the latest in paving machines and weather-resistant asphalt. The list was almost endless.

"There was a huge demand for everything," Cescotti said.[75]

4

A BORDERLESS WORLD ARISES

Reagan initiated globalisation with Thatcher. Their big emphasis was fighting the Soviet Union. The fact that these countries willingly turned toward markets was a huge gesture, symbolically and practically, toward globalisation.[1]

This is the BRICS syndrome, when you have companies looking at markets from an economic perspective and forgetting that they're countries.[2]

Timing is everything

Russia's emergence as a fledgling country and a primitive market came when the leaders of the world's largest companies were starting to think about their businesses in a far more expansive, and expansionary, manner. As the 1990s unfolded, these executives had begun to feel confident they could do business in markets they had once considered too exotic, distant or risky.

Russia's arrival as a business destination was firmly within a broader context and a strong, new, global commercial trend. It's worth spending a small amount of time to place Russia in that wider environment.

This international business trend had a name.

"'Globalisation' has become the buzzword of the last two decades. The sudden increase in the exchange of knowledge, trade and capital around the world, driven by technological innovation, from the internet to shipping containers, thrust the term into the limelight," *The Economist* wrote in 2013.[3]

Since then, globalisation has come to mean a lot of things. It's a business plan for growth or a scapegoat for business failure. It's a trend to be defended and protected, or it's an evil to be unwound and avoided. A few decades ago, it was all the rage and changed the way business and geopolitics worked.

In his discussion of geopolitics and political risk, the author and former UK ambassador to Belarus Nigel Gould-Davies breaks globalisation down to four main features. First, the scale and significance of cross-border trade had grown enormously since the 1980s: "[F]rom 1988 to 2017, the total stock of foreign direct investment ... rose from 8 percent to 40 percent of global GDP."[4]

Second, these cross-border capital flows became more diverse in the activities they supported, Gould-Davies writes. What started as more straightforward, "loans, trade in goods and primary production," evolved into something qualitatively different, including "global manufacturing supply chains, equity investment, data, and trade in services."

Third, Gould-Davies—now a senior fellow at the International Institute for Strategic Studies in London—said cross-border investments became geographically more diverse. "From 2000 to 2014, flows of FDI into developing countries rose from 20 percent to 55 percent of global FDI."

Finally, international financial flows became more complex. Money began to flow from emerging markets into developed markets. China became an international lender. "From 2000 to

2013, FDI flows *from* developing countries rose from 10 percent to more than 30 percent of global FDI."[5]

Gould-Davies' statistics bolster his convincing argument that growth in the volume and changes in the character of cross-border financial flows exposed investors to increasing and increasingly complex levels of political risk. Time has borne him out.

The enormous rise in global FDI travelled peaks and valleys, but the direction of travel was only up. Global FDI in 1994 was just under USD 205 billion. That number peaked in 2015 at just over USD 2 trillion. The Russia figures are similarly buoyant. In 1994, FDI into Russia was USD 690 million. FDI had two high points in Russia: in 2008, the number was USD 75.8 billion, and in 2014, the number was USD 53.3 billion.[6]

Despite this global surge, Gould-Davies points out that FDI as a share of global GDP did not return to pre-1914 levels until after 2004.[7] This further bolsters the assertion from Jeffry Frieden that the world was most globalised on the eve of the First World War. It took almost a century of commerce—including more recently the advent of technology that can distribute data and dollars in nanoseconds—to return international trade to an era facilitated primarily by the telegraph.

Ready, set, go

For business, the collapse of the Soviet Union and the end of the Cold War was one of globalisation's loudest starting guns.

The twentieth century was bracketed by periods of deep economic interdependency. "Problems and all, the end of the century was reminiscent of its beginning dominated by globe-straddling markets. ... The global capitalism of the start of the century had returned," Frieden wrote.[8]

The early phase of globalisation saw the formation of two trading blocs: NAFTA, the North American Free Trade Agreement (now known as the USMCA, the United States–Mexico–Canada Agreement), came into existence in 1994, as did Mercosur, the Latin American trading bloc. These were, respectively, the world's second and third largest trading alliances, behind the EU.

"It started in the 1980s, but it really took off in 1990," said Mitchell Orenstein, professor of Russian and East European Studies at the University of Pennsylvania.[9]

Evidence abounded that a world where trade barriers fell and borders between countries faded could experience stunning economic growth. "Between 1993 and 2000, American trade with its NAFTA partners grew nearly twice as fast as trade with the rest of the world, from under USD 300 billion to over USD 650 billion," Frieden wrote. Mercosur became the most important destination for inbound investment among all developing economies, and trade among Mercosur members increased by 500 per cent in the decade since its founding.[10]

By the late 1990s, foreign companies were investing USD 35 billion a year into China. Vietnam began an aggressive integration campaign with the global economy and saw its GDP increase by 300 per cent in fifteen years.[11]

Eastern Europe, too, profited from the global expansion of American, Asian and European companies:

> Corporations flocked to the region. Western European firms moved quickly to rebuild commercial ties that had been cut for decades and to carve out production sites and markets in the EU's rediscovered hinterland. American and Asian firms seeking a low-cost springboard to the EU market also took up the opportunity. Daewoo spent USD 1.5 billion to build two Polish auto plants; Sony set up state-of-the-art factories to make consumer electronics in Hungary; Goodyear took over a Polish tire maker; Volkswagen bought up the Czech Republic's respected Škoda automaker. Sweden's Electrolux, the world's leading producer of kitchen appliances, turned a musty Hungarian state refrigerator producer into one of the region's industrial showcases.[12]

Globalizatsiya

Russia was both a driver and a beneficiary of globalisation. The country opened, and investors flooded in. The rush took all comers—big business, chancers, even people with criminal records came to Russia hoping at best to wipe the slate clean or, at least, to find refuge. The Pittsburgh Penguins NHL hockey team even financed Russia's Central Red Army hockey team in the hopes of scouting players from inside the Russian sport.[13]

"Moscow by then was crowded with foreigners eager to help Russia and get in on the ground floor of a great social and economic change. Entrepreneurs, consultants, lawyers, bankers and academics with foundation grants, as well as fast-buck artists and swindlers from all over the world, swarmed across Russia looking for a piece of the action," David McClintick wrote in his explosive magazine piece, "How Harvard Lost Russia." "The atmosphere was charged with possibility and fraught with danger. Financial transactions were mostly conducted in cash; cities were awash in roubles. Kidnappings were common, as was gunfire and even bombings. Organized crime darkened the already grim picture."[14]

Russia was an "inbound" market, but it was much more. It was a resource-rich nation with enormous export potential. Analysts who tend to describe Russia as a petrol station with nukes, to paraphrase a simplistic and reductive approach, fail to grasp the role that Russia plays in the modern, global economy. To be sure, in per capita terms, Russia's economy once compared unfavourably to places like Portugal and Spain.[15] But Russia's role in strategic sectors has been critical for decades now, as we have all come to learn following the disruptions to commodity markets in the aftermath of the full-scale invasion of Ukraine.

"In 1992, literally thousands of Western entrepreneurs and businesses flooded into Russia looking for deals, joint ventures and any number of opportunities to set up their own companies in what seemed a frontier economy," reporter Larisa Vostryakova wrote in *The Moscow Times* in the mid-1990s.[16] The primary thrust of this article was a description of how Western businesspeople began taking positions in Russian companies, a phenomenon that developed as the Russian market did.

Russia became a place to sell things, to buy things and, later, even, to make things. Investment went in a cycle. In the very early 1990s, international companies sought to export things onto Russian shelves. Food, clothing and personal care products all topped the list of items that began progressively to appear in Russian stores or, latterly, in the branded outlets of Western stores.

Following its recovery from the 1998 government default, discussed later in this book, Russia became a place where companies started to make larger, more strategic investments. Instead of exporting to Russia, companies built factories in Russia to produce goods in and for Russia. Joint ventures slowly gave way to the creation of stand-alone businesses in Russia that were fully owned by an international parent company.

The world's greatest rebranding?

In 1981, IFC economist Antoine van Agtmael coined the phrase "emerging markets."

In 1991, Russia became one.

In 1996, the World Trade Organization (WTO) granted Russia MFN status.

By 1997, Russia was in the G8.

The G8, of course, later spat Russia from its ranks following the invasion and annexation of Crimea. Russia remains in the broader G20 group, though Putin is typically unable to travel to international gatherings in connection with a warrant for his arrest by the International Criminal Court. His attendance at a 2014 G20 summit in Australia, prior to the warrant, saw him lectured and eventually shunned by his international peers. He famously ate lunch alone at the summit before departing prematurely.[17]

The term "emerging markets" was designed to replace "third world country," described by the IFC as "a term that connoted extreme poverty, shoddy goods, and hopelessness to many at the time. But 'emerging markets,' van Agtmael would later write, 'suggested progress, uplift, and dynamism.' It reframed the picture, in time becoming the universal term used in the financial world to describe developing economies."[18]

In short, "third world countries" were not investible; van Agtmael was sent to rethink the term after a presentation to an investment bank. "Emerging markets" seemed so much more appealing. Mostly, they were the exact same places.

Linguistic interlude

"Van Agtmael invented the term as a marketing ploy. His job was to get investment into South East Asia," said Philip M. Nichols, professor at the University of Pennsylvania's Wharton School and a specialist on law, ethics and Russia. "The invention of the term has no meaning, but there was this phenomenon going on all over the world—it needed a name, and that name was emerging economy."[19]

Nichols makes a distinction between an emerging market and an emerging economy and prefers the latter: "People who live in those countries don't want to feel like they're just a market." Nichols cautions against seeing this as a rebranding. In the WTO, for example, there are meaningful distinctions to how countries are labelled: "That's why China fought so hard to get the developing country status when it joined, even though politically, they hated the word developing country. There are connotations and baggage with that."

With time, however, the term emerging market or emerging economy became accepted global shorthand for a country experiencing rapid economic growth and developing away from a weak market or pre-market system.

And the phrase just seemed so much more ... polite.

"A big bang moment"

Linguistics aside, the term caught fire.

"The notion that billions of people suddenly became interesting—that was like a big bang moment," the investment banker Sucher said.

Prior to that, the third world country label evoked an entirely different response in many investors. They were, Sucher added, "poor places that no one had to worry about unless they were causing a war or other disruption. Now it's an opportunity that fund managers and corporate executives were duty-bound to learn about and find a way to make money on."

This was not to be the first time that financial services terminology revolutionised how investors looked at countries.

Who's in control?

Companies thrived in an environment where goods, capital, people and information could move quickly and more freely than ever. Globalisation was a way to optimise costs, to locate production closer to resources and inputs and to get finished products closer to customers. Companies began to dream about, believe in and ultimately urge forth a borderless world of frictionless trade.

Governments loved what globalisation was doing for GDP growth. With time, though, companies started to generate revenues rivalling some of those GDP figures. As globalisation accelerated, the technology companies, media companies and international retailers with their complex supply chains and borderless markets waded into globalisation on nearly equal footing with policymakers in their home governments and their host countries. In this increasingly amorphous world, public and private sector priorities resonated in some corners but conflicted in others.

First among these conflicts was the mounting pressure globalisation placed on political sovereignty.

Dani Rodrik of Harvard's Kennedy School made this pressure the centrepiece of his 2011 book *The Globalization Paradox*, where he introduced the globalisation "trilemma": countries cannot at the same time be (1) hyper-globalised, (2) democratic and (3) sovereign. For the state to work in a traditional liberal, democratic fashion, he argued, something had to give. His suggestion was that hyper-globalisation, expressed as an intense economic interdependency, had to suffer for the state to function properly.[20]

This framework contains some of the language and views seen in the divergent perspectives on how companies viewed Russia. Some companies saw Russia almost entirely as a globalising playing field where the trilemma was resolved in favour of economic integration.

Others saw Russia as a political entity firm in its Putin-backed sovereignty and with only a passing acquaintance with democracy.

Debate raged, and rages to this day, over whether Russia became an emerging democracy in the immediate wake of its Soviet past. Those conversations, both now and then, were highly politicised and usually revealed as much about political analysis as they did about Russia.

Whatever progress Russia might have made toward democratisation, Putin long ago shut it down. He and his advisors in the early 2000s started calling Russia a "managed democracy,"[21] a structure with a rigid central spine called the "power vertical."[22] In this pastiche of democracy, a strong president hollowed out the political institutions typical of robust, competitive political systems. Power in Russian democracy flowed down from the Kremlin, rather than up from the voting public.

Four little letters

In November 2001, the investment bank Goldman Sachs forecast that the weight in global GDP of four economies—Brazil, Russia, India and China—was set to increase dramatically. A research paper by Jim O'Neill, then the bank's head of global economic research, called "Building Better Global Economic BRICs,"[23] was an economically robust marketing exercise for Goldman Sachs' asset management division.

Goldman Sachs' research generated interest far beyond the portfolio investment community. Two years later, in 2003, a second Goldman Sachs paper, "Dreaming with BRICs: The Path to 2050," forecast that the GDP of those four countries would by 2039 overtake the GDP of the world's largest economies.[24]

This second piece of research went off like a bomb. When one of the world's leading investment banks deems a country investible, the investing world drops whatever else it's doing and pays attention. Goldman's analysis landed like a legitimising benediction on the very term emerging markets, the rapid acceptance and expansion of globalisation and, in the case of Russia, the relatively rapid recovery from a devastating default on domestic government debt and a dramatic internal financial meltdown in 1998.

"The BRICS concept reaped bountiful publicity and prestige for Goldman Sachs, so in that sense it was a stunning success: analysis by acronym," read a slightly snarky retrospective of the term from the Lowy Institute of Australia. "It also brought the potential of emerging economies to the notice of the rich-countries [*sic*] financial sector which was narrowly focused and parochial."

Prior to the emergence of the BRIC acronym, the institute wrote, "Wall Street thought of developing economies in terms of Latin America's chronic under-achievers and serial bankrupts, or Africa's endemic poverty."[25]

Goldman's magic acronym made investing in Russia—not just financial investments, but also bricks-and-mortar investments—a lighter lift in corner offices and boardrooms around the world. With Goldman Sachs' analysis backing you, investing in Russia became the closest thing you could get to a no-brainer.

In business circles, the acronym was everywhere. Books dove into the phenomenon of the BRIC economies. Seminars and conferences deciphered the meaning and the potential of the four big letters. The expression became part of international investment jargon. The phones started to ring off the hook in law firms, among mergers and acquisitions teams at investment banks, at risk consultancies and at accounting firms and management consultancies. Vice presidents of emerging markets—a job title that scarcely existed a decade ago—became extremely busy and wildly popular. Everyone took their calls.

Globalisation went into overdrive.

"Absolutely. I'm surprised the BRICs acronym came so late," Baker McKenzie's Melling said. Russia benefitted, he said, from being in the same acronym as China, something Wharton's Nichols confirms.

"If you have a passing familiarity with those countries, lumping them all together kind of makes them look all the same," Nichols said. It was a signal to investors: "These five countries [including, latterly, South Africa], these are the ones."

The second, and very much related, BRIC by-product was an enormous exercise in risk transference. Executives around the world were able to cite Goldman Sachs' research and say that investing in Russia was not only worth it but also passed the risk/reward test. Risk transference is one of the ways that companies can treat, or minimise, risk. Typically, risk transference involves things like buying insurance policies against war or nationalisation.

In this case, the Goldman Sachs report was the insurance policy. This is not to say that companies recklessly cancelled their political risk policies, but some of those risk management exercises may have become slightly less rigorous, or might have been carried out at a less senior level. Goldman had already done all the heavy lifting. Goldman's report named the preconditions and assumptions underlying its forecasts, including concerns about political stability and transition. The investment bank prudently cautioned that, for its forecasts to materialise, a lot of things had to go right.

A lot of that caution was treated as fine print.

More timid executives could confidently cite the acronym and offload all the risk, at least symbolically, on to Goldman Sachs. The acronym was a halogen-strength green light for companies to invest in emerging markets.

As a result, Russia—and most visibly, Moscow—exploded.

Goldman's own history in the Russian Federation is marked with starts and stops. The bank initially opened an office in 1994 but reduced its presence as part of a broader retrenchment. Goldman returned more prominently to Russia on the eve of the 1998 default and once again left the country, keeping only a small staff and a starkly reduced office in place. Goldman's then-president, Lloyd Blankfein, still new in role at the time, moved to bolster the bank's presence in Moscow starting in 2006. He met Putin and Dmitry Medvedev when Medvedev was president and Putin was prime minister. The bank ultimately developed a full-service presence in Russia and for Russian clients outside the country. In Russia, Goldman Sachs had a broker-dealer licence, and a banking licence. It was investing in Russian companies as a private equity investor and was also helping Russian companies issue debt and IPOs.[26]

Red hot chili peppers

Once companies had grown accustomed to doing business in the BRIC countries, they were served up a new menu to digest: "frontier markets." Again, note the emphasis on market, rather than country.

The geopolitical risk envelope was being freshly pushed from the inside, much in the same way Amazon tells its shoppers to try products similar to something they just bought.

In 2018, Goldman Sachs' O'Neill labelled a new group of promising economies "the Next Eleven." Further country-group acronyms variously known as MIKT, MIST and, latterly, MINT (Mexico and Indonesia, for example) later emerged. None of these abbreviations really gained any traction among investors.[27]

Each iteration of these acronyms bore a higher level of risk compared with its predecessors. It's interesting to consider whether the emergence of these new acronyms, along with monikers like frontier markets, was an invitation to take on increasing levels of risk or instead reflected a growing appetite for risk. Building up a tolerance for high-risk transactions and risky markets, after all, is similar to how the human palate adjusts to, and then craves, increasing levels of spice. After learning to live with jalapeños, you move on to habaneros. Before you know it, you're at the Carolina Reaper.

5

THE WALLS COULDN'T TALK, BUT THEY COULD LISTEN

It was heady times—it was amazing running a hotel. We had 110 per cent occupancy. We were struggling to keep up with demand. Every hotel was in the same position—to get a hotel room in Moscow was a miracle.[1]

I bought a loaf of bread and I bought a giant sausage. And then breakfast, lunch, and dinner was a slice of bread and a slice of sausage.[2]

The Radisson Slavyanskaya

When is a hotel not a hotel? When it's the Radisson Slavyanskaya Hotel and Business Center, on the banks of the Moscow River in the centre of the capital. It's difficult to describe how vital the zoo-like atmosphere of this dreadful, soulless, but somehow familiar institution was to the lives of many expats (and more than a few Muscovites) in the early and mid-1990s. The hotel's utilitarian, boxy exterior was no preparation for what went on inside.

Part of the Radisson complex was a hotel that came reasonably close to international standards and played home-from-home to an endless stream of visiting political and celebrity delegations. Part of the complex was a business centre housing the Moscow outposts of a cluster of international companies. You knew these places were plush because they had fax machines. The offices were also home to the BBC and NBC News' Moscow bureaux, among a few others. The Radisson Slavyanskaya had an indoor swimming pool. Oligarchs would use the hotel's press centre to speak to journalists in early versions of Russian press conferences.

The Radisson Slavyanskaya's most prominent feature, however, was its vast marble lobby, a small slice of Western Europe, or maybe even America, in still-barren, post-Soviet Moscow. It had bars, restaurants, shops, probably one of Moscow's first and only ATMs, and the all-important currency exchange to convert crisp, fresh dollars into roubles.

Changing dollars to roubles in Russia was a twisted treasure hunt: Russian currency exchanges would only accept spotlessly clean dollar bills to swap for roubles. It was endlessly maddening. For locals, having crumpled or pockmarked dollars in your pocket meant roaming the streets looking for a rare, lenient exchange booth. That, or it meant pleading with friends to swap your literally dirty money for anything brighter they had in their wallets. You would approach them gingerly: maybe they were leaving Russia on a trip and wouldn't mind taking your wrinkled money out with them. Businesspeople coming to Russia on short trips to Moscow were forced to beg their companies' finance departments to provide spanking new currency for their travel expenses.

The hotel had a global crossroads feel. It was also the kind of place where you could get a serviceable steak or meet a friend for an easy, if expensive, after-work beer. If the movie *Casablanca* were ever to be remade and set in 1990s Russia, the lobby of the Radisson Slavyanskaya would probably feature.

But some saw the hotel as the backdrop for a different movie.

"I still think of it as the *Star Wars* bar scene," Sucher reminisced.[3] He remembers the time of day he met investment bank Troika Dialog founder Ruben Vardanyan to talk about the emerging Russian stock market:

> The Radisson Slavyanskaya at 10:30 in the morning was just filled with these outrageous figures. You literally had stereotypical Texas cowboy oilmen in black and white cowboy hats and cowboy boots. You had these dark-skinned, heavily bearded muscle men from the Caucasus. You had a dizzying number of girls in cocktail dresses and high heels at 10:30 in the morning. And scurrying around was the beginning of a corporate and financial community, because it had a business centre and the Dialog Bank branch where most of the blue-chip corporates were doing their banking.

Sucher is a robust character who takes things pretty much in his stride. The panorama at the Radisson gave him pause.

"During the course of our conversation, I kept looking around at this scene that just didn't make sense. What are all these people doing in this picture? How do all of these people fit into my field of vision at the same time?" he said.

Hotels good enough to welcome international guests in Russia struggled with their roles as global watering holes. The Radisson brand started in Russia with the Slavyanskaya in 1991 and in 1993 built the Radisson Lazurnaya in Sochi. The Lazurnaya had a sports club and a large lobby bar so overrun with prostitutes in the 1990s that management levied a USD 1,500 membership fee at the sports club; only paid-up club members and hotel guests could visit the lobby bar. Russians are nothing if not resilient: the prostitutes—or more likely the thugs running the prostitution rackets—ponied up the cash, and the women joined the sports club. Russians knew business continuity just like everyone else.[4]

The legendary Metropol

Across town from the Radisson Slavyanskaya was its architectural antithesis, the Metropol Hotel. The Metropol was a stunning, vast, art-nouveau pile just a quick stroll from Red Square. Lenin once held meetings in its lobby and rooms; it was briefly home to an early Soviet ministry. It is an elegant, jewellery-box of a hotel with one of Europe's most beautiful atrium dining rooms. Like the Slavyanskaya, it was an East–West crossroads, but in a slightly more hushed manner. Even though it had the same carpetbaggers, arrivistes and Gucci-loafered Swiss bankers, it had an old money feel.

Despite all that beauty, history and intrigue, it was dead empty until Gorbachev got pushed out of the Kremlin.

"Come September of 1991, the business just exploded," Hugh Hallard said. Hallard was an Australian transplant to the role of director of sales and marketing at the Metropol. He came from a job in Sydney with no previous exposure to Russia.

The August putsch against Gorbachev brought a media scrum to Moscow and its few tolerable hotels: "We were inundated with television crews and media and everyone coming in to get a piece of the gold rush."

In short time, the Metropol once again became a major Moscow hub of commerce and diplomacy. The International Monetary Fund's (IMF) first, informal Moscow office was on the hotel's second floor.[5]

"There were these massive delegations from the World Bank and the IMF and the EU and everybody, everybody pouring in," Hallard said.

The hotel handled the onslaught, though the entire enterprise would have come crashing down if it wasn't for what the staff commonly referred to as "the truck." The Metropol was offering caviar brunches at a time when the shelves were empty everywhere else in Moscow. In 1990, the George H.W. Bush administration in the US was shipping in frozen chicken legs as food relief for Soviet citizens. They were affectionately known as "Bush's legs."[6]

"We purchased some things locally—eggs, milk—but twice a week, and then I think it became three times a week, a truck would come in from Poland. And we waited for that truck. We would say to each other in the morning meeting, 'Where's the truck? What's happening? Is the truck on schedule?' because the truck would come in with, you know, everything," Hallard said.

The truck was the equivalent of a supermarket—no, more like a department store—on wheels. Wine from France and Italy. Meat from Germany. Pasta from Italy. Butter from Denmark.

"A lot of money changed hands at the border to get things through," he said. "We were very dependent on the Russian partners." If the truck failed to show, the hotel wouldn't quite shut down, but the Metropol had an orgiastic breakfast buffet that attracted locals as well as hotel guests. Without that truck, it was back to the Soviet Union.

"We could have run the hotel a bit like ... the Intourist hotels," Hallard said, naming the infamous Soviet travel monopoly, "with cold sausage and boiled eggs for breakfast, and perhaps stale bread and a tea bag or instant coffee or something like that."

The wine, cheese, meat and supplies of all sorts might as well have been diamonds and gold ingots in early 1990s Russia. And a lot of it went walking.

"We had to turn a blind eye to the staff taking home a kilo of meat or a tray of eggs. We knew this was going on, but it wasn't only food. It was cutlery, crockery, sheets, towels, the lot, I mean, they could have taken the chandeliers off the ceiling, though that would have been a bit obvious," Hallard said.

It was theft, but times were tough outside the walls of the Metropol, and inside, Hallard said the staff were like actors on a stage. They'd come to work ahead of their shifts and put on a uniform as if it were a costume and then pretend their world was filled with splendour. On the outside, they were shopping for essentials on folding tables outside metro stations. "Certainly, at the beginning, we just had to go with the flow, shall we say."

Roger Canton was a junior banker with Credit Suisse First Boston (CSFB) in London when he made his first trip to Moscow and was booked to stay at the Metropol. While still at Heathrow, he had a call from his boss, who was stuck in traffic on the M25 and was going to miss his flight. Canton got on the plane and followed his boss's new instructions for a late arrival: "Meet me in the bar," his boss told him.

So he did. Canton recalls how far he had come from his home in rural New Zealand: "I get to the bar. Within twenty seconds I've got a gorgeous woman sitting on my left and a gorgeous woman sitting on my right and I said, 'This never happens to me.'"

Hallard's friend Tony Gambrill was a fellow Aussie also in the hotel business in his home country. He had a series of options for an internal move; one of them was Moscow. Hallard tried to talk him out of it, to no avail. So he met Gambrill at the airport.

"I left Australia, and it was 38 degrees Celsius. When I arrived in Moscow it was minus 15," Gambrill recalled.[7] He arrived in Moscow in January 1992—days after the emergence of the Russian Federation—to assume a role as director of training and development at the Metropol:

> The drive in was fascinating, because you could have shot a gun down every road you drive on. There were no cars, which I found astounding, considering the width of the roads. Then we got down to Gorky Street [one of central Moscow's main roads, now called Tverskaya Ulitsa]. I'm starting to see civilisation and shops. The first thing that struck me was I saw one shop that had something to sell, and that was a jar of green tomatoes. That was the only thing I saw going down Gorky Street that was tangible to buy.

Then he saw the Kremlin towers.

"I'm not political or anything"—Gambrill was twenty-seven at the time—"but it just had this magical aura and mystique about it. And then we turned the corner and went round to the Metropol Hotel, and I was now home." About thirty-five expat employees were meant to train somewhere between 500 and 600 local staff. The Metropol was freshly affiliated with the Intercontinental brand, and there was work to do.

"Our challenge is to try and move them toward an international style of hotel," Gambrill said. "And their move was to try and steal as much as they could from the hotel. The silverware you'd see for sale at Izmailovsky Park [a famous Moscow flea market], not just one piece here and there, a whole truckload. It was all quite openly known." Items went out the back door in employees' pockets; funds were siphoned from contracts.

In the throes of all this petty and not-so-petty theft, items would sometimes magically materialise out of nowhere. Gambrill lived on the premises, and once after returning to his room at the end of the day he noticed that there were no matches in his room's ashtray. He complained out loud, to no one. Moments later, there was a knock on the door and a member of staff to deliver a fresh box of matches.

"Every room was bugged," he said. "It's very obvious." Even though the Soviet, and then Russian, intelligence community was in a state of total upheaval at the time, hotel rooms for international visitors were typically bugged by domestic intelligence operations.

Management of the Metropol changed hands in 1994; the Intercontinental brand was stripped from the building, and the hotel was transferred to local owners and local management. Gambrill had already moved on; Hallard was out of a job but quickly moved to a similar role at the Grand Hotel Europe in St Petersburg, the 1905 venue for negotiations for the tsarist government's financial lifeline.

This was not the only moment of historical continuity and importance at St Petersburg's grande dame. More than eighty years after the landmark tsarist loan, the hotel was a joint venture with St Petersburg City Hall, which owned the property. Hallard delights in telling that his joint venture partner at the time was Vladimir Putin, then the head of international relations for the city of St Petersburg.

"I can say that I actually worked for Mr Putin for two and a half years," Hallard said. He admits he's stretching things a bit. "Look, he came in occasionally. But he was so quiet and inconspicuous and low-profile compared to, I think it was, Sobchak." Anatoly Sobchak was the mayor of St Petersburg at the time and Putin's boss in City Hall.

"When Sobchak came into the hotel, my God, you know, it was like a royal visit and we'd all be standing at attention," he said.

"I left at the end of '94, and I sort of completely forgot about him," Hallard said of Putin. "I was running a business in Australia, and ten years later, it must have been about 2004, 2003 or something, we had a ten-year reunion of the expats who had been working there, and someone said to me, 'Mr Putin has done well, hasn't he?'"

Sheremetyevo Airport

One of Moscow's more revered and loathed places bears brief special mention: the suburban Moscow hulk that is Sheremetyevo Airport, and, most specifically, the metallic human warehouse once called Sheremetyevo-2, the terminal built for the 1980 Summer Olympics and left virtually untouched until a renovation almost a generation later.

For about two decades following the Olympics, Sheremetyevo Airport was the grimy funnel that processed almost all arriving international visitors. It is a prominent character—but rarely the protagonist—in almost everyone's stories about travelling in and out of Moscow. It was not the sort of place that made an arrival, or even a departure, enormously auspicious.

It was dreadful. The floors were a sullen, mottled granite that could have been the discards from Lenin's mausoleum. For some inexplicable reason, the floors were perpetually covered with a powder-fine layer of dirt. Periodically, cleaners would move this dirt from place to place with rags thrown around wire frames at the end of a wooden pole. The place was cavernous and dark; the air was thick and stale enough to taste.

Frequent visitors in the late Soviet and early Russian periods complained endlessly and floridly about Sheremetyevo as part of a deep, love–hate relationship. Arriving into Sheremetyevo was a full sensory reminder that you were back in Russia. Departing held the promise of hot showers, white tablecloths or a family embrace, whichever mattered most. Road warrior stories always included the time spent in passport queues, the interminable wait at baggage reclaim or the utterly random and useless selection at duty free. Navigating Sheremetyevo was a pain: the two pairs of escalators connecting the arrivals and departures floors were out of service for more than five years in the 1990s.[8]

It was the sort of place that was an expat conversation starter and even the periodic subject of bragging rights. Dinner table conversations sometimes included the following dialogue: "You waited an hour at passport control? Ha! That's nothing. Last time I went through, I waited two hours!"

For a while, British Airways' morning departure from Heathrow to Moscow landed at Sheremetyevo shortly after a flight from Vietnam, guaranteeing an almost endless wait at passport control. Visitors from outside Europe were treated with time-bending scepticism at the tiny glass booths that constituted passport control, and some of the arrivals from Vietnam were suspected of supplying Moscow's lucrative black-market economy.

It was not unusual for the most reserved British business traveller—often dressed in suit and tie, even though the afternoon arrival time made meetings that day almost completely impossible—to sprint inelegantly toward passport control, just to lodge himself at the head of the queue, only then to briefly stare around self-consciously at the indignity of it all. Sitting toward the front of the plane, that much closer to passport control when you landed, almost justified the extortionate cost of a British Airways business class ticket.

Sheremetyevo-2 had a few legendary features. One was its massive, hanging arrivals and departures board with flip-over letters and a mesmerising array of destinations. It was more Warsaw and Tashkent than London and New York, but for expat visitors and even for most Russians, it embodied exoticism.

There was the departures area Irish Bar with the promise of as much draught Guinness as your departure time would allow. It was the sort of place where delayed flights, if not quite welcome, were easy to drink away. The Irish Bar was part of a Soviet–Irish joint venture that included a duty-free store in central Moscow with a second, nearly identical Irish Bar next door.

Sheremetyevo's ceiling was a dusty, hanging honeycomb of deep, dark, copper rings that everyone referred to as "the coffee cans." Some of them were used as light wells. Sometimes, the lights even worked. Morning, noon and night, Sheremetyevo indoors was always set at twilight.

Calling the coffee-can ceiling a legend is not an exaggeration. During the 2008 global financial crisis, as one expat executive packed his office to leave the country for good, the floor was littered with the memos and memorabilia of a long tenure in Moscow. Among the items prioritised for shipment home was a box with two or three of the coffee cans. One didn't dare ask how he got them. The ceiling pieces from Sheremetyevo were so precious, this executive left behind a case of wine to make room in his cargo container.

Finally, Sheremetyevo's toilets were the thing of legend, for all the wrong reasons. This is a polite book; the description of Sheremetyevo ends here.

Hospitality was for the home

The first time Paul Moxness made a trip to Moscow, he was providing security advice to a Danish investor opening a chain of restaurants in the capital. One of his first tasks was to release one of the restaurant managers from a walk-in freezer, where he had been briefly imprisoned for having scolded a waitress. The rest of the trip, which included meetings with representatives of the city fire department, and other safety bodies, went much more smoothly.

"They were way more accommodating than they would be in almost any other country," Moxness said of the public officials. They helped Moxness and the restaurant chain understand how the authorities managed emergencies and what to expect in the event something went badly wrong at one of the restaurants.

Moxness, who later became global head of security for Radisson Hotels, confirms observations by his colleagues in the hotel industry that the last thing you wanted to do when setting up a hospitality business in the new Russia was hire anyone who had experience of working in the old Soviet Union. Russians are among the most hospitable people you could ever encounter, but their warmth and generosity are mostly reserved for the kitchen table at home, rather than a hotel dining room.

Moxness tells a story about how, on arrival to Sochi, a group of uniformed men boarded the plane, pointed to him and his fellow travellers, and delivered that terrifying "come with me" gesture. Rather than being taken to the police for a potentially disastrous document check or a corrupt shakedown, Moxness and four other men were asked to haul the baggage trolley to the terminal. The tractor that normally hauled the off-loaded bags had broken down.

"I think they upgraded the airport before the [2014 Winter] Olympics, so maybe they bought a new tractor," Moxness said.

It was not unusual to hear stories about animals on board Aeroflot planes following the breakup of the Soviet monopoly airline into dozens of so-called "babyflot" airlines. This does not mean dogs and cats or support animals. In the early 1990s, goats, sheep and chickens sometimes travelled on board, next to paying passengers.

No laughing matter

The people who passed through the doors of some of Moscow's and St Petersburg's more prominent hotels—whether local or expat, hustler or banker—were part of a nation in the making. Hallard was right, in a sense, that these venues were stages that hosted an endless programme of performances.

Some of these hotels were also home to some of post-Soviet Russia's more tragic moments.

The Slavyanskaya's mobby reputation stemmed in part from a June 1994 police raid in the hotel's lobby, as officers armed with automatic weapons searched for an organised crime gang. The police held their fire but made ten arrests.[9]

That reputation tragically worsened when the Slavyanskaya—or more precisely an underground walkway a few metres away—was the site of the murder of Paul Tatum, the hotel complex's general manager. Tatum was at the centre of a three-way joint venture between Radisson, Intourist and Tatum's company Americom. In 1987, just as joint ventures with foreign companies became legal, Tatum set up shop.

Following the collapse of the Soviet Union—newspaper accounts say that Tatum loaned a mobile phone to an aide of Yeltsin while Yeltsin was barricaded inside the nearby government building[10]—Tatum's government joint venture partner became the Moscow city property committee, and the city named Umar Dzhabrailov its representative.

Dzhabrailov and Tatum never got along; disputes at the joint venture escalated. Tatum hired bodyguards, started living in his hotel office and eventually took to wearing a bullet-proof vest. At the same time, the lobby became ever more like Sucher's vision of the "Star Wars bar." One of Tatum's bodyguards was stabbed with a penknife. The Russian Interior Ministry labelled Dzhabrailov "a known contract killer" and a Chechen mafia leader.[11]

Tatum was murdered on 3 November 1996.[12] Ownership of the Slavyanskaya passed into Dzhabrailov's Plaza Group, which owned several other hotels in Moscow.[13]

Without wanting to overstate the problem, hotels saw more than their fair share of criminal action.

A "hail of bullets" killed John Hyden, a British consultant for the European Bank for Reconstruction and Development (EBRD), in February 1996 at the Nevsky Palace Hotel in St Petersburg. Hyden, a Scottish attorney, was sitting in a lobby café and was caught in the crossfire during an assassination attempt on a Russian businessman. Two Russian off-duty police officers working as bodyguards for another Russian businessman were also caught in the crossfire; a third police officer was wounded.

The Moscow Times article describing the killing also discussed at length the debate around installing metal detectors at the entrances to major hotels. Some hotels installed the airport-style, walk-through scanners as an additional security measure. Others were steadfastly against the measure, lest they scare away guests and visitors.[14]

Violence on the streets

Paul Klebnikov, the US-born editor-in-chief of the Russian edition of *Forbes* magazine, was gunned down in Moscow in July 2004 in an unsolved crime that bore all the hallmarks of an organised crime hit.[15] Klebnikov was a driven investigative reporter who came to Moscow from the US edition of *Forbes* and brought a hard-hitting brand of journalism to a business community that sometimes hit back. Von Flemming took the helm of *Forbes* in the wake of Klebnikov's murder. She asked everyone at the magazine if they wanted to keep going and was impressed with their response.

"The very brave decision of Maxim Kashulinsky, who was the second editor-in-chief to step in, said, 'Yes, we will go on,'" von Flemming recalled.

Elizabeth Krasnoff[16] was hiding behind the bar—it was 1995, she recalled—as shots rang out at the Moosehead Bar, a popular pub on the south side of the Moscow River close to the city centre. She had moved to Russia with USD 300 in her pocket and a list of contacts from a fellow waitress she met while working in New Jersey, all after graduating with an honours degree in Russian studies and fluent Russian.

Krasnoff's first job was as membership director at the start-up American Chamber of Commerce in Moscow. One of her initial tasks was to publish white papers on Russian government policy to help American companies get a grip on what was happening around them.

Once she had a job, she and a girlfriend rented an apartment that cost them each USD 85 a month, which she scraped together until her first pay cheque came.

Krasnoff recalls breaking down one night, out of money and food. That's when she learned resilience from her Russian roommate, Olga:

Olga opened the refrigerator and she said, "What are you talking about? There's food right here," and I looked in there, and all I saw was a head of cabbage. I just kept crying, and she took it out and cut it up, and salted it, and peppered it, and fried it on the stove with some onion, and we had dinner.

Later, Krasnoff was the spokesperson for Dermajetics, the skin care division of Herbalife, a multi-level marketing brand that, for a while, seemed to conquer Russia. Krasnoff travelled to almost every major Russian city to deliver presentations to audiences across the country. It was a world without rules; deals were made on a handshake. Krasnoff gave the impression that sometimes these deals stuck, and sometimes, they didn't.

"To me it just seemed like such a game of well, to use an apt metaphor, Russian roulette," she said.

It had its lighter moments, too.

Krasnoff recalls travelling to Sakhalin, in Russia's far east, to the north of Japan. She was giving a seminar on using her company's face-peel product and reminded the audience to wash the mask off with hot water. About 800 people erupted in laughter, she said.

"They were, like, 'We only have hot water on Mondays, Wednesdays, and Fridays,'" she said.

Organised crime

The downfall of the Soviet state and the atrophying of its law enforcement infrastructure produced a parallel enforcement system entirely independent of any of the constraints—and responsibilities—of the state. An underpaid and outgunned police force was subjugated to, penetrated by or partnered with organised crime, and sometimes all three.

Russia's mean streets and brutal boardrooms did not come out of nowhere. Under the tsars and under Soviet party bosses,

Russia was rife with criminal elements—some of them violent murderers, some of them more subtle fraudsters. Both genres of criminality thrived in environments where the state was weak and corrupt. In the years immediately following the collapse of the Soviet Union, the Russian state was both. "In the 1990s, it may have seemed for a while that the criminals were in charge," Mark Galeotti writes in his encyclopaedic history of Russian organised crime, *The Vory: Russia's Super Mafia*.[17]

Galeotti's book discusses criminality in Russia as early as the years of Ivan the Terrible in the sixteenth century. Few of Russia's imperial rulers, he said, were equipped to combat crime. The police reacted to crime, rather than preventing it, and themselves were deeply criminalised.[18]

The chain between contemporary Russian organised crime and the tsarist or Soviet past, however, is not continuous. Criminality in pre-industrial Russia, Galeotti writes, differs from criminality in the urban, industrial Soviet Union. Theft and violence in a country where everything belongs to the state differs from theft and violence against private property.

But the symbiosis between criminal activity and the state in Russia presents a continuous strand through history. Galeotti writes that "the Bolsheviks—and Stalin in particular—were willing to use criminals as allies and agents," a union that helped dictate the sort of Russia that evolved in the aftermath of the Soviet breakdown.[19] Corruption flourished under Brezhnev; Gorbachev's market reforms created the perfect playing field for gangsterism.

"It is a perverse irony that the true midwives of organised crime in today's Russia are to be found in an unlikely and disparate trinity of Soviet general secretaries: Stalin the tyrant, Brezhnev the manager and Gorbachev the reformer," Galeotti wrote.[20] The Soviet economy and the criminal economy were not parallel worlds. They were interdependent worlds.

Nature abhors a vacuum. Crime thrives in it

The difference between the Soviet and capitalist periods was unmistakeable. The Soviet system could not work without the grease of criminality, even under the best of circumstances. A command economy built on the political imperatives of the five-year plans had dysfunction built in from the start. Bribery, fraud and theft were not bugs in the system; they were a feature. A capitalist system in Russia, at least in theory, could have worked without all that cheating. But capitalism in Russia wasn't born under laboratory conditions. It was born in a vacuum of governance.

When the Soviet Union died, Galeotti writes, that interdependency did not die with it. The relationship between the criminal underworld and an emerging Russian elite retooled for the budding capitalist melee of the new Russia. In the 1990s, it seemed that criminal elements were everywhere. For example, sometimes, when the tax police came to your door to audit your books, the audit was a pretext. In reality, the tax police had come to seize your company and transfer it to a criminal gang. And at other times, criminals were brought into rivalries among elites, just to add a bit of extra muscle. Violence, some of which played out in very public car bombings or daylight murders, was everywhere.

But before you think there is something inherently violent in Russia or Russians, consider this: "There is a danger to viewing the explosion of organised crime as pathological—as a society of chaos, or as all kind of spiritual diseases invading the country," University of Toronto's Gunitsky said:

> There was a much more rational, economic explanation. When the state is too weak to do basic functions like contract enforcement and property protection, the state needs another actor to step in. Violence became an adjudication method in the absence of a strong state. That's

how you solved disputes in the absence of formal institutions. Private agents of violence performed functions that the state was unable or unwilling to do.

The sheer volume of reporting on Russian organised crime, and the periodic outbursts of extreme violence—more Russian-on-Russian than Russian-on-expat—terrified foreign executives. Stories of unvarnished brutality proliferated on the pages of international newspapers, along the streets of every Russian town and in the minds of almost every businessperson doing business there:

> Just as the 1990s saw Russia go through financial and political crises as it tried to define itself and its place in the world, its underworld spent most of the decade expanding rapidly into every corner of the economy and society but also getting involved in running turf wars as gangs rose, fell, united, divided and competed. This was a decade of drive-by shootings, car bombs and the virtual theft of entire industries, in which the forces of order seemed powerless. In 1994, President Yeltsin declared that Russia was the "biggest mafia state in the world."[21]

The stories were outrageous. Readers saw pictures of the elaborate tombstones of organised crime figures gunned down in service to their gangs; the central Russian city of Yekaterinburg was famous for its ornate mafia cemeteries. We read about how some gangsters were buried inside their favourite car.

The business community's fears were understandable, if not slightly misplaced. In Russia, the perception of violent crime was far, far greater than the reality, at least as it concerned international executives. Even when foreign companies were targeted by organised crime and the confrontation escalated to violence, more often than not, Russian executives took the heat.

That said, in the 1990s, everyone in Moscow, expat or otherwise, lived in an environment where violence was cheap, routine and almost casual. Cars were being blown up on the streets, bars and restaurants became shootout saloons and, in one case, an office argument between a local employee and an expat ended with a threat against the expat: "It only costs 300 bucks in Moscow to have someone killed."[22]

It might be glib to say that "only a few" foreigners were killed in organised crime hits. But the most flagrant and intentional of those attacks typically followed relatively clear and predictable escalations that usually carried numerous warnings along the way. This is not to blame the victims. On rare occasions, the patterns were hard to spot, or even more difficult to believe.

Protect yourself

Like kids bulking up to ward off a schoolyard bully, international companies in Russia did the corporate equivalent: they took on outsourced (or even in-house) security forces. Most of the time, this was enough to stay out of physical trouble. The periodic attacks on security providers, though, were among the signs that a criminal opponent had the intent and capability to deliver on a threat.

Though the brute force was the terrifying aspect, the more subtle ways that organised crime penetrated the finances and the operations of international companies inflicted much more damage. In this sense, the international community's borderline obsession with organised crime in Russia was entirely justifiable.

Certain industries in Russia were known to be highly criminalised; it wouldn't surprise anyone to learn that among them were the tobacco and alcoholic beverage businesses. Trucks full of cigarettes or whiskey might as well have been trucks full of cash—these high-demand items were easy to move and easier to sell. They were also extremely susceptible to counterfeit activity, a key revenue stream for organised crime inside and outside of Russia. International companies that were domestic producers or importers of these products knew that their distributors more than likely contained criminal elements. These were legitimately dangerous businesses.

Some of the most banal and boring sectors of industry were also of interest to organised crime. Anything that could be stolen, sold on the black market, counterfeited or parallel imported was a potential target. Any company with cash in the office or a leaky finance department was a valuable mark. The possibilities were endless, and criminal forces in Russia were increasingly creative. Every international company wanted to know whether their joint venture partner, distributor, landlord, security company, catering company or finance director was a member of, or beholden to, a criminal gang.

This meant background checks. Dozens of them. Hundreds of them, some of them highly detailed, others narrow and cursory. The most careful of companies would conduct background checks on the people who cleaned their executives' apartments. This level of scrutiny was rare and expensive, but by no means unheard of.

Cover me

The way international companies protected themselves from organised crime, however, was sometimes as dangerous as the criminal gangs themselves. The cure was as bad as or worse than the disease.

Many international companies were convinced—how and by whom remains unclear—that they needed a *krysha*, or roof, to protect their business from criminal influence. Kryshas came in a variety of flavours, depending on the organisation providing the cover. There were police kryshas–these were sometimes referred to as "blue" kryshas. There were FSB kryshas–these were sometimes called "red" kryshas. Or there was the criminal *krysha*, which should be referred to as the "stupid" *krysha*.

And then there was the ultimate *krysha*. This was the roof over the head of the German business community.

"When Putin came to power, the German business community was the most loved one. He has a big [soft] spot for Germany. He speaks fluent German, his daughters went to the German school. He owes Germany a lot. By the way, according to rumours his granddaughters are still going to the German school in Moscow, you wouldn't believe it," von Flemming said. "So the German Chamber of Commerce always had a special card in this sort of investor community. The chamber always had a phone number we can call when a company was getting pushed, bullied, racketed."

"Until 2022," von Flemming said, "when Germany started delivering weapons to Ukraine."

Other companies went the DIY route: their internal security departments almost uniformly came under the direction of high-ranking military, KGB or police alumni. These were individuals who were accustomed to wearing a tie to work and had at least some basic notion of how to structure a security department and stuff it with reliable individuals. Most importantly, these were people whose former networks were useful for crisis management purposes.

These security departments were part muscle, part brain, and in delicate situations, they were part diplomat—making sure relations with the criminal world, or criminal elements in the business world, stayed below the threshold of concern. It was usually better not to ask how this sort of diplomacy was conducted. It didn't necessarily involve violence, but it was the sort of thing you probably wouldn't want to put past your audit committee.

In the worst of all cases, an outside security company was a front for a criminal organisation. The money you paid every month—sometimes on an invoice, sometimes not, sometimes by bank transfer, sometimes not—went straight into the pockets of a protection racket. Companies gave into the problem to help solve the problem. As you might imagine, this usually didn't work very well in the longer term.

Dropping like flies

Crabtree, the former IFC executive, went to visit a former Soviet factory he thought would make a great candidate to buy, improve and sell to a Western investor. At the time, ownership had been transferred to the management.

"So I proposed this to the general director, and he refused," Crabtree said. "I think within forty-eight hours he was dead, killed by a sniper."

This was not Crabtree's first run-in with organised crime. Nor was it his last.

"There was this guy I was dealing with on the State Property Committee, and I had to give him money for a feasibility study"—this was early in Crabtree's time in Russia, when he was in the construction consultancy business—"it wasn't a huge amount of money, it was like USD 5,000, but before I could get it to him, he was shot, for whatever reason."

It gets worse. Crabtree took a group of American investors to an industrial site to view how a German company had set up shop in a sector similar to the Americans'. "We went over to show them, and it had been burned down, and they tied up the people in it and burned the place down as a warning to the Germans not to get involved."

Lest you get the wrong impression, Crabtree's experience was not exceptional.

"If there was ever a sense that we were to be left alone, it is clearly gone now," Richard A. Conn Jr, a Moscow-based lawyer with Latham & Watkins, told *The New York Times* in 1994. "I still consider it safe for Westerners to work here, and I encourage them to do so all the time. But the growth of the mob has been dramatic, and there just isn't a pass for American businesses from the mafia anymore."[23]

Russian organised crime became the topic of national security discussions at the ministerial level in governments around the world. Russian criminality, the argument went, had the potential to destabilise Western institutions as more expansion-minded Russian gangsters wove themselves into international criminal activity. Here, too, though, as Galeotti points out, Russian organised crime was becoming more business-like and sophisticated and more interested in making sure the West remains a stable environment for their investments, let alone as a place of residence for their wives and children.[24]

Casual observers could spot the infantrymen of Russia's organised crime gangs almost everywhere. They had a distinct, easy-to-identify plumage. Criminal foot soldiers were the size of refrigerators, topped with precision-trimmed crew cuts. They had gym-built necks that were handy for supporting the trademark gold chains dangling on their chests. They often wore turtleneck sweaters, topped by what was uniformly referred to as the *malinovy pidzhak*, the maroon-coloured blazer, though the jackets were sometimes emerald green or, on a bad day, mustard yellow. Often, those jackets had a visible lump on the side, where the outer fabric hid a shoulder holster.

These were thugs, plain and simple, used as bodyguards and heavies to protect and to drive their bosses around town, to supervise hotel-lobby prostitution rings and to scare the crap out of everyone. They drove ostentatious, souped-up Jeeps; long, low, black Mercedes-Benzes; and BMWs fresh from Bavaria. Tinted windows were standard.

In the lobby of the Radisson Slavyanskaya, these thugs were almost as common as suitcases. How these men could look at each other as they strutted around the hotel or drank beer in the lobby bars and not burst out in laughter at the sheer self-parody of it all was astounding. Russian organised crime gangs tended to be built around territorial or ethnic structures. The hotel was, in a horrible ethnic slur, nicknamed the Radisson Chechenskaya, in twisted homage to one of Russia's nationality-based organised crime gangs. Others traced their origins to veterans' organisations, to sports-based affiliations or to relationships built in the Soviet, and later Russian, prison systems.

The frisson

Candidly, if a little cold-bloodedly, living in Moscow in an orbit separate from, but parallel to, a very dark criminal underworld delivered a slight electric charge. You were sometimes close enough to touch it. At expensive restaurants, dining companions with a sharp eye would be able to point to a neighbouring table and say "there's a sit-down happening over there." There were restaurants in Moscow that were known mafia hangouts; walking quickly past the darker recesses of the dining room sometimes brought a small, cheap thrill, as long as you avoided eye contact. This was only worth it, of course, if the food was really, really good.

This is not to make light of a dangerous situation. Organised crime's penetration of the business environment and subversion of the police and government was toxic and corrosive, not to mention blatantly murderous. Business in Russia—expat and otherwise—had a body count.

6

JOINT ADVENTURES

You could smell hope in the air.[1]

*It's a certain kind of person who enjoys Russia, because of
course, you know the saying, "You have to take Russia as it is."
You don't see that as a disadvantage, but you just take it the
way it is and you tackle the problem.*[2]

Appearances can be misleading

The Soviet Union was gone. In the immediate aftermath, there
was nothing to replace it.

Sure, every morning, thousands of government employees
got dressed for work and went into ornate or, in other cases,
completely dilapidated buildings with shiny brass plaques at the
front door declaring the serious purpose of the institution inside.
Very little governing got done in those buildings. Chaos was the
only item on any agenda.

Also, it was hard to do serious work when your salary wasn't
being paid.

Confusion ran rampant among and within ministries, and among and within the newly independent republics. Some of those new states descended into civil war. In Russia, the end of the Communist Party's monolithic status gave way to a noisy political marketplace that was a raucous circus of legitimate and crackpot voices.

Similarly, millions of newly minted Russian citizens—they still had passports from a country that no longer existed—got up every morning and went to work. Some wore suits and ties, others put on factory uniforms, everyone else wore something in between. There, too, very little real work got done. Thousands of enterprises, all still state-owned, came to a screeching halt. As in the government ministries, salaries weren't being paid on factory floors or down dim, fluorescent-lit office corridors. Finding food and taking care of the basics—difficult tasks in the late Soviet period—became even more urgent. The Russian economy was even descending into barter—companies paid each other with their products. Some companies got paid in barrels of oil, some got paid in undergarments.

Millions of families, particularly those outside Moscow and a few other major cities, fell into abysmal poverty. It was not unusual to see factory workers or elderly men and women standing by the sides of major roads, or at the exits of metro stations, setting up small stands to sell the harvest of their subsistence gardens, or what little output their factories produced. In the early 1990s, trips along Moscow's main highways were like driving past makeshift, open-air malls. At one moment, you'd drive past a forlorn battalion selling pots and pans. A few minutes later, mattresses. Beyond that, perhaps, plumbing supplies.

Selling these items, rather than working a daily job, is what brought in a salary.

It was tragically convenient. Goods were cheap; payment in a hard currency brought a discount. Pop open the back of the car and fill it with whatever you needed, no questions asked. Buying these wares felt a bit like scavenging—picking over the detritus left in the wake of a natural disaster.

A "monster" awakens

The first Moscow employee of Ernst & Young, now the professional services giant EY, worked in a private apartment. Ernst & Young, when it opened in Moscow, was in its infancy in more ways than one—the firm had only just come together following the 1989 merger of Ernst & Whinney with Arthur Young.

"We had both, just before that, begun to understand that this monster was going to wake up, and we needed to assess what our role should be," said Paul Ostling, who came from Arthur Young, became a key player for EY's Russia business and ultimately became the firm's global chief operating officer.[3]

Working from an apartment was unorthodox but by no means unheard of. Western-style office buildings barely existed in Russia at the outset—there were few premises that could support the requirements of an international professional services firm. As early as 1993, that made Moscow one of the world's most expensive places to do business. The combination of scarcity and runaway demand combined to make office space per square metre in Moscow more expensive than in New York and only slightly less expensive than in Tokyo.[4] Growth in the Moscow market for office space was to come later, as were many of the other features of international professional services, like submitting honest timesheets.

"Partners were submitting time and expense reports with their credit card bills, and there were some very strange claims being made," Ostling said. "There were some really weird things happening. Obviously, it was the Wild West. There were no professional standards in Russia because there was no profession—it didn't exist."

Ostling's first business trip to Moscow, in 1993, triggered a re-evaluation of several of his assumptions about the Soviet Union and Russia. He had served in the US Marine Corps during the Cold War and grew up knowing the Soviet Union as an existential threat. Then, he went and saw for himself. Among other things, he said he noticed the crumbling cement on Dynamo Stadium, one of Moscow's most prominent sports facilities.

It left him unimpressed. He recalls thinking: "Maybe they could get a missile off the ground, but they could never hit what they were aiming at."

Two FBI agents briefed him prior to his first trip. "They gave me this lecture: 'Don't wear your best suits, wear your worst suits, don't walk on the streets, blah, blah, blah,'" he said. "I violated every rule they gave me."

So did his Russian driver at the time.

"I remember driving in from the hotel to the office, and I remember the glovebox in the crappy little car the driver was driving opened up and, you know, a revolver popped out."

Surviving the trip to the office was the easy part. Once he arrived, Ostling and his colleagues started building an accounting profession entirely from scratch.

"We were bringing all these young people in and literally teaching them—hopefully teaching them—how to be accountants, or auditors, or consultants, or tax people," he said. "And they were very smart, and they wanted very much to learn. There was this rising mass of young people yearning to be free and learn. And I have to tell you, they were great."

Around him, Moscow was febrile. Everyone from everywhere was piling into Russia. Ostling called them "carpetbaggers."

"Every company coming in [was] making whatever deals are made with locals who they thought could open a door and had some connections," he said. "It was all about connections, of course. And they were cutting corners."

Cabin pressure

Cutting corners, Ostling explained, was a euphemism for, among other things, bringing in suitcases of cash to cover local expenses. The practice was widespread because there was almost no other way to get hard currency into Russia; the Russian banking system was in its infancy, and no one took the rouble seriously. But the costs of starting and running a business in Russia added up quickly. On top of that, a lot of companies lured in new employees by promising to pay their salaries in US dollars.

At the beginning of the 1990s, Russia went through a period of eye-watering hyperinflation; the only hedge was to hold dollars. Some salaries were paid in a combination of roubles and dollars. The roubles were on the books, the dollars often weren't. Some dollar salaries were simply handed over in paper envelopes. Among the Russian employees of domestic and international companies, it was common to ask whether, or how much, of a person's salary came *v konverte*—in an envelope. The more, the better.

The easiest way for an executive to get cash into their Russian office was to pack it in carry-on luggage. Some companies brought in the legal amount, if anyone—including Russia's customs officers—knew what it was at the time. Other companies brought in as much as they could and held their breath at customs. Others perhaps left a small amount at the border with a customs officer prepared to look the other way if they were bringing in sums large enough to raise suspicion.

One UK executive was stopped at Heathrow by the British security services when he was discovered to have USD 50,000 in a carry-on bag. Ever vigilant, the officials suspected money laundering. Upon arrival in Moscow, he was asked to count the money out in the open on a table in the arrivals hall, and then let through, no questions asked. At Heathrow, that amount of cash raised suspicion. At Sheremetyevo, it didn't.[5]

A "watershed moment"

To Ostling, this practice was a watershed moment, early as it was to declare anything a watershed in Russia's development.

The problem wasn't the specific practice of bringing suitcases of cash into Russia. What mattered, Ostling said, was the idea that international and domestic businesses in Russia could bend the rules up to and sometimes beyond the breaking point, and then carry on as usual.

These sorts of workarounds, he said, eventually hardened into accepted practice, embedded deeply into the business mentality across the country.

The Russian economy was ashen with what were called grey practices—the almost-legal, sort-of-illegal and better-close-your-eyes business practices that made things work in a system where it was often quite difficult to follow the law even if you wanted to.

Digesting all of this, let alone working in it, burned a lot of brain cells.

"The cognitive dissonance was extraordinary," Ostling said. In more traditional markets, professional service firms had libraries filled with policies and procedures, and in developed economies, rule books were meant to be taken seriously. That entire culture was absent in Moscow in the early 1990s.

Ostling discovered these practices and more at his firm and cleaned house. He said he swapped out the free-wheeling, credit-card flashing leadership for someone from Minneapolis whose parents were missionaries.

A more modest initiative

One of Russia's earliest enterprises with foreign capital was the St Petersburg *Yellow Pages*, the famous business directory printed on tinted paper. The idea to bring the *Yellow Pages* to Russia initially belonged to publishing magnate and erstwhile *Daily Mirror* owner Robert Maxwell, who died in an unexplained boating accident in 1991.[6] Robert Sasson, whose career ultimately spanned the entire arc of business in Russia, starting in Maxwell's publishing business, kept the idea alive by working with some of the late Maxwell's partners and by securing financing to print and distribute the book.

Sasson and his team put a map of St Petersburg up on their office wall and divided it into about 100 sections. "And then we had this team of, I don't know, 500 students and literally went door to door collecting information," Sasson said.

Subscribers took a bit of convincing at the outset, and an extra nudge was required to get businesses to pay 20 dollars for a bold-face listing that would help them stand out from their competitors. St Petersburg's entrepreneurial class told Sasson's sales force there was no need to be listed in a business directory. "Everyone who needs to know about us already knows about us," Sasson said, paraphrasing the pushback.

Sasson did Russian language and Soviet studies at university in the UK and did a language course in Russia as well. For him, the *Yellow Pages* project was a chance to bring his studies to life. Many Brits who studied Russian before and after the Soviet period did it in the city of Voronezh, about 500 kilometres south of Moscow.

Sasson took a different path and went to Krasnodar, in the heart of Russia's wine country.

"It was during the Gorbachev years, and there was no alcohol," he said, referring to Gorbachev's sobriety campaign. "In Krasnodar, they had wine."

Joint ventures—an unstable molecule

Joint ventures, which traced their origin to Gorbachev's reforms, were a popular model for companies looking to do business in emerging Russia. They seemed to be safer: pairing with a Russian partner meant an investor had a sherpa for the local market. The legal structure of the business also reduced some of the foreign partner's exposure to the vagaries of Russian law. A joint venture was not quite as "jump in with both feet" as opening a full, free-standing Russian subsidiary, for example.

Joint ventures by their very nature, though, made for highly unstable molecules. Someone always had the upper hand; true 50–50 joint ventures were rare and seen as something to avoid.

Joint venture management was often split unevenly and contentiously between local employees and expats—most international businesses would insist on having the CEO and the CFO roles, as insurance policies. In some cases, Western technological know-how and capital conferred the upper hand. The Russian partner, however, owned the local networks and the local market expertise, not to mention the home-field linguistic advantage. Throw in all the other pressures of doing business in an emerging market, and you can see why joint ventures had the potential to get fractious. Numerous joint ventures ended in disaster or with the Western partner losing control.

Cultural considerations

Most foreigners would say "Russia is a relationship country," meaning that getting along with your partner was more important than the contracts you would sign. Outside Russia, the exact opposite was the case. If you signed a contract, you had the rules for how a relationship would work. If the partners liked each other, it was a pleasant bonus, but not required. The contract said it all. And if one of the parties failed to hold up their side of the bargain, then there were legal paths to determine the appropriate remedy.

The relationship aspect of business culture in Russia has roots in how relationships were created and maintained in Soviet times. Their expression in the Russian context made for a sharp distinction between insiders and outsiders. The membrane between the groups was porous, but for a very long time, few businesspeople could pass through it in either direction.

There have been any number of attempts to explain, quantify and chart the differences between standard international and Russian business practices; the gap between the two in many cases narrowed with time. The more open the Russian economy became, and the more Russians went abroad for MBA degrees, the easier it was to straddle the two business cultures.

Before that happened, though, companies often undertook outrageous measures to bridge the gap. These efforts often involved vodka. There was wining. There was dining. There were hunting trips. There were joint holidays. Western companies, their employees and their employees' livers usually suffered as a result: no company nor individual could ever become *plus russe que les russes*.

"Businesses wishing to succeed in Russia need to socialize with their Russian counterparts and attend social events, dine together, and even consider taking vacations jointly as a means to strengthen their emotional bonds and build trust as a foundation for business success,"[7] one source of advice read, sounding a bit like a Baedeker guidebook for Russia. That advice was quickly followed up by precautions not to allow any of the above gestures to run afoul of anti-corruption legislation.

There was a certain cycle to how joint venture partners got along. Relationship-building takes time, and the business world in Russia, especially given the compressed in-country tenure of the typical Moscow expat, couldn't always make it work. Some of the mechanisms used to short-circuit the relationship-building life cycle—gifts, bribes, trips, kickbacks—got companies into trouble. More importantly, they didn't always work. Imagine the company that "invested" in a series of expensive trips and lavish gifts for its Russian counterparties and then lost a bid or failed to sign a contract.

Russia's biggest, best and scariest joint venture

There has been no larger investment in Russia than TNK-BP, the 50–50 joint venture between the British energy giant BP and Russia's oligarchic TNK. It was, at the outset, one of the boldest, and by a mile the largest, foreign investment in Russia. It was a study in strategy, bare-knuckled negotiations, epic chutzpah and, ultimately, a lesson in the hardball politics of the Russian energy sector.

BP, known as British Petroleum before globalisation took country names out of company names, was an early mover in Russia. Even before its first investment in oil production, it opened a chain of petrol stations in Russia, following the trend for mini-market-plus-car-wash-plus-coffee-shop petrol stations along highways and high streets across Western Europe and the US.[8]

BP knew that Russia was a strategic player in global energy markets—the country had one of the world's largest reserves of oil and gas and, in the 1990s, was poorly equipped to extract those resources efficiently.

In 1997, BP paid Vladimir Potanin, one of the most powerful men in Russian business, USD 571 million for a 10 per cent stake in an oil company called Sidanco, which under the umbrella of Potanin's Interros holding company held the lucrative and productive Chernegorneft subsidiary.[9]

From here, it gets complicated. Books, newspapers and magazines are full of the story of TNK-BP. The following is a greatest-hits version.

About a year after BP's initial investment, TNK used Russia's sledgehammer bankruptcy laws to smash up Potanin's debt-ridden Sidanco. In 1999, TNK took Chernegorneft out from under Potanin and Sidanco and moved it under TNK's control. TNK belonged to a consortium of Russian companies led by a group of billionaire businessmen including the Russian oligarch Mikhail Fridman and his Alfa Group, a massive and powerful holding company with activities across Russian business and industry. With Chernegorneft gone, BP's investment in Sidanco lost half its value.[10]

"Welcome to Russia, BP," Bloomberg wrote, parenthetically, in a summary of the transaction.[11]

By 2001, BP, Potanin and TNK were close to resolving their tripartite dispute. TNK would take full control of Sidanco from Potanin and add Chernegorneft back into Sidanco, where BP maintained its stake.[12] In other words, Sidanco became whole once again, but now BP's partner was TNK, rather than Potanin. TNK's owners were a Russian consortium called AAR, standing for Alfa–Access–Renova, owned by Alfa's Fridman and German Khan, Access's Leonard Blavatnik and Renova's Viktor Vekselberg.

The entire saga was a massive black eye for BP but also for Russia's reputation as a stable place to do business. The transaction was constantly in the headlines; everyone took a beating. The US government even intervened to force TNK to resolve the transaction.[13] BP's other, smaller activities in Russia outside of Sidanco were also subject to minor challenges.

No matter. BP ploughed ahead and intensified its relationship with TNK. In 2002, BP increased its stake in Sidanco from 10 to 35 per cent, knitting itself even more tightly with TNK. The two companies publicly exchanged pleasantries about cooperation and sharing know-how and expertise. Accounts at the time said this move was the equivalent of energy sector foreplay to an even more intense relationship between BP and TNK. Whatever the meaning of the gesture, it cost BP USD 375 million.[14]

The foreplay paid off. A year later, BP and TNK announced the terms of the largest equity deal in Russia's history. BP would contribute USD 8 billion in cash, shares and assets toward a company that would consolidate Sidanco and a series of other Russian energy assets with TNK's energy empire, creating a colossus worth USD 18.1 billion. The move launched BP into the big leagues of the energy industry, placing its expanded footprint on a par with companies like ExxonMobil and Royal Dutch Shell (as it was then called).[15]

The deal was a landmark beyond its price tag. It was the first deal between a Russian and international company of this magnitude that was entirely 50–50 in its ownership structure. This arrangement was said to have concerned Putin, who feared losing control over a critical asset in Russia's strategic natural resource sector.[16]

That didn't prevent Putin from travelling that year to London for a state dinner at Buckingham Palace with Queen Elizabeth II, followed by a signing ceremony in the presence of TNK-BP executives and UK Prime Minister Tony Blair. Again, public pleasantries abounded about how the Sidanco conflict was firmly in the past. Russia, Russian business and the Russian business environment were all on the mend. Analysts and executives alike said that BP was armed against any corporate "shenanigans" and that "Russia is a very different place under Putin than it was under Yeltsin."[17]

The deal became lucrative for both companies and is still referred to as one of BP's best investments, but scale alone couldn't save it from conflict between the partners and, ultimately, between the partners and the Russian state. Strategic misunderstandings began to emerge when TNK accused BP of treating the tie-up as a mere subsidiary. BP chafed when TNK voiced ambitions to take the company's combined might into new and more distant ventures.

Differences simmered until 2008, when challenges over control, financial performance and money more broadly were "starting to bear all the hallmarks of a hostile takeover, evoking an era of cut-throat capitalism in Russia that BP thought was long past," the *Financial Times* wrote.[18]

From there, the relationship turned bitter, dysfunctional and ugly. BP executives were harassed and threatened. Expats assigned to work in the company's Moscow office couldn't get visas. Foreign executives feared they were under electronic surveillance; the state put the company under investigation for a series of alleged infractions. The CEO of TNK-BP, Bob Dudley (who later became CEO of BP), was rumoured to have received death threats and discreetly exited Russia—his departure was announced only after his aeroplane was in the sky.[19]

Speculation was rife about the source of the intensifying conflict. Some observers speculated that TNK was attempting to squeeze out BP. The government investigations were believed to be made-to-order by TNK's owners.[20] Others said TNK was just seeking the control that a 50–50 partnership could never really bestow. Still more speculation suggested that the Russian government was sending a signal to both parties in the company, a reminder of who the real boss is when it came to hydrocarbons. When BP entered discussions with state-owned Rosneft in a separate transaction regarding Arctic exploration without TNK, the TNK-BP dispute approached open corporate warfare.[21]

Analysts began writing obituaries. "We're now in the War of the Roses stage and one person has to leave the house, dead or alive," Moscow investment analyst Steven Dashevsky told the *FT*.[22]

They say that in corporate conflicts, the only winners are the lawyers. In the case of TNK-BP, the winner was the Russian government. State-owned Rosneft ultimately bought TNK out from TNK-BP in March of 2013, bestowing billions of dollars on the already indescribably wealthy individuals at Alfa, Access Industries and Renova, the owners of TNK. For BP's troubles, the Russian government paid it USD 12 billion in cash and awarded the company an 18.5 per cent stake in Rosneft, Russia's national champion in the oil sector.[23] The move also served as a signal to everyone else with a stake in the Russian energy complex: the state—Putin's state—would always be in control.

BP's experience in Russia was enormously painful but could generously be called bittersweet. Its stake in Rosneft provided billions of dollars in dividends and, of course, a stake in the company's production revenues. It was BP's worst and best investment, until, of course, 2022.[24]

Russia's list of Russian corporate conflicts, particularly those pitting oligarchs against Westerners, is long. Many of the battles include Alfa Group and Fridman.[25] For years, Fridman was a caustic irritant for Telenor, Norway's national telecoms operator, in their joint venture in VimpelCom, in matters concerning both Russia and Ukraine.[26] That battle included a raid on Telenor's Russian office by court marshals and armed men[27] and a hostile lawsuit from a shell company with only a 0.002 per cent stake in the joint venture.[28] Scandinavia saw even more of Alfa in the long-running conflict with TeliaSonera, the Nordic telecoms giant, over their investments in Turkcell in Turkey and Megafon in Russia.[29]

The Moscow Times described Fridman's Alfa as "admired and feared in equal measure for the ruthlessness with which it does business."[30] Alfa also used a defensive merger in the Russian supermarket business to block Walmart's market entry.[31] Walmart closed its Moscow office in 2010.[32]

Rodzianko recalls a lunch with the owners of Alfa Bank when JP Morgan was applying for a licence that would allow retail banking in Russia. Rodzianko can't precisely recall who was sitting opposite him, but he remembers how one of Alfa's owners turned to him during the meal and said "Look, we know we can't stop you, but we're going to try to slow you down as much as we can."

The oligarchs—it wasn't just Alfa and Fridman—threw everything they had at their Western partners: from political connections and business relationships to the native ability to navigate a business landscape saturated with legal and financial mines.

The oligarchs were bolstered by the best international legal advice money could buy—the most magic of London's magic circle firms and the whitest white shoes of New York's legal upper crust all worked for Russian clients. Everyone, they would say, is entitled to legal support, and more than that, business disputes everywhere often bear the same hallmarks. Working for an aggressive mergers and acquisitions raider in New York wasn't all that different from working for a Russian oligarch bent on dominating his sector. Western law firms during the go-go days in Russia weren't there to play games. The expat legal community was high-octane; stomach linings were thick and strong.

After the beginning of the full-scale invasion of Ukraine, Fridman and his partner in Alfa Petr Aven were both heavily sanctioned by the US and the EU. The two won a limited appeal against the EU sanctions, which they continue to challenge. Fridman, who left the UK for Israel after the full-scale invasion, has since returned to Moscow. Aven reportedly resides in Latvia.[33]

Joint ventures—the theory

Two veterans of the Russian oil and gas industry, James Henderson and Alastair Ferguson, have put a theoretical framework around how joint ventures functioned, or didn't, in Russia. Their experience is based in their area of expertise—the energy sector. But much of their book *International Partnership in Russia: Conclusions from the Oil and Gas Industry* is relevant beyond that sector:

> [T]he history of BP's investment in Russia provides in one example a microcosm of the experiences of international companies over the past two decades and demonstrates the changing reality of partnership in a country where the shifting power of institutions and influence of individuals has been difficult for foreign companies to interpret and understand.[34]

Henderson and Ferguson raise the interesting question of the inequality and imbalance between two parties who each bring something of considerable value to their partnership. In Russia, which was worth more: the capital and know-how the foreign partner brought, or the insider knowledge of the Russian partner? Neither could work effectively without the other; each side probably valued its contribution more highly than the other's. Foreign partners surely thought their Russian counterpart would be unable to re-create decades of business know-how in the fledgling Russian market. The Russian partner was likely thinking that all that imported capital was worthless when the foreign partner couldn't read a restaurant menu in Russian.

But the domestic partner's role, crucially, didn't stop there. It's what the partner did with that on-the-ground network and local knowledge that is the most interesting. Henderson and Ferguson say that "this key skill was used not only to gain competitive advantage in the domestic market ... but also as a key bargaining tool with foreign investors."[35]

What makes the process so interesting, Henderson and Ferguson wrote, is when each partner begins to acquire the other's knowledge. In general, this is a good thing. Partners want each other to become better at what they do. Henderson and Ferguson point out, though, that it was probably easier for knowledge to flow from the international partner to the Russian partner than in the other direction. It's easier to learn about an industry sector than it is to gain a deep understanding about Russia.

The behaviour of local partners in Russia was sometimes entirely opaque to their international partners. In some cases, this arrangement was more than welcomed by both parties. If it worked and no one had any complaints, great. And if it was a bit ugly beneath the surface, also great—the Russian partner was trusted best to know where the red lines were when doing business in Russia and not to cross them. In fact, it was sometimes a relief to outsource some of the difficulties of doing business in Russia—meeting government officials, filing regulatory paperwork, travelling the country's great distances— to a local partner.

One large investor in Russia once said, in a private conversation: "What we don't know, we still don't want to know."

Other international companies wanted more granular visibility of what their Russian partners were doing, and how they did it. Often, this was because regulators in their home jurisdictions required it. That usually involved asking a series of awkward questions that could deliver uncomfortable answers. Asking these questions involved striking a delicate balance. Partners have to respect each other; asking whether a local partner was involved in questionable business practices carried the risk of fracturing that trust. For the international partner, sometimes just asking the questions was showing enough effort to satisfy regulators.

Other international partners insisted on a high level of transparency and sometimes got it. That sort of accomplishment represented a meeting of the minds between a Russian and an international partner that wasn't unheard of but was hard to come by.

For the avoidance of doubt, Russians complained about their foreign business partners, too. Russian parties to joint ventures surveyed by Henderson and Ferguson said their international partners were not always of the highest calibre:

> The best people aren't always available for postings like Russia, especially if they perceive that it is not a major priority for the company and that their careers might be better enhanced elsewhere. You need to be very careful that you don't just get average people looking for the financial benefits of a hardship posting.[36]

Ouch.

Ferguson worked for eight years as head of gas for TNK-BP and said that the venture started with the best of intentions. The partners diverged, however, on issues of culture. BP had a strategic outlook, Ferguson said. TNK and its owners had a more short-term outlook and mentality, something he said reflected the view of most Russian entrepreneurs.[37]

Ultimately, the joint venture ran aground on the issue at the core of Henderson and Ferguson's book—the positions of the venture's partners:

> BP had seen the worst of what the Russian business environment could throw at it and was very realistic about what protection it would need going forward. AAR had proved that it had the skills to get things done on the ground where any foreign partner would have encountered major difficulty. Inevitably, it is of course natural that the domestic players not only understand this but also protect their competitive position. The perpetuation of the chaotic business environment was clearly to their advantage, and I would say they were happy to make it difficult for any foreigner, including their partner, to operate in that environment.[38]

Mostly, Ferguson said, co-existence with AAR and TNK came down to choosing battles carefully.[39]

A joint venture with the KGB

Derk Sauer and his wife moved to Moscow in 1989 with a six-month-old baby and a sense of optimism. Sauer first founded *Moscow Magazine*, followed by a company called Independent Media, where he was the publisher of *The Moscow Times*—the publication that for many visitors and expats was a staple of life in the capital.

Because he moved to Russia before the end of the Soviet Union, Sauer was obligated to start *Moscow Magazine*, modelled loosely on *New York Magazine*, as a joint venture.

"You need to team up with some state organisation, which in practice, in Russia, meant basically the KGB or former KGB people, who I would say were the most entrepreneurial people around, because they knew the West better than anyone else," he said. "They understood, a little bit at least, what private business was. So the first joint venture I got involved in was with the Union of Journalists, and, you know, here comes this group of ... at least they claimed to be journalists, and said, 'Let's start a magazine together.'"

It didn't go very well at the start. The publishing company Sauer worked for at the time put up the magazine's start-up funds, but Sauer's Russian partners were supposed to cover the local costs—things like rent and salaries.

"So this was my first experience with Russian business. It was like a cold shower," Sauer said. His Russian counterparts envisioned Sauer and his company to be capitalist fat-cats who smoked cigars and had "money coming out of their ears." Before the magazine's first edition was published, Sauer's Russian partners asked when they would be going on holiday to Spain and "When do we get a car?"

"The idea that you had to work for something never entered their head"; they just thought "'Now we are part of a capitalist company,'" Sauer said. "I quickly found out it was totally useless, because these people were not journalists, but they were all on the payroll of the KGB."

Sauer started paying cash to writers on the side who would populate the magazine with the articles that made it a standout in Moscow journalism, while his joint venture partners watched it all happen. The arrangement suited both sides fine.

"It was a very weird arrangement," Sauer said.

What he learned, though, was that the Soviet Union was not ready to work. At all.

"If you grew up in a system where basically everything is taken care of, you know everything from the moment you're born to the moment you die. The state decides where you live, where you work, where you go to school, where you go on holiday, and so forth," Sauer said, describing the cradle-to-grave socialist utopia the Soviet Union aimed to create. "That you can make your own choices is very intimidating. A journalist has never been in an environment of business. In fact, no one had been in an environment of business. So I would say everyone above thirty basically was lost."

The arrangement was unsustainable, and about two years later, Sauer's Dutch backers pulled the plug to focus on other projects. Sauer was still so taken with the size of the opportunity in Russia that he stayed. Expats were streaming into the country; they would become his new audience. "So I started my own business," he said. *The Moscow Times* was entirely foreign owned.

Cheese gets the job done

The Moscow Times' early journalists—a team of Russians and expats—worked in an office on Ulitsa Pravdy ("Truth Street"), the Soviet era home of the Communist Party daily newspaper, *Pravda* ("The Truth"), which was cranked out on presses for a daily circulation of about two million copies. Sauer asked the printers if they could squeeze in a print run of about 30,000 for *The Moscow Times*. They laughed at the notion.

But *Pravda*, like so many large Soviet enterprises, was at the heart of an entire micro-economy meant to support its workers. That economy included a dairy farm that needed help. Sauer was Dutch, so the *Pravda* bosses immediately assumed he knew everything about cheese-making, which, well, he didn't. But when Sauer promised to introduce the *Pravda* dairy farm to a Dutch cheese-making consultant, *Pravda* promised to print *The Moscow Times*. Sauer also vowed to pay for the print run in full and on time, which sealed the deal. *The Moscow Times* was distributed for free to hotels, offices, bars, restaurants, the airport and anywhere expats hung out.

"The nipple agreement"

Sauer's industry-changing breakthrough was an agreement with Hearst Magazines of the United States to license Russian-language editions of an entire stable of glossy monthly magazines, the most famous being the blockbuster women's magazine *Cosmopolitan* and the title best known, of course, for its articles: *Playboy*.

Cosmopolitan, Sauer said, launched into a market where the only previous women's magazines had been *Working Woman* and *Peasant Woman*.

The Russian edition of *Cosmopolitan* started in 1994 with a print run of 40,000. Two years later, it had a circulation of more than one million.

"It was like printing money," Sauer said. When Sauer sold the company at the top of his publishing business, it had forty magazines in its portfolio. "It was a dream market. Everything you launched was a success."

In a profile published in 1999, *The Economist* noted Sauer's strong leftist political credentials—the magazine said he was a "former member of the Dutch Marxist–Leninist party"— before calling him "Russia's most successful publisher."[40] In a biographical piece in *The Moscow Times*, Sauer mentioned having reported from Northern Ireland and "Vietnam, Cambodia, Angola, Mozambique, South Africa, Nicaragua, El Salvador, Beirut."[41] The *Financial Times'* Simon Kuper was able to write his biography of British double-agent George Blake partly thanks to Sauer, who introduced Kuper to Blake in Moscow.[42]

Getting *Playboy* on the magazine racks in stores and at kiosks around Russia involved turning the entire country on its head. In the Soviet days, Sauer said, smuggling a copy of *Playboy* into the country was "the ultimate trophy."

When it came time to display the magazine openly for sale, the Russian Press Ministry turned out to be a prude.

"All these bureaucrats, they were extremely nervous for the cover," Sauer said. *Playboy* had already decided not to include full nudity in the magazine.

The "nipple agreement" put their fears to rest.

"We would not show nudity for sure, but also the nipple would be at least a little bit covered," Sauer said.

An entire new media industry was galloping across Russia. Radio stations, television stations, newspapers and magazines jammed the airwaves and sidewalk kiosks. In 1992, *The New York Times* launched a twice-monthly Russian-language edition, with advertising from companies including "American Express, Archer Daniels Midland, the Coca-Cola Company, Estee Lauder International, Goldman Sachs, IBM and TWA."[43] Ultimately, these advertisers pulled out; *The Times'* Russian-language version ceased publication twenty-two months after it began.[44]

Along the way, Sauer launched *Vedomosti*, a national business newspaper, in a tripartite joint venture with Pearson, which at the time owned the *Financial Times*, and Dow Jones, owner of *The Wall Street Journal*. The Russian media market remained attractive until a 2014 law restricted foreign ownership of any Russian media company to 20 per cent.

Von Flemming's tenure at Axel Springer ended on 1 January 2016, at the end of the two-year grace period following the introduction of the restrictions. That law reportedly targeted *Forbes* and *Vedomosti*, two of Russia's most influential media outlets, specifically.[45] The crackdown came partly in protest at the negative coverage Russia was getting over its role in Ukraine in 2014, particularly from media outlets with foreign ownership.[46]

Von Flemming made the decision to stay in Russia, however, but rather than work for a single employer, she began to serve on boards. When von Flemming started serving on the boards of Russian companies, she said she was one of eight such women. When she left, she was one of thirty-eight.

"I'm extremely grateful for the opportunities I think I had as a woman. I wouldn't have made such a career in Germany, on this scale," she said. "And I think I was supported by other strong women."

The Russian edition of *Forbes* magazine was a powerhouse brand. The title attracted high-profile Russian journalists, broke big stories and was always stuffed with expensive advertising. The magazine even sent a restaurant critic to London to let readers know where they had to be, next time they were in town.

Forbes' high-profile takes on Russian business periodically got the company into the kind of trouble that made people want to hire bodyguards, including the dispute over a quote on the cover of the magazine from Yelena Baturina, the billionaire wife of then-mayor of Moscow Yuri Luzhkov.[47] Von Flemming had her own security detail as that conflict unfolded. She installed an emergency button in her office and was not the only Moscow executive to have one.

Sauer felt the tightening on freedom of speech in Russia and in 2005 sold his holdings to a Finnish media company. The following few years were turbulent ones both commercially and politically for the media business, particularly as Kremlin interference in the sector grew. Sauer again became the owner of *The Moscow Times* eight years after selling it.

Cosmopolitan was a publishing sensation in Russia with few parallels, but four years later, in 1998, another publishing bombshell dropped: *Vogue* came to Russia. Two years after the launch, Condé Nast sent Robyn Holt to Moscow from Australia, where she had worked in the company's magazine portfolio, to be the new president of Condé Nast's Russian operations. Holt said her Russian colleagues eyed her sceptically at first—she didn't speak Russian, and she stepped on a few toes as she tried to audit and clean up some of the looser practices around the company.

"It was a hard, hard slog, but I wouldn't have changed that experience for anything in the world," she said. Holt launched *Architectural Digest* in Russia and revamped Russian *GQ* from "being a magazine of raunchy women" into the magazine for Russian men increasingly eager to know about wearing the right watches, buying the right suits and networking in the business world. Holt called it "the bible of how to look like a young Westerner with heaps of dough."[48]

Glamour magazine was the final achievement in Holt's six-year tenure in Moscow. The magazine started with a print run of 400,000 editions, and to her great relief, Holt kept the original plates, just in case. After the first run sold out, she reprinted another 600,000 editions before taking it up to a total of 800,000.

Holt puts the success of the first run to an error in *Glamour*'s cinema advertising campaign, which placed an ad at the end of the Russian showing of *Bridget Jones's Diary*, before the movie's credits.

"It looked like *Glamour* was part of the movie," Holt said. Holt was happy for the inadvertent mistake, but what happened with publishing in Russia was no accident.

"It was mind blowing. It was just the right mood, the right time," she said. "I think we in the publishing industry, picked up on that energy of adventure that was there in that generation."

The "insider"

Heidi McCormack, whose thirteen-year career with General Motors (GM) culminated in the role of executive director—new ventures, Russia and CIS—worked on one of the highest-profile ventures in transatlantic manufacturing. The project was the joint venture between GM and AvtoVAZ, the Russian automotive behemoth founded as VAZ in the 1960s and manufacturer of legendary Soviet brands like the Zhiguli and, later, the Lada. The joint venture between AvtoVAZ and GM produced the Chevy Niva, an updated version of the Soviet workhorse mini-SUV.

"That was my baby," McCormack said, as if the 2001 transaction had happened yesterday. "That was my first really, really big deal."[49]

McCormack was a natural to lead GM into Russia—she was on the deal team at Bear Stearns, a New York investment bank that worked on privatising AvtoVAZ starting in 1991. Bear Stearns became a casualty of the 2008 global financial crisis, but before that, McCormack travelled into and out of Russia for two years, on a three-weeks-in, two-weeks-out schedule. After that, she lived for three years in Irkutsk, deep in Siberia near the shores of Lake Baikal, as part of a group that started one of Russia's first private equity firms.

Yes, Irkutsk.

"That's where I had my first shareholder meeting where I got locked out because they changed the venue," she said, "because they didn't want the foreign investor showing up."

The private equity firm had a short-ish shelf-life, and McCormack went to work for GM. Her early roles involved cleaning up the importation of car parts and seeing sales skyrocket as Russia climbed out of the 1998 financial crisis. Over the course of her career there, she worked on the AvtoVAZ joint venture, an assembly plant in Kaliningrad and a greenfield automotive factory outside St Petersburg.

The AvtoVAZ joint venture was a backbreaker. Across the table, some of McCormack's Russian counterparts wanted nothing to do with her and GM.

"Somebody's been sitting across the table from you for fifteen or twenty years, in different incarnations. He looks at me and he says, 'I've done everything in my power to stop this JV [joint venture] from ever happening. And you didn't do bad, McCormack, you won,'" McCormack said.

"Fifteen fucking years. Sorry. You've gotten drunk with them, you've stayed up all night with them. You've done the power weekends with the lawyers and the accountants, to have someone say to you they tried everything they could to stop the JV from happening. Why?" McCormack asked.

Here's why. Senior management at AvtoVAZ were all making money from the business AvtoVAZ did with its suppliers.

"They all had ownership interests in suppliers. Suppliers are all subject to due diligence," McCormack said. That due diligence discovered that AvtoVAZ's suppliers were fleecing the company, and AvtoVAZ executives pocketed the proceeds.

"It all went out the window, but they tried to sabotage it," she said.

Once the joint venture started, the sabotage didn't stop. McCormack said the AvtoVAZ–GM joint venture had an abnormally high rate of parts loss off the assembly line. McCormack and her colleagues went through two security companies before discovering a tunnel under the Niva assembly line that was 2 kilometres long, used to siphon off parts. McCormack wanted to report it; she said her security company told her she'd be killed if she did. During a standard, two-week break for scheduled repairs to the assembly line, McCormack said GM had the tunnel filled with cement.

GM officially opened a new assembly line outside St Petersburg in 2006 and found the experience entirely different from what happened at AvtoVAZ. St Petersburg Governor Valentina Matviyenko, McCormack said, did everything she could to make GM's factory happen. She built roads out to the site. She built metro stations. She lured other auto manufacturers and their suppliers to the region.

"She said, 'Do it,' and it was done—poof!" McCormack said.

The GM plant started to grow before it was even finished, a sign of GM's intent in Russia and an optimistic forecast for automobile sales. GM's sales in Russia were growing closer to the company's sales in Germany and the UK, its largest European markets.[50] The economy was growing, car loans were becoming popular and the mid-market, affordable cars GM made under the Opel brand in the St Petersburg region were a big hit with buyers.[51]

The global financial crisis of 2008 nearly defeated GM. In 2009, the company declared bankruptcy in the US and re-organised.[52] By 2011, the re-organisation reached McCormack, and she left GM to work for a consulting firm run by former FBI Director Louis Freeh, working on financial monitorships.

By 2015, GM was out of St Petersburg amid a broad downturn in European sales, complicated in Russia partly by Crimea-related sanctions, weakness in the rouble and a slowing Russian economy.[53] The company exited the joint venture with AvtoVAZ in 2019.[54]

What were the alternatives?

The alternative to an unstable joint venture or an export business run by remote control was to open a fully owned subsidiary in Russia. This was a format that offered the highest level of control for the parent company and the enticing opportunity to grow a business inside the Russian Federation. The primary drawback, however, was that the Russian subsidiary of an international company was solely responsible for its behaviour on the market and bore the full responsibility for its successes and failures. There was no joint venture partner to hide behind. There was no distributor to throw under the bus or terminate when things went wrong. The exposure to the parent company was high.

Corruption

One of the greatest concerns for international companies was that a direct presence in Russia would expose them to unmanageable levels of corruption. Opening a full subsidiary took out a lot of the intermediaries whose presence could act as a buffer between the corrupt Russian business environment and an international company from a highly regulated home jurisdiction.

In interviews with dozens of people for this book, corruption was regularly presented as an acute problem—Russia was drowning in bent businesspeople and crooked bureaucrats. But corruption was always mentioned as something happening to someone else. In a country where everyone had their hand out and where corruption was the grease in the gearbox, how could it be that everyone heard about it but no one was really involved in it, touched by it or affected by it?

The reality is a bit more subtle than that. Some international companies were so large and so high profile that it was difficult for even the most mercenary of Russian bureaucrats to ask for a bribe. Other companies developed reputations as uncorruptible; politicians with their hands out went somewhere else. And at some point, corruption began to separate into layers. It was less frequent at the higher reaches of government, more common at the building-permit level. It was there, without question, but it could be avoided.

"To run the business in an ethical way was easier than I thought," said Harry Itameri, who was between 1995 and 2001 the head of Russia and later most of the former Soviet republics for Novo Nordisk, one of the world's largest manufacturers of insulin. "I had this impression that when you went to Russia, you had to pay everyone. Overall, that wasn't the case."

But corruption was present and pervaded nearly every aspect of business. The Russian economy of the 1990s could be depicted as a Venn diagram with overlapping circles labelled "politics," "business" and "crime."

"There was a time when it was a perfectly legitimate strategy in Russia to say, 'We're going to hire Mr X. We're going to pay him USD 50,000 a year. And his job is to make our problems with customs go away,'" Melling said. "That was a perfectly legitimate speciality."

"For every company that wound up in *The Moscow Times*, there were 500 companies that didn't," Melling said, meaning there were indeed companies that had their house in order. "But even those companies had problems."

As testimony to the fact that Russia was still a corrupt business environment that either ensnared or invited foreign participation, below is just a partial list of companies around the world involved in Foreign Corrupt Practices Act (FCPA) regulatory actions in Russia and elsewhere.[55] These are not, by the way, cases of executives getting caught walking into ministries with briefcases stuffed with cash. The schemes to disguise these payments could be enormously elaborate.

- Juniper Networks – The California-based telecommunications company agreed to pay more than USD 11.7 million to resolve violations of the FPCA's internal accounting controls and recordkeeping provisions in China and Russia. (August 2019) According to government records, "[t]he SEC took into consideration Juniper's cooperation and remediation in determining whether to accept Juniper's offer of settlement.[56]
- Teva Pharmaceuticals – The global generic drug manufacturer agreed to pay USD 519 million to settle parallel civil and criminal charges that it paid bribes to foreign government officials in Russia, Ukraine and Mexico. (December 2016)[57]
- AstraZeneca – The UK-based biopharmaceutical company agreed to pay more than USD 5 million to settle FCPA violations resulting from improper payments made by subsidiaries in China and Russia to foreign officials. (August 2016) According to SEC records, AstraZeneca neither admitted or denied the agency's findings.[58]
- Nordion Inc. and employee – The Canadian-based health science company and a former employee agreed to collectively pay more than USD 500,000 to settle FCPA charges. Mikhail Gourevitch, an engineer, arranged bribes to Russian officials for drug approvals and received kickbacks in return. Nordion lacked sufficient internal controls to detect and prevent the scheme. (March 2016) The government noted that Nordion self-reported the violation and then cooperated extensively with authorities.[59]
- Bio-Rad Laboratories – The California-based clinical diagnostic and life science research company paid USD 55 million to settle FCPA charges filed by the US Securities and Exchange Commission (SEC) and the Department of Justice (DoJ), following accusations that its subsidiaries

made improper payments to foreign officials in Russia, Vietnam and Thailand in order to win business. (November 2014) Bio-Rad self-reported the violation and cooperated extensively with authorities.[60]

- Eli Lilly and Company – The Indianapolis-based pharmaceutical company agreed to pay more than USD 29 million to settle the charges its subsidiaries made improper payments to foreign government officials to win business in Russia, Brazil, China and Poland. (December 2012) Lilly did not admit or deny the allegations in consenting to a final judgement.[61]

This is all entirely aside from the seismic Siemens case, which saw the company pay more than USD 1.6 billion in penalties for what the US SEC described as the

widespread and systematic practice of paying bribes to foreign government officials to obtain business. Siemens created elaborate payment schemes to conceal the nature of its corrupt payments, and the company's inadequate internal controls allowed the conduct to flourish. The misconduct involved employees at all levels, including former senior management, and revealed a corporate culture long at odds with the FCPA.[62]

As Putin began to institute a state based on (his version of) law and order, corruption and gangsterism took on a more complex, "symbiotic" relationship with the state.[63] Some of the street-level extortion subsided. Subsequent developments in E-government made some progress toward denting the impact of corruption in things like the customs service and state procurement, though it's almost as easy to rig an electronic bid as it is to rig a paper one.[64]

Top government officials put their hands out less often, or did it less blatantly, and some of them were even caught taking bags of cash in carefully choreographed stings designed as a deterrent.[65] In some cases, government officials were targeted for prosecution not just because they were taking bribes but because they were failing to share the bribes around. Corruption in Russia had supply chains and distribution networks. Still, as these sorts of cases emerged, they were evidence of another important trend: corruption was discussed publicly. It was no longer a nasty secret whispered quietly while glancing over one's shoulders. It was hard not to talk about it in Russia.

Despite Russia's reputation, or its abysmal place in the Transparency International Corruption Perceptions Index, it's entirely possible that big deals in Russia got done without money in paper bags changing hands. But perhaps that's the wrong way of looking at it. Money in paper bags is, after all, so very 1990s. More likely than not, the corruption evolved into something more high-minded like dinners in Courchevel, the elaborate elbow-rubbing in Davos or the awarding of contracts down the line to friends and relatives of key Russian decision-makers.

Companies also learned they could polish their reputations on the market in more polite and acceptable manners. Supporting charities became popular, as long as the charity wasn't run by a politician's relative.

The cash box

When Cescotti got to Russia in 2006, he noted that many publicly listed companies were still doing business from a "cash box." "The cash box was still common, even with listed corporations," he said. Executives were still bringing cash in suitcases, usually once a month, to take care of expenses that were, he said, "difficult from the point of accounting, including commission payments."[66]

Saying no to requests for bribes and kickbacks is, to put it mildly, awkward. Companies did it variously. Sometimes, it meant letting deals die from benign neglect. In other cases, companies sought legitimate and auditable measures of community engagement to help create win-win situations when everyone else wanted a zero-sum game.

Cescotti was blunt.

"If you don't want to cover this policy, you have the wrong employer," he told his employees. "You're getting a salary; you bloody well comply."

Yes, there were what Cescotti called "grey zones." It's not unexpected in a place like Russia:

> I had compliance breathing down my neck more than once in those fifteen years. Whistle-blowers turn up and you have to prove that nothing is going on. That can be very difficult. I was clean, but I had to go to efforts to prove it. That was part of the job—that was part of the minefield. You're clean, but you have to prove it.

The pressure came from both sides of transactions.

"On the one hand we were under pressure to perform corporate results," Cescotti said. But on the other side, Russian customers were asking Cescotti "to help him with his homework." "Homework," Cescotti explained, was the expression his Russian counterparts would use to discuss kickbacks.

Cescotti recalled a real-life example.

A tender worth more than EUR 7 million had been secured to deliver equipment for a chemical plant. This was a big win. And then, Cescotti recalls, the contract partner said:

> Oliver, we researched about you, and we know that you know Russia very well, and we know that we can talk directly and openly with you without the interpreter. Listen, you know what business is like in Russia, but we would like to close the contract with you for EUR 8.5 million and we would like you to transfer 1.5 million euros somewhere.

The details, Cescotti said, would have involved paying its client EUR 1.5 million for services the client would never perform and did not exist. The money would go "somewhere," to an affiliated company. That "somewhere" was most likely a personal account that belonged to the client in a low-disclosure jurisdiction where his name was not directly associated with the account. Otherwise, the money could pass through an elaborate system of shell companies, converted to cash and then distributed to the beneficiaries.

Cescotti refused, and suffered a rare, lost contract. He said the episode ended collegially—the client came to respect Cescotti's position.

He used a relatively well-worn excuse, saying that even though he was the managing director for Russia, he worked for a publicly listed German company that had a "zero tolerance" policy that ruled out these sorts of transactions. "Please understand, my hands are tied," he said. This was the simplest and most effective way to deflect the heat to a distant HQ.

Cescotti said he was fortunate. His firm provided equipment and services that were not widely available from competitors. Often, buyers came to him, rather than the other way around. The business he was responsible for in Russia was highly profitable.

"I was in the lucky position, as MD, to nearly always have a very competitive product to offer," Cescotti said.

"Sometimes there was no way to bypass us as a technology provider, and the 'homework' was not addressed to us as over time our 'zero tolerance' reputation grew," Cescotti said.

This reflects the experience of other businesses in Russia. Just as some companies earned reputations for paying bribes, others earned reputations for not paying bribes, and the opportunists moved to other targets. When Cescotti's salespeople told him the company would lose business if it didn't play ball, he reminded them of this.

Cescotti's experience in this environment came at a time when government officials were being locked up on corruption charges across Russia. He explained that these arrests targeted politicians who broke the unwritten code that they share their spoils. At the same time, other politicians known for their alleged corrupt activities remained untouched. The client Cescotti lost explained it to him this way:

"He said, 'Oliver, it's very simple. *Svoim, vsyo. Ostalnym zakon*,'" Cescotti recalled.

If you're one of us, you get it all. Everyone else gets the law.

"In the end, you're either part of the system or you're not. And if you're not part of the system, the system sacks you." If you're inside the system, he said, there are no limits.

The international executives and professionals doing business in Russia—in joint ventures or otherwise—had to do so much more than what they thought would be their day jobs. They had to be tour guides. They had to be drinking companions. They had to be cultural ambassadors and diplomats, even if they never set foot inside an embassy. It was part of the challenge; it was part of the burden. It was, in the end, part of the job.

A lot of the time, they had to be sheriffs. And that was a full-time job. Corruption was only one symptom of a system that could not police itself consistently or reliably.

"There fucking well is no law the way we understand law. That's just the fact. There is no rule of law and that is for me the end of society. There is no contract between the government and the population," Cescotti said. "There is no social contract in Russia. It is a self-service supermarket of an elite that goes shopping and runs the country like it's their personal supplier and they extract the revenues from there in whatever convenient way."[67]

7

INSECURITIES

*There are people who devoted their lives to building up the
capital markets. I know it sounds odd to some people—
bankers are parasites and thieves and all that—
but for me it was a holy cause.*[1]

*Hey look, there's this American here. Maybe she can help us
with privatisation.*[2]

The Party's over. The party's starting

The Bolshevik Biscuit Factory had been filling Russian cupboards
with small pleasures since 1855. The striking red-brick factory
complex just outside Moscow's central ring road, built originally
as the Adolph Siou and Co. confectionery factory, survived the
Bolshevik Revolution, the source of its modern name. It survived
the entire Soviet period and even the demise of the Soviet Union.
The conveyor belts that churned out beloved brands like the famous
"Jubilee" biscuit kept rolling even during the turbulent 1990s.

Getting stuck outside the biscuit factory in contemporary
Moscow's infamously sclerotic traffic brought a moment of relief

from urban life: the air around the complex was always rich with the promise of something to dip into a cup of tea.

It's no surprise, perhaps, that the Bolshevik was chosen as the first enterprise to go under the hammer in Russia's decade-defining privatisation process. It was a high-profile enterprise but not a sensitive, strategic site. It would be a popular company for Russia's emerging class of investors. (And privatising a factory with the word Bolshevik in its name must have been too good to resist.)

Russia had to rid itself of government ownership and create private property and a securities market where none had existed before. Starting with the Bolshevik would get everything off on the right foot. We will return to the biscuit factory's privatisation a bit later.

Privatise this

One of the most profound changes to the new Russian economic landscape rested on, and sprang from, a programme that took thousands of large, state-owned enterprises, each of them zombie-like after the collapse of the Soviet state, and transferred them into private ownership: voucher privatisation.

This sweeping, national endeavour was engineered to give just about every Russian citizen a coupon they could exchange for a stake in a state-owned enterprise as those entities came up for sale in a public auction. Privatisation vouchers had a RUB 10,000 face value and could be bought and sold before being submitted at an auction. The value of a voucher fluctuated, depending on the nascent market where they were traded; their real worth depended on inflation.

The ticket to capitalism cost each Russian 25 roubles to cover the overhead costs. In 1992, 25 roubles equalled about 26 US cents.

The Russian government hired CSFB, the investment banking arm of erstwhile Swiss giant Credit Suisse, to help design and execute the programme. Credit Suisse was one of the biggest early movers to Russia in financial services in the early 1990s, spurred on by Hans-Jörg Rudloff.[3] Boris Jordan, a US citizen of Russian heritage, ran CSFB in Russia after a stint in the Russian government's Privatisation Centre. Stephen Jennings, a New Zealander, joined him. Jennings arrived for a six-week assignment and stayed for twenty years.[4]

Goskomimushestvo, the State Property Committee known by its Russian initials GKI and led by then Deputy Prime Minister Anatoly Chubais, ran the privatisation effort with CSFB's banking and technical support. A wide range of related agencies, including the Ministry of Finance and the Privatisation Centre, joined in.

Sticker shock

Voucher privatisation, which took place between 1992 and 1994, was just one component in a spectrum of economic reforms in the 1990s aimed at various former Soviet ailments. The immediate liberalisation of prices, a move known as shock therapy, was another essential, if highly controversial, element. This step came courtesy of advisors from Harvard University and the Yeltsin government under then acting Prime Minister Yegor Gaidar, an economist and supporter of Gorbachev's perestroika.

Harvard's presence in Russia was prominent in the years following the end of the Soviet Union, in part due to relationships between professors at the university and US government officials, according to a prominent account of Harvard's work in Russia. Academics from across the university and consultants they hired worked on privatisation, democratisation and the development of a commercial, legal and regulatory framework for the Russian securities sector. Representatives from the John F. Kennedy School of Government, the Russian Research Center, the university's economics department and the Harvard Institute for International Development, known as HIID, were all working on Russian reform projects. The HIID's programme was perhaps the most expansive; it was funded by the US Agency for International Development, or USAID.[5]

The irrelevance of prices in the planned economy—but their centrality to a market economy—was one of the most urgent corrections the Russian government needed to introduce. Prices in the Soviet Union never reflected the dynamic between supply and demand. Their static nature drove the country's perennial shortages and infamous queueing. Hindsight is a powerful analytical tool, but even at the time, economic planners had to understand that allowing, overnight, the price of goods to float freely was an invitation to crisis-level inflation. That's exactly what happened on 1 January 1992.

The impact was brutal in the market for consumer goods. Prices skyrocketed instantly and then persistently. The price tags on basic staples at Russia's ubiquitous outdoor kiosks rose between morning and evening—it was cheaper to buy a container of orange juice on the way to work than on the way home. As the rouble slumped, anyone who could get their hands on hard currency—or who was lucky enough to get paid in dollars—got richer by the hour in rouble terms.

Most Russians rapidly became fluent in exchange rate mathematics; everyone learned to hold on to dollars and convert them at the last moment to pay, for example, rouble-based utility bills that came due on a fixed schedule. The longer you waited, the more roubles you could get for your dollar. It was also routine to roam the streets of Moscow, by then dotted with tiny—and always slightly shady-looking—currency exchange holes in the wall, to shop for the best exchange rates.

Voucher privatisation was central to the international presence in Russia because it helped create the Russian financial services sector, a nascent industry that sought to mimic its Western predecessors but under the most primitive, frontier conditions. The international team of powerful brains behind the voucher privatisation programme quickly, if imperfectly, created a market economy in a country that was about two years old and had never so much as bought or sold a pair of shoes at retail.

Experts came from all over the world to work on the project. "I had only been to the Soviet Union—I had never been to Russia before, and sitting here was just ridiculous when everything was happening," said the executive director of Harvard's Davis Center, Alexandra Vacroux. When she went to Russia, Vacroux was a PhD student at Harvard and was invited to join Professor Graham Allison's team supporting democratisation. Allison, one of Harvard's more renowned professors, was a Defense Department official in President Bill Clinton's government and a former dean of Harvard's John F. Kennedy School of Government.

"I kind of had the privatisation beat," she said. Vacroux tells the privatisation story with enthusiasm and energy.

Vacroux's first job was to write a memo about the political forces arrayed around privatisation. Her bosses liked it, so she just kept going. Before long, Vacroux was writing grant applications to USAID to fund a national public relations campaign boosting privatisation. Part of the reform task was not only to implement privatisation but to define and promote it.

A "voucher?" A "share?"

Russian citizens had no idea what a stock market was. They had no idea what a share was. They barely knew what a privatisation voucher was. The Russian economy was heading south fast, and the idea of trading a voucher to invest in a company seemed not only improbably exotic but exceedingly unappealing.

"We were kind of working on campaigns that were designed to explain to people how you pick up your vouchers, who's eligible for the voucher and the way to deal with it," Vacroux said. "You could invest it in a voucher auction, sell it or invest it in a fund."

The advertisements hoped to appeal to a Russian popular sensibility and in some cases, Vacroux said, relied on Russian folklore phrases. One campaign included traditional Russian words of caution, "Measure seven times before you cut," prompting Russians to consider their options carefully before using their voucher.

"One of the big discussions, for example, from a PR point of view was, 'Do you put a value on the vouchers?'" Vacroux said. "Ultimately, the decision was to put 10,000 roubles, because that was what a Volga was worth." The Volga was the bulky, lumbering car that was a status symbol of the Soviet elite. "That would convey to people that these things have value. Never mind that with hyperinflation, soon that was worth nothing."

At the outset of the voucher programme, RUB 10,000 were worth about USD 32. Low as that may seem, it was then six times the average weekly wage in Russia. Nina Yerokhina, a seventy-nine-year-old Muscovite, told a correspondent from the *Los Angeles Times* that she would cash in her voucher without hesitation and renovate her apartment.

"This voucher thing is my only chance to have my crumbling apartment repaired, so I can spend the remainder of my days in relative comfort," she said.[6]

Other voucher holders grasped the concept.

"This is great, this is fantastic!" Akop G. Kirakosyan, forty-four, told the *Los Angeles Times*. "This is the first time we've become masters of our country!"[7]

The Russian government needed as many Kirakosyans, and as few Yerokhinas, as possible. The more people who cashed in their shares to renovate their apartments, the less "public" the privatisation would be.

If you were more interested in buying a loaf of bread than buying a share in a bakery, people standing at folding tables in underground crosswalks in Moscow and elsewhere across Russia would eagerly buy your voucher for cash. These buyers were often harvesting and consolidating vouchers to sell them onwards to Russia's first brokerages and the founders of Russia's securities industry.

"That's where you had the brokerages that formed, because they started buying these individual vouchers. Probably not from the guy in the subway, but like the guy in the subway who started re-selling them on to brokers who were then accumulating them. They were also going to the factory gates and buying them from workers, because all the workers got [vouchers]," Vacroux said.

Privatisation was the pathway along which some of Russia's best surviving Soviet enterprises ended up in the hands of some of Russia's earliest entrepreneurial players. Voucher privatisation, among other things, was part of the primordial soup from which Russia's oligarchs would emerge.

"A dartboard and a basketball hoop"

Tony Gambrill's time in Moscow was emblematic of what could happen to a person who had an appetite for risk, spoke some Russian and had a sense of adventure. Plenty of people came to Russia as one sort of person—professionally speaking, at least—and left as another. After a year at the Metropol, Gambrill moved briefly into property management and then logistics before he plunged into the brokerage business. Gambrill's trajectory was not traditional, but he was by no means an outlier. Even as early as 1992, Russia presented transformational opportunities, as described in a 1992 article by Joanne Levine in *The Moscow Times*:

> Jessica Perera came to Moscow four years ago to work as an au pair. Today she is a tax consultant for Ernst & Young.
>
> Marty Zug was sitting in university classes a year ago. He is now planning to orchestrate the opening of one of Moscow's first Western dry cleaners.
>
> And Cami McCormick, once a radio broadcaster in New Orleans, has made herself into a household name in Moscow.
>
> These three Americans have little in common, other than their peculiar choice to migrate to Moscow to stake out fame and fortune.[8]

While Gambrill was in the logistics end of a company in the fertiliser industry, his employer was looking for something to do with a serious amount of cash on hand. Gambrill suggested they invest some of the company's funds in privatisation vouchers.

"We had a lot of cash sitting around, and the stock market was beginning," Gambrill said. "I said to my boss, 'It was a bit like buying candy.'"[9]

An initial investment of USD 100,000 in the Russian voucher market generated a 100 per cent return within a month. Gambrill pocketed a bonus; his boss developed an appetite for more. "We do this for a few months, and we start to do really well," Gambrill said.

He turned his company's knowledge of the Urals region, a centre of the Russian fertiliser industry, to a new advantage. "I start sending people out with USD 500,000 in cash in a suitcase, and a fold-up picnic table and a chair. They sit outside the factory gates of the places where we want to buy privatisation vouchers and bring them back to Moscow to convert into shares and to keep what we want. And then I started selling the remainder to Brunswick," he said, naming one of Russia's homegrown brokerages, and the place where Vacroux became head of sales. Vouchers were useful at the initial privatisation auctions. Once a company was privatised and shares were issued, they were also tradeable.

Gambrill said his relationship with Brunswick was mutually beneficial. Brunswick, via Gambrill, bought shares in companies in the Urals where it wanted to develop a stake. "'Do you have anyone at this factory?'" Brunswick would ask, in Gambrill's words. "I'm like, 'We can find somebody at that factory. We'll send somebody off.'"

"So that's what I used to do," Gambrill said.

It wasn't all breakneck capitalism. Along the way, Gambrill became a trustee of a charity in Moscow for children with Down's syndrome. But capitalism never really went on holiday. Gambrill said he once had a gun pointed at his head, after an escalating series of threats from a criminal syndicate in search of an unpaid loan taken out by a colleague.

Gambrill's success did not go unnoticed. After establishing a track record in a sector that barely had a track, he was hired into the investment arm of a Russian energy company:

> When I started there, my job was to open a brokerage. I do a little bit of quick reading through textbooks, just to see what a brokerage is and how it functioned. I set up a trading floor with a dartboard and a basketball hoop and all that sort of thing. Some days we might buy or sell USD 100 million-worth of stuff. Other days we might do nothing. But I'd gone from being in a hotel five minutes ago to now doing this.

Trading in Russian privatisation vouchers and shares was not for the faint-hearted; most of the activity from the international community came from experienced investors who knew they were taking on potentially enormous risk. If the voucher privatisation programme failed to take root, or if privatised companies failed to thrive—as sometimes happened—any investments in vouchers or shares would turn to dust.

"You're basically taking a flyer on Bitcoin or something like that," Vacroux said, underlining that it remained a high-risk investment. "It's not that unusual to be in an emerging market situation and see an opportunity and know that they could go to zero."

Getting everyone on board

The risk that the entire privatisation programme would do exactly that—go to zero—was high.

"I don't think anything, or anyone, was 100 per cent sure, but they thought this was the only chance," Vacroux said.

The risks were not strictly economic. Political opponents had encircled the privatisation programme. GKI, the State Property Committee, was in a former Soviet Ministry of Finance building on Nikolsky Pereulok, near Red Square in the heart of Moscow's imposing government quarter. Most of the people in the building, all former Soviet Finance Ministry staff, were opposed to privatisation. GKI's offices on the third floor were surrounded by detractors.

"And there were foreigners running all over the place, which they were still kind of freaked out about," Vacroux said. "We were not super popular." This was a time, however, when Russia—or at least parts of the Yeltsin administration—were open to Western support and assistance. President Putin would now call this sort of support "interference" or a loss of sovereignty.

Starting in 1992, most of the measures taken in connection with privatisation were managed by presidential decree, rather than via the hostile Russian parliament.[10] Even supporters of privatisation, among Russians and their Western advisors, split into camps. Some advocated for the privatisation models used in the former Czechoslovakia or in Poland, which at the very least moved more slowly.

The (former) Soviet C-suite

Enterprise directors—the biggest and most powerful were called the "Red Directors"—were dead set against privatisation, which they feared would sell their factories out from under them. These were powerful directors who never had to worry about making a profit or really managing a business during the Soviet period of central control and five-year plans.

"Never mind that they don't even know what profit is," Vacroux said. "They had no interest in reforms."

In their offices and behind their desks, these Soviet managers were rulers of all they surveyed, in positions of power and privilege commensurate with the size of the enterprises they ran. They were brought on side by getting a stake in their enterprises.

It didn't always work.

The director of Permskiye Motory—Perm Motors, one of the Soviet Union's signature industrial enterprises—picked up the phone and screamed down the line at Vacroux. Privatisation, and the vagaries of a system that caused a company's value to rise and fall, he insisted, did not suit him.

"I had the director calling me and saying 'What do you mean my effing shares are worth like 2 kopeks? We have 30,000 people here. We make jet engines. How can our shares be worth so little?'"

Explaining to a director of his stature that an algorithm determined the value of his shares did very little to soothe his managerial ego. "'This is terrible! I'm worth more!'" Vacroux recalls him saying.

He had little choice in the matter—his enterprise was privatised.

Patti Baral remembers coming to Moscow from rural Canada at twenty-two years old with a degree in international economics and a desire to do something to improve the environment. She had few illusions about the Soviet or Russian relationship to the environment—it was non-existent—but she saw an opportunity for change. Russia was latticed with leaking oil and gas pipelines. If she could help bring investment into that sector, it could make a difference.

"I seem to recall that the entire market capitalisation of Russia was probably like the equivalent of Disney World at the time," she said, only half joking.[11]

After an immersion course in Russian and time at a Belgian food importer, Baral became a senior manager at a Russian brokerage firm. Before long, she was taking clients to meet the big bosses at enterprises deep in provincial Russia.

"All of my clients were foreign investors, and at the beginning were hedge funds," she said. Like all sophisticated investors, Baral said her clients wanted to talk about economies of scale, corporate governance and return on investment. It didn't go down well. The companies were being privatised; the bosses, less so.

The Russian government's privatisation manual even had a section called "Know the Trade-Offs!" where it helped explain the difference in expectations between the Russian enterprises being privatised and the foreign investors buying them.[12] In short, the Red Directors' position on privatisation could be summarised as "give us your foreign money, but we won't be giving you any control."

"It was clear that the concept of 'ownership' by foreign shareholders of the company that they manage was obscure, and having foreign investors asking pointed financial and operational questions had them hesitate to answer," Baral said. She recalls taking a client to meet the director of a regional telecoms company, in a communist-era, Art Deco building palatial in size and imposing in stature. The manager was equally imposing.

"It appeared that he was meeting a Western foreigner for the first time," she said. "This man was absolutely huge, and he sat around the table, and he was sweating buckets, like sweating, sweating, sweating buckets."

For the directors of Russian enterprises early in the privatisation process, meeting a broker, an analyst and a Western hedge fund manager was fever-dream material.

"I surmised that some management were practically insulted to have foreign investors coming in asking penetrating questions about their operations," Baral said:

> Foreign ownership of the companies they managed was a concept they didn't fully embrace. Certainly since prior to privatisation companies were owned by the state. Having outside investors required them to adhere to profitability standards dictated by the West. But what does this profitability standard look like? A standard they had no prior lived experience in.

On the topic of no prior lived experience, Baral's clients found themselves in rural Russia with suitcases full of cash. At the time, the investment process was primitive, and, well, highly analogue.

"In order to purchase shares in Russian companies, one had to send a delegate to physically go with suitcases of cash, go to the company register in the region, and register the foreign investor," she said. Even when Moscow's stock market began to emerge, brokers were still travelling to pick up share certificates in exchange for cash.

The need for speed

Though he described the environment at the time of voucher privatisation as a "jungle," Maxim Boycko, once Yeltsin's deputy chief of staff, a former deputy prime minister and an architect of privatisation, said there wasn't that much he would do differently. As one of the key designers of voucher privatisation, Boycko said the programme's overriding principle was to prevent Russia from collapsing back into the Soviet Union. He is now a visiting lecturer in economics at Harvard.

"The biggest concern of many people, including myself, was that we don't want the country to go back to the communists," he said. As Russia spun out of control economically and politically, the Communist Party of Russia was gaining in popularity. "Because, really, life under communism was not nice, just from experience."[13]

Boycko chose his words with great care. There was a window of opportunity, he said, and "you need to probably not beat around the bush."

The Yeltsin administration was in firefighting mode.

"Chubais and Gaidar really thought that if they didn't move very fast, that the communists were going to come back and seize power," Vacroux said. "This was not just words; they were convinced of it."

Every element of the privatisation programme involved critical trade-offs, many of which had the potential to alter Russia's trajectory as a nation. Among the issues at stake was whether privatisation—designed to enrich and fund the Russian state— would instead impoverish it, Vacroux said. Polish enterprises, for example, were first reformed under state ownership and privatised when they were financially more robust. Vacroux wondered what would happen to all the other state functions—healthcare, for example—when a strong, Western, neoliberal ethos was urging lightning-fast privatisation.

The Russian government also resisted offers from Western investment banks only too happy to take the privatisation programme off the government's hands, Boycko said. Among various banks' proposals was a plan to privatise Russian enterprises one at a time. To Boycko, this envisioned a privatisation programme that, with slight exaggeration, might still be at work today.

Depending on your perspective, and more to the point, your politics, privatisation was either a resounding success or a botched attempt at bringing a socialist corpse to life as a market economy. It was a triumph of democratic reform or an exercise in political window-dressing. If your most important criterion was removing companies from state control, privatisation was a triumph. Thousands of companies were taken private. If your most important metric was establishing an open market where assets had accurate values established in a transparent fashion, privatisation was a catastrophe. Thousands of companies were bought via inside deals at knock-down prices.

"They basically consolidated everything to a very, very small group of hands," Baral said.

Daylight robbery

In the run-up to Yeltsin's 1996 presidential re-election campaign—another perceived make-or-break moment to keep the new Russian state from falling under the control of Gennady Zyuganov's Communist Party—the loans-for-shares operation was one more striking and enduring distortion of the Russian economy. It was a staggering piece of economic chicanery, mildly put, for the sake of a larger political triumph.

The exchange of campaign cash for shares in Russia's most valuable companies has been explained in painstaking detail in several books, perhaps most compellingly in *Sale of the Century*, by then *Financial Times* Moscow bureau chief Chrystia Freeland. Freeland is now finance minister and deputy prime minister of Canada.

To summarise, Russia's emerging oligarchs agreed—while they were at Davos, no less—that they would loan the Yeltsin administration hundreds of millions of dollars to finance Yeltsin's re-election campaign. In exchange for these loans, they were given enormous blocks of shares in Russia's most strategic companies. The government promised to repay the loans; the shares were meant to serve as collateral.

The loans were never repaid. The shares were never returned. There were auctions to make it all look kosher; it was anything but. A group of businessmen small enough to fit around a dinner table became the owners of the Russian economy's crown jewels at unconceivable discounts, awarding them hammer-like political and economic power. It would be wrong to call this the birth of the oligarchs. It was more like their coronation.

In 1997, Bloomberg labelled then thirty-six-year-old Vladimir Potanin, one of the architects of the loans-for-shares schemes, "the most powerful man in Russia"—a title usually reserved for a country's president. Bloomberg wrote that the companies comprising his business "empire" were collectively responsible for almost 10 per cent of Russia's GDP.[14]

"These are highly collusive, closed deals which they are working out," a source told *The Moscow Times*, which aggressively covered the loans-for-shares transactions and was on to their fraudulent nature from the start, though the scheme's function as a campaign finance programme was initially less clear. Reports in *The Moscow Times* and elsewhere covered the fiery bargaining and high stakes negotiating underpinning the scheme. "It was clear that people were saying: 'This is mine—stay away; you can have that one, I'll stay away from you.' There's collusion built into the rules, but there's collusion just built in generally."[15]

Wharton professor Philip Nichols is prepared to give voucher privatisation a passing grade, but his appraisal of Russian economic reform in the 1990s turns darker when it comes to the outrages of the loans-for-shares arrangements.

"More and more people are realising that until you get to loans for shares, which was just despicable, until you get to that point, given that no one, none of us, had ever dealt with anything like that before, the transfer of assets went pretty well," he said.

"But loans for shares? Criminal. Criminal. There's no excuse for how that happened," he said. "The implications have tripped up Russia ever since. There is no question, no question about that."

A US General Accounting Office (GAO) report expressed the view that by the time the West realised the degree to which the outcome of the loans-for-shares programme could further undermine reform objectives, it was too late. According to a former World Bank official, the only person capable of persuading the Yeltsin administration to abandon the programme would have been the US president. Others stated that effective opposition could have been easier to muster. According to the GAO report, "one former senior Russian official [described] the overall western reaction to the program at the time as a conspiracy of silence."[16]

Not surprisingly, privatisation was frequently referred to in Russian slang as *prikhvatizatsia*, or "grab-it-isation."

The post-mortems

Debates about the efficacy and the outcome of the privatisation process raged endlessly from all quarters and every constituency. Western journalists who breathlessly reported the sale of state assets and declared privatisation the second coming were accused of being gullible and worshipping the cult of Chubais.[17] Investment bankers were charged with hyping the companies they were auctioning while downplaying just how messy the process really was. The Russian government was either irreversibly corrupt, in a terrible hurry, hopelessly naïve or vigorously scheming. The team from HIID comprised either geniuses or gangsters. Take your pick.

None of these viewpoints are mutually exclusive. The privatisation programme was vast enough to contain a bit of everything—corrupt, sweetheart deals; smooth, efficient transfers of ownership; rapacious and unforgiving greed; and a bit of fairness. Other countries' privatisations were cleaner and, more importantly, put more money into their states' treasuries. Few of those countries had the bazaar-like free-for-all that visited Russia in the 1990s.

"Well, privatization was done in the 1990s in a very bad way. But the problem is that I have seen no single postsocialist countries [*sic*] where the population would be satisfied by the way in which privatization was done," Gaidar said in reflection at a 2004 conference:

> We had the choice of either stopping privatization and then having a mess when the managers whom we were unable to control are stripping assets, creating new companies for their wives, transferring under the laws—the assets—or to start a very inefficient—we knew—there was a lot of enthusiasm at the time—we knew very well that the voucher privatization will not be an extremely nice experience.[18]

The West applauded Yeltsin and his privatisation plans. While documenting the breakneck speed of the process—thousands of companies were said to have been privatised every month—the international media led cheers from the sidelines. The *Los Angeles Times'* Moscow correspondent wrote that "Marx must be turning in his grave, Lenin revolving in his tomb," because Yeltsin was bringing the "bourgeoisie" to Russia.[19]

"And the triumph of the bourgeoisie means progress. Yeltsin may be no economist, but he knows that private ownership makes for a materially advancing society, not only in the United States and Western Europe but in Japan, South Korea, Taiwan, Singapore and other countries of Asia," the *Los Angeles Times* wrote. "He is determined to bring that kind of progress to Russia. That's why he has pushed economic reforms, bringing free-market economists into his government and enraging those who would slow reform in favor of an imperial Russia dominating the former Soviet republics."

David Hoffman, a prominent and insightful chronicler of Russia's early days from his position as Moscow bureau chief for *The Washington Post*, produced a pithy summary of the process:

> [T]he massive transfer of property to private hands, a necessary step to create a free-market economy, has turned into a vicious struggle for wealth in which the rule of law has never been established. Former Soviet bureaucrats, factory directors, aggressive businessmen and criminal organizations have all made a grab for the bounty through insider deals, bribery and simple brute force.
>
> Russia's economy has taken on an oligarchic structure, in which large business conglomerates, often allied with groups of powerful politicians, compete for grand fortunes—and sometimes resort to violence.[20]

Team Navalny, the group carrying on the work of the late Alexei Navalny and his Anti-Corruption Foundation, known by its Russian initials as the FBK, lays the blame for Russia's current state of affairs squarely at the feet of Yeltsin and his entourage in the 1990s. In a multi-part documentary film re-examining the 1990s and based on a social media post from Navalny shortly before his death in February 2024, FBK chair Maria Pevchikh draws a straight and unbroken line from the chaos and corruption of the Yeltsin administration to Putin's Russia of 2024. The film is titled *Traitors*.

"Russia could have been completely different. Everything could have been different. And it should have been different," Pevchikh says to the camera, in a film full of tension and the vivid production values that made Navalny's social media work so resonant.[21] The documentary sparked controversy within the Russian opposition, where Navalny, who survived an assassination attempt via poisoning in August 2020 and died in a Russian penal colony in 2024, had been so prominent. Critics wondered why Pevchikh was dredging up ancient history, why she laid so much blame specifically on Yeltsin and whether she had overplayed the influence of Boris Berezovsky on the Kremlin.[22]

Personalities are important, and the 1990s in Russia produced more than its fair share of characters who left their mark on the country and, without exaggeration, the world. But people come and go; an unshakeable Soviet hangover likes to blame individuals and let heads roll but does nothing to change the fundamentally flawed ecosystem underneath it all. To be sure, we will not soon forget the individuals who played in the drama called 1990s Russia. But the people were only part of the problem.

"Lawyers and theoreticians"

Among the domestic and imported government officials, bankers, academics and lawyers, each knew a piece of what they had to do; collectively, none of them had the experience to make it work in a place that had no recent history of capital markets.

In a lengthy interview with the PBS programme *Commanding Heights*, then CSFB Russia head Boris Jordan noted that Mexico and Argentina, for example, could bring in Ivy League-educated Mexicans and Argentinians to restructure their capital markets. But Russia was structuring, not restructuring, and the number of Soviet citizens who had Ivy League educations was, for the time being, tiny.

"Russia didn't have that resource at the time, and so it was working with people who read textbooks," Jordan said. "So the process that they embarked on was in many ways naïve and more of a survival tactic":[23]

When we were hired, we were asked to implement a legal process that was developed by a group of both American and Russian advisors to the Russian government. Harvard University was involved with this. Jeffrey Sachs and a group of Russian advisors were involved as well and put together a legal structure and a legal framework for the privatisation of Russian assets. The problem lay in the fact that these were largely lawyers and theoreticians who did a fantastic job putting the framework together, but to put that into practice, none of them had the experience.[24]

He was not alone in his thinking. It was hard to overestimate just how isolated the Soviet Union, and now Russia, had been from international markets.

"Back then, only two professors in Moscow and about ten people working at Vnesheconombank [Russia's state foreign trade bank] had a solid understanding of what the stock market was and how it operated," Troika Dialog's Ruben Vardanyan wrote in a personal blog post many years later.[25]

The brokers

One of the sophisticated investors who came to play was Bernie Sucher. And he put his money down at Troika Dialog.

"I had found my way out to ulitsa Krasina [Krasina Street] on the third floor, where Troika's office was, and I had walked in prepared to invest some money in the vouchers," Sucher said. "I was met by this young man, and he was, it turned out, twenty years old and still at university. And when he wasn't at university he was at Troika."[26]

"I told him in English that I wanted to invest USD 20,000, and the kid nearly fainted," Sucher said. "He said he couldn't take the responsibility of accepting that much money."

Sucher briefly thought Troika Dialog itself probably didn't have 20,000 dollars to its name. In truth, it did, courtesy of

American banker Peter Derby, a Troika co-founder. But it was still early days. The student, Sucher suspected, was probably making about USD 100 a month; his boss was probably making something like USD 500 a month. So the student did what keen junior employees do everywhere.

"He called his boss and said, 'We've got a big one here and you've got to help me land it,'" Sucher recalled. Before long, Sucher was a Troika co-founder.

Later, Troika's Vardanyan wrote that he was making it up as he went along.

"When I got a licence to start the business, I had no idea what I would do. My main vision was not about the company, it was about the country and the change that was starting in Russia," Vardanyan said in an interview. "I wanted to prove that a successful business could be built in Russia in five or ten years. I believe that was a major reason why we were so successful. The second reason for our success, I would say, is the support of our first shareholder."[27] Derby had contributed USD 35,000.

Once the company was up and running, Troika still didn't know what to do with the money pouring in. There was no Russian expression for "client onboarding."

"So I'm sitting here with Ruben and he's lit my world on fire with this vision, and among the first things that we were trying to deal with was, 'How do you accept the money?'" Sucher said.

"What are the rules of the game? Someone like me walks in the door, what are you going to do?" Sucher's first task was to edit Troika's trifold brochure and take out the spelling mistakes. "That was the first of tens of thousands of documents that I started editing."

The opportunity, they decided, was as a broker in the voucher auctions—buying and selling vouchers and, later, shares to and for foreigners:

This was really, really basic blocking and tackling, but none of it was more urgent and long-term important than the mentality of these young people, and getting them on a track where they could develop—with minimal resources—but nonetheless develop quickly into the kinds of people who could be bankers and brokers and a support staff that would have to face off with Credit Suisse First Boston, and with Merrill Lynch, and the hedge funds.

Troika, in other words, aimed to work with and compete against the big boys. It would buy vouchers and sell them into the high-risk, high-reward investment community. Those investors lived and worked far from Russia and worked with investment bankers from London, New York and Zurich.

"If I go out and I say to Merrill Lynch 'We can do this for you,' they're going to come after me if I fuck up," Sucher said. "I have to make sure that these people are incredibly responsible and honest and effective."

Sucher was in Boycko's jungle, and it was scary.

"For two years, I was terrified," he said.

Sucher came from Goldman Sachs, so he had some idea of how to structure a securities market. Even so, he said he had very little idea how the back office worked. Many—most, Sucher says—of the first players in the Russian capital markets had very little experience in the front or the back office. If you were a big foreign bank, with a sophisticated global operation, a brand and a reputation, you could go to your clients and tell them you could, potentially, make them rich.

But someone on the ground in Russia had to make it happen.

"We started trading vouchers and putting up vouchers for securities, and there was a long delay in the time between people buying vouchers in 1992 and getting registered Russian securities in 1994 and 1995," Sucher said. "During that entire time, the potential for error and fraud was gargantuan, let alone if the government just screwed it up. The number of things that had to go right for that privatisation voucher to become a deliverable, unencumbered Russian security in, say, 1994–1995 is mind boggling."

As the business evolved, brokers began to distinguish themselves with their levels of service and how accurately they could interpret the market for investors. Brunswick, where Vacroux worked, was known for its research. It was primitive, but in a primitive market, it stood out. Brunswick sent students into the field to pound the pavement; information came back for review among more senior, experienced, expat bankers.

All of this, bear in mind, in the days before the internet came to Russia. "We had a chalkboard where we would write prices because, remember, no internet," Vacroux said.

Baral ultimately understood that getting to know a company's fundamentals, such as they were, was important, but there was something even more important: information. Formally, she was a sales executive, but she was also an analyst, an interpreter. An article in the *FT* could move the value of a company more than any corporate governance exercise.

"At the time, equity markets in Russia were rather illiquid, and information flow shifted the market significantly. It is safe to say that the content and power of one written article in London, credible or not, had a significant impact on the market," she said. Baral said she often found herself having to square the coverage of Russia with what she knew was happening on the ground and relay that nuance to her clients.

Beyond that, it was Las Vegas with snow.

"The responsible thing to do"

Companies knew that Russia and the countries of the former Soviet bloc posed risks as well as opportunity. The challenge was quantifying the balance between the two. "The mental makeup of decision-makers who came to the Czech Republic, or Russia or South East Asia, these were people who said, 'I have an opportunity to take advantage of an historical moment for my company or my investors, and I'm eager to try,'" Sucher explained.

This was a time in the business community—it did not last forever—when investors had almost a free pass to invest on unfamiliar turf. Everyone was doing it; it was part of how the global economy worked under the guiding principles of globalisation. The risks associated with investing in emerging markets were not, at least not initially, framed as governance or reputational risks.

"If you were a corporate decision-maker and you were going to commit real capital into a pre-law environment like Russia, obviously that's a risky thing to do," Sucher said. "But I think a lot of people felt like they had the responsibility to try. It was, like, it could be really good for the world, and it could be really awesome, really good, for the company."

"The responsible thing to do was engage, despite the risks," he said.

In Russia, that attitude faded as the 1990s came to an end. The buccaneering spirit that accompanied equally buccaneering times—a feeling of both invincibility and impunity—was replaced by a type of corporate caution and an understanding that Russia was becoming the kind of place that could ruin a career. Or a company. That was when Sucher was being headhunted to work at Merrill Lynch in Moscow.

"CEOs like John Thain at Merrill Lynch, they wanted to know who I was because they knew that I could be responsible for a business that could destroy their careers. You didn't have that attitude in the early 1990s," Sucher said.

"It's a completely different mentality as reflected in corporate thinking and investor thinking over that decade," he said. As an aside, Sucher was also responsible for bringing the Starlite Diner, a 100 per cent replica of a traditional American diner, to

Moscow. When US expats discovered a place that had decent burgers and milkshakes, it became an instant institution.

Taking the biscuit, in detail

Much like their peers across Russia, managers at the Bolshevik Biscuit Factory had no interest in being privatised. Jordan, in the PBS television interview of 2000, described how he overcame the resistance: "[W]e had long lessons in the offices of the Bolshevik Biscuit Factory, where I would be explaining the concept of private ownership, the benefits that would bring the company and the benefits that would bring to them as managers," he recalled.[28]

There was explaining, and then there was convincing:

> In the end, it was a very old, simple process that got these guys to agree. We had to basically, I wouldn't say bribe, but incentivise them by giving them stock. And so the programme that was developed gave managers of their factories, and the employees of the factories, about 50 per cent of the stock in the company that would get distributed, based on the amount of years you worked at that company.

The balance of the shares would be sold to the public via the vouchers.

The most widespread form of voucher privatisation was the "Type Two" format, which gave managers and employees the opportunity to purchase 51 per cent of their company's shares. Those two groups could acquire shares in their companies with those vouchers or even with cash, among other options. As privatisation developed, more experienced investors simply brought suitcases of vouchers to the auction site and swamped the auctions.[29]

The biscuit factory went under the hammer in a convention hall stuffed with an army of young Russians hired to ensure things went smoothly.

"Finally, on December 8, 1992, we opened up the first official auction of a Russian company to the public market. It was a big exhibition hall, but, you know, it was very difficult to get people interested," Jordan said in the interview:

> People in the street didn't believe it. They felt that if the voucher could buy them two bottles of vodka, then that was a lot better than something called equity. And most of the people that were actually standing in line were employees of the company that not only got stock through the internal subscription that gave it to them, but they also then got their voucher from the state.[30]

The auction's main takeaway was a revelation that turned into a sensation.

The number of vouchers bid for shares in the Bolshevik Biscuit Factory was low; demand was weak. Even though managers and employees already had their shares, no one else seemed hugely interested. Jordan recalled the opening price for the Bolshevik Biscuit Factory, based on the auction, was USD 684,000.

A year prior to that, Jordan's colleagues in Poland sold a nearly identical biscuit factory for USD 80 million. Russian assets could be had at a tiny fraction of their potential value. Investors who felt confident in that potential value stood to make a fortune.

"[W]hat we realised after that first auction closed is that these assets were going to go out tremendously undervalued, and that word started to spread very quickly through the very undeveloped financial community in Moscow," Jordan said. "And all of a sudden, brokerage firms started to pop up everywhere. People were buying these vouchers and were going to auction centres, bidding for these companies because they realised they could get them real cheap."

The air outside the biscuit factory is no longer sweet with temptation. In short, here's what happened at the Bolshevik Biscuit Factory. Fridman's Alfa-Capital, a part of his once sprawling Alfa Group, dominated the flagship privatisation and in December of 1992 took control of Bolshevik for USD 1 million. Alfa-Capital bought out the biscuit factory's employees' shares, after convincing factory management they were doing this for the factory's benefit. They even arranged a special schedule for employees to queue up to sell their shares, out of concern that a stampede would shut down the factory's production conveyer. Employees got USD 250 for every share that had a face value of 1,000 roubles.[31] Even if they only had a small amount of shares, these were dizzying sums of money for a factory worker.

Two years later, Alpha sold the factory to Danone for USD 30 million.[32] Danone, in turn, sold Bolshevik and its entire global biscuit business to Kraft in 2007 for EUR 5.3 billion.[33] In 2011, Kraft closed the Bolshevik plant and moved production to the Vladimir region. The former factory is now a meticulously restored and renovated office and apartment complex and home to the Museum of Russian Impressionism.[34]

There were other, howling distortions to Russia's privatisation process. AvtoVAZ, the sprawling automotive enterprise, wrote its own privatisation rules, seeking to substantially suppress participation by foreign investors. At the time of its voucher auction, AvtoVAZ employed more than half a million workers and produced 7 per cent of Russian GDP. When it was privatised, the share prices set at the auction valued the factory at USD 45 million. A year prior to its privatisation, Fiat reportedly offered USD 1 billion dollars to buy AvtoVAZ.[35]

The Russian energy giant Gazprom excluded "foreign and professional buyers" from its voucher auction, yielding a company valuation of USD 228 million. Boycko writes that this was "one thousandth of the value put on it by foreign investment banks."[36] Later in its evolution, Gazprom briefly became one of the world's most valuable companies.[37]

The list of Russian industries privatised on the cheap is long. The implication is that whoever bought these industries at the outset later became phenomenally wealthy—shareholders became millionaires, if not billionaires—when shares were traded on an open market that could assign them real value.

Russia's instant millionaires flouted the rules and flaunted their wealth. The Russia of the 1990s produced a garish stereotype called the *Novy Russky*—the new Russian. These were capitalism's first winners, and like their nouveau riche predecessors elsewhere in the world (the linguistic similarity is absolutely not accidental), they were the sort of folks who had more money than taste.

Looking back over the course of privatisation based on the value of vouchers over twenty months, the grand total of the entire effort was set at about USD 12 billion. "That is, the equity of all of the Russian industry, including oil, gas, some of its transportation sector, and most of manufacturing, was worth less than that of Kellogg or Anheuser-Busch," Boycko wrote.[38]

Heady days. Moscow was up to its neck in high finance, and there were still no restaurants or proper offices in town. Jordan ran his operations from a hotel suite in, of course, the Metropol. He paid the hotel to run extra phone lines into the rooms.

"We went out and in on airplanes and brought in fax machines. We literally had to come in on a weekly basis with a suitcase of USD 25,000 or USD 50,000 or USD 100,000 in cash just to finance this whole operation and put it together," he said.[39]

Kids those days

There was no payroll, no HR, nor any of the stultifying induction programmes typical of modern companies. Still, Jordan found plenty of smart, young people to work the Bolshevik auction. It seemed as if everyone who worked in the nascent Russian financial services industry was young. They had mathematics degrees, they had physics degrees and some of them spoke a bit of English. These were the hallmarks of the Moscow educational elite who, whatever you threw at them, grabbed it and ran. Everywhere you looked, the new entrants into business seemed like the student Sucher met at Troika Dialog. Most of the bosses were from this group, too. Some of Russia's early business elite came from the influential and well-connected circles of Soviet youth in the Komsomol, the Soviet Communist Party youth organisation.

Vardanyan was twenty-two when he set up Troika Dialog.[40] Jordan hadn't hit his thirtieth birthday yet.[41]

You had to be young to pull this off. Every privatisation auction—the important ones, at least—repeated the battle at Bolshevik: convince the bureaucrats, win over the management, hoover up the vouchers, take a deep breath and bid.

"I don't think I'd ever take that on again," Jordan said. "We were real kamikazes, putting that together."

Jordan and Jennings left CSFB to create Renaissance Capital in 1995 in a move that lit the Russian financial services sector ablaze. RenCap, as it was known, became an instant powerhouse.

"From the first day, Renaissance Capital was a high-wire act, a collection of colorful and super-aggressive money men banded together by vaulting ambition for wealth amid the land grab that was Russia in the 1990s," Sucher wrote in a column for *The Moscow Times* when Jennings left the firm. "That ambition was feral, just barely restrained by the superior, concentrated professionalism that became the firm's competitive attribute. Renaissance, inspired by Jennings' beloved Kiwi rugby tradition, was in your face: muscular, fierce, fast and intimidating."[42]

Running the sums

By 1993, around 72,000 companies had been privatised, compared with 1,352 from the previous year, an astonishing increase of around 5,000 per cent. More than 20 per cent of the country's industrial labour force then worked for private firms, and due to voucher privatisation, another 35 million became shareholders among Russia's 149.5 million people at the time.[43] By July 1994, when the voucher privatisation programme ended, two-thirds of Russian enterprises were privately owned, Russia had a "booming" stock market and 40 million Russians owned shares, either in companies or in mutual funds.[44]

Harvard heads for the exits

In 2000, after three years of investigation, the US DoJ accused some of Harvard's most prominent participants in the Russian reform effort of insider trading and misusing public funds in their work in Russia, alleging damages of up to USD 120 million.[45]

In 2006, the university and two of the HIID staff involved in Russia reached a USD 31 million settlement with the US government. HIID closed in 2000.

The payout

The men and women who built the Russian financial services sector became the rock stars of the early to mid-1990s and in some cases for years to come. The newspapers called them "Tsars,"[46] or robber barons, like Russian Rockefellers. Many, if not all of them, stayed in the Russian capital markets and founded their own firms.

Market consolidation shook loose astronomical sums of money. Mikhail Prokhorov's ONEXIM Group bought 50 per cent of Renaissance in 2008 in a deal that valued RenCap at USD 1 billion. He took full control in 2012 for an undisclosed sum.[47] By that time, Renaissance had already merged with Potanin's MFK Bank.[48]

Russia's national savings bank, Sberbank, announced in March 2011 that it would acquire Troika Dialog for USD 1 billion, including a 36 per cent stake bought in 2009 by South Africa's Standard Bank.[49] This was the firm founded with USD 35,000 from Peter Derby and where Sucher showed up at the front door with USD 20,000.

Deutsche Bank acquired a 40 per cent stake in United Financial Group, a brokerage co-founded by American Charles Ryan and former Russian Finance Minister Boris Fyodorov in 1994, for a reported USD 70 million in 2003.[50] Deutsche completed the acquisition by buying the remaining 60 per cent in 2005 for a reported USD 400 million.[51]

That same week, Dresdner Bank bought a stake in Gazprombank for USD 1 billion.[52] SBC Warburg, then the investment banking division of the former Swiss Bank Corporation, now known as UBS, created a joint venture with Brunswick.

Sucher and Jordan are now, separately, engaged with cannabis companies in the US.

8

APPLES AND ORANGES

They embraced the idea of markets the same way they embraced capitalism. No holds barred. Even though they made a hash of it. They made a hash of it from the get-go.[1]

The common assumption among western leaders was that Russia's conversion from a Communist state to a market economy within a democratic state would bring long-term stability within Russia and between Russia and the West.[2]

Not so peaceful co-existence

For ten years, a gigantic, 6.5-ton replica of the three-pointed Mercedes-Benz emblem rotated lazily atop the infamous House on the Embankment on the edge of the Moscow River, a few metres across from the Kremlin. The House on the Embankment, a massive, imposing monster of a building that is almost a city unto itself, was once home to the Soviet Communist Party super-elite and is filled with the legacy of officers and bureaucrats purged during Stalinism. The stories of life in the House during Stalin's reign of terror are legendary. Its residents were famously plucked from their prestige apartments and sent to the gulags on spurious charges of being enemies of the state. Residents would come home in the evenings and not take their coats off until they knew the day's round of arrests was over.

Latterly, the building had become a bustling hive of rich expats with lavish relocation budgets and Moscow millionaires desirous of its panoramic city views. As part of a 2011 City Hall crackdown on outdoor advertising, the revolving Mercedes logo was taken down.[3] (A similar, but shorter-lived, episode saw a nearly 2-storey-tall Louis Vuitton trunk removed from Red Square in November 2013.)

One of the West's most famous brands for a decade sat atop one of the Soviet Union's most famous buildings. But the combination could not last. It was a graft from one system on to another that could never take root.

The clash

The international business community arrived in Russia and met a social, political and economic system that had formed in almost complete isolation from the West. What happened in Russia starting in 1991 wasn't even an awakening from a period of dormancy. A Rumpelstiltskin analogy here would be convenient, but wrong.

The point of departure for most of those executives, though, was a Western, or international, system that was becoming increasingly consistent, transparent and, most importantly, formalised. Where they came from, the rules of the game were published, agreed and (mostly) enforced.

To the extent that Russia took on some of the exterior trappings of international business—comfortably carpeted conference rooms, business cards with raised lettering and invoices and contracts emblazoned with company logos—international businesspeople were at least on some level under the impression that Russian business culture was increasingly mirroring theirs.

On the surface, emerging Russian business practices did begin to resemble the way Western people do business. But it remained that way—a resemblance. Underneath was a system with origins deeply rooted in the dysfunction of the Soviet centrally planned economy. Making that economy work at the macro level relied almost entirely on a network of informal practices and relationships on the micro level. Those informal relationships were the grease that made the rigid five-year plans work.

When the Soviet Union went away, the informal practices and relationships stayed.

"Russia and the former Soviet countries were not a developed economy or a developing country, but more of a misdeveloped country, due to the legacy of communism and state-planning," said Michael Calvey, one of Russia's most prominent investors.[4]

"Too many people, who perhaps should have known better, expected the independent Russia emerging from the debris of the Soviet Union to become a normal country rapidly," Martin Gilman, the head of the IMF in Moscow, wrote in his *No Precedent, No Plan*.[5]

This is not to say that expat executives—well, not all of them, at least—were fooled by ornate meeting rooms and fancy office coffee. But that happened, and some market players say it's still happening. This is also not meant to minimise the number of international companies that did robust, clean and mutually beneficial business in Russia to high international standards. That also happened.

Both extremes—the informal and the rules-based—were present, but by and large they were just that, extremes rather than the rule when doing business in Russia. The ocean of commerce within these extremes existed in a deep, grey area between the informal practices of Russia and the formal practices of international business. Expat lawyers have referred to the moments when they were asked to leave a meeting room so their Russian counterparts—or their Russian colleagues—could discuss the aspects of a transaction that a Westerner shouldn't have known about and might have objected to.

At times, investing in Russia and trying to make it work felt like pinning an orange to an apple tree and hoping it would blossom.

Professor Alena Ledeneva of University College London colourfully portrays many of these informal practices in her book *How Russia Really Works*. Ledeneva describes what might be characterised as the softer elements of the informal economy, including things like interpersonal relationships, and the harder elements, including practices like double-bookkeeping and outright fraud. Ledeneva also describes in detail the distortion of law enforcement and the use of *kompromat*, or compromising material, as an extortion tactic.

Robert Starr, previously a partner at the law firm Salans and formerly of counsel at Dentons, recalls the origins of the system and saw it in person.

"The old Soviet market operated on *blat*," Starr said, using the Russian word describing the system of favours and influence that lubricated the dysfunction of the Soviet command economy. "'I know a guy, he owes me a favour.' It wasn't about a payoff; it was basically just a system which operated to be able to get around."

Starr started making trips to the Soviet Union in the 1970s, during détente, and has watched business and legal developments through the Soviet invasion of Afghanistan, the collapse of the Soviet Union and the start of the war in Ukraine. He was actively advising clients until the invasion in February 2022.

"In a system where businesses were state-owned, people could close their eyes to illegal activity and often engage in it," Starr said. "People could steal state property, perhaps thinking that there was no victim."

One of the more notorious informal practices of the Russian economy was the once widespread use of *odnodnevki*, or one-day companies. These were legal entities formed expressly for the purpose of executing a single transaction and then liquidated—with neither official trace nor tax liability—the day after the transaction. Company formation agents in Russia produced these sorts of companies by the thousands, many of them registered to post-office boxes or mass registration addresses. It was not unusual to see companies registered to "owners" who were either dead or whose personal details had been sold or stolen.

Another of the "grey practices" in the Russian economy was conducting business in off-the-books cash, referred to in Russian as "black cash." The extensive use of black cash in the Russian economy meant that the declared accounts and the actual turnover of a Russian company could be wildly disparate. This sort of cash was usually generated via false-invoicing schemes involving one-day companies and the withdrawal of cash from a complicit bank.

"Companies established practices which they wouldn't have accepted in the French market, for example, or the German market, or the Canadian market, or whatever it happened to be," said Richard Prior, formerly of investigative company Kroll's Moscow office. "I mean, OK, this is Russia, and they do things differently there. So it doesn't matter that a very large proportion of business is conducted in cash, which then has to be recycled and banked with a bank that also understands that they do things differently in Russia."

This generated some difficult conversations between Moscow and headquarter offices in places like France, Germany and Canada, among others.

"Absolutely, but I think that people appreciated their Russian businesses because they were generating huge amounts of cash," Prior said. "People liked Russia because it produced growth."

Russian companies also took advantage of the opacity of offshore company registration, which provided a spectrum of benefits. Among them were the masking of beneficial ownership, which kept aggressive regulators, tax authorities and acquisition-hungry rivals at a safe distance. They also allowed combinations of tax minimisation and tax evasion.

Customs fraud schemes were widespread in the earlier days of business in Russia. One of the more prevalent schemes went like this: a Western company paid a Russian customs broker to shepherd its goods across the border. The Russian broker would charge the Western company for the full cost of importing a modern, high-tech item that might attract high import duties. But when the Russian broker declared these goods to the customs service, it declared the goods as older, outdated technology that attracted lower fees at the border. The customs brokers kept the difference.[6]

Robyn Holt, who ran the Condé Nast publishing business in Russia in the early 2000s, once got a call in the middle of the night telling her that the truck bringing her magazines into Russia from Germany—where the printing quality was superior—had "disappeared." In truth, it was being held for ransom. "Surprise, surprise, if a certain amount of money was paid in a certain amount of time, we knew the truck would appear again."

Holt fixed the problem herself with a small sleight of hand on the last of each month's trucks full of magazines: "I'd leave the back door unlocked. When it was at the border, they'd be able to take a pallet of the magazines, which they would then ship and sell and keep the money," Holt said.

Can we really get along?

The expat business community diverges on how well these two systems worked together. Some saw Western executives as something like commercial missionaries, trying to run a profitable business while at the same time trying to teach the Russians how to work to international standards. In the eyes of some, the mission succeeded.

Trying to do business and teach business at the same time requires twice the effort and put international companies at significant disadvantage. Perhaps the size of the Russian market made it worth it, and perhaps it was also a part of a post-Cold War moment of rapprochement. But German executives doing business in France don't have to play that role. In Russia, foreign investors had an additional burden. They tried to play by the rules; many Russian companies didn't.

Beyond this was perhaps an even more fundamental misunderstanding in Russia of what a business really was. The late Patricia Cloherty, once the CEO of the US–Russia Investment Fund and Delta Private Equity Partners, said in public appearances in the formative years of the Russian business environment that most Russian company executives saw themselves as "owners of cash flows" rather than as owners of companies.[7]

Were Russians capitalists?

In the early days and even later, observers argued that Russia could never become a capitalist country because Russians weren't capitalists.

Boycko liked to point to a broad study he and colleagues conducted in 1991 to test Americans' and Russians' grasp of market principles and democracy. He found both groups' understanding of how markets worked to be roughly equal and used those results to show that Russians were—or at least could be—capitalists.[8]

Vacroux met capitalists every day in her work and beyond.

"Anyone running a little shop, anyone offering violin lessons, and the fact that there was barter at one point, was framing for people," Vacroux said. "Everything is commodified."

After that, though, came another question: whether the broader Russian business community understood or embraced the underpinnings of capitalism—the principles that drove it and its cultural, legal and ethical rules and norms.

That sort of experience, the argument goes, can't be learned in a semester or two or by writing a few annual reports. Being a capitalist involved being exposed to, absorbing and ultimately adding to experiences formed over generations.

That's why Russian business leaders were able to participate in capitalism without necessarily building it.

Ostling thinks about the Tower of Pisa when he thinks about how modern-day Russia rests on its Soviet past.

"I don't know whether the tower started to lean the day it was finished or not," he said. "But it was obviously built on the wrong spot." He conjures the images of the towering skyscrapers in the part of Moscow called Moscow City, a nickname borrowing purposefully from London's financial district, known as the City.

"We built all these ... what look like skyscrapers, Moscow City," he said. "They look like skyscrapers, and they are. But I think we omitted those steps that baked in a framework of governance and integrity."

Financial scandals were not invented in Russia, nor were they perfected there. But Ostling places much more confidence in the towering edifices built in the West.

"It's driven by millions and millions of processes and millions and millions of people, and investors, and regulators, and it's the sum total of 100, 200 years of corporation existence and governance and market," he said.

In Russia, the exact opposite transpired. Everything happened all at once. There were no millions of millions of processes or people. What's more, Ostling suggests, the companies and institutions that were the products of generations of experience left it all at the border when they came to Russia.

"The big law firms, the Big Four, we've all been complicit," he said. "We've gone about our business, and we've put the best French perfume on a pile of manure. Everybody who's doing anything in-country has, I believe, a basis to believe that if you dig far enough down in the P&L and balance sheet, you're going to find crap."

Doing business in Russia, then, amounted to a certain suspension of belief perhaps on both sides of the border, but perhaps materially more on the side of international businesses. It involved a lot of advisory contortion, as the professional class stood on its head, squinted hard and tried to see what it wanted.

This partly explains why so much business between Russian and international companies was conducted offshore, in jurisdictions with reliable legal systems and competent, liquid banks. It also explains why so many contracts in Russia were governed by English law or carried provisions for international arbitration.

How did Russia learn business?

Vladimir Borodin, the former *Izvestia* editor, left journalism to become one of Moscow's more prominent entrepreneurs. He and his partners' popular chain of steakhouses in Moscow were the sort of places you name-checked to impress your friends, if you were lucky enough to get a table. He is now based in New York.

"What I loved about these times is the speed of change every day, especially being in dailies [newspapers]," he said about the 1990s and the 2000s. "Every day, something happened—the speed of change and the events themselves were absolutely like nowhere else probably."

Borodin breaks the Russian business environment into three phases.

In the beginning, he said, foreign executives set the trend for almost everything—most of what was happening in Western markets was entirely absent in Russia. In everything from fast food to office furniture, foreign players dictated the market.

Foreign executives, he said, "were like little gods, coming to earth and saying 'What shall we do?' So from the Russian perspective, we were looking at them as 'OK, we basically need to mimic what they were saying and what they were trying to do in the market.'"

That phase did not last long. Whether you believe that Russians are innate capitalists or not—there are as many opinions as there are capitalists—the market learned quickly.

"Stage two was when Russians learned, and they started competing. We're ready to create our own brands, and we're ready to talk about market share," Borodin said.

But capitalism collapses without a shared understanding of the rules of the game. Within the Russian business community, there might have been that sort of understanding about a Russian set of rules. Those rules, however, were neither fully shared with nor visible to the international business community.

There was an arc to this story, too, and it involved the gradual—though by far not complete—obsolescence of foreign businesspeople in Moscow.

"By that time, Russians got their MBAs," Borodin said. "And they got back and were effective enough for Western standards. And it was the time when less and less foreigners were in demand for companies in Moscow." Expats started to become obsolete and rare in the aftermath of the crisis of 2008, when it also became incredibly expensive to send expats to Moscow. The combination of salary (in some cases augmented by "hazard pay"), an expat housing package, flights home and school fees, was starting to pile up.

Abdullaev is a 2004 master's degree graduate from Harvard's Kennedy School of Government. He said he was part of a cohort of students from Russia earning advanced degrees across the university, especially at the business school and the Kennedy School.

"The thought never crossed anyone's mind to move somewhere or stay in America," he said. "Everyone went back to Russia. We knew it was a bonanza."

The wheel took one more turn, though, Borodin said.

"But then what happened is that Russians started to kind of push back and started to dominate in the market by affiliating themselves with corrupt politicians and officials and they basically started dictating to the foreigners and foreign investors," he said. "It flipped—they were setting the standards for Western companies to follow."

This is another topic where a multitude of viewpoints co-exist without necessarily contradicting each other. They add great depth to the understanding of how business functioned—or malfunctioned – in Russia.

Roman Zilber, who was until 2022 a member of the management committee at Raiffeisen in Russia, sensed a moment when Russians took on increasingly senior roles inside international companies.

"In the middle of the 2000s, companies started to place trust in their Russian employees," Zilber said. "This was an important moment and was the source of serious growth. Russian managers were more aggressive."[9]

It was, Zilber explained, the arc of a natural progression. When international companies first arrived in Russia, they had to teach their Russian staff everything. The training must have been endless, ranging from how to use a company's IT systems to how to file a vacation request with HR.

"For us, the moment came when we had learnt most of the things they could teach us," Zilber said. Remember, many of the Russians who first worked inside international companies—even as administrative assistants—came from Russia's educational elite.

"In 1991, they hired people with English as secretaries, and who were the people with English? They were the graduates of Moscow's top universities," Zilber said. "In four or five years, these people became managers."

Still, no matter what the level of language, education, experience and training, turning a company's Russian business over to local management took an enormous leap of faith from the international side.

"It was a mind shift for them," Zilber said.

Zilber's experience was that Russian managers were able to drive business even more successfully than their Western predecessors. This explains why, in some companies, their Russia operations were among their best performing.

Political cover

Surveys, barter, violin teachers or otherwise, the rest of the world was told that Russia was not only an emerging market economy but was also an emerging democracy. Companies were encouraged to support Russia, politically and financially, to help the country along its path to liberal democracy.

"The way they made a hash of it was covered up by international institutions," Penn's Orenstein said:

> By 1993, it was clear. It was obvious things had gone badly wrong by then. The Clinton administration was in power at the time—from [1993] to 2000. During that time, [Clinton] basically persuaded everyone that Yeltsin was a democrat when Yeltsin had just fired on the parliament building, blowing up the democratically elected parliament

and sort of instituted this crazy oligarch capitalism and was dealing with the most massive recession in world history.

Democrats don't shoot at parliaments. (An American onlooker at the events of 1993 suffered near fatal injuries.[10]) But Russia's parliament was full of communists, so Yeltsin got a free pass. Western patience with Yeltsin faltered periodically: diplomats were concerned about the flawed and fractured efforts toward democratisation. But the alternatives always seemed worse.

Between 1992 and 2000, US presidents—first George H.W. Bush and then Clinton—met their Russian counterparts—first Yeltsin and then Putin—more than twenty times, either in head-to-head summits, during G7 meetings or on the sidelines of other international gatherings.[11]

The early and mid-1990s were meant to set Russia firmly on the path to becoming a multi-party, market-oriented country. There were those who assumed—hoped might be a better word— that with enough time, money and encouragement, Russia would somehow evolve into a liberal democracy. Among other things, a country's legal system is meant to evolve when it embraces private property and the rule of law and develops a middle class. There was no shortage of politicians cheerleading from afar, labelling Russia an emerging democracy that needed investment, political support and general international bonhomie from all corners.

From German Chancellor Helmut Kohl in 1993:

Boris Yeltsin is the democratically elected President of Russia. His name stands for a new Russia that has opened up to freedom, democracy and a market economy. We want this new Russia to be a reliable and stable partner that plays the role it deserves in the community of nations. A weak, internally torn Russia would be in no one's interest. The same applies, of course, to the other successor states of the Soviet Union. For us Germans this must mean: Anyone who follows the path towards more democracy, a social market economy and constructive international cooperation can of course count on our support in the future.[12]

From UK Prime Minister John Major, in a speech praising the efforts of his Conservative Party in 1992: "Who has taken the lead in holding out a hand to the new Russia and to Eastern Europe's new democracies?"[13]

From French President Jacques Chirac, in Moscow, in 1997:

> Here appears a democratic Russia, at peace with all its neighbours, and which occupies its full place on the international scene. A Russia that is opening to the market economy, wants to fully integrate into world trade and will gradually regain prosperity. A Russia with which everything becomes possible again, with which the French wish to build the future.[14]

From US Deputy Secretary of State Strobe Talbott, one of the country's most respected experts on Russia, in 1997:

> The initial signs are auspicious. The new Russia has already gone a long way toward repudiating the old Soviet Union's delusions that autarky and self-isolation are even options for a modern state. Russia today plays an active role in organizations of which it was a founding member, such as the UN and the OSCE [Organization for Security and Co-operation in Europe]. It is also knocking at the door of those from which it has been excluded. Over the past two years, it has become a member of the ASEAN [Association of Southeast Asian Nations] Regional Forum and the Council of Europe, agreed to join the Paris Club, and it has strengthened its ties to the European Union.[15]

To international business, the net effect of this international drumbeat—even if a lot of it was the flattering language of global diplomacy—was a strong signal that Russia was a safe, emerging market.

Whether they meant it or not, or whether they pinched their noses while saying it, politicians around the world were telling their business communities—the merchant diplomats of the globalised late twentieth century: Go to Russia and help move it along the way toward becoming like us. American executives in Moscow confirmed this—the US government actively encouraged their companies to invest in Russia.

The message landed squarely.

"It was a triumphalist message: we won, and Russians are going to be like us," Gunitsky said. "That gave the Russian transition a greater heft than was actually the case."[16]

The heft rested on what Gunitsky called the "giddiness" and the "triumphalism of American politics in the 1990s." The United States, after all, had won the Cold War.

"It was essentially trying to build a new economic infrastructure on a political base that was never meant for that sort of system," Gunitsky said, adding that a market system cannot take root "in the absence of a state that can perform the functions of a market system."

The optimism was flawed, and the flaws were there to be seen—if we wanted to see them.

There is an important point to make here. Investing in Russia was not a "mistake." Companies don't make moves this complex and this expensive by accident. The amount of time, money and effort it took to engage with Russia, from a distance or on the ground, was too important for it to be spent in caprice. Companies went into Russia with their eyes wide open. They may have, however, been looking at the wrong things, or not looking everywhere they needed to.

"This post-Soviet experiment of Russia, and its interactions with the West, largely the United States, but also the United Kingdom and others is an experiment of—whether it's mismatched expectations or hope over practicality—there was this idea that we could make Russia rich enough that they become our friends. And that was fundamentally flawed from the get-go," said Brian O'Toole, a former US Treasury Department officer and now a non-resident fellow at the Atlantic Council.[17]

"And it took us a long time to realise that, through successive presidents and administrations and seeing deep into Putin's soul through his eyes, all of the resets and all of that stuff," O'Toole said:

> There was this theory that was supported by economists—open markets don't go to war with each other, and we don't want to be at war with the Russians. We just spent the last fifty years being completely at odds with them during the Cold War. It's hard to find fault with the optimism and the academic thinking that formed the basis for that set of theories.

O'Toole has a point. Among other things, US defence spending as a proportion of overall government spending dropped significantly in the wake of the Soviet collapse.[18]

The primary problem was this: just as international investors were eyeing Russia's potential as a market for everything from long-haul aircraft to fluoride toothpaste, Russia was becoming anything but a liberal democracy. Its political processes, long before the advent of Prime Minister and then President Putin, were distorted, subverted and corrupted.

"More fundamentally, there were a lot of assumptions made about Yeltsin that proved not to be the case, not the least of which was that he was committed to democracy," said an individual formerly inside the US government who asked not to be named.[19]

On the surface, or from a safe distance, these processes looked democratic. Russia had elections. Participation was voluntary. There was more than one name and more than one party on the ballot. Clinton leaned on the IMF to provide a loan to Russia in support of Yeltsin's reform efforts and, as a result, in support of Yeltsin's re-election. American advisors even worked on the

Yeltsin campaign, though *The Washington Post* said the team had "marginal influence."[20]

But the 1996 presidential election that returned Yeltsin to the Kremlin was so laughably rigged that even the most passionate, optimistic and pro-Russian political observers gasped quietly at the conduct and the outcome of that year's balloting.

Much like the suitcases of cash that breezed past customs, once this electoral precedent breezed past the voting public and the international community, it would be impossible to unwind.

Everyone looked the other way. Returning Yeltsin to the Kremlin at any cost was worth it, not only to Yeltsin's Russian elite but to the international investors and politicians who had already thrown their support behind the incumbent. The other option—the presumed return of the Communist Party—was completely unacceptable, even if that's what a legitimate vote tally might have delivered. Russia did not produce a functioning democracy; it created an electoral sausage factory.

Boycko wrote that privatisation and the other elements of the early economic reform programmes would not be, and were not meant to be, a panacea. He expected that ownership in the economy would, at some point, drive even further reform.

"While Russia will not turn into a law-and-order paradise in the near future," he wrote in 1995, "the interests engendered by privatization are using their economic and political resources to press hard for international reforms." Without the price reform that triggered hyperinflation, "there would still be very little food or consumer goods on store shelves."[21]

Official money rains down

The largest international organisations and some of the world's richest countries poured billions of dollars into Russia and what were then referred to as the Newly Independent States of the former Soviet Union. The primary sources of this funding—loans, investments, grants and technical assistance—were the World Bank, the IMF, the EBRD, the US and the European Union. According to one comprehensive study on the amount of foreign aid sent to Russia between 1991 and 2000, these multilateral and bilateral arrangements sent a total of around USD 36 billion to Russia. That study adds that the overall amount of money sent to Russia, including billions of dollars provided by Germany alone, brought the total amount of international assistance to Russia to more than USD 66 billion. Taking into consideration assistance from other organisations and countries like France, Italy, the UK and Japan, the overall sum is likely higher.[22]

Cash from Uncle Sam

The United States' share of that money, USD 2.3 billion, came as part of a programme called the Freedom Support Act (the FSA), signed into law in October 1992 by President Bush. The FSA sent money to Russia initially as humanitarian aid, but its longer-term purpose was to support market reform and democratic transition. More than twenty US government departments and agencies were involved in the assistance programme.[23] USD 58 million was spent on the design and execution of the voucher privatisation programme;[24] support for privatisation came from other lenders, too.

"[R]ecent developments in Russia and the other independent states of the former Soviet Union present an historic opportunity for a transition to a peaceful and stable international order and the integration of the independent states of the former Soviet Union into the community of democratic nations," the text of the law read.[25]

The US sent planeloads of consultants to cities across Russia to midwife its journey toward democracy; they'd pop up at parties all around Moscow. They worked for USAID, or they worked for companies with USAID grants. They were lawyers. They were accountants. They were business development executives. They were every stripe of management consultant.

Cash from the EU

The EU's share of aid to Russia was delivered via a programme called TACIS—Technical Assistance to the Commonwealth of Independent States. The programme promised a total of USD 2.7 billion in support to the broader region between 1991 and 2000; of that sum, USD 1.6 billion was disbursed in Russia.[26]

The TACIS programme shared the same goals as the US and the multilateral agencies: a democratic, market-oriented Russia would make for a peaceful neighbour. The difference was that the EU emphasised training and technical programmes rather than direct funding for, say, infrastructure projects.[27]

TACIS provided policy advisors to government agencies. It offered training and advice to the private sector. It sponsored internships and funded studies (market research and pre-investment plans, for example); it supported regulatory reform and programmes designed to link EU and Russian institutions. Between 1991 and 2000, TACIS implemented almost 500 projects.[28]

If more than USD 60 billion was transferred to Russia, but the US and the EU jointly were responsible for just under USD 4 billion of that money, it's clear that most of the cash came from the multilateral organisations. That was partly by design. The US and the EU were reluctant to spend too much taxpayer money on projects with potentially uncertain outcomes. The IMF, the World Bank and the EBRD collectively sent many more billions of dollars into Russia under various guises.

Debate raged at the time and sometimes even surfaces to this day about where all this aid went and what it did. Was it a programme designed to support the Russian reformers and bolster them and their methodologies—at any cost—to prevent Russia from backsliding into a Soviet Union 2.0? Was it a programme designed to put money in the pockets of American and European consultancies? The two are not mutually exclusive.

The answers to these questions matter but may never come. Their signals to the international business community, though, were unambiguous. The world's largest market democracies were pouring extravagant sums of public money into Russia. The world's biggest countries and multilateral organisations were Russia's friends and supporters. And their reference to putting Russia on the path to a market democracy was meant to suggest that Russia could, in some unspecified timeframe, become just like us. Some supporters of Russia's transition economy even went so far as to say they anticipated Russia becoming a "normal" country.[29]

The EBRD

The documents creating the EBRD were signed in 1990; the first meeting of the bank's board of governors was in 1991. Its heavily marbled headquarters once sat on the northern edge of the City of London; the EBRD is now in Canary Wharf, London's purpose-built financial centre.

From the beginning, the EBRD was an unusual animal. First, among all the multilateral lending institutions, it was the only one that had an explicit mandate. Article 1 of the agreement establishing the bank said it was committed to "foster the transition towards open market-oriented economies and to promote private and entrepreneurial initiative in the Central and Eastern European countries committed to and applying the principles of multiparty democracy, pluralism and market economics."[30]

"In 1991, when the EBRD was created, it was expected that every country emerging out of the former Soviet Union would be moving toward a liberal democracy and a market economy. So there was no question," said Oksana Antonenko, who worked as a senior political counsellor at the bank from 2011 to 2016. "To the extent the private sector existed [in Russia], the EBRD was a big player in it."

After launching the *Yellow Pages* in St Petersburg, Sasson moved to the EBRD for a large portion of his career in Russia:

> All of the very early team were deep believers in a mission that you can achieve something through applying various conditions on financing which move people in the right direction, which encourages business to move to a market economy, which helps the democratic process. There were a lot of people who really believed, myself included, that we were doing the right thing.

The idea that business could be at the leading edge of democracy was part of the "vector of democracy."

"Every time you saw a new store open, it was a sense that politics was moving in the right direction," said William Burke-White, founding director of Perry World House at the University of Pennsylvania and a professor at Penn's law school. "The EBRD was going to be the best way to liberalise Russia."

It was an idea that both the business and the academic world supported. "And then it began to seem that there was a disjuncture between the two," Burke-White said.

For Russian companies, getting a loan from the EBRD was an enormous seal of approval on the recipient—the bank had stringent credit conditions and conducted extensive due diligence, including the use of external consultants, prior to committing funds. Working with the EBRD was also a form of political risk insurance. Once a Russian company was on the EBRD's books, it became more or less untouchable politically. The affiliation with a powerful international financial institution was meant to keep corruption and criminal activity at bay.

The EBRD did a lot of "due diligence and integrity work," Sasson said. "A lot more probably than other financing organisations would provide. Plus the local knowledge of people on the ground who knew who to work with and who not to work with and who were the good guys. The financial due diligence was very significant."

The EBRD was unique among similar institutions in that it was, from the outset, designed to be temporary. It had a mission to rebuild the economies of Central and Eastern Europe, and once those countries were well enough on their way, the bank could slowly put itself out of business. In theory.

"There is no such thing as temporary institutions," Antonenko said. "Turkeys don't vote for Christmas." The EBRD suspended new financing to Russia following the invasion and annexation of Crimea.

Russia's full-scale invasion of Ukraine and the fallout within the international business community has resurrected discussion among foreign participants in the Russian economy about where, or whether, the West went wrong with foreign aid to Russia. Westerners who were on the ground in Russia or involved with Russia from a distance have said they found the amount of money sent to Russia to be "stingy." The West should have implemented a "Marshall Plan for Russia," invoking an investment of the breadth and depth of the financial support that rebuilt Europe after the Second World War. Others said the West should have forgiven the Soviet debt that it forced Russia to repay. That gesture alone, the thinking goes, would have allowed money used to pay old debts to be invested in a new economy instead.

The sum total

The General Accounting Office (GAO), the US agency that tracks whether US taxpayer money is well spent, was diplomatic but clear in its 2000 appraisal of all the public money spent on Russia's first decade. There is one word that appears consistently in the language used to describe the effectiveness of all the lenders' programmes: "Mixed."[31]

Officials at lenders the GAO interviewed for its report at least partly blamed themselves. The programmes their money supported could have been better designed, better implemented or better monitored. But most of the blame in the GAO's report fell on Russia. There were no democratic or market traditions to be revived. There was no political will, or if there was, it was weak and isolated. There was a revolving door on government offices; ministers moved in and out of roles too frequently to expect any sort of continuity. Lenders across the board underestimated the depth of the problems in Russia and the amount of time it would take to right them.

But most importantly, the GAO report acknowledged that the Russian economy was too corrupt and too distorted by vested interests to develop into a functioning market, at least not within the ten-year period the report discusses. The development of oligarchic capitalism in Russia as engendered by a privatisation programme that favoured insiders, and capped with a loans-for-shares programme that trounced the principles of transparency and good governance, were heavy blows.

This is one view in one report. That said, it contains the collective comments of numerous officials, and the GAO is known for its exhaustive, authoritative and, most importantly, politically neutral research and reporting. Again, depending on your point of view, these programmes were a raging success, but perhaps against more modest goals. Also, even if Russia failed to become a thriving liberal democracy, consolation came as Russia at least became less of a strategic military threat.

The EBRD undertook a survey in 2006—six years after the GAO report was issued—and still couldn't declare whether economic and political transition in Russia was a success.

"Has the transition been a success? It is impossible to give a definitive answer at this stage. For a start, transition is not over. Even in the most advanced countries of the region, there are still a number of challenges to be addressed," wrote Erik Berglof, then chief economist of the EBRD. It is notable that the bank first undertook a major survey of transition in 2006, fifteen years after it started working in Russia.

"More fundamentally," he continued,

> a judgment about whether transition has worked must involve more than economic issues, such as income, trade or employment. Ultimately, for transition to be declared a success, it should lead to a measurable improvement in people's lives, with the principles of democracy, pluralism and the market economy deeply embedded in societies.

"These concepts are difficult to measure," he concluded.[32]

The men and women who lived and worked in Russia took their own measures.

"They would fly people over here, projects advising the Russian government on a new property registration scheme for Moscow; seven, eight, nine, ten law firms bidding," Baker McKenzie's Melling said. "Someone would win for some astronomical amount, fly over fifteen lawyers for the better part of a year and a half, drowning in overpriced alcohol at the bar at the Metropol Hotel."

"At the end of the day, the work was put on a shelf and no one read it," he said.

Von Flemming tongue-in-cheek can point to more concrete results than some of her consulting peers from the 1990s. She was first posted to the Russian Privatisation Centre in Moscow, where she worked in anti-asset stripping compliance, a role that must have been akin to working on anti-snowfall measures in winter. She was then posted to St Petersburg in 1992 for a factory privatisation in a part of town close to the Hotel Sovietskaya, where she lived for three months. While living at the Sovietskaya, von Flemming said she became friendly with the women who worked in the hotel's "erotic show" and translated for them when it came to their off-duty activities.

"The prostitutes liked me, and I translated and negotiated the pricing," she said: "The foreigners were asking, 'How much?' and they couldn't speak English, and I looked at the girls and looked at the agony foreigners and said, '100 dollars,' and the ladies of course were grateful because I increased their pricing triple and they didn't have to work the following day."

Beyond government money

Beyond the taxpayer money that was sent to transform Russia, how many private sector players felt an ideological commitment to what they were doing?

Having been raised, like all Americans, on a consistent, anti-Soviet, Ronald Reagan "evil empire" diet, Sucher saw the Kremlin as a global centre of malice. He saw the banking and financial system as "a grass roots bulwark that would overcome the evil in the Kremlin."

"A big part of what I set out to do in the beginning was to bring the benefits of banking and finance to ordinary Russian people on the now failed, I guess, theory that if people had the ability to grow their own prosperity, and to develop wealth, and to use their growing financial literacy to make choices as individually sovereign citizens," they could have become a force for political change, Sucher said.

Sucher goes back to that early conversation with Vardanyan in the Radisson Slavyanskaya, when, as Sucher paraphrases, Vardanyan told him: "I know this is not a normal country, and maybe it never will be. But if we build a normal business, and if other people build normal businesses, then maybe we will find that we have built a normal country."

This is a weighty remark, given the linguistically loaded meaning of the word "normal" in Russian. It means much more than just "standard" or "typical." In this sense, it also meant "like everyone else" or, as Russians also like to say, "civilised." This idea of Russia being a normal country is something that comes up regularly in discussions of its transition from the Soviet period. And no matter how amorphous the concept of normal may be—in reality and in the mind of the speaker—it almost always meant becoming more like the West. Specifically, more like Europe.

Sucher said his conversation with Vardanyan was transformative: "To me that was the most electrifying call to action. It was the articulation of the mission of my life. It was exactly what I thought, but I had never put it in such compelling terms. It changed my life, and I was lit on fire."

Sucher understood that it would be a herculean task. But he believed an incremental approach would work. He likened the process to building "islands of sanity."

"You build a little business, you create something that is sort of routine, and you expect certain standards every day, and you minimise the zones of chaos," he said, referring to the lawlessness of the 1990s. "And you just imagine other people doing that in their own way, and then sooner or later all these businesses start touching each other and you're closing out the chaos."

Idealism run amok

No one thought Russia could be fixed in a day. The early years had a palpably experimental feel to them.

"For some of these young consultants coming out of graduate school, basically, twenty-something-year-olds, newly minted PhDs, there may have been some idealism from them. There may also have been a somewhat, almost tone-deaf, kind of graduate seminar approach that, this is like an interesting theoretical problem. It's a laboratory. I can't help but think of the neocons in looking at the Middle East," economic historian and investment manager Malik said. There was a lot of high-minded language about what good work the West was doing in Russia. "It's a question for me. Were they driven by idealism? Or was it almost like a graduate school seminar or something?"

Statecraft in Russia in the 1990s had it all backwards, University of Toronto's Gunitsky said, recalling the debate between the idealists and the realists in political science in the aftermath of the First World War. The idealists said that if you get the laws and regulations right, then good politics follows. The realists said that "in the real world, it was the other way around," Gunitsky said. "You have to get the politics right, and only then do you get the laws and regulations right."

The flotilla of consultants that came to Russia in the early 1990s were behaving like idealists. They spent years helping to reform Russian legislation, hoping that a functional state and a transparent market would follow. "But what they didn't take into account is that you have to get the politics right to enforce the laws. None of the laws matter if the politics aren't there," Gunitsky said.

The lawyers back him up.

"They enacted numerous legal codes and extensive legislation, but people felt that there was no real rule of law offering them protection, in the sense that we understand the 'rule of law,'" attorney Robert Starr said.

Russia in the 1990s and beyond was, to a certain degree, attracting the same sort of people who felt the pull—or were pushed—more than a century ago.

"The place is attractive for a lot of people," said Tom Firestone:

> If you learn how to work the system, you can do very well for yourself. For a lot of Western individuals and businesses, it turns out to be a pact with the devil. That's what I felt—what I loved about Russia was the craziness. You live by that, you die by that. If I wanted a more peaceful life, I wouldn't have worked in Russia.

Firestone worked in the US embassy as a resident legal advisor and later as an attorney with a law firm in Moscow. In 2013, the Russian government expelled him from the country, allegedly for refusing to cooperate with Russia's domestic intelligence agency.[33]

The craziness of life in Russia was undeniable. Even so, a lot of businesspeople went to Russia for compelling reasons that were entirely logical.

"It was impossible to sit in one of the top centres in the world for grain trading, and not see Russia as a major, important player. So we had to be involved in Russia," said Andrew Glass, a former executive with a major US commodity trader in Russia. Avoiding Russia, he said, "would be extremely negligent."[34] Glass's company had been involved with Russia for years prior to investing on the ground in the mid-1990s and expanding from there.

"People always saw Russia as a key component," Glass said:

> They'd been through the Soviet era, they wanted Russia to succeed, and they wanted to help Russia succeed. So there was no way we were not going to be involved in that country. I think the BRIC story, the GDP growth per capita, certainly helped us go in as well. It was a very positive outlook at that time [from 2000 to 2008].

For every company, including Glass's, that saw Russia as an attractive market, a second factor brought them into the market: their customers. The buyers of Glass's products wanted their ingredients produced locally.

"They needed to de-risk their supply chains by sourcing locally manufactured food ingredients to Western standards," Glass said.

If Glass's company was at least to some extent pulled into Russia by its customers, there was another major driver behind the urge to do business in Russia. There were enormous competitive pressures.

"The reward is too attractive. But as importantly, the fear of missing out was terribly strong. If you were Cadbury Schweppes, for example, and you saw Danone absolutely sweeping up in Russia, you'd think, 'Bloody hell, why aren't we here?'" said Prior, the business intelligence executive.

"An insane asylum for egomaniacs"

When describing the kinds of investors that went into Russia without the security of the rule of law, the IFC's Crabtree recalls the words of an associate: "It was an insane asylum for egomaniacs. You could go around with these grand plans that would never come to fruition."

And then he recalls one of his favourite quotes, from the eighteenth-century correspondence between Emperor Joseph II and his mother, Maria Theresa of Austria. Russia had recently won the Russo-Turkish War. Joseph II and the Russian Empress Catherine the Great were touring a new city on the Black Sea and the site of a cathedral to be built. Joseph writes to his mother: "I've done a great thing today. Catherine laid the first stone of the great cathedral, and I laid the last."

The quote perfectly encapsulates the difference between appearance and reality—or perhaps between intentions and results—in Russia. International business based a lot of its decisions on the assumption that "the great cathedral" would be built. Instead, the project never really got very far past the cornerstone.

"We had this naturally ideological view that everything leads to liberal democracy in the end," said Firestone. When the Soviet Union collapsed, he said, we were ready to pick up the pieces, the thinking went. "Now they're going to be back in our fold, and they're going to be exactly like us."

Francis Fukuyama, the American political scientist, popularised this line of thinking with his argument—which resonated widely as the Soviet Union teetered toward collapse—that the path of history followed the ascent of liberal democracy as the world's predominant form of governance. Once the Soviet Union was out of the way, he suggested, we were in the clear as far as political evolution was concerned. Game over.

These optimists, Firestone said, "underestimated the resilience of local practices, structures, institutions, ways of doing business. The euphoria was completely misplaced."

"Not to fall into the trap that it was inevitable, but the enthusiasm was misplaced in the early days," Firestone said. "Now we're coming back full arc."

A sulphuric taste

Russia's modern experiment with capitalism left a sulphuric taste in its citizens' mouths. The transition to a market economy was supposed to be good for Russia in the same way that syrupy, bitter medicine is supposed to be good for a cough. None of it tastes good, and it doesn't always work.

"Even the word business had a negative connotation," said Timothy Stubbs, a partner at the international law firm Dentons, who started in Russia at a predecessor firm in 1991.[35] Young

Russians who followed commercial pursuits—*biznesmen*, in Russian—were considered somehow unclean, driven solely by money. Money was not meant to be important—late Soviet banknotes were ugly and small.

Fertile ground?

The most important outcomes here are, first, that Russia did not produce a functioning democracy in the way its Western supporters would understand it. Second, it did not build the foundations of a market economy in the way most businesspeople would see it.

Against that backdrop, international business—companies whose home and foreign markets were primarily democracies—came to call.

Some of these companies were reasonably well appraised of the shortcomings of Russia's democracy and the flaws in its economic system. It was hard not to notice them. The world's media outlets were focused intensely on the new Russia; its hormonal early years were documented by a global army of foreign correspondents. Other companies were less aware—or less concerned—about Russia's particular state or stage of development. Both types of companies, however, paid more attention to the economic opportunity of an emerging market than they did to the politics.

Economics mattered, but what mattered more than anything else at the time was the emergence of a consumerist society that was starving for everything from the most basic domestic commodities to, shortly thereafter, the most extravagant of luxury goods. The size of the prize in the Russian economy far outweighed its defects. The risk–reward equation worked strongly in favour of market entry and expansion.

"There were 1,000 per cent, 10,000 per cent profits—it seemed like everybody came and no one at all was thinking

'Is this going to be a democratic country or a non-democratic country?'" said Alexander Gubsky, the former deputy editor in chief of *Vedomosti*, Russia's leading business newspaper.[36] He's speaking here of the securities market: "What did they have there? They had beautiful, cheap prostitutes, cheap vodka, and 1,000 per cent profits." Gubsky's remarks also help summarise why, particularly in the earlier days, the Russian market was so attractive to male executives.

It's 1998 and we (almost) all go home

In 1997, the Russian Federation struck landmark deals with the Paris Club and the London Club, groups of creditors owed billions of dollars by the Soviet Union that Russia promised to pay. In September that year, Russia agreed with the Paris Club of government creditors to "reschedule $40 billion in Soviet debts owed to foreign governments over 25 years." And in October, Russia came to an agreement with the London Club of commercial creditors to "pay off USD 33 billion of Soviet debt over 25 years" after having initially defaulted on that debt in 1991.[37]

The deal was trumpeted by Russians and international observers alike as transformative for Russia's reputation on international markets, coming as it did after years of rolling over billions of Russian and former Soviet debt to G7 countries that Russia couldn't pay. Russian politicians publicly trumpeted the country's new commitment to financial hygiene.

"Today leaders of the biggest banks in the world recognised the irreversibility of our reforms and the prestige of Russia in the international community," then First Deputy Prime Minister Anatoly Chubais told a press conference. Chubais, who became one of the most hated politicians in Russia and was blamed for having sold the country to his friends for a fraction of its real worth, proclaimed that the deal with the London Club "opens the door to a non-oligarchic capitalism in Russia."[38]

"By summer of 1997, non-resident investors appeared ready to buy just about any asset with Russia stamped on it," the IMF's Martin Gilman wrote.[39]

This all started to smell like victory. Russia was a darling of international markets. Yeltsin was meeting regularly with heads of state around the world. The country looked less and less like a military threat, and observers with a "glass half-full" outlook on life could still trumpet the country as an emerging democracy, even if that glass might have been half full with vodka.

"Russia was finally on its way to becoming a normal country," Gilman, in reflection, wrote in 2010, echoing Vardanyan almost two decades previously.[40]

We all know where this is headed. The Russian financial markets imploded in 1998. The entire country and its beleaguered currency became toxic until the early 2000s, when companies and investors with a strong stomach for risk started to edge back in.

Hold the bubbly

As Freeland wrote in *Sale of the Century*, 1997 was "Champagne too soon."[41]

While Western money was coursing into Russia, the country's nouveau riche were hauling cash out of the country as fast as they could to the safety of banks in the West. The contrasting behaviour of international and domestic investors was instructive. The West was diving in; the Russians were heading for the exits. This divergence in the level of confidence in the Russian financial services sector gave rise, Gilman suggests, to the creation of the massive offshore payments schemes developed by institutions like the Bank of New York (BNY), as it was then called, among others.[42]

Bear in mind, as does Gilman, that these investment patterns reflected the behaviour of organisations that were investing cash, primarily in financial instruments like government debt. This behaviour—the movements of so-called "hot money" in search of high rates of return—is often distinct from the behaviour of direct investors.

Russia's massive, chaotic and dysfunctional banking system— the country at the time had thousands of banks liberally licensed by the Russian Central Bank—was one of the main players in the crash. Most of these banks—they were called "pocket banks"— were really just extensions of company owners' wallets, designed to optimise financial flows (including capital flight) in the most opaque manner possible.

A brewing financial crisis in Asia—and the drop in oil prices it triggered—did not help,[43] nor did the tar pits of Russian politics, where infighting and scandal had for months been roiling the government and its key supporters.[44]

The main driver of the 1998 crisis, however, was Russia's inability to collect taxes and control spending. The country simply could not make its citizens or its companies pay what they owed the state and as a result was unable to make ends meet. The government made a bad situation even worse by allowing companies to defer their tax payments or to offset them by offering services to the state more or less for free.

There were a few small victories along the way to disaster— hyperinflation had come down, and Russia famously recalibrated its banknotes. Three zeroes were erased from notes printed when inflation was soaring and the cost of even simple household items was counted in the thousands of roubles. The new Russian rouble came in at 1:1,000, meaning a 1,000 rouble note now represented 1 rouble. To everyone's surprise, the Russian public took the redenomination in its stride; there was neither panic nor mass confusion.[45]

But the appearance of stability at the end of 1997 and the beginning of 1998 did not even last as a veneer. Yeltsin sacked Prime Minister Viktor Chernomyrdin in March, sparking a carousel of change in the government that brought the relatively young newcomer Sergei Kiriyenko to power. Kiriyenko's young looks and surprise ascent to office earned him the nickname "Kinder Surprise"—the name of an Italian company's children's chocolate.[46] The chaos extended to August, when Yeltsin kicked out Kiriyenko, too.

The late spring and early summer of 1998 brought a massacre on Russia's financial markets. The interest rate on Russia's domestic debt skyrocketed, investors started pulling out of the stock market, Russia sought to crack down on tax cheats and Russia's dirty banks were threatened with regulatory truncheons.

In July, the IMF packaged up a consortium of lenders to provide Russia with a USD 22.6 billion financing bailout. It was enough, Gilman said, to allow Russian officials to make summer holiday plans.[47]

In the end, no one really went on holiday. Panic on the Russian markets resumed by the end of July, and August is when Russians usually get out of town. Russia was unable to convince the international financial community that it was in control, and in his scorched-earth telling of the crisis, Gilman said: "It is notable—and remarkable in hindsight—to what extent the Russian authorities themselves were flying blind going into the crisis."[48]

A last-minute meeting was held in central Moscow with representatives from the IMF, one of whom was staying at—where else?—the Metropol. The meeting failed to stave off the collapse of the Russian financial markets, and on the morning of 17 August, the government announced (1) a new exchange rate for the rouble that wiped out most Russians' savings in an instant, (2) a freeze on the repayment of Russian banks' external debt and (3) a default on the Russian government's domestic debt.

The times were frantic and more than a bit chaotic. *Forbes'* von Flemming recalls stories of disappearing banking records: "This was also the hilarious time when complete trucks were drowning in the River Moscow with documentation about the Central Bank," she said of the frenzied atmosphere the crisis generated.

Kiriyenko's replacement, and his replacement's replacement, were both in and out between 1998 and 1999, until the appointment of Vladimir Putin as prime minister in August 1999.

Crabtree watched it all unfold, live:

> It was a shock, honestly. I had spoken to the Canadian ED [executive director] of the IMF in June of 1998. I saw Chubais at Kennedy Airport and he was looking grim. I knew there were negotiations about a bailout, and I thought there would be some brinksmanship but eventually ...

"I remember waking up and looking at the stock market. It went to 6 per cent of its value or some crap like that," Crabtree said. "It was a complete wipeout. It was incredible. I've never seen anything like it."

Crabtree put the crash down to a drop in oil prices that coincided with record Russian spending. "All you had to do was look at oil prices," he said. "Other than the fact that they were overspending, which they were, but oil [drops], and they're finished, always." A little more than a decade earlier, in 1986, the price of a barrel of oil was around USD 10, Crabtree recalled. Soviet oil extraction was extremely inefficient—low prices meant drilling at a loss. That economic equation, Crabtree said, was one of the accelerants of the collapse of the Soviet Union.

There were several immediate effects following the 1998 crisis. First, the Russian banking system froze, making routine operations difficult for companies and individuals. The Russian government owed these banks billions of roubles in government debt called GKOs; the default ensured the banks would never get that money back.

"Everyone thought that the GKOs would be high yield and that they would pay off," Zilber, formerly of Raiffeisen, said;[49] 1998 "was hugely painful because every possible risk materialised. The market for GKOs collapsed. The value of the rouble plummeted. Currency controls were introduced," he said. "Everyone in the game went bankrupt immediately."

Russian banks collapsed like dominoes, taking their clients' money with them. The rouble became so weak that imported goods became unaffordable. And finally, but perhaps most importantly, the investment community lost confidence in Russia's financial management. That said, anyone buying raw materials from Russia had a windfall, if they could buy those inputs with hard currency. This would eventually sow the seeds of Russia's recovery from the crisis.

In the meantime, Russian government debt, called "Russian paper," in investment lingo, was quite literally seen as radioactive. No one wanted to touch it. Adam Elstein, then the managing director of Bankers Trust in Moscow, famously told the *Financial Times* that most foreign investors "would probably rather eat nuclear waste than buy Russian paper again for the foreseeable future."[50]

"The golden days"

"In 1997, it was like the golden days. Money was dropping on us from everywhere. Anything you did made money," said Rodzianko, who at the time was building up the Russian Markets team at JP Morgan's London office. He and his colleagues were trading primarily in domestic Russian government debt. "All of a sudden, there's this bump in the road," he said, referring to the Asian financial crisis preceding the Russian default.

A "bump in the road" sounds a bit euphemistic, but Rodzianko carries with him the genetic imprint of several bumps in the road in Russia. US-born Rodzianko's paternal great-grandfather was the president of the Russian Duma, the parliament, when Tsar Nicholas II abdicated. His father's family emigrated to Serbia in 1920, where his father was later born and raised.

His mother, whose family has origins in the pre-revolutionary Russian aristocracy, left the Soviet Union in 1935, before the worst of Stalin's purges, and eventually settled in Germany. Rodzianko grew up in the US speaking Russian as a child and going to Russian school on Saturdays, when his American peers were all out playing. He's a graduate of Dartmouth College and Columbia Business School. He went to Russia from 1995 to 1996 and returned again in 1998. He left only after the full-scale invasion of Ukraine.

In 1997, he and his colleagues felt something wasn't quite right.

"I kind of felt it was going bad and started selling my Russian positions. And then I had to leave for the weekend for my sister's wedding," he said. "So I flew to New York. I sold as much as I could. I got back on the red eye Monday morning. I get in at ten o'clock and all the rest of my position had imploded."

"We had had a great year up until that point, and then it went down to still making money, but not very much," he said.

The following year, 1998, carried on in much the same fashion—"flat, short, flat, short, flat, short the whole year," Rodzianko said. "Then in early summer of 1998, the IMF announced a large support programme which we thought gave us an opportunity to invest in Russia. Within a month, things were not going so well." Rodzianko basically put the bank in damage control posture, reflecting his slightly pessimistic view on the year ahead.

His bosses were not impressed.

"I remember my boss saying, 'Look, if you're so negative on Russia, I'm not sure you're the right guy to set up the business,'" he said. The bank made money until August 1998.

Rodzianko's team relocated to Moscow from London and settled into new premises exactly two weeks before the crisis hit. Rodzianko said he had even chosen the office furniture. He and his team had their Monday morning meeting in the wake of the IMF announcement of its support package. Rodzianko thought the package would delay the collapse of the Russian economy for about six months. But even early in the bailout, the market started to spin out of control. Interest rates were "skyrocketing," he said. He and his team started to think that "something was wrong."

"And for the next two weeks, as much as we could, we sold everything we could. And it got us down from, like, 200 million to 40 million," he said. "We essentially got out of the way of most of the damage. The day that the default happened, we had to book a loss of USD 40 million."

These are large numbers to perhaps anyone other than an investment banker, but JP Morgan had made about USD 30 million before the write-off, so they kept their losses to what was quite minimal for a trading desk. These were losses on the bank's own account. Clients who believed in the IMF package and were more bullish on Russia lost much more.

Rodzianko's boss told him that he didn't normally pay bonuses to bankers who made a loss, but since he did better than the rest of the market, he could keep his job.

"And then, you know, the whole thing collapsed. No more trading. Everything is frozen. Cash machines weren't working," he said. "It was a bloody mess."

Rodzianko held his nerve and ultimately started to bet on an upswing. The so-called "resource supercycle" had begun, the price of oil was rising and Russia was once again a superstar market. The supercycle refers to a manufacturing boom that drove galloping demand for Russia's subsoil chemical and mineral wealth. The toxic waste he had gathered in 1998 had morphed into financial pheromones. Rodzianko in 2000 told his bosses to go big on Russia, but this was right around the time that Chase Manhattan Bank bought JP Morgan, to form the JP Morgan Chase powerhouse. Chase wasn't interested in Russia, and life got boring for Rodzianko. He moved to Deutsche Bank for the go-go days of 2001–6 and later worked for Credit Suisse and a Russian investment bank.

Rodzianko became head of the American Chamber of Commerce in Russia in 2013, when US–Russian relations were approaching an all-time low.

As the 1998 bloodbath unfolded, Western governments started to worry about political stability in Russia.

"The direct impact of Russia's turmoil on the world economy will be slight, of course: Russia's gross domestic product is smaller than the Netherlands', its stock-market capitalization smaller than Belgium's," *The Wall Street Journal* wrote. "Although the devaluation could increase investor gloom over emerging markets, the more worrying concern for the West is Russia's political stability, the perennial focus of Western policy makers ever since the collapse of the Soviet Union in 1991."[51]

The 1998 crisis also delivered an entirely new risk to international companies—the "can't pay/won't pay" dilemma. Some Russian companies couldn't pay invoices issued to them by Western suppliers. They couldn't scrape together enough roubles. Or they prioritised other payments. Or they were broke.

Other companies, however, hid behind the crisis—the *krizis*—and played poor, when they may have had the money to pay partners. Some Russian companies stripped the paint off the walls before shutting down. Rather than pay debts to Western partners as they came due, some Russians in the teeth of the crisis asset-stripped their companies and stashed the most valuable assets offshore.

The riskophiles

Raiffeisen's authorised capital—the maximum value of shares a company can issue—at the time of the crisis, Zilber said, was somewhere in the neighbourhood of USD 15 million. To stay afloat and to restore the bank's creditworthiness, Raiffeisen needed an injection from Vienna of USD 150 million. It happened, and Raiffeisen started to boom. It was, for a while, the only bank that could connect Russia with the outside world—a role the bank had been playing again in the aftermath of the full-scale invasion and the exit of most international banks from Russia.

"To be successful in business in Russia, one of the essential elements is that you have to be a riskophile," Zilber said. "Maybe it's like that in all new markets. I don't know. But for a number of reasons this was totally uncharted territory and very hard to understand."

After the 1998 crisis, companies flocked to Raiffeisen. Russia's billionaires—every one of them, Zilber said—became clients. This, despite a company policy that said private individuals could only become clients via referrals from bank employees or other clients. Zilber's phone rang off the hook.

"It started with a really brave decision. It was a leap of faith," Zilber said. "You remember the fear in 1998. These people were riskophiles."

The 1998 crisis was a body blow to foreign investors. FDI into Russia sank like a stone. Recovery began early, but slowly. FDI returned to pre-1998 levels only in 2003.

It was not unusual to hear executives discuss the default in apocalyptic terms.

The "neutron bomb"

"The business community feels like it was hit by a neutron bomb, and we've all been irradiated ... We are alive today, but in 30 days, 60 days, 90 days some are going to die," Scott Blacklin, the then-president of the American Chamber of Commerce in Russia, told *The New York Times*.[52]

Casualties mounted quickly. *The New York Times* went to Boris Jordan at Renaissance Capital, now called MFK Renaissance following a merger with another entity.

"Most of the bank's capital has been wiped out, most of its assets are nearly worthless, and the firm, like many other investment banks that not so long ago were speculating in Moscow's booming markets, is scrambling to stay afloat," which it ultimately did.[53]

The *Times* laid Russia's default squarely at the feet of voucher privatisation, which it described as a massive insiders' heist. The newspaper pointed out that Jordan, in his CSFB days, was one of the architects of the voucher privatisation and was reaping what he sowed.

The Financial News carried on with the body count. Citing the UK's *Independent*, it said that "up to forty per cent of the 4,000 or so staff employed by Western investment banks in Moscow have been sacked, and London headhunters are receiving calls from those who have worked in Moscow."[54]

The statistics just kept coming: "By the estimates of one Moscow recruiting agency, about 60,000 professionals in Moscow have been either laid off, sent home on 'temporary leave' or seen their salaries cut by as much as one-third."[55]

United Financial Group, another of Russia's mighty domestic financial firms, "cut staff and dropped its salaries by an average of 30 percent, with senior executives taking cuts of 50 percent,"[56] *The New York Times* wrote.

Crying into your beer in Russia became costly. A Heineken importer and distributor started laying off staff and re-negotiating his commercial leases, while his financial transactions were stuck in Russian banks.[57]

At the sharp end of the alcohol supply chain—the bar stool—customers were drying up.

"This is the quietest night of the quietest week," Martin Bainbridge told *The New York Times* in 1998. Bainbridge was the manager of Moscow's Chesterfield Café, which the *Times* described as "a popular watering hole for Moscow's high-living young professionals."

"For a week and a half, I have had people coming in here, saying this is their last drink in Moscow," Bainbridge said. "But it is worse for the Russians, who are at the bottom, watching their ruble literally disintegrate."[58]

Even the mighty Credit Suisse, whose vigorous appetite for risk brought it into Russia before almost anyone else, took out the hatchet. The bank cut 103 jobs in its Moscow office—32 per cent of its Moscow staff.[59]

Andrew Ipkendanz, head of global emerging markets for CSFB in Moscow, told *The New York Times*: "Frankly, all of us made a bet on the ability of the Government to get its fiscal house in order ... They didn't; we lost money, and so you move on."[60]

Gambrill's career in Russia—it started at the Metropol and progressed to financial services—gradually wound down after the 1998 default. He was on an ocean liner crossing the Atlantic when he got a call that the Russian market had melted down.

"I got a phone call saying there's been a banking crisis in Russia and everything has collapsed," he said. There was little he could do—he was at sea.

So was Russia.

The Washington Post's David Hoffman, writing with a colleague, summarised the entire sordid affair as follows:

> Those sorry results now stand as a cautionary tale about the new global economy and its treatment of developing nations. Russia, like many developing and formerly communist countries, acquired the trappings of a market economy in the early 1990s—bonds, stock markets, people in business suits and a boom psychology. But like a number of emerging markets around the world, Russia's new capitalist veneer hid deep unresolved problems from the old era. Its underlying economy was still rooted in cronyism, lacking rule of law, and hostile to the long-term direct investment it needed most.
>
> Western investors, in their haste to seize a new market, overlooked or wilfully ignored these realities. And while the wave of capital they supplied temporarily buoyed stock prices, enriched the politically well connected and papered over the government budget deficit, little of it went into new plants or equipment that might have helped Russia grow. When the investment managers suddenly lost confidence this year, their money flowed out of stocks and bonds with bewildering speed, leaving the Russian economic terrain scorched.[61]

Foreign investment was down, but not zero. If a company had the stomach for it, there were bargains to be had. In truth, investor sentiment was divided. Businesses that had longer-term plans for Russia, and businesses whose model allowed them to take advantage of the cheap rouble, stayed.

Iwan Williams, Coca-Cola co-president for Russia at the time, said: "We plan to overcome these complications, not doubting for a second our long-term prospects in this country ... Coca Cola will invest in Russia for the next 100 years."[62]

9

THE VALERIAN DAYS

I look at my period in Russia as split into two periods;
2005–2008 [were] the glory days. It was just insane, there was
so much money in this.[1]

There are two days that you cry in Russia. The day you
arrive, and the day you leave.[2]

Itchy feet

On the eve of his departure for Moscow, David Grant had itchy
feet. He was a Londoner with a London education and wanted to
get out. For many UK university graduates, a job in Australia is a
popular option, but for Grant, the popular route was something
to avoid. He wanted somewhere far, far from his comfort zone
to work on himself and his CV. He narrowed his choices for his
first post-graduate year to Tokyo and Moscow, and then slowly
ruled out Tokyo.

"You know, I thought, I'm not ready to walk down the street
and be pointed at," he said, assuming what life as a Westerner

might be like in Japan. "Little did I know that I would stand out like a sore thumb in Moscow in '02, anyway."

On top of that, there was the language. "I thought, I'm never going to learn Japanese in a year. Turned out I wouldn't learn Russian in a year either."

It hit him in the departure hall at Heathrow. He was going to a place he'd never been to before, where he didn't know a soul and where he didn't speak the language. All he had was a job offer to teach business English.

"We're not in Kansas anymore," he said. But after a trip to Red Square and a commute on the metro, "You could feel the growth and the development and the dynamism."

He stayed for another year. He made friends. He joined an expat website and then became its administrator, becoming the guy who organised pints on a Friday night. And he stayed some more, until the full-scale invasion in 2022, when he crossed the border into Finland on the early morning bus.

The early 2000s, and the relatively rapid recovery from the crisis of 1998, was the start of another growth spurt, when someone with a good education, a curious mind, some Russian language skills and a good sense of timing could become involved in something interesting. By 2006, Grant was evaluating real estate sites for an international hotel chain looking to expand across Russia.

"So you spend the first year in disbelief at how everything works (or doesn't), and the second year trying to change it, in utter futility," Grant said. "And if you make it to the third year, you get to the point where you can say 'Yeah, I get it now. We can actually start working.'"

As he put it, people were starting to get used to Putin, and the 2008 global financial crisis had yet to strike. He met local oligarchs with bear-skin rugs across their office parquet. He was offered a Kalashnikov as a gesture of appreciation (thoughts of customs at Heathrow got the better of that gesture). He met investors, property developers, hoteliers and people who just owned land and wanted to build.

"You could feel this growth, and it seemed, talking to people, that every international company wanted to be in Russia. Suddenly, everyone was talking about Russia. It was a place where people were seemingly making millions out of the wildest ideas," Grant said.

Companies stung by the 1998 crash returned on exploratory trips to Russia. The economic indicators were good enough again to start weighing them against the risks. Business wanted to know about the changes in the political landscape in the transition from Yeltsin to Putin. They wanted to know how, or whether, the legal and regulatory environment had improved. They wanted to know whether it was any easier to do business. Some companies were still licking wounds from their experience in Russia in the 1990s. It wasn't that long ago that they had closed representative offices or liquidated local companies. High-level executives came—the decision to return to or to enter Russia was not taken by sherpas or junior colleagues.

Gould-Davies, the former UK ambassador to Belarus, recalls talking with an investment banker in 2003, when the news broke that Russia's debt had returned to investment grade.

"What was it that caused companies to pile in? It was being given investment grade," he said. And as the price of oil continued to climb, investors were seeing

IPOs almost every month in Russia, even as the country was becoming more repressive domestically.[3] This is the interesting thing—the state is becoming more corrupt and exerting more control over domestic business, constraining them in various ways. It was really the growth story—the growth on the back of oil prices [that attracted investors].

Russia achieved another important milestone in the mid-2000s that further burnished its international reputation. The Russian Federation finally paid off the Soviet Union's debts—the debts that had been restructured in the 1990s. The amounts were overwhelming—the final payment was in excess of USD 25 billion, not including USD 1.3 billion in servicing costs, and brought the total sum paid in 2006 to USD 40 billion. The debt was paid on the eighth anniversary of the 1998 default and was paid in full fourteen years early, saving Russia further billions in costs.[4] This was a great act of financial hygiene from the Russian government as its coffers swelled with oil money. These were the debts that many blame for hobbling Russia in its post-Soviet infancy.

Cognitive dissonance, 2000s style

Gould-Davies encapsulates one of the primary contradictions in the "growth story" he refers to above. Business was booming in Russia, but so was the business of authoritarian politics. For international investors, the economic story had the upper hand.

Did business deliberately overlook the politics? It was hard to ignore that the decade-long, free-for-all of Yeltsin's brand of Russian politics had come to an end. The business community welcomed Putin enthusiastically as a law-and-order president and a relief from Yeltsin's debilitating chaos. At the same time, everyone also knew that Putin was from the KGB, an atypical source of liberal reformers.

That's contradiction number one. The economy was booming, but the people at the top are not the sort of people you'd have over for dinner. Lots of countries, including a democracy or two, work that way.

But the contradictions multiplied. The economy was booming, but it was permeated by corruption—even if the jewel-tone blazers were gone and the gangsters were sending their kids to boarding school in England. The law as written was improving, accounting standards were improving and the Big Four were everywhere in Russia, but was this the guarantee of propriety that it seemed to be?

Once again, international companies walked into these contradictory spaces. Some did it knowingly and tried to bridge the contradictions. Some companies worked comfortably in these grey zones. You had to be living under a rock not to know that Russia was a low-transparency jurisdiction paved with visible and less visible risks.

There were endless seminars on "best practice" in corporate governance in Russia. They talked about conditionality for Russian companies, meaning that cooperation with, or loans from, Western partners should be contingent on corporate clean-ups on the Russian side. Western companies had to behave, too, in Russia and not facilitate bad behaviour in the Russian business environment. Zero-tolerance policy was a familiar phrase, but that sort of stance was easy to preach and hard to execute. Some Western companies were terrified by the volume of grey area in Russian law. Others took advantage of it.

One of the largest investors in Russia once said, privately: "Poor corporate governance can be dealt with. Malicious corporate governance can't be dealt with." In between those two zones, investors had to find leadership on the Russian side that was willing to clean up.

These seminars featured rubbery blueberry muffins and platters of smoked salmon on 50-metre-long breakfast buffets and served up talk about the role of independent directors. They stressed that good corporate governance created added value—updating a company's corporate governance structures was like updating its manufacturing equipment. Access to Western capital markets would improve Russian corporate governance because listing agencies in New York and London insisted on it.

"Every million that is shunted from a company into a villa wipes a billion dollars off that company's market capitalization," speakers would say from the podium.

Most of the time, Russians looked at these seminars as a colossal waste of time and resented the fact that pressure for improved corporate governance was always coming from the outside world, which, among other things, generally hadn't been covering itself in glory when it came to keeping its own house clean. On compliance, the attitude was more, "Show me the forms and I'll fill them in." This is perhaps too broad a generalisation, but anyone who read the statements of risk in the prospectus of a Russian IPO will understand that corporate governance wasn't high on most executives' lists.

But all of this missed the point. The lack of corporate governance was core to the Russian business environment. Modern Russian business folklore had a phrase along the lines of, "Only a fool makes a profit." Asking a Russian company to disclose its beneficial owners was like asking a billionaire to give his PIN to the tax police.

This is precisely why Russians kept billions of dollars in capital outside of Russia.

The intermediaries in all of this were the auditors who worked in the Moscow offices (and elsewhere) of the world's largest accounting firms. Part of their job was to weld together two different business worlds. These were highly diversified advisory businesses, but a lot of their work focused on helping their international clients do business in Russia—called "inbound" work—and auditing the books of Russian companies.

"So I think on the inbound work a decent job was done, because those people had to answer back home, not just in Russia," EY's Ostling said. "But I do think there was a lot of squinting, you know, narrowing of eyes, putting a finger in one ear to think things through, to get legal letters, cold comfort, and I'm not saying it was pure." (Cold comfort letters in this context refer to letters from a parent company in support of a subsidiary.)

Rent-a-lord

Some accountants fixed companies with a very British toolbox.

"Every Russian is smart enough to know that if he wants to list his shares, he needs to get some 'pigeons' from London, at least. Lord Haw-Haw, whatever," Ostling said. He is referring here to the periodic use of what became known as the "rent-a-lord" schemes, whereby Russian companies put a member of the British aristocracy on their boards and in so doing added a posh lustre of credibility to their brands.

They were called "pigeons" for a reason.

"They come in four times a year, shit on the statues, and then fly out," Ostling said.

These schemes were a mirage of governance. There was no serious oversight, there was no serious regulation, there were no serious penalties and whatever was on the books was not enforced.

"Unless you have that kind of shit, governance doesn't mean a fucking thing," Ostling said. "We didn't have that in Russia. We had the dinners, and the wine, the tables with the names, but we didn't have the process where there was really a regulatory regime in Russia that was going to punish people for not doing the right thing."

"I think we mediated that as a profession," Ostling said. "We did it maybe with the best interests—we employed a lot of people and trained a lot of people and made a lot of companies. But when you have something like this happen," he said, pausing for emphasis to show that he's referring to the war in Ukraine, "it all comes out in the wash."

What were we supposed to know? What were we supposed to see coming?

Ostling was not alone. He cites papers by the Organisation for Economic Co-operation and Development (OECD) about governance in Russia, and publications by other professional services firms—to which he contributed—as long ago as 2012 or 2013 asking "Who is going to stand up for corporate governance in Russia?" Ostling said.

He illustrates the willingness to overlook certain Russian realities, including Russia's invasion and annexation of Crimea in 2014, with an anecdote:

> At the same time that Crimea happened, at the same time sanctions were being applied, I went to a dinner at the UK ambassador's residence, where there was a group of lawyers and big guys who are going to list, around the dinner table, and he's trying to convince them to list in London.

It was, to Ostling, a stunning level of dissonance:

> If you're in the Land of Nod, where you know, there's all these beautiful women, all this money, and you could be 90 per cent honest and the 10 per cent grows your business, you find a way to look at the 90 per cent where you're doing the right thing, and minimise the 10 per cent. And I have a hard time believing that anybody who was anybody didn't understand that there was at least a 90/10 rule.

In principle, there were ways to forensically examine the accounts of Russian companies, but they relied on Western investors asking for an enormous amount of potentially sensitive information from their Russian counterparties. These were big asks, and they ran the risk of alienating potential partners. Moreover, not all Russian companies would comply with these requests. And finally, an international company could never be sure that the information it was getting from its Russian partners was an accurate depiction of the business. If most Russian companies in the 1990s (at least) were cooking the books they showed their own government, imagine the fictions they were sending to foreign business partners.

Pouring oil on the fire

At the turn of this century, Russia was beginning its recovery from the 1998 default and rouble devaluation, and of course President Yeltsin famously stepped down on the eve of the new millennium. Not long after that, Russia became the second letter in the BRIC countries.

In geopolitics, the 11 September 2001 terrorist attacks on the World Trade Center in New York City, the Pentagon outside Washington and on United Airlines flight 93, followed by the Gulf War of 2003, were transformative events. First, 9/11 revealed that the plumbing of the global banking system was polluted with terrorist money. The US, the UK and governments around the world vowed to clamp down on dirty cash.

Second, energy prices are sensitive to geopolitical instability: the threat of conflict is also a threat to the supply of oil and gas. The 9/11 attacks triggered a sharp and enduring increase in the price of oil, a development that saw torrents of cash flow into Russia's treasury. Finally, the world was entering a resource supercycle beyond oil and gas.

An economic transformation that showed enormous promise took on even more generous proportions. According to Jeffry Frieden: "Per capita output in Russia nearly tripled between 1999 and 2014, almost entirely due to the natural resources boom, as the country's exports ballooned from USD 100 billion to USD 600 billion." Russia joined the WTO in 2012.[5]

Russia's economic growth went into a delirious sort of overdrive that made the state, the oil sector and the broadest circles of people who serve it phenomenally wealthy. Russia became a star performer for companies with global footprints, and a Western company thriving in Moscow was a sign that a business had its act together.

"Success in Russia for a foreign company generally shows two things. One, that the company is good at hiring and empowering local staff, because those are the people who make the best decisions in Russia. Second, that the company has a strong culture of compliance and anti-corruption, because those are needed to withstand pressure for bribes from the Russian environment," said Tom Adshead, head of research at a strategic advisory consultancy who after years in Moscow left at the start of Russia's full-scale invasion of Ukraine. "Western companies that got too Russian and paid bribes tended to come unstuck sooner or later."

The move to Russian companies

In the 2000s, expats started making more money inside Russian companies than at international companies. These sorts of career moves removed all the frustration of having to explain Russia to headquarters overseas. Once you moved to a Russian company, you didn't have to place a long-distance call for deal approval.

"They loved being employed by Russian companies," the recruitment executive Sergey Vorobyev said, "because they were paid a lot more and they were able to make any deal."

It was a time of fluidity between and among Russian and international employers and employees. Within the tech ecosystem, for example, senior and junior employees of all sorts of nationalities moved around among Microsoft, Amazon, Facebook and Yandex, Russia's homegrown online giant.

"Yandex was kind of an incubator, in a good way," said Anton Shingarev, a former vice president at Yandex and Kaspersky, now serving as an adjunct professor at the University of Texas. Yandex would hire the overachievers of Russia's elite universities and then see them poached into the likes of Google. "Google was a very strong competitor in Russia. And it always kept Yandex in very good form. Constant competition with Google was really important for Yandex."

Russia was on its way to becoming less exotic. Economic historian Malik moved there in 2005 to work for Troika Dialog. He even deferred the start of his Harvard PhD to allow more time in Russia.

"Russia was starting really to become more on the beaten path," Malik said. "But it really skyrocketed in popularity between '06 and '08. I mean, '08 was insane." These were the years of "peak-market signals" and "opulent conferences." It was, he said, miles away from the 1990s, when the Russian market was run by a "lot of these individuals that know each other," toting suitcases of cash.

The beaten path in the sky

British Airways went big on Moscow. Outside of the 1998 default and the 2008 global crisis, the UK flag carrier's flights were perennially packed. On the busiest flights, business class sometimes stretched to fill almost half the plane.

For a while, British Airways flew a 747 to and from Moscow on one of its three daily flights,[6] an unusual move for what was still considered a longish short-haul route. The sight of a British Airways 747 at Moscow's Domodedovo Airport was a visual anomaly—it looked like an aircraft carrier had pulled up to the gate. Flight attendants did not have permission from the Russian government to overnight in Russia—this was likely the result of bilateral conditions—and in most cases were not even allowed off the aircraft in Russia. It was not a favourite route for the crew—it was one of BA's longer intra-European routes, and it was there-and-back in a day.

Aside from the 747, BA sweated countless Airbuses and Boeing 767s rammed with the men and women of UK plc. The wide-body 767s were heavy, big-bellied beasts—notorious for their rattling discomfort, for the rivers of gin they dispensed onboard and for flying—at their peak—one of the most profitable routes on BA's entire global network.

When the *Financial Times* wrote about the return of Western investment banks to Russia in the wake of the 1998 financial crisis (and, as it happened, on the eve of the 2008 crisis), the newspaper cited a certain frustration with running investment banking in Russia from London.

"One of the main constraints on the business is the number of seats on a Boeing 767," the newspaper said, quoting an investment banker based in Moscow.[7]

And this, from 2005: "A senior German banker complains that if you want to fly with British Airways or Lufthansa from London or Frankfurt to Moscow you now have to book more than three weeks in advance—and that includes economy class."[8]

British Airways in 2003 had moved its Moscow service from the decrepit Sheremetyevo to Domodedovo, a lavishly refurbished airport in Moscow's distant south. History had come full circle. Prior to the collapse of the Soviet Union, British Airways and the Soviet government were contemplating a joint venture to be called Air Russia that would be based at Domodedovo.[9]

The evening flights, even more so in the winter when the entire route took place in darkness, were quieter affairs. At other times, it was a flying pub. It was impossible not to run into someone you knew—a client, a supplier, a neighbour or any of those people who you always seem to run into on aeroplanes. During school holidays, British Airways' business class ferried

Russian students commuting to and from classes at England's fabled public schools.

There was, of course, the time when up to three BA aircraft were thought to have traces of the radioactive material suspected in the poisoning of former Russia spy and exile Alexander Litvinenko. One or both of the individuals allegedly dispatched to London to murder Litvinenko with polonium 210 were believed to have travelled on British Airways from Moscow and contaminated the aircraft as they flew.[10]

Lufthansa also made Russia a priority. In 2002, on the thirtieth anniversary of the start of regular flights between Frankfurt and Moscow, the company's regional director for Russia said the company aspired to fly to all of Russia's "main industrial cities."[11] American Airlines and Delta both offered a non-stop service to Moscow from the US; American discontinued service in 2009,[12] and Delta pulled its flights in 2015.[13]

Following the 2012 demise of British Midland's Moscow service, low-cost carrier easyJet flew to Moscow for a while, certainly one of the brightest (orange) indicators of just how busy the London–Moscow route was.

"Moscow is a landmark route and one we are delighted to be able to serve. Russia is the world's largest country with a growing economy. Offering frequent and affordable flights enables easyJet to play a key role to aid trade links between the two countries," Carolyn McCall, easyJet CEO, told *The Guardian* at the time.[14] At one point, the airline was offering flights to Moscow from both London and Manchester.

Service was suspended from Manchester in September 2015; easyJet flights from London ended in March 2016. The airline told *The Moscow Times* that demand was weakening and visa regulations between Russia and the UK were tightening, further dampening demand.[15] This was, of course, after Russia's illegal annexation of Crimea and the start of hostilities in Eastern Ukraine.

The Aeroflot flights, too, were almost like a shuttle service.

"My family has been living in London since 2008," Alexei Evgenev, formerly of Alvarez & Marsal in Moscow, said. "So I've been between London and Moscow for a pretty long time. You know, the Aeroflot flight was like a commuter bus, you knew everyone who was flying."

When "shopping" became a Russian word

In 1985, the US hamburger chain Wendy's ran a television commercial reminding viewers that it offered customers a wide range of choice. To drive the point home, Wendy's depicted what it thought a Soviet fashion show would look like. The fashion show featured "daywear," "eveningwear" and "swimwear," but for every look, the same, rotund Soviet model plodded along a mock runway wearing the same outfit: a stiff, boxy, grey smock. Each "outfit" was greeted with tepid applause from a group of onlookers dressed in their Politburo finest.

By 2011, Russians were spending USD 5.3 billion a year on luxury goods; 30 per cent of that figure was spent on fashion. And this was only shopping in Russia—holiday shopping and duty-free purchases were not included.[16]

And what Russians couldn't wear on their backs they wore on the roads. Imported cars, by value, made up about 80 per cent of the Russian automobile market by 2008, an increase from 8 per cent in 2000.[17] Moscow's tiny side streets and horizon-busting boulevards became a live-action showroom of some of the most expensive cars in Europe. Sales of Bentley automobiles available across seven dealerships in Russia peaked in 2019, at 341 vehicles, up from a low of 120 in 2010.[18]

If central Moscow's roads were a luxury car showroom come to life, its offices, restaurants and nightclubs—even the aisles of its more expensive supermarkets—all sprang from the pages of Holt's

Vogue. Starting slowly in the 1990s, Moscow—which by some statistics was 85 per cent of Russia's market for luxury goods—went through the sort of transformation that happens when the *Wizard of Oz* switches from black and white to Technicolor.

Not surprisingly, perhaps, the first brand reportedly to move into Russia was Versace, in 1991. This roughly coincided with the birth of the *Novy Russky*, who liked to swaddle themselves in designer goods from head to toe—the more bling the better. Before embracing the Savile Row aesthetic *GQ* suggested, Russian men wanted heavy watches, Italian leather goods and bold patterns on everything. This excludes an interim period when every Moscow middle manager was trussed up in sleek threads from minimalist German designer Hugo Boss. For a while, it felt like Boss was everywhere in Moscow, but it was even better, of course, if you bought Boss at Berlin's ultra-luxury KaDeWe department store. The ultimate accessory, *natürlich*, was an Audi A6, Moscow's default company car.

Russian women wanted body-hugging dresses, constellations of jewellery and sky-high heels. Manolo Blahnik and Christian Louboutin both had stores in Moscow.

The gravity-defying acrobats from Cirque du Soleil would blush in front of the Russian women in stiletto heels navigating Moscow's lunar landscape of sidewalks, most of which are pocked with ice for half the year. Then again, if you're dressed in high heels and head-to-toe Versace, you're more likely to be cruising through town in the back of a BMW than to be clambering out of a metro station.

Less is more, but keep it expensive

More than a decade after the first boutique bearing her surname opened in Moscow, Donatella Versace reflected on the progress of her Russian clientele.

"Russians have started to learn that less bling is better, that more sophistication is in," Versace said in an interview. "The women here learn this slower than the rest of world, but they're learning for sure."[19]

Versace moved into Russia via a distribution partner who took care of the business on the ground and sent a slice of the revenue back to Milan. This was the common format for a great number of luxury brands in Moscow: three distributors towered over the high-end retail business; only the largest and most powerful fashion brands ran their own stores in Russia.

Whether in partnership or alone, every luxury label you could imagine stormed into Russia.

"Just when it looked as if Russia's fashion elite couldn't fit another logo on its collective rump, Italian powerhouse Gucci rolled its double G's into town for the grand opening of its new boutique on Kutuzovsky Prospekt," *The Moscow Times* wrote in 1997.[20] Kutuzovsky Prospekt was a choice address for Muscovites with elevated tastes and the bank accounts to match.

Some fashion brands opened at least a small, experimental presence in Russia before the crash of 1998. Christian Dior came to Moscow in the same year that the crushing debt default laid waste to most of—or the rest of—Russia's economy.

"Christian Dior understands that Moscow is the kind of city that needs to have a Christian Dior," a company representative told *The Moscow Times*.[21]

The rest came afterwards and caught the rebound. Fendi caught the start of the upswing in 1999 and showed its seasonal fur line at Moscow's legendary Bolshoi Theatre in a show thronged by *le tout* Moscow.[22]

The surge in the price of oil that started around 2002 and drove the Russian economy into a dizzying upward spiral of growth in personal income and consumer spending drove 11 per cent annual growth in retail spending for about eight years, according to estimates from the Brookings Institution.[23] "Real wages and incomes almost tripled from mid-2000 to mid-2008," Brookings wrote.[24]

Brookings is referring to Russian wages. What was happening to expat wages at the same time was a separate story. Investment bankers in Moscow were being paid multiples of what their colleagues earned in New York, London and Frankfurt.

"Russia has been spectacular in terms of wage growth for western-trained, Russian-speaking bankers," Yiannis Demopoulos, a recruiter at Delta Executive Search, told the *International Herald Tribune* in 2007. The article went on to say that "pay packages of $7 million to $10 million are common for managing directors in Moscow."[25]

In the spring of 2007, when Ralph Lauren opened a 3-storey, 720-square-metre flagship store in central Moscow, the shop sold out of crocodile handbags at USD 21,580 a pop on the first day of business. That sort of shopping enthusiasm prompted one analyst to say that the Russian luxury market would be 10 per cent of an overall USD 270 billion Russian retail market and was expected to grow 17 per cent in 2008.[26]

Moscow in 2007 also played host to an annual roving retail conference known as "Supreme Luxury," sponsored by the *International Herald Tribune*. The event was held at central Moscow's Ritz-Carlton Hotel. Tom Ford flew in. Fashion critic Suzy Menkes was there. Donatella Versace made an appearance; French fashion corporate mogul Bernard Arnault of LVMH and his son Antoine sat in the front row. Between flashes from the local and international paparazzi, the cream of Moscow society mingled with folks who set the standards for extravagance around the world.[27]

The luxury brands just kept coming. Dolce & Gabbana had ten venues in Russia by 2010. Tom Ford, Cartier, Tiffany, Oscar de la Renta, Prada and Chanel were in town, too. It was easier to make a list of luxury brands that weren't in Russia. In 2013, even Brooks Brothers, known for its starchy, preppy, corporate look, opened a store in Moscow.[28]

There were monobrand stores, department stores, urban malls and suburban malls. Barvikha Luxury Village, a collection of ultra-elite brands, was the most famous of the suburban retail playgrounds, tucked away in a painstakingly designed mall (the word doesn't really do it justice) in the woods outside Moscow. The town of Barvikha is at once easy to describe but almost impossible to capture. In terms of sheer wealth, and its place in the Russian imagination, it's a cross between Beverly Hills (a power address, but with pine trees instead of palms) and Greenwich, Connecticut (for its air of enormous, but quieter wealth). Some of the folks who live in and around Barvikha have second homes on the lavish Cote d'Azur. Others have mansions in England's horsey Surrey. Some might have had both.

The growth, the sales and the profits were stratospheric, even though luxury goods in Russia were far more expensive than they were in their home markets or elsewhere: import taxes and the cost of doing business in Russia saw to that. A fluctuating rouble also hurt or helped local shoppers. Never mind. "Russians spent USD 7.3 billion on Italian luxury goods in 2012, a 9 per cent increase in the previous year," *The Moscow Times* reported, citing Italian sources.[29]

The big labels grabbed most of the headlines, but Moscow's international retail scene wasn't all crocodile and cashmere. Marks & Spencer, purveyor of goods to Britain's middle classes for more than a century, came to Russia in 2005, via a Turkish franchise operator.[30] Everyone in Moscow seemed to know that the city's first lady Elena Baturina, despite her billionaire status, liked to shop in the M&S flagship store on London's Oxford Street.

IKEA, of course, also came to Russia. The arrival of its famously pragmatic but stylish Scandinavian brand of furniture was nothing short of sensational in Moscow. IKEA's entrance came when Russia was pulling out of the 1998 crisis and home renovations gripped the nation. IKEA was one of Russia's largest and most successful retail investors, though its tenure generated excitement and controversy in equal measures. When the first store opened in April 2000, traffic backed up for miles to bring more than 40,000 visitors to ogle the flatpack bookshelves, simple ceramic dishes and the practical but inviting sofas.[31] Many of IKEA's visitors dressed up for the occasion and took pictures against the backdrop of its famous sample rooms.

But IKEA's landmark presence attracted landmark controversy. In 2004, IKEA's Lennart Dahlgren said he was "living in fear of his life"—he was under a series of threats that came to a head in connection with the deeply troubled opening of the Mega-2 shopping mall in north-west Moscow.[32] The company had to wage bureaucratic war with the city of Moscow to build a highway overpass into that store. IKEA was in 2010 charged with allowing contractors to pay bribes allegedly to resolve a dispute over the supply of electricity to stores in St Petersburg.[33]

The global financial crisis

Almost exactly ten years after the 1998 default, the global financial crisis of 2008 dealt Russia another near knock-out blow. If the 1998 crisis was largely homemade, the roots of the 2008 crisis were external to Russia. But by now, Russia was no longer isolated from external shocks. In a globalised world, the collapse of the US financial services industry bloated on collateralised sub-prime mortgages didn't stay local for long.

As the global economy contracted, so did demand for the energy and raw materials that were the drivers of the Russian economy. As banks re-evaluated their loan portfolios and re-assessed inter-bank lending—the *kredit kranch*, as it was called in Russian—growth funding evaporated. The price of oil collapsed, and with it the rouble and Russian GDP. The price of a barrel of oil in Russia was the highest it had ever been in the summer of 2008. By the end of the year, the price had fallen by 70 per cent.[34] When the price of oil went down, it took retail sales with it.[35]

Russia – and its expat bankers—was in much better financial condition in the run-up to 2008 than in 1998. Public debt in Russia was low, and foreign currency reserves were high. But the economy had failed to diversify away from its dependence on oil exports. As a result, 2008 hit hard.[36] The Russian government launched a USD 50 billion bailout programme that first rescued Russia's oligarchs and the strategically significant companies they owned. Oleg Deripaska got USD 4.5 billion to pay back a loan to a banking syndicate led by BNP Paribas. Had he missed the payment, he would have forfeited the 25 per cent of Norilsk Nickel serving as collateral.[37]

Sources told *The New York Times* that Fridman and Alfa "were minutes away" from losing 44 per cent of mobile telecoms giant VimpelCom in a margin call to creditor Deutsche Bank. The same government bailout rescued that transaction. In a rare confluence of conflict, Alfa's long-running dispute with Telenor might have blocked Deutsche Bank's margin call on VimpelCom.[38]

The Russian Central Bank made sure that the ATMs in the country's retail banking system continued to spit out roubles.[39] Russians withdrew cash from private banks and either stuffed them under their mattresses or transferred them to safer, state-owned banks.[40]

The situation was grim, everywhere. Moscow suffered, but "the periphery," as it is sometimes called, faced "oblivion."

"Now advertising banners and billboards offer 'anti-crisis' discounts on everything from mattresses to Lada sedans. Nightclubs stage 'anti-crisis' parties. Jokes about the crisis are legion: 'Daddy, is it true we're facing a crisis?' "No, Son. It's the oligarchs who are facing a crisis. We are facing oblivion,'" Bloomberg wrote. That same article described how the freezing of global financial markets cut off Russian companies and banks from life-saving short-term credit; layoffs were widespread; and Russia was burning through its hard currency reserve to bolster the rouble.[41] Financial investors in Russia took about USD 148 billion out of the Russian economy by the end of 2008,[42] and FDI dropped from USD 75.85 billion in 2008 to USD 27.75 billion in 2009.[43]

Some companies left; some expats went home. But there were always companies and executives who took the longer view.

"It's not going to change anyone's desire to be in Russia in the long term," David Thomas, president of Volvo Cars in Russia, said in the Bloomberg article.[44]

The Cup runneth over

It is almost jarring to recall that in early 2014 the Winter Olympics were in Sochi and the World Cup was staged across Russia in 2018. These are the sorts of events that demonstrate the host country's prominence and status among advanced, or at least advancing, nations. As part of the public relations exercises that usually precede these global events, Putin went on a short-lived charm offensive that included the release from prison of Yukos CEO and Putin critic Mikhail Khodorkovsky. But before the Winter Olympics were over, unmarked Russian soldiers invaded Crimea. Russia occupied the peninsula and in March 2014 held the sham referendum leading to Crimea's annexation.

As an aside, the Sochi Games later became notorious for the discovery of an elaborate, state-sponsored doping scheme that illegally enhanced the performance of "dozens of Russian athletes."[45]

The World Cup four years later, long after the annexation of Crimea, was of an entirely different magnitude. The world's largest party was in Russia, and when the tournament started, the Russian capital convulsed in ecstasy. Voting to award the tournament to Russia was widely believed to be tainted;[46] the few protests about holding the event in Russia post-Crimea went nowhere. The entire month of the tournament was an enormous triumph for Russia. Everything about it went viral, including scenes of spontaneous samba festivals in the Moscow metro and the coats of high gloss applied to Moscow's urban contours.

The other big playing field

The 2014 Winter Olympics and the 2018 World Cup were enormously symbolic of Russia's arrival on the world stage. Both events came decades after Russia had last hosted an event of similar magnitude—the 1980 Summer Olympics in Moscow. An international boycott of the Games in connection with the Soviet Union's 1979 invasion of Afghanistan marred the occasion.

Beyond the athletic playing fields, the other massive international showground for Russia was not a sports stadium but a financial arena: the London Stock Exchange. Starting in 2002, with the listing of energy giant Lukoil on the LSE, more than two dozen Russian companies listed on the exchange, transforming them from private ownership to companies with shares that could be owned by the public and traded freely. The London exchange vibrated with Russian money—the European financial capital was seen as an easier place to list a company than New York, where scrutiny of public companies was more microscopic in nature. Plus, London was already well on its way to becoming a suburb of Moscow.

"[London] already hums with Russian money—wealthy Russians have bought up some of its most expensive real estate and its leading soccer team, and its high-end boutiques are now staffed with Russian-speaking employees," *The New York Times* wrote in 2006.[47]

London, with USD 13 billion in listings in 2005, and New York with USD 15.4 billion, were both popular venues for companies from emerging markets to come to public markets, but in 2006, London was expected to outstrip New York.[48]

Investment banks and law firms queued up to lift Russian companies onto the exchange; the flow of work was a bonanza to London. The process was equally a windfall for Russian companies. By selling shares, Russian companies earned billions of dollars in investment. Russian companies were only part of a stampede of companies from emerging markets listing on the London exchange.

In the 1990s, Christine Wootliff was in Berlin, organising trips to Germany for Russians who wanted—and could afford—anything from dental implants to heart surgery. The logistics were crushing, but business was good.

"It was the leading business for Russians travelling to Germany, and we covered everything," she said.[49]

Years later, Wootliff was involved in an analogous business but on an entirely different level: arranging the road shows for Russian companies launching IPOs on international stock exchanges. Road shows are the gruelling, multi-city tours companies undertake to persuade investors to buy shares when they debut on a public exchange. It's sort of like a pop star's concert tour, except the performances are usually in conference rooms at the top of skyscrapers with floor-to-ceiling windows. Also, unlike a rock concert, most road shows come on the heels of the issuance of an investor prospectus, which extols the virtues of the listing candidate but also enumerates the risks.

Clients would ask the company Wootliff worked for to support them with complex itineraries around the world's financial capitals. Multi-million-dollar budgets. Private jets. Five-star hotels. A logistics manager would travel in advance to make sure the fridges in the hotel rooms were stocked with all the clients' favourite snacks. Wootliff's Russian clients wanted to be chauffeured everywhere they went; their eyes widened with astonishment when Wootliff said the only way to keep to a tight schedule in London was to take the tube. In other cities, the only way was to take a helicopter. At moments like that, Wootliff would turn to her "bible" and dial anything from helicopters-for-hire to emergency dry cleaning.

Often Wootliff was the only woman on a plane with a team of Russian businessmen. It was, in the end, fun. Manic, insane fun, but a real charge. It was also something close to an MBA, the hard way, for Wootliff, for her clients and for their bankers. Western investment banks were still relatively new to Russia, or at least they were new to taking Russian companies public. The Russians were new to investment banking. Both happening at the same time at 30,000 feet was something to behold. Wootliff hastened to add, though, that all road shows, as the name implies, are high-stress, high-impact events, regardless of the client's nationality.

"I mean, it's not pretty. It's not," she said. But still, "it was fun, you know. We did something like eight of these a year." Wootliff would wake up in one city and fall asleep in another. "You don't know what your name is when you wake up in San Francisco."

Was it "normal?"

Russia almost did become a normal place to do business. Vardanyan's plea to Sucher in the lobby of the Radisson Slavyanskaya—let's build a normal country by building normal businesses—almost came true.

"I used to say to people that from 2000, maybe a tiny bit later, until about 2015, I did deals in Russia exactly the same way with the exact same documentation that I'd done them in the US for years," said Holly Nielsen, a director on the funds' board at Baring Vostok Capital Partners, the private equity firm in Russia. "We really lived in a very normal world. We expected [Russian] courts, and they usually did, to uphold those contracts, you know."

Russian law, as it existed on paper, became in most ways equal in quality to its European or American peers.

As time wore on, the business community sought to update how it looked at Russia. This raised a series of deeply challenging questions for international investors, above all in the client acceptance processes of banks and professional services firms, but across all sectors.

When was it appropriate to start applying a discount—to write down or write off, if you will—to a person or a company's past? When would an oligarch's "sins" be forgiven? And who was doing the forgiving? The business community struggled with this question—was there a statute of limitations on the way people did business in Russia in the 1990s? As ever, companies resolved these issues differently. Some used a strict interpretation of what the law would say. Others forgave and forgot.

It was normal. But it wasn't boring.

"It was still Russia. There was always a little bit of this or a little bit of that around the edges, and the people were kind of colourful, but it was very normal, is the word I'd use," Nielsen said. "I know that there's no definition of that, but it was normal."

10

TIME OUT

You would think me drunk if I sat down and told you what Moscow nightlife is like today. It is, in a word, delirious. And, in other words, it's sexist, chauvinistic, painfully loud, flashy, wasteful, boastful, swaggering, libidinous, overpriced, decadent, sometimes dangerous.[1]

No rules

All it took was a few IPOs to turn Moscow from a city with no real restaurants into a city with thousands of them. And you still couldn't get a table on Saturday nights.

Moscow nightlife had very few rules. First and foremost: whatever wasn't expressly prohibited was permitted. Encouraged, even.

Second, if it's never been done anywhere else, Moscow wanted to do it first, biggest and best. This is the sort of attitude that delivered night clubs with trapeze acts over the dance floor. It's entirely possible someone else thought of this first, but it was still pretty remarkable for Moscow.

Third, money was irrelevant, assuming you had lots of it in the first place. The more, the better. Sometimes, that was the entire point. The more outrageous the decor, the more expensive the menu and the more extravagant the dress code, the better. At some places, entry-level drinks like gin and tonics would start at about USD 30. Patrons at clubs like Diaghilev Project claimed it was easy to burn through USD 40,000 in one night,[2] starting with fees in the thousands for booking table service in advance.

Finally, make sure it was exclusive. The velvet ropes that kept the likes of you out of clubs in New York, the clipboards clutched at the front doors to London clubs or the bouncer at Berlin's Berghain had absolutely nothing on the merciless, withering social Darwinism of Moscow's "face control." This was an entirely new expression for the brutal winnowing of the crowds clamouring to get into the clubs whose names you desperately wanted to sprinkle into Monday morning conversations. There was nothing you could do to pretend you were good enough to get into certain Moscow bars and clubs. The guardians at the doors of Moscow's most elite venues had X-ray vision. They sized up your visual pedigree, they saw right into your wallet, and, if it didn't add up, go home.

For a while, expats had a certain—but not unlimited—amount of *carte blanche* at Moscow's better clubs. And not just any expat, mind you. Bankers raced to the head of the queue. Lawyers did OK. Corporates, not bad. Journalists, hmmm. Nordic folks? Very good. Darker skin? Not so good.

Imagine, if you can, the humiliation when, sometime around the 2008 global financial crisis and beyond, Moscow began to tire of expats and their entitled attitudes, and investment bankers started getting sent to the back of the queue. This was also around the same time that anyone who was anyone, locals included, would leave Moscow for the weekends to go clubbing in Ibiza, Verbier, St Tropez or, indeed, at Berghain. Aeroflot was already flying to Nice. Flights started in 1995.[3]

The competition to be labelled Moscow's most exclusive club was so cut-throat that the only way to be successful, it would seem, was to admit no one.[4] That was exactly the sort of rumour that club owners and party organisers wanted on the streets. White-hot word-of-mouth had personal assistants working the phones for hours to get their bosses on to VIP lists. Of course, if you had a certain surname—say, you owned a football club—you were on those lists without asking.

Decades before all this outlandish excess, Russia and Russians were always, without fail, able to have a good time. For a birthday, for New Year's Eve or even just for a Saturday night get-together, there was a time when very little went a very long way. Imagine the possibilities, then, when money and food were available in bottomless quantities, at least in certain circles. Chefs came from all over the world. Fresh fish for sushi and sashimi came via air freight from the waters off the coast of Japan.

Disney on a plate

Moscow perfected several restaurant formats that were hard to find anywhere else in the world. Outlandish and outrageous themed restaurants—Disneyland on a plate—were a particular Moscow speciality. There was the Soviet movie-classic restaurant that recreated the Central Asian desert; the Georgian restaurant styled as a quaint Caucasus village complete with a babbling brook through the middle; the Armenian restaurant called Noah's Ark; and the absurdism of a restaurant whose interior resembled a wedge of Swiss cheese. Moscow also featured a small chain of meticulously curated holes-in-the-wall made to look like perfect foreign dive bars but were wide of the mark by being just too pleasant and too creative.

Moscow's Café Pushkin, a multi-storey restaurant where the prices, the nineteenth-century splendour and the exclusivity all rose as the birdcage lift ascended from one floor to the next, was the unofficial staff cafeteria for white-collar Moscow. The ground floor recreated a pharmacy shop; corporate credit cards got some of their most high-impact workouts in the "library" floor above it. When the boss came to town, a visit to Café Pushkin was higher on the list than a trip to Lenin's mausoleum.

That was the case at least until Turandot arrived on the scene, just a few doors down from Pushkin. Turandot was unflinchingly operatic in scale. If it were possible to imagine what it might be like to dine inside a Fabergé egg, it was Turandot. The thick layers of gold leaf and 10-tonne chandeliers—not to mention the servers in period costume, for no restaurant was complete without that—were embarrassingly grand and deliberately over-the-top. According to *The New York Times*, the 65,000-square-foot restaurant cost USD 50 million to deliver. Part of the cost included demolishing the centuries-old mansions that already stood there and replacing them with something designed to look like a baroque palace.[5]

From the Department of Irony Never Dies, there was a restaurant in one of Moscow's best neighbourhoods designed to look like the inside of a Soviet apartment. A very nice Soviet apartment, mind you. Visitors were greeted at the door by an elderly man wearing a tracksuit and bedroom slippers, the off-duty uniform of millions of Soviet men. The food was Soviet chic, as if the famously lush, Stalin-era cookbook *The Book of Tasty and Healthy Food* had leapt vibrantly and expensively to life.

One of the pleasures of going out in Moscow were the real holes-in-the-wall. The Vietnamese restaurant in a random apartment in south-west Moscow. The fish restaurant in the middle of a tower block courtyard that took reservations via an unpublished phone number and had no menu. The live music bars that were damp, sticky, crowded and, in wintertime, smelled like wet overcoats. The poetry slams in draughty, forsaken, candle-lit rooms.

Moscow's more relaxed but still respectable clubs, the ones that let people in without too much fuss, were known as *demokratichniye* ("democratic") for their more liberal door and pricing policies. They were a blast, the kinds of places you could easily recommend to your more pragmatic friends, even if your investment-banking friends hung out at the Soho Rooms.

Moscow also had more than its share of inventive, creative entertainment spaces, many of them warehouses converted from the capital's overflowing stock of abandoned Soviet-, and even tsarist-era, factories. Like the tiny black grains at the bottom of a caviar dish, nothing went to waste; Moscow's clubbing scene got its start in these very places.

A Moscow weekend was a seventy-two-hour affair. Friday night became Saturday morning without pausing for thought. Dinner became dancing, and both seamlessly led to breakfast and double espressos at places like *Kofemania* at the Tchaikovsky Conservatory, on a leafy lane in the middle of Europe's biggest city. Taking hangover cures on *Kofemania's* outdoor terrace at the conservatory in the summer, within earshot of the world's best pianists in rehearsal, was nothing short of sublime.

Sleep came sometime between breakfast and a late lunch. Rinse. Repeat.

There was a seamier side. Drinks got spiked. Expats out "on the pull" woke up on the outskirts of towns in their underpants and little more. But absent from central Moscow was the kind of slurred, public drunkenness and lager-fuelled hooliganism that punctuated the streets of, say, London. In Moscow, if you wanted to get so drunk that you couldn't speak Russian or your mother tongue or either, you did it with friends at home in the kitchen or made sure you were securely in the back of a chauffeured Benz before opening the first bottle.

Money bought more than dinner and drinks in Moscow's nightlife. The ability to splash a bit of cash magically amplified the attractiveness of expat men who should have years ago hung up their disco shoes and joined a book club. These were the guys who you'd see at Night Flight, a bar with quite possibly the worst reputation in Moscow. It was a place for expats, but it was also a place for business travellers; it was the kind of bar where businessmen thrust their wedding rings deep into their pockets or left them in the safe at their hotel. It was a rare example of a perfect clearing market. Supply and demand for companionship matched seamlessly. No one went home alone unless they wanted to.

The Hungry Duck was Night Flight's only rival in the hard-fought Moscow contest for World's Most Louche Playground. The Hungry Duck was the kind of place where at some sort of undefined witching hour—after common sense but before total blackout—all hell broke loose. The Hungry Duck was the host of a recurring frat party driven by what seemed like a combination of hormones and jet fuel, delivering the sort of levitating abandonment that drove people to do things they would only do after getting fired or divorced or both at the same time. The only difference was that the regulars did this week in and week out at the Hungry Duck and then went back to work at Moscow's investment banks and consulting firms. The club, owned by a Canadian expat from Nova Scotia, was famed among other things for its strip shows that combined performers and patrons.

"The floor was generally a sticky mess of blood, vomit, beer, dirt and sweat," *The Moscow Times* wrote in a story eulogising the Hungry Duck after a visit from a group of parliamentarians precipitated its closure. As the group of deputies from the Duma walked in, "a male stripper from Nigeria was dancing on the bar with a female customer while the sound system blasted the Soviet national anthem."[6]

Apparently, everyone has their limits.

Vanity Fair, in an exhaustive profile of *The eXile*, the bad-boy expat rag that everyone who could read English devoured but would never admit it, called the Hungry Duck "Caligulan."[7]

One of the surest metrics of a cosmopolitan city's night life is the quality of its gay scene. At its peak, somewhere after the 1990s and before the passage of sweeping anti-LGBT legislation in 2013 and punishing anti-gay laws in 2023 that put life on edge, Moscow's gay scene was the sort of escapist euphoria it was everywhere else, but more so.

Its beginnings were modest enough: the very first gay club nights were clandestine, furtive, surreptitious events mostly in forlorn outlying venues, or carefully curated, need-to-know-basis parties in private apartments. In the early days, gay-bashing— known as *remont*, Russian for *repair*—was a popular local sport among the usual neighbourhood hoodlums. Still, the secrecy of these gatherings was matched only by their outrageousness. By the late 1990s and early 2000s, Moscow's gay scene had erupted into one of Europe's most effervescent party landscapes, gay, straight or otherwise. It was not unusual to start the weekend with an off-Broadway quality drag performance of Chekhov's *Three Sisters* and end it on a dance floor under the spell of a celebrity DJ.

Some of Moscow's venues were ingenious enough to morph almost seamlessly from one purpose to another. Propaganda, one of several central Moscow venues associated with the late, bohemian-leaning, Moscow nightlife legend Irina Papernaya, had an unofficial gay night on Sundays. For most of the evening, Propaganda was a low-key restaurant with a serviceable menu, though no one went there for the food.[8] This was a place to sit, watch and be watched, but in a discreet manner in stark contrast to the eye-popping, neck-straining people-watching at Vogue Café a few streets away.

As Sunday evening progressed toward very early Monday, the dinner tables at Propaganda began to disappear. The background music came to the foreground; a beat began to rise in the way high tide climbs the beach. And the demographics began to shift, at first imperceptibly. All the while, a queue at the front door extended like a long strand of DNA containing mostly Y chromosomes.

Face control was, as always, merciless. Punters were rejected because their shirts were untucked. Others were bounced because their shirts were tucked in. Groups of friends held their breath at the door to make sure they'd get in together. And, like most of Moscow's gay bars, once you were in, you were anywhere. Aside from the prices in roubles and the drink orders shouted in Russian, you were everywhere.

Beauty's where you find it

"Restaurants like Vogue Café near the Kremlin are draped with 18-year-old models toying with their miso soup and the 'modelizers,' mostly Russian executives and bankers, who pursue them over Moët," *The New York Times* wrote.[9]

Condé Nast's Holt created Vogue Café to reinforce and amplify the magazine brand. The licence for the restaurant went to Arkady Novikov, a youngster at the time who later became one of Russia's most famous restaurateurs. The atmosphere was meant to be international and sophisticated, with a bar at the front and a white-tablecloth restaurant at the back with a London-clubby feel.

This was another place that no one really went to for the food. Gordon Ramsay came out for a first anniversary party and, in Holt's telling, had a very on-brand reaction to the kitchen.

"He came to me and he said, 'Who and what have you been serving for the past year?' He was just horrified when he went into the kitchen," Holt said. It didn't really matter. Vogue Café in the evenings was packed. Holt grasped for words when describing how beautiful Russian women were, and how Russian men suffered the comparison. "You've got these girls with legs up to here that are so beautiful to look at."

But was it "Moscow?"

Here was the essential paradox of Moscow in the 2000s. So often you would hear someone look around, slack-jawed, at a bar, restaurant, club, office building, theatre, apartment complex and say, "This is so not Moscow," and mean it as a compliment.

The comment would at first elicit agreement: most of the expats in Moscow had already seen it all in Stockholm, Tokyo or São Paulo. But never before in Moscow.

A moment of reflection, though, provoked a re-think. The place you were admiring for being so-not-Moscow was, in fact, so-very-Moscow.

Moscow became a world-beating capital city. Rumours used to swirl regularly that Jennifer Lopez or someone similar was in town singing at a Russian bank's New Year's bash, or at an oligarch's birthday party. Only the border guards knew for sure; Moscow was a prolific producer of rumours and gossip.

A handful of chart-topping singers periodically did come to Moscow. They were paid millions of dollars to sing a few songs, at rates that turned out to be tens of thousands of dollars a minute.[10] The 2016 wedding of oil billionaire Mikhail Gutseriev's son drew a stable of performers, and more than a dose of sarcasm, to the event.

"It's not every day that Sting, Jennifer Lopez, Enrique Iglesias and Alla Pugacheva give concerts in a restaurant outside Moscow's

Third Transport Ring," the Russian website Gazeta.ru coughed.[11] Moscow's relevant world fell off a cliff outside the third beltway around the city, at least until you got to some of the wealthier suburbs. For die-hard Muscovites, the world ended outside the Garden Ring, a fairly tight belt around the very centre of Moscow.

Naomi Campbell and Elizabeth Hurley were known to periodically turn up in Moscow. Campbell even took up light housekeeping for a while with one of Russia's most prominent property developers—Vladislav Doronin. He is the only person known to have commissioned a private residence from the late architect Dame Zaha Hadid.[12]

Yes, there was the world-famous Bolshoi Theatre. Yes, there was the renowned Tretyakov Gallery—two of them, in fact. And of course there were the universities, the conservatories and the vast intellectual and cultural heritage. But none of those places served a decent mojito. At the Bolshoi, the dancing was on the stage, not on the tables.

Reality check

Anything and everything happened in Moscow, but it didn't happen everywhere or all the time.

Moscow is a vast city, Europe's largest by a substantial measure. But only the very centre of town and its better burbs were captured by a globe-trotting, truffle-munching jet-set. The real picture of Moscow included working-class families, an expanding but modest middle class, pensioners, students, internal migrants and workers from countries around Russia's periphery. The average city-wide salary for Moscow in 2000 was USD 125 per month. That number peaked in 2022 at USD 1,780 before starting to drop off in 2023.[13]

Moscow was internationally renowned for its excesses. But that tells you more about who was watching Moscow from afar than it does about what was happening on the ground.

Where to?

Before taxi apps became popular, hailing a freelance cab was one of the best ways to get around Moscow and followed a fixed ritual: Hold out your hand, wait for a car to pull up, open the passenger-side door, stick your head in and negotiate a fare as if you were working a hostage exchange.

Riding in a freelance taxi was like attending a theatre performance on wheels, but you never knew which play you'd bought a ticket to. You could have drivers who were off-duty government chauffeurs. They drove the monstrous, black Volgas and offered quick-witted, off-the-record political monologues better than the front page of any newspaper. You could get picked up by an off-duty ambulance. You could get picked up by just about anyone who wanted to make a few roubles or a couple of dollars. When the rouble was down, it was easy to feel like a Rockefeller. Fares were cheap, supply exceeded demand and you could name your price and destination.

You could smoke, most of the time.

Drivers from former Soviet republics offered insights into life in Russia without blond hair and blue eyes, and unspooled tales that pushed the boundaries of tolerance. Drivers would rail against any—no, every—ethnic group they didn't belong to. For expat passengers who were Russian speakers, these were immersion-style lessons in linguistic diplomacy or in how to ask to turn on the radio. When your accent gave you away, the roving performance of the day would be about your home country, your family and, of course, what taxis were like where you were from.

Seatbelt wearing was uniformly discouraged; fishing around for a buckle and a latch was a dead giveaway you were not from these parts. In the best of circumstances, there was a seatbelt, it worked and you could convince your driver that, well, you were the cautious sort. In the worst of circumstances, your driver would take offence at wearing a seatbelt, as if you were expressing doubt at his—ninety-nine times out of 100 it was a man—driving skills. Also ninety-nine times out of 100, the seatbelt was a very good idea. Freelance taxi drivers used to call their off-duty work "bombing," which roughly described how passengers were dropped off at the end of their journeys.

Lots of expats drove their own cars—or company cars—in Moscow; they were all insane. The only way to travel safely by car in central Moscow was to have a local driver who was crazy in the exact same way as everyone else on the road. Only a certain type of native-driver ESP prevented most crashes.

Expats, twenty-first-century style

Like their nineteenth-century predecessors, some expats were sent to Moscow under duress as part of a relocation strategy; they had little to say in the matter. These were a minority—you'd like to think that no company forces anyone to live anywhere. But it happened. "The people who went to Moscow because they were sent there for business and had no Russian, knew nothing about Russian history, they just lived in an expat world," former EBRD banker Nicolas Ollivant said. "Getting things done and going places was a huge challenge the whole time." Some expats went voluntarily but also failed to integrate.

Ollivant makes an important distinction among expats. Russia was full of expats who chose to live in Russia, because they were interested in the language, the history and the culture, on top of whatever their career or professional aspirations may have been. More than a few expats stayed long enough to move out of the expat phase.

"It's sort of a love–hate relationship, loving parts of Russian life and not loving other parts," Ollivant said. "Most of the expats were there not just because it was a good job, but because they were interested in being in Russia. It was a fascinating time to be there."

Moscow started to take on a high sheen in the aftermath of the 2011 and 2012 protests on Bolotnaya Square, protests that were unusual for their size, for their location in the centre of the capital and, perhaps most prominently, because they were protests of middle-class Muscovites. The people who came out on to the streets in the winter of 2011 and later in the spring of 2012 were not political activists. They were not labour union members. They were not senior citizens protesting pension reform. The protesters on Bolotnaya were Moscow's professionals—the kind of people who work in office buildings that have a Starbucks on the ground floor. They came to the protest well dressed and carrying late-model iPhones. Some of them were pushing prams. They came to protest a number of issues, but they were primarily catalysed by then-President Dmitry Medvedev announcing in 2011 after serving one term that Putin should return to the presidency. They were also motivated by the Duma elections in December of 2011, by the presidential elections in March 2012 and by Putin's inauguration in May that year.[14]

These were the individuals with whom Russia—and Putin—had made a compact. You stay out of politics, he told them, and I'll leave you alone, too. This was a deal struck most prominently with Russia's business elite, but it was meant to resonate nationally. I'll let you grow wealthy—across the economic classes—but don't even think about protesting.

The middle-class Muscovites who travelled frequently were forever comparing Russia to everywhere else, but held Western Europe in the highest esteem. Was Moscow's shopping as good as in Paris? Was the cultural scene as good as in London? Was the public transport as zippy as in Munich?

Moscow promised to make sure the answer to all those questions was "yes," in part because providing competent public services is what governments do but also because it was part of the social compact. The more time you spent marvelling at Moscow's new park benches and cycle-hire scheme, the less inclined you were to trample them in protest.

During prominent public holidays, and year-round on certain central thoroughfares, the city is decorated within an inch of its life. In the run-up to every New Year, the city sparkles with elaborate displays. Year-round, the capital is home to pedestrian zones with fanciful overhead lighting. The legitimately laudable Moscow metro has added dozens of new stations in recent years, many of them polished to a high sheen.[15] Residents and visitors alike looked at the city and marvelled.

There was, a greater cynic might argue, an inverse relationship between Moscow's appearance and the general state of Russia's economy and political system. One got better as the others worsened.

11

"WHO'S THE BOSS?"

*By the time you get to the end of the Yeltsin presidency, it was
not an unconsolidated democracy, it was an unconsolidated
autocracy. And Putin picked up those strands. I didn't think
that Russia was on the road to democracy, but I didn't
think that Russia was on the road to what we
have today, which is tragic beyond belief.*[1]

Geopolitics was bad, but business was good.[2]

Off to a good start

It all started so promisingly. Or at least it seemed that way.

Yeltsin resigned as president of the Russian Federation on
the last night of the outgoing millennium and appointed then-
Prime Minister Putin, in post for less than six months, as his
successor. Prior to that, Putin had served as the head of the
Federal Security Service (FSB), the successor organisation to the
Soviet KGB.

It was largely assumed that Yeltsin's inner circle, which
included his family members, their high-ranking spouses and

associated political and business hangers-on including a group of oligarchs, crowned Putin as a compromise-and-continuity candidate. He would clean up the country, but he wouldn't disrupt the vast network of vested interests the country's business elite had cultivated during the Yeltsin administration. At least that was the expectation. Putin installed an impressive line-up of top economic and political advisors to show he was serious about reform.

The start of the Putin presidency is an obvious inflection point in Russia's modern history. At its outset, though, it wasn't clear just how sharp an inflection point this moment was. In fact, early assumptions were that if anything, Putin would be a stabilising, reform-minded leader. The divergence between the early assumptions the business community made about Putin and the outcome of his record-setting term in office is what makes an exploration of his presidency so important to the story of international business in Russia.

The (in)famous question

At the very beginning of Putin's first term as president, US journalist Trudy Rubin addressed a panel of Russian officials at Davos and famously asked them, "Who is Mr Putin?" No one on the elite panel ventured a response.[3]

It took twenty-two years to get an answer.

It is more than slightly dumbfounding that over the decades of the Putin presidency, this complex yet elementary question remained the subject of high-profile and highly politicised conjecture that never really yielded a fixed or satisfactory answer. Russian politics is notoriously opaque, even to the closest of observers. But it was never encouraging to see the analytical community periodically revert to old school Sovietology to try to understand the man in the Kremlin.

Some people—Russians and expats—say they knew from Day One that Putin was Bad News. How could anyone who worked for the KGB be anything else? Others saw his ties to the Yeltsin clan as a fatal flaw. How could anyone associated with a group as corrupt as the Yeltsin family ever set the country straight? Others thought Putin grew into the person he is now: he is a different person and a different president than upon his appointment.

"I don't think people realised at that stage," Richard Prior, the business intelligence executive, said of the early Putin days. "The first Chechen War was really a shocking event in many ways," Prior said, referring to the 1994–6 invasion by the Russian army of the Chechen Republic, a part of the Russian Federation feared as a breakaway region and a threat to Moscow's supremacy. "And so the warning signs were there, but it was later that one realised that the security apparatus was something to fear, as much as the criminal apparatus that preceded it."

Security service background notwithstanding, Putin represented stability, which came as enormous relief in the wake of the Yeltsin era. His background was a source of reassurance—a law-and-order president who would crack down on the excesses of the '90s was long overdue.

"Let's just say that by the time Putin showed up, there were a lot of people who were like, 'This sucks, law and order is totally worth it, we'll give up some of these freedoms we have if people are not getting shot on the street,'" Harvard's Vacroux said.

Black belt; no shirt

Putin's devotion to judo and his tendency to periodically appear shirtless stood in stark contrast to Yeltsin's bulging belly and debauched condition. Putin would be an active, present head of state. Yeltsin's declining health debilitated his presidency; news he had suffered a heart attack between the two rounds of the 1996 election emerged only after he was returned to office following bypass surgery.

Yeltsin's episodes of public drunkenness were legendary. In 1994, following what must have been an exceedingly relaxing lunch with then-German Chancellor Helmut Kohl, Yeltsin grabbed the baton from a German police orchestra and started conducting. The same year, Yeltsin failed to leave his aircraft and meet the Irish prime minister during a stop in Shannon, Ireland. He was reportedly tired but believed to be drunk.[4] Yeltsin in 1995 was also reportedly found drunk in his underwear on the streets of Washington, DC trying to hail a cab in search of a pizza, according to a biography of US President Bill Clinton.[5]

Putin avoided alcohol. What a relief.

"There seemed to be a sort of moving in the right direction. There was a coherent president who was, let's say, sober all the time and appeared to be doing the right sort of thing," Ollivant, the former EBRD banker and business intelligence executive said. Putin became famous for his team's financial reforms, introducing a flat, 13 per cent income tax, a rate that started to fill state coffers. "Prior to that, nobody paid taxes. Out of the 145 million people in Russia, about 3 million paid income tax."

A "pro-Western leader"

During a visit to Berlin following the 9/11 attacks on the US, Putin addressed the German parliament in fluent German to periodic outbursts of applause. Many of his remarks addressed combatting terrorism and terrorist financing: he sought a more prominent role for Russia in the challenges facing Europe and the international community. Putin was developing a remarkably, some commentators would say suspiciously, close relationship with German Chancellor Gerhard Schroeder, but his visit to Berlin impressed the German legislature and the German public.

"Of course evil must be punished," Putin told a capacity audience in the Bundestag. "But we must also be aware that reprisals alone cannot replace a complete, focused and well-coordinated battle against terrorism. In that, I am in full agreement with the American President."[6]

Putin was reportedly the first international leader to express his condolences to then-US President George W. Bush immediately after 9/11 and went beyond that by offering to share intelligence and open Russian airspace to humanitarian relief flights.[7] Relations between the US and Russia were at a high point.

"In the early 2000s, Putin was a pro-Western leader by all accounts," Baker McKenzie's Melling said.

This was very much the prevailing wisdom at the time. It is a sign of just how distorted Russian politics had become at the end of the 1990s, however, that a leader who was the product of the Soviet security service and chosen by a cabal of his predecessor's close relatives and associated billionaires was seen as a law-and-order, pro-Western president.

Putin's appointment completely subverted the notion of the democratic process in Russia, such as it was. Rather than opening the presidency to a legitimate contest following Yeltsin's resignation, Russia's next president came pre-packaged. Russian voters made it official in March 2000, electing Putin president in the first round with 53 per cent of the vote, but the referendum conferred very little genuine legitimacy on the new Putin presidency. The international business community broadly welcomed the outcome.

Soviet elections never really pretended to be anything more than the ratification of a single-candidate slate. Russian elections in the wake of the Soviet collapse appeared, at least, to be competitive, multi-party exercises in democracy. In reality, they rarely were, particularly at the presidential level. Most of Russia's presidential elections, starting with the 1996 contest and even more so since, are thoroughly, elaborately and sometimes very clumsily rigged.

Ballot-stuffing during the presidential elections of 2018, for example, was caught on the CCTV cameras installed in precincts to deter ballot-stuffing.[8] That election returned Putin to office with 77 per cent of the vote. Subsequent elections aggressively minimised the participation of opposition candidates and thwarted grass-root candidate registration drives. The appearance of alternative candidates on the ballot usually comes with the Kremlin's blessing. Putin's 2024 re-election campaign returned him to office with 88 per cent of the vote.[9]

Companies that want to make long-term market plans crave stability and consistency; after a decade of anything but, Putin was a balm on everyone's nerves. As long as he stayed sober, healthy and in office, a lot of foreign investors didn't pay excessive attention to who Mr Putin was or, for that matter, what he did. This was years before companies were meant to have a public stance on politics. All the business community wanted was to know that the same guy would show up for work at the Kremlin every day.

Putin worked on the micro level: "Those of us who came in the '90s, we remember the chaos, the destruction, the banditry, and although the '90s were fun as hell for us, it was the Putin days in the 2000s that allowed us to build careers and build wealth for ourselves," said Joshua Tulgan, an investor relations and corporate finance executive with more than two decades of experience in Russia.

And, thanks to increasing oil prices, Putin also worked on the macro level: "Many watched the deterioration of Russia's once promising market economy with chagrin, yet economic growth returned, in large part because of higher oil prices but also in part because Putin's centralising reforms worked. They created an institutional structure to manage a new capitalist economy, albeit in a corrupt fashion and top-down manner. For most citizens of Russia, Putin's form of capitalism functioned well. Growth returned. Poverty rates fell," Penn's Mitchell Orenstein and Kristen Ghodsee wrote.[10]

A corrupt and top-down manner

Here's the thing: Putin was a law-and-order president, just not in the way that most fans of liberal democracy would describe it. The 1993 Yeltsin constitution, a topic of controversy when it was adopted, gave the Russian presidency wide-ranging power. Putin jumped into the role with great vigour.

Financial reforms aside, the early Putin years left two big, early marks on Russia and its business environment. First, Putin built a strict, top-down, "managed democracy," a contradiction in terms where democracy by its nature is meant to deliver authority from the bottom up.

Second, Putin re-inserted the state into the economy. The Putin presidency, long before the nationalisations and asset transfers following the start of the full-scale war, saw an incredible consolidation of state ownership, or at least state control, over Russia's most important industries. According to some estimates, by 2018, more than 50 per cent of Russian GDP was generated by state-owned enterprises.[11]

Putin joined a small but increasing group of authoritarian leaders around the world who showed that their countries could have market economies—even with the distorting role of the state—without a democracy.

By the time Putin had solidified his control over the country, lawyer and private equity executive Nielsen said, asset ownership in Russia came at the pleasure of the Kremlin, most pointedly in connection with large, oligarchic capital. Whatever you owned, and whatever your attitude to it, it could all go away at the stroke of a political pen.

Nielsen came to Russia from Houston in 1992 to open the Moscow office of Baker Botts, well known for its work in oil and gas. Since then, she has had a career that has spanned nearly every significant bend in the arc of international businesses' journey through Russia. Nielsen's career started, as it did with so many people who moved to Russia in the early 1990s, with an academic interest and a dash of happenstance.

"This was the reason I got to Moscow: I was in Houston, Texas. The Berlin Wall comes down. Russia adopts its joint venture law in November 1987. And every energy company in Houston wants to go to Russia and try to do a joint venture, right?" she said. "So, every lawyer in the firm is saying 'I'm not going,' and I had done Russian as a minor in college, and then had a tutor at Rice University who was a Russian woman. I kind of kept it up as a hobby."[12]

"So I jumped in. I'm a young partner with basically nothing to do at that point, because they didn't know what to do with the women," she said. "I'm looking for a *raison d'être*, and so I opened the Baker Botts office in 1992."

Nielsen went on to work for the Harvard project in Russia and helped to build the Russian equivalent of the US SEC; she basically wrote the book on Russian securities law. After that, she worked for a series of New York law firms, and by 2006 she was general counsel of Baring Vostok Capital Partners. Her work there gave her a nuanced appreciation of how Russian business worked. The participants in Baring Vostok's private equity deals, she said, were "all foreign institutional investors and North American, European, Middle Eastern institutional investors, who wanted a piece, just a little piece, please, of alternative investments in Russia."

"And you know, it was a magnificent time. I mean, we had internal rates of return of 20 and 30 per cent, much better than you could get anywhere else in the world," she said. Baring Vostok, at the time, invested in companies that had not been privatised; they were greenfield projects in sectors like media, financial services, healthcare and consumer goods.

Nielsen makes two critical distinctions about how investments in Russia worked at the time.

First, she pushes back against the notion, sometimes found in academic texts, sometimes found among the early commentariat, that big deals in Russia required permission from the Kremlin, both under Yeltsin and later Putin.

She told one of the more prominent members of that commentariat, "I've done twenty-five deals in Russia. I have yet to even think about going to the Presidential Administration or getting their approval for anything. We do USD 200 million deals all the time, and we're not required. Nobody cares."

"There were two entirely different, I used to say to people, economies, but definitely two different business worlds," she said. The dividing line between the two was not, however, the more traditional and widely accepted distinction between strategic and below-the-radar businesses. Instead, Nielsen saw the line as between privatised and non-privatised businesses. Baring Vostok fished in the latter pool, where the rules were different.

When it came to privatised industries, Nielsen comes to her second distinction about how Russian business worked.

"I think privatisation may have been a little bit of a misnomer for what happened," she said:

> If you were Western, you thought [privatisation] really meant ownership had changed and was yours. I think what happened when Putin came in and he told the oligarchs, "This is the way it's going to be," and he said to them, "You may keep your wealth. You may keep your companies, but get out of politics." I think all he was doing was re-instating the way it had always worked, which was the state owns everything, we allocate and get to decide from time to time who has the right to those cash flows, who can manage the company, and thereby get the cash flows, until we decide you can't.

Nielsen thinks the Russian business community understood this transaction. Westerners didn't.

"Westerners thought, 'Oh great. Now it's private property that we can enforce and will always be ours and no one can take it away,'" she said. "Wrong."

In 2004, former Prime Minister Gaidar gave a talk at his eponymous Gaidar Institute for Economic Policy where he was asked "what Mr Putin wants." After saying that the question was best posed to the president himself, Gaidar continued:

> I have a quite clear view on this. He's for a liberal economy, but he's very skeptical about democracy in Russia at the present stage. It doesn't mean that he's genuinely against democracy or that he's genuinely against democracy in Russia ever, but he doesn't think, from my point of view, that Russia needs a functioning democracy. Of course, democratic entourage, yes, but functioning democracy, when the people really decide, no.[13]

In their book on joint ventures in Russia, Henderson and Ferguson had an even more direct, yet nuanced, view: "Despite Putin's claim to have strengthened the Russian state, we argue that in reality, the institutions of state have been hollowed out and used as a front for the continuation of the informal practices seen in the 1990s, but under a different guise."[14]

Tulgan, the corporate finance executive in Russia, saw it all happen on the ground: "Russia has the rule of law, but the indeterminate, inconsistent application of the rule of law," he said.

Russia's middle class

Russia in the 2000s started to develop a robust, urban middle class. Russians were now working in successful, large, domestic companies and had solid management jobs in international companies. Russia's middle class had mortgages. They had a car, perhaps acquired with the help of a bank loan. They had Visa and Mastercards. They took package tours to Europe and elaborate, custom trips. It was no longer remarkable to sit next to Russians on a tour through Stellenbosch wine country or to hear Russian in a Buenos Aires café.

Certain economic and political developments are meant to accompany the emergence of a middle class. These are the individuals who, after all, are meant to be interested in growing, preserving and then passing on their wealth. And they are meant to support the development of an economic and political system that supports and protects those ambitions.

That never happened in Russia because the middle class bought the political trade-off. Have all the cars you want. Visit every wine-growing region you like. Grow your mining and metals companies big and strong. But do not voice a political opinion and do not attempt to influence the course of politics, whether you're a partner in an accounting firm or you own a platinum mine.

The social contract—get rich but don't complain—was only one of the brakes on the development of genuine democracy in Russia. Political scientist Bryn Rosenfeld, an assistant professor in the Department of Government at Cornell University, discusses this theme in her book *The Autocratic Middle Class: How State Dependency Reduces the Demand for Democracy*.

Rosenfeld, a specialist in Russia and other post-Soviet countries, writes that a middle class whose wealth is contingent on the public sector, rather than the private sector, is not a natural ally of democracy. In fact, in authoritarian states where the public sector controls a substantial part of the economy—Russia is an excellent example—the middle class can be more interested in preserving autocracy than in promoting democracy.[15]

This sort of social contract was likely an admission from the Kremlin that economic wealth can breed political rivals. It was also a very clear description of the Kremlin's comfort zone—as political monopolist. The message went out at a meeting of the oligarchs in the Kremlin on 28 July 2000, early in Putin's first term.[16]

The most important thing Putin said at that meeting was that he would not touch the results of the loans-for-shares privatisations of the 1990s, which had delivered the commanding heights of Russian industry into the oligarchs' hands. But by leaving the 1990s untouched, he hinted that the 2000s would involve a heavy state hand in everything else, which was still considerable. This included things like paying taxes.

"It was a really powerful message that Putin was sending— that you need to stay in your lane and let me do what I need," Gunitsky said. "As long as you do what I tell you to do, I won't bother you. That is when the rule of the '90s is officially done; when the oligarchs are officially done."

The missing pieces

Why and how did the development of a middle class—and a super-elite of astronomical wealth—fail to produce a legal system and business culture that was more transparent and better regulated? Dozens of conversations with Russia watchers and participants reveal dozens of suggestions.

One Russia observer in the US government, who asked that his name not be used, noted that throughout Russian history there were opportunities for market-based economic reform that never delivered.

"If you look at the broad sweep of Russian history, economic reform stimulates a sort of activity that the ruling elite begins to see as a threat," he said.[17]

Putin may have provided a certain amount of macroeconomic stability in the Russian economy, buoyed by the unslakable thirst for Russia's leading export, oil. He may have driven reforms to the tax code that the business community found helpful. While he was in the Kremlin, if not entirely because he was in the Kremlin, Russia became wealthier than ever before.

But Putin never helped diversify the Russian economy away from natural resources. Nor did he build an economy that provided opportunity for small and medium-sized businesses. These are the sorts of activities that might have brought forth rival power centres, or the decentralisation of economic power.

Perhaps even more importantly, Russia's elite abandoned the cause. What happened to the millionaires and billionaires who, presumably, wanted a safe, stable business environment that would allow them to keep their fortunes and pass them to their children, or to whomever else they wanted?

They found that environment somewhere else.

Russia's ultra-high and high-net-worth individuals didn't need to build a stable business environment in Russia. The parts of their businesses that needed protection by the rule of law moved to countries that already had it—the US, the UK, the EU and offshore jurisdictions that followed Western legal principles. Russian oligarchs and the other phenomenally wealthy business owners sought protection in armies of international lawyers, bankers, public relations agencies and professional service providers all over the world.

When and where they needed the rule of law, they had it. Outside Russia.

The parts of their business that remained in Russia were there precisely because there was no rule of law, or, as has been pointed out, there was the rule of law on paper, but it was selectively applied. And, as Russia's super-elite, they could guide that selectivity, within the rigid political control of Russia's business community. Yes, they had physical assets that couldn't be moved—platinum mines are not portable—but they made the very best of where they were.

Could the West have helped?

In light of the war in Ukraine, an old conversation has become newly fresh in circles outside Russia that the West could have done something—many things, perhaps—differently. The West could have forgiven Russia's Soviet debt and not held Russia to crippling repayments. NATO might have been a bit friendlier. Still other conversations revolve around the quantity and quality of Western financial assistance to the young Russian Federation of the 1990s.

Nielsen thinks the US missed its chance: "The US never came through with the sort of Marshall Plan analogy that serious thinkers thought would be required to really change Russia," she said. "I'm not so cynical that I think we did it in some sort of Machiavellian way to, you know, colonise Russia. But I think we, the US, were really chintzy in the amount of money and time and effort we spent."

"I think we always sort of treated them in a very condescending way," Nielsen said, "and I don't think anyone ever spent the time or the money to truly bring them into the fold."

Then again, bringing Russia into the fold might mean treating the country like an equal. It was easy to try to bring an Angola or a Ukraine into the fold, Nielsen said. But a powerful and successful Russia was a completely different matter in the eyes of the US.

"A big and powerful successful Russia would have been a threat," she said.

Nielsen acknowledges shades of nuance. The US may not have led a Marshall Plan to rescue Russia, but foreign governments dispensed billions of dollars in aid to Russia, some of which, Nielsen said, was treated by some Russian politicians like "largesse for them to hand out."

But even some of those same Russian politicians wanted Russia to work.

"I think there was a group that really hoped for a US-like, a European-like market and country," she said:

> And that just wasn't gonna happen. They had a moment in time about five years on under Yeltsin, in the chaos, to try to make it happen. And I think they were genuine about it. But there was way too much hangover from the Soviet system to make that radical kind of change.

"And I can remember Chubais saying, 'Well, we have to do privatisation while we can, while there's any kind of political will, and then market discipline will take over.'"

"Well, no," Nielsen said, "the Kremlin took over."

It all came so close to working.

They've come for ...

Starting about six months into his term, Putin raked through the business and political communities with a wave of investigations, accusations, arrests and other political pressure. *Kommersant*, one of Russia's leading business newspapers, for months ran story after story with headlines saying "They've Come For ..." and inserted the surname of an executive, a company or a government official. It was language redolent of the times when Stalin would cull the elite from the House on the Embankment. The pressure campaign was meant to bring big business to heel.

In part, it worked, though the oligarchs' individual and collective economic power still made them important players.

"Russia's business elite is growing in power and influence despite efforts by the President, Vladimir Putin, to curb the political ambitions of the oligarchs, *The Russia Index*, a leading guide to the movers and shakers in the world's largest country, suggests," *The Times* of London wrote in April 2004. "Business tycoons now account for the majority of the 50 powerbrokers named in the 2004 edition of the *Index*, a reflection of the increasing concentration of economic power among a small group."[18]

In a twist that just about defies logic, *The Times* argued that Khodorkovsky was one of the more influential men on that list. By this time, of course, he was in jail.

The Yukos affair

Khodorkovsky was arrested in October 2003 as his private jet set down for refuelling in Novosibirsk. Much has been written elsewhere about the Yukos affair, the nationalisation of a private oil company and the imprisonment of its CEO.[19] Seizing Yukos was not an evolution in the Russian business environment. It was revolutionary.

Initially, it was not clear quite how revolutionary the change was or would become.

Khodorkovsky's arrest and the Russian state's hostile clasp on Yukos drove a wave of panic through international company headquarters and their branches in Moscow. The move was an unmasking of Putin's attitudes toward business; Khodorkovsky was arrested and his energy business dismantled because he broke the "stay out of politics" deal.

Questions remained about how much more was yet to come, for Khodorkovsky and for everyone else, too.

Companies and investors were unsure whether Putin's move on Yukos was a domestic matter, or whether signals were being aimed at international investors, including the obvious but unintended signal to be extremely careful when choosing Russian business partners. Yukos had dozens of foreign partners of all sizes. Those companies were doing business with the Russian government now. For as long as the nationalisation of Yukos remained contentious, it thrust the company's business partners into a vast grey area.

The bigger questions were strategic in nature and more difficult to decode. Did Putin take aim at Yukos only because Khodorkovsky was becoming political? Did Putin take aim at Yukos because it was involved in talks with Exxon that could have led to foreign investment in a strategically important company? No one initially knew—no one still knows—the answers to all these questions.

A sort of misguided panic took root within the investor community and gave off a vibration that sounded like this: *Will my company be next?* The market initially had no way to understand where the limits of the Yukos affair ended. No one knew who should be nervous and who shouldn't. It was an unsettling, disruptive time. Everyone was talking about it.

Risk consultants, lawyers, auditors and management consultants did what they could to reassure their international clients that they or their Russian partners were not the next Yukos.

"What I told them is that if you're flying under the radar and not pissing anyone off, you're probably going to be fine," Reichert, the attorney formerly based in Moscow, said. "I can't guarantee anything, but you can't guarantee anything anywhere."

The other topic on the investment community's mind was Khodorkovsky himself. While at Yukos, he had become a corporate governance evangelist. Yukos had all the trappings of a well-governed company, including a slate of foreign directors, quarterly reporting to international financial standards and ownership disclosure statements. Yukos was one of the earliest, and biggest, companies to do exactly what all the corporate governance seminars had been preaching. On paper, Yukos looked in better shape than a lot of its international peers.

But despite its international listing and all the annual reporting, Yukos was very much Khodorkovsky's company. And its operations were still in a country where the rule of law was weak. There was, in the view of some, ample room for violations of corporate good behaviour, or, at the very least, investors in Yukos shares should have been on alert to that potential.[20]

As the adrenaline slowly drained from the business community, an uneasy consensus began to emerge. Yukos was attacked because its landmark status meant any deviation from national energy politics had to be quashed. From this, international executives and their bosses in headquarters began to understand that the greatest risk was attached to companies of strategic importance. Shampoo manufacturers everywhere heaved a sigh of relief.

But if shampoo was safely outside the realm of strategic sectors, what sort of company was strategic? Who and what was in that group and should continue to be nervous? The Russian government wanted to issue a clean line, Russian oligarchs wanted the Russian government to issue a clean line—and one that would keep foreigners out of their industrial holdings—and international business also wanted clarity about where they were and weren't wanted.

Prior to the Yukos disaster, foreign investment in Russian enterprises was largely uncontrolled. An audit by the Russian Accounts Chamber in 2004 showed that the State Antimonopoly Committee had never rejected requests from foreign—or foreign-controlled—entities to acquire controlling stakes in strategic enterprises.[21]

As Putin started to consolidate power, Russia increasingly started to restrict foreign investments. In 2004, the Russian government published a list of strategic enterprises,[22] preventing them from privatisation[23] and restricting foreign ownership to 25 per cent.[24]

In 2005, Putin asked the government to draft a law that would codify foreign companies' investments in defence- and security-related enterprises. It took three years for the law to move from Putin's request to submission to parliament and then to passage, as rival parties within the government and within industry fought their corners. Hardliners wanted international companies kept entirely out of certain sectors, including the energy sector. More liberal factions sought to ringfence only military-industrial enterprises.[25] The law was also discussed at the high-level Foreign Investment Advisory Council in Russia,[26] an indication of the level of concern the legislation generated.

In other cases, Putin allegedly took matters into his own hands. In 2005, he reportedly blocked Siemens' plan to increase its stake in Siloviye Mashiny ("Power Machines"), a massive industrial company that had contracts in the defence sector. More likely, Putin was said to be protecting Deripaska's bid for the company from outside competition.[27] In any case, Power Machines' status as a company with a large domestic military order book—and the lack of any guidance on foreign investment in strategic industries—was both a problem and a resolution in the proposed transaction with Siemens. The government denied the move on security grounds. A second Siemens bid to buy out a stake held by Potanin's Interros was denied in 2007.[28]

The final legislation on foreign investment in strategic sectors created a long list of industries where a foreign stake above certain limits—from a private or government investor—would require advance permission or notification after the fact or otherwise could be entirely banned. Emphasis, as expected, was heavy on the defence and energy sectors, but the list of dozens of fields of activities included broadcasting, the print media and fishing, among others.[29]

Liberal democracies and market economies all around the world restrict or control investment in strategically important sectors of their economies, even in what is meant to be a freewheeling private sector. And even in otherwise transparent markets, the screening of foreign investment into strategic sectors can be highly opaque. This was a common complaint against the

Committee on Foreign Investment in the United States (CFIUS) regime in the US, at least until legislation in 2018 toughened the CFIUS regime but made it more transparent.[30]

There was, however, a palpable shift in how the international business community started to view the complexion and character of the Russian economy.

The 2005 version of the *Russia Index* said it all. That year's equivalent of the *Who's Who* in Russia contained the following passage:

> Many of the new faces are politicians rather than business people, reflecting a swing in power back from business to the state, a result of events of the past year, such as further centralisation of power. Nevertheless, it would be foolish to draw any simple conclusions as to the long term impact of this change, as these new entries represent a variety of different ideologies, and include some of the youngest in the book.[31]

Keep calm and carry on

As Yukos travelled its tortuous path through the courts toward complete state absorption, everyone else recalibrated and moved on. Khodorkovsky was in jail, Yukos was in pieces and life went on. The goalposts had shifted, but for the time being, the international business community could find them again. Business as usual for the oligarchs was over. Business as usual for international companies became slightly less confusing.

The aftermath of Yukos's nationalisation sparked the sort of head-scratching that again revealed how slippery the reference points were for risk. What makes a strategic sector, and does that definition vary from country to country and, within a country, from administration to administration? In a business environment as opaque as Russia's, how does anyone even begin to understand the size and shape of the playing field?

There were also some uncomfortable, but potent, questions. Wasn't Khodorkovsky the Russian oligarch who discovered before everyone else that reputations can be laundered through painstaking PR campaigns or a series of well-placed and generous philanthropic gestures?

Did Khodorkovsky have it coming? Did his political ambitions and his overtures to the legislature break the unwritten rule about business keeping its nose out of politics? Were Khodorkovsky's claims to be a champion of transparency and corporate governance little more than the happy talk Western investors wanted to hear? Can you champion corporate governance while you're trying to sway parliament? Hadn't he benefitted from the loans-for-shares debacle?

These are inelegant questions, but they were widespread because it went directly to the issue about whether change in the Russian business environment was taking root or remained cosmetic.

"Some thought there a sort of karmic justice for Khodorkovsky," Stubbs, the international attorney formerly based in Moscow, said:

> I mean, you had this loans-for-shares scheme, where certain people got enormously wealthy, which was effectively wrongful to the Russian people to see all these assets taken off of the books of the government. And some wanted to see them go back on the books of the government so that the people would benefit from that.

For the avoidance of doubt: Khodorkovsky's singling out for a momentous and cruel prison sentence was itself unjust, corrupt and riddled with vengeance. But hadn't it been levied on a businessman who should have known where the red lines were?

If Khodorkovsky's embrace of corporate governance was only superficial—an empty gesture aimed at a Western audience—then a critical question dangled threateningly: how much confidence could the international business community place in the masses of less stellar Russian business partners who also claimed they were trying to clean up their acts?

Khodorkovsky disputes that he was ever an oligarch by the strict definition of the term, and that he ever had any political power in Russia. He was, instead, a wealthy businessman whose influence was limited entirely to the energy sector. The oligarchs, he insisted, were Putin's cronies, who genuinely combined phenomenal wealth and unassailable political power.[32]

And what did all this tell us about Putin? The Yukos debacle came relatively early in his presidency, when he seemed to be doing the right thing on the surface, without introducing—or maybe even wanting—any real, deep reform.

"There was substantial 'legal reform,' particularly to meet the needs of business and financial markets after the end of the Soviet Union and as modern Russia developed," senior legal professional Robert Starr said. "But it never became a system governed by the rule of law as we understand the term ... the Khodorkovsky case demonstrated that."

It was mind-bending. Putin cracked down on the poster child for corporate governance. He accused him of cheating on his taxes by applying tax laws on Yukos in ways they were never meant to be applied.

"From a legal standpoint, it was disturbing," Stubbs said of Yukos:

> And then you live in a state of cognitive dissonance where you have this one very disturbing event that you've seen happen to a taxpayer, which is inconsistent with the way the tax code is actually written and interpreted, and inconsistent with creating a rule of law and predictability for investors.

"And then you think, 'Well, Holy F,' right?" Stubbs added. He called the Yukos decision, which was based on tax law, "just off the wall. They came up with this concept specifically to nail Khodorkovsky with it, and on that basis, to create basis for a fraudulent bankruptcy in which to steal Yukos's and its investors' assets."

For Stubbs, the way forward was to continue to advise clients and to stay close to them. He felt it was his role to "open investors' eyes to the fact that there is some element of unpredictability within the system," he said.

International companies would have to hold several thoughts in their head at the same time. The system was unstable. A wary posture was in order. And maybe Khodorkovsky stuck his neck out too far. Finally, perhaps, as with every market and every transaction, there is at least a small leap of faith: "We would tell clients, hopefully, it's a one-off event, but this cannot be guaranteed," Stubbs said.

Foreign investors with a decent appetite for risk were able to hold all these thoughts in their head at the same time and still get business done.

"Some Western companies were very, very capable of accommodating bad things. This was very much in their expectations," Prior, formerly of Kroll, said. "They expected the worst, they were dazzled by the opportunity, they were able to accommodate some quite disturbing things."

Russian partners, after all, knew everything.

"In many cases, they knew not just where the bodies were buried, but how they got there in the first place," Prior said.

Firestone, formerly of the US embassy in Moscow and a lawyer in private practice, concurs.

"Yukos was the beginning of the end for liberal Russia," Firestone said. "The state is always more powerful than the private sector and that's what makes Russia Russia and not the UK."

Some Western investors were less sensitive to the corruption and broader political environment. Businesses can sometimes make a lot of money in authoritarian countries. But that carries an elevated level of risk.

"They recalibrated after Yukos," Firestone said. Companies adjusted their risk appetite and moved on.

"The lure of business opportunities, particularly in the energy sector, led Western oil companies to take big risks, perhaps because they felt they couldn't afford not to," Starr said.

Russian FDI statistics show a minor dip from 2004 to 2005 before resuming robust growth up to the global financial crisis in 2008.[33] Whatever post-Yukos dip there might have been, it's difficult to show that it had anything to do with Yukos or the energy sector. Business shrugged and moved on.

"What it comes down to at the end of the day, I always told people, like anything, it's all a question of risk appetite," former Moscow attorney Reichert said.

While this was happening, the Western business press was busy praising the Russian business environment for becoming, well, normal:

> But since Vladimir Putin was elected president in 2000, the business environment has gradually become more normal. The oligarchs whose companies are still afloat have shown that they can run businesses, not just assemble assets—or they have hired professional managers. Virtually all publicly listed companies have adopted international accounting standards, enabling investors to track once-amorphous cash flows. Violence has all but disappeared from big business; competing oil or metals barons now take their disputes to court. Imported Western executives and a new generation of Western-trained Russians have dramatically improved senior managements, even as top-flight talent remains scarce lower down.[34]

But wait. In this article lauding Russia's most admired managers, *Institutional Investor* reminds its readers that "[t]o be sure, the Russian business landscape still resembles an untamed frontier," and

[g]raft and corruption are commonplace. Russia tied with Mozambique for 86th place out of 133 countries ranked in Transparency International's corruption perceptions index for 2003. The line between organized crime, which runs its own shadow economy, and the legion of small businesses that deal only in cash to avoid taxes remains blurry. Confidence in the financial system is so shaky that the Central Bank's shutdown of a tiny bank accused of money laundering in May set off a depositors' panic that threatened the biggest privately owned commercial institution, Alfa Bank, whose president, Pyotr Aven, was picked by investors as best in Financial Services.[35]

How carefully does a logical reader have to parse this message? Russian business leaders perform to global standards, yet when it comes to corruption, Russia feels like Mozambique. Russian managers now pay salaries on time and have brought juice boxes and mobile phones to Russia, but they're doing this in a place where a minor regulatory activity triggers mass panic. It's almost as if Russia, as a large, emerging market, is being held to a standard that is at once complimentary and hypercritical. It's a story of "look how far this place has come in such a short time" combined with "it's difficult to describe how much further there is to go."

The arc begins to bend

Things changed for investment banker Sucher around 2007. He was reading the front page of *Vedomosti*, one of Russia's leading business newspapers, and saw that a state holding company called Russian Technologies had been formed by presidential order and was going to be run by someone Sucher had never heard of. At the time, Sucher was working at Alfa Capital with some of the most powerful people in Russian business. They were supposed to know everyone.

"I was completely blindsided. We're complaining about privatisation slowing and the bad signals coming because of the fucking thing at Yukos, and what is this? This isn't privatisation, this is deprivation," Sucher said. "The fucking KGB is going to be running 600 companies. Where did this come from? I was flabbergasted."

"The needle had already punctured the balloon and I was becoming increasingly concerned about the risks and I stopped being a prominent member of the 'rah-rah chorus,'" he said. "I was growing concerned about what was happening politically and how that was going to affect the economy and investments."

Sucher put his head down and got on with his job:

> That was perfect. I didn't have to put my heart out there and pretend that I was thinking that everything in the future was going to be great. I had a job, and the job was to build the local financial infrastructure of an international investment bank, and I still believe very much in building more local infrastructure for finance. And on top of it I was being paid more money than anyone had ever paid me before, and no one was really asking me whether I thought this was a good investment or not. I was just there to do a job. And as a result, I had a lot of fun.

Russian business carried on, too. Russia used the advantage available to many developing economies. It took well-tested best practice from everywhere else, added a bit of Russian ingenuity and made it work at home. Russians and expats both liked to extol how easy certain things were in Russia. Routine interactions with the government, with banks, with utilities were streamlined to a few clicks. As long as you were, say, under fifty years old, Russia was a country of early adopters. Russians hoovered up technology solutions as quickly as their fingers would let them tap their credit cards.

"Apple Pay in Russia was number two, globally," Tulgan said. In 2020, *Vedomosti* trumpeted the app's success in Russia.[36] "I believe that what we built in Moscow—'we' as a very expansive term—will one day be the halcyon days for everyone."

"What is unique about Russia and its capital markets—you have local IPOs, you have rouble debt. Those of us living there had really ambitious ideas of Russia, and the EU, and Moscow as a capital centre of countries from Central Asia who couldn't make the grade in London or Amsterdam. We had all the ideas," Tulgan said. "What we were building in Moscow was as good as anywhere else. The sophistication was something of which we were really proud. Things you don't see in China, in Saudi, etc."

And again, from one of Russia's most experienced investors, Michael Calvey:

> They lacked a lot of the infrastructure that affects grassroots type of business and small businesses and entrepreneurial activity. And it takes time to develop those. But I think that if you look at Russia say, five years ago, it still had a vibrant entrepreneurial community with people, managers of businesses and entrepreneurs who understood value creation in the same way that talented entrepreneurs in the United States or Israel or India or China do. Businesses with unbeatable value propositions for customers with great brands and sustainable potential to grow and make money so that all of the stakeholders are happy about it.

The Americans were bullish on Russia.

"We made great progress, because the Russians considered American and foreign business to be a good thing, foreign investment to be a good thing, as long as we minded the line between business and politics," said Robert Courtney, a founding board member of the American Chamber of Commerce in Russia. "That line got much more tightly drawn the further we got into the Putin administration."[37] Courtney came to Moscow in 1992 to run the American Medical Center, the clinic in Moscow that delivered services to a US standard and made expats—and later Russians—feel all the more comfortable just for its presence.

Crimea

The events in Kyiv in 2014 that ousted President Viktor Yanukovych following his refusal to sign an association agreement with the EU triggered a landmark moment in Russia's evolution in the international community: the invasion and annexation of Crimea.

The Crimean Peninsula, jutting into the Black Sea from Ukraine's southern coast, is a historically popular summer destination for generations of Russian and Soviet families. It is also the traditional homeland to the Crimean Tatars, a people whom Stalin deported to the Uzbek Soviet Republic during the Second World War. In 1954, Nikita Khrushchev moved Crimea from the Russian Soviet republic to the Ukrainian republic by decree.

Crimea is not just home to millions of childhood memories of hot, seaside summers. It is also home to the Russian Navy's Black Sea fleet. The protests in Kyiv in 2014 and Yanukovych's eviction from power brought a level of instability and threat to the peninsula's status that Putin could not tolerate. Putin infamously sent in a battalion of "little green men"—so called because they wore army fatigue-coloured clothes without any markings or signs of affiliation—to start the takeover of the region, and then he sent the army. A laughable referendum put a comic semblance of legitimacy on Crimea's return to Russia.

World leaders watched in disbelief; sanctions followed, and a peace process began, even as Russian proxies both in Ukraine and from across the border in Russia assaulted the Donetsk and Luhansk regions in Eastern Ukraine.

For a part of the international business community, the annexation of Crimea—and the sanctions that followed it—was another beginning of the end. Russia was an aggressor state that had hacked away a strategic chunk of Ukraine's Black Sea coast and was waging war in Eastern Ukraine behind the thinnest of denials.

The rest of the business community carried on mostly as if nothing had happened. The strictest interpretation went like this: the sanctions related to Russia's annexation of Crimea were tightly drawn and restricted in scope, as sanctions are meant to be. As a result, the sanctions barely grazed big international businesses; few of them had interests in Crimea. Most Americans wouldn't be able to find Donetsk or Luhansk on a map; the casualties in the conflict were anonymous. The US embassy in Moscow shrank, as did the Russian embassy in DC. The business of diplomacy became difficult.

Geopolitically, Crimea was small. Commercially, Russia was still massive.

"The Russian market became one of the largest in Europe, and in some positions still is, that's why they didn't want to leave after Crimea," former recruitment executive Vorobyev said of international businesses. For some sectors, he said Russia "was their largest business in Europe."

For Evgenev, formerly of Alvarez & Marsal in Moscow, Crimea was the thin end of a wedge that promised increasingly severe consequences:

> For me, the junction point is that Russia took over Ukrainian territory. And that creates a situation in which no country has a way to go back. No Ukrainian president will ever admit to Crimea being Russia. No Russian president will ever admit to Crimea being Ukrainian. So, you know, this is a situation that has no solution.

For Anton Shingarev, who was working for Russian anti-virus software provider Kaspersky at the time, Crimea was a big deal for him and his business.

"It changed after Crimea," he said. "We started experiencing reputational problems and questions. And in the beginning, we thought 'Come on, it's gonna pass.' But then it was really painful."

Shingarev said that Kaspersky's US- and UK-based business partners were deeply disturbed by what was happening in Crimea. German and French partners, he said, remained stable.

"Relative to what has happened since, Crimea was a blip," Shingarev said. "It's changed now. Back then it was fine. And politics came and balkanised the world, the IT world," he said.

When Crimea happened, Reichert was at a law firm in Moscow whose management committee was already nervous about remaining in Russia.

"They just said, 'You know, we're done,'" Reichert recalls from behind a new desk in a new city. He looked out the window at a polyglot megapolis of gleaming skyscrapers, thought of Moscow and sighed: "You know, when I look out my window at Dubai," he said, "it was supposed to become this."

Expats drained from Russia. The number of Germans— traditionally one of the largest expat populations in Russia— dropped by more than 50 per cent, from 350,000 in January 2014 to 112,000 in December of the same year. US citizens, too, saw their numbers thin substantially, from 221,000 to 48,000. The British population plummeted. At the beginning of 2014, there were 179,000 UK citizens in Russia. By the end of the year, 29,000 remained, according to Russia's Federal Migration Service.[38] From 2012 to 2013, FDI had been on an upward trend in Russia; between 2013 and 2014 and through to 2015, FDI dropped sharply.[39]

Sanctions associated with the illegal annexation of Crimea triggered an economic slump and tragicomic countermeasures from Russia: the country banned agricultural imports—but not booze—from countries that imposed Crimea-related sanctions. Russia experienced its first critical shortage of Parmesan cheese, which quickly became the hot item shoved into Moscow-bound suitcases, like dollar bills had been in the 1990s. Import replacement became a bit of a joke as Russia attempted to make its own Brie. Eventually, a lot of the goods banned by Russian sanctions against the EU found their way into Russia via Belarus. Russia's neighbour was not under sanctions, and there was no customs border between the two countries.

Baseball, hot dogs and a disconnect

The American Chamber of Commerce, like all international chambers of commerce, was a membership association with a broad mission. It was a community of businesspeople with common concerns, in some cases common backgrounds and, in most cases, common goals. It was a social network. It supported charities. And it represented the US business community to the Russian government when the government was proposing legislation or regulations that could harm US business interests.

Following Crimea, the US government became one of the US business community's biggest problems.

"My directors come to me and say, 'Look, at our board meetings, we have representatives of the US embassy. They come, they sit, they listen and they take notes. We talk about things that are going on in our lives, and then they go back and use them to create sanctions against us," former chamber CEO Rodzianko said, recalling that conversation. "They were out to get Russia, and sanctions were the weapon of choice."

So Rodzianko agreed not to invite an embassy representative to the chamber's next strategy session. The move triggered an outburst from the US ambassador that Rodzianko remembers to this day.

"It was a very heavy meeting," he said. But after a heated exchange, the air was cleared. "That's a curious thing. I mean, you would have thought that the relationship should be more symbiotic."

The AmCham also lobbied the Russian government hard to help secure Calvey's release from prison. Calvey, a US citizen who grew up in Oklahoma, started working in Russia in the 1990s and left an acceptance to Harvard Business School on the table when he moved to Moscow to work, initially for the EBRD.

Baring Vostok

Calvey, the founding partner of Baring Vostok Capital Partners, was arrested on fraud charges in February 2019 and held for two months in pre-trial detention. Calvey was one of the international investment community's most successful, prominent and longest-running investors in Russia. He had a pristine reputation built on decades of experience. Baring Vostok was an early investor in Yandex, the Russian online powerhouse; its exit from the company reportedly earned Baring Vostok billions of dollars.[40]

The Russian security services accused Calvey and a small group of other individuals of "conspiring to defraud Vostochny Bank, a Baring-owned top-30 lender" specialising in Russia's far east. The *Financial Times* reported that the sum of the alleged fraud was USD 37.7 million. Some of Russia's most respected business figures publicly defended Calvey in a story that made national headlines in Russia and was discussed among its most powerful politicians.

Baring Vostok and other market participants said the company was being targeted as part of a business dispute with Vostochny Bank and among broader efforts to eliminate foreign investors from the Russian business landscape. An unnamed source close to the situation at the time told the *FT*: "This is transformative. This kills FDI stone dead forever ... This sends the message, can you use the security services against your business rivals over a few million dollars? Yes, you can."[41]

Baring Vostok by that time was managing funds invested by some of the world's highest-profile investors, including the EBRD and CalPERS, the California state employees' pension fund. Calvey is widely regarded as a careful, smart investor. He was not an expat; Russia was home. He and his company stayed in Russia through all the economic, political and geopolitical events the country served up.

According to an editorial in the *FT*, Calvey avoided investing in sensitive sectors and steered clear of controversy. His case was part of the ongoing abuse of the legal system by commercial rivals and a hardening of Putin's attitude toward foreign investment.[42] Russia's image as a destination for foreign investment was worsening after Crimea; Calvey's arrest was a severely damaging blow to the country's international image. Putin backed the case against Calvey and was said to have taken personal control over its disposition.[43]

Calvey had been a staple at the St Petersburg International Economic Forum and had registered to attend the 2019 conference prior to his arrest. After being transferred from detention to house arrest, he asked to attend the conference but in the end did not. In his absence, he was one of the significantly diminished forum's main topics of discussion.[44] His case continued to deliver blows to Russia's reputation: the conditions of Calvey's arrest complicated cancer surgery he underwent at a clinic where Baring Vostok was an investor.[45]

According to the *FT*, Baring Vostok settled the corporate dispute that Calvey had said was at the core of the criminal case against him. The charges against him were reduced; the terms of his house arrest were relaxed. In August of 2021, the Russian courts found Calvey guilty of embezzlement but handed him a suspended sentence, a sign the charges largely came to nothing. Calvey left Russia; the damage to the country's reputation remained.

Calvey asked not to discuss the case, adding only that he and his funds had taken the decision to exit Russia completely. The transactions finalising Baring Vostok's exit from Russia completed in the first half of 2024.[46]

Back to the peninsula

The annexation of Crimea froze the EBRD's growth in Russia. "We then ourselves helped to put the nail in the coffin," former EBRD political advisor Oksana Antonenko said. In the wake of the full-scale invasion, the EBRD "decided to suspend access to the Bank's resources by Russia," and closed its Moscow office.[47]

Stubbs looks at Crimea within a longer narrative.

Russia, he said, "was a pretty good brand. Moscow was like the hottest city in the world. Best place to live in the world, even post-Crimea." The post-annexation period featured celebrations from people who called themselves *Krym Nash* (Crimea Is Ours), but even that died down after a while. "At least up until 2022, Russia did really well. After the [2008] financial crisis, it came right back up."

For other companies, business continued almost as normal, including the annual ritual of ratcheting up targets and key performance indicators. Cescotti, the German executive, said that the messages coming from headquarters were conflicting: Russia, bad. Business in Russia, good:

> The temperature was rising after Crimea. It slowly went up and many said "Oh yes, corporate headquarters was wagging their fingers, this is bad what is being done with Crimea, but nevertheless we think you have the potential to increase the sales forecast for next year another 5 to 10 per cent. You could also squeeze out another nice percentage of EBIT [a financial performance measure]," this kind of absolute lack of integrity saying "it's not good, it's not nice, but business is good. We don't like what Russia is doing, but business is good, so let's increase our business."

The language was fairly clear-cut: "We know this isn't right, but we'll follow the sanctions and let's move on," Cescotti said. "It's about business in Russia. It's about really good business in Russia."

So most companies did what they could to avoid sanctions—more due diligence, more monitoring, more legal advice—and carried on. If they steered clear of sanctions and could prove it to their regulators, there was no other business reason to leave Russia. Most companies had very little business in or with Crimea, so the trade-off was relatively simple.

"We were fully compliant with sanction legislation—nothing going to Crimea or Donbas, Lugansk or Donetsk," Cescotti said. "No impact on our business. We were fully compliant."

Red lines

Companies draw their red lines individually. For some, those lines are thick, solid and bright. For others, they are thin, flexible and pale. Some companies aren't sure where to put red lines, or whether they should have them at all. Still other companies have them only when it's too late.

Most customers, shareholders and broader stakeholders in international businesses didn't consider the Crimea incident to be significant. Crimea used to belong to Russia. Russians liked it. It was populated with ethnic Russians and Russian speakers. At the end of the day, it was sort of like Russia's invasion of Georgia in 2008. Bad, but not bad enough.

Not too far beneath the surface, though, in certain quarters Crimea was bringing fairly heavy heat on the international presence in Russia.

"I think there was an inflection point, post-Crimea," said Prior, who by then had left Kroll to open a risk consultancy in the UK:

It wasn't a total withdrawal from the servicing of oligarchic needs, but I do remember, for the first time—to my surprise—big law firms were saying "We're not getting involved," because there was tremendous pressure from government sources here, in this country, and I guess in the US as well.

Those voices, Prior said, were telling the business and professional services communities, "'You're servicing the interests of aggression by providing legal services and other professional services to Russian-owned businesses. That started in the aftermath of Crimea.'"

That pressure seemed to have limited results. In 2017, Russia's EN+—a major, oligarch-controlled energy company—listed on the London Stock Exchange.

"We continued to welcome them," former ambassador to Belarus Gould-Davies said of the EN+ 2017 listing. "We're still welcoming huge sums of Russian money without any significant reform of domestic regulatory arrangements, just jumping into the City of London, into London property markets and into our overseas territories as well." Recall Paul Ostling of EY's comments about dinner at the UK ambassador's residence around the time of Crimea's annexation and the call for Russian companies to list in London.

On an even deeper level, this was another mark on a spectrum of behaviour that had its roots in the previous decade. The Russian business climate had just added a new element of caution, much in the same way that the Yukos episode set executive teeth on edge. But perhaps in the exact same fashion, business recalibrated and moved on.

In 2006, Russia deployed a radioactive toxin in a foreign country to poison and kill Litvinenko, a Kremlin critic living in London. In 2018, Putin used a nerve agent to try to kill Sergei Skripal and his daughter Yulia, this time in Salisbury, England.

"Putin's Russia had a risk appetite to do things that, frankly, it was hard to believe, including the use of a nerve agent on the

UK's homeland," Jeremy Fleming, the then-departing head of Britain's GCHQ told the *Financial Times* in 2023.[48]

Much as some people thought that the West should have given Russia an even warmer embrace in the early 1990s, some think that come the 2000s, it was time to turn that embrace into a choke hold.

The Atlantic Council's Brian O'Toole said that instead of the huge emphasis on sanctions in the wake of the annexation of Crimea, the US could have gone after some of the oligarchic money that facilitated Putin's ascent in the first place.

"If we had gone after that money in, you know, 1999 to 2002, what would Putin's power base have been, then? Would it have been more fractured and fractious?" O'Toole asks. "Would he have been able to hold on to power in the same way, by bribing people, by taking Khodorkovsky's company, as dirty as Khodorkovsky's company may or may not have been?"

O'Toole knows he has the luxury of time and perspective.

"I think these are somewhat navel-gazing questions, because hindsight is 20/20, but I feel like we would have had a better chance then of stopping his kind of pure consolidation of power in Russia," O'Toole said.

"It was entirely sensible"

In a 2023 interview with Times Radio in the UK, former UK Prime Minister Tony Blair looked back at his, and the international community's, relationship with Putin and said it all made sense at the time.

"It was entirely sensible to try to pull Russia towards us," he said. "Putin used to turn up to NATO meetings, as did Yeltsin before him. I don't think we were wrong to try to bind Russia into the world order." Blair, for context, said that the West's efforts to embrace Russia undermine Putin's argument that he authorised the full invasion of Ukraine in February 2022 because the West was trying to isolate Russia.

That said, the relationship between Russia and the West, Blair said, began to sour around 2008, when in Blair's words Putin started to give up on economic reform. He had actually started to give up on economic reform much earlier.

"When I first knew him, you would have thought there was a possibility of Russia operating in reasonable cooperation with the West."[49]

First impressions can be misleading.

12

THAT TIME COMPLIANCE WAS SEXY

For the average Russian businessman, the rule of law was whatever you could get away with. If I can get away with it, I'll do it, and if I can't, I won't.[1]

There is such a wide variety in how well people go into emerging economies. There are people who go in just as stupid as can be, and there are people who go in really well.[2]

The kleptocracy

It all got so much more difficult when the gangsters started wearing good suits.

Putin's crackdown on the rampant criminality of the 1990s and the return of the state to a central role in the economy brought gangsterism "in house." The main source of corruption and the more polite form of gangsterism was, in the end, the Russian government. The government had not quite monopolised criminality in Russia, but it had certainly harnessed it. The corruption that remained in the private sector usually had the blessing, or the patronage, of the state.

"When I started at the CIA, a lot of the talk was about Russian organised crime," O'Toole said. "When I left in 2008, there wasn't Russian organised crime, there was just the state."

The nationalisation of criminality and corruption made them both harder to detect. And precisely when these two issues became less visible to the naked eye, regulators all over the world were asking Western companies to work harder and harder to find them. The tension between these two trends merits discussion because compliance became something close to religion in the 2000s.

Not everyone attended church with the same level of zeal.

Just as companies in the 1990s created job titles like "vice president of emerging markets," in the 2000s they were creating job titles like "chief compliance officer." Professional services companies, too, grew exponentially to support companies' efforts to meet increasingly onerous and complex regulations.

Even under law-and-order Putin, doing business in Russia remained far from straightforward. Russia remained, Melling said, in

> the legal equivalent of the Twilight Zone, where you could find yourself in a position where nothing was working as it should, where everything was going wrong, and you're getting hassled and you don't know why, and there's nowhere to turn. There was always that possibility right the way through, including under Putin, but more so under Yeltsin.

Most expat executives could name their number one concern in one word.

"Transparency," said Laurie Fry, a senior finance executive in Russia for one of the world's largest brewing companies.[3] Any business in Russia—any globalised business, really—involves a complex network of counterparties at the best of times. Developing some level of comfort about how those companies behaved was an ongoing challenge.

It spanned almost every sector imaginable.

"The biggest challenge was opacity," said the CFO of an international property company who asked to remain nameless. His business naturally enough depended on access to land, and this executive said he was never sure if offers from potential Russian partners were too good to be true:

> You could go and have a meeting with some of these people, many of whom would be connected to the mayor's office or had been connected to the mayor's office, and you would have no confidence whatsoever that what you were being told was the truth and no confidence whatsoever about the provenance of what they're offering you.[4]

Doing business in an opaque commercial and legal environment was like throwing darts blindfolded. Foreign executives had to work a lot harder in Russia to try to establish the level of comfort they required about whom they were doing business with and how their Russian partners conducted their affairs. Transgressions carried the risk of an expensive, reputation-crushing regulatory headache at home. Handling criminal capital or coming too close to political relationships were bright red flags to regulators, most vigilantly in the US.

Money laundering's motherlode

Everyone knew that Russia's economy existed partly in Russia, partly in Switzerland, partly in the UK and partly in a cloud of cash that was constantly moving from country to country and bank to bank. But the event that placed the complex, opaque and sometimes criminal web of international finance into common parlance is commonly referred to as "the Bank of New York scandal."

This story—*The New York Times* broke it in 1999—put BNY and a small group of its senior employees at the centre of a network that brought billions of dollars out of Russia and into the US banking system via accounts housed at BNY. The case brought criminal charges against, and a guilty plea from, a senior bank employee and her husband, who managed the accounts that processed the massive extraction of cash from Russia.[5]

The story dominated business coverage for a while in the late 1990s and early 2000s, as the case wound its way through the financial community, an extensive international law enforcement investigation and the courts. It was an important case not only because of its size—newspaper accounts said that initially USD 4.2 billion and then as much as USD 7.5 billion flowed through BNY accounts.[6] The BNY case was important for other reasons, too.

First, the story was presented as a scheme that laundered funds associated with Russian organised crime. In other words, BNY was accused of helping to disguise the origins of money tied to criminal activities. Money laundering is a loud phrase but describes practices that make the proceeds of crime look legitimate.

Second, among the individuals initially suspected of wrongdoing were two Russian émigrés living in the US. This drew attention to the potentially pernicious involvement of individuals outside Russia in illegal activity based inside Russia. One of the BNY executives, in fact, was married to a Moscow resident who was once a high-ranking government official and later a senior executive in Russian banking. These two individuals were not charged with crimes. Third was the use of offshore accounts whose ownership was disguised.

Finally, though, a more thorough examination of the entire episode painted a more pixilated picture of how financial flows from Russia worked. Indeed, some of the money flowing through BNY was traced to criminal origins and specific criminal individuals. Some of the money, however, was transferred "to evade Russian taxes on legitimate business transactions" and "to avoid Russian customs duties on imports."[7]

None of the characters in this story, including BNY—which paid penalties and compensation but was never prosecuted—came out looking very good.[8] The almost instant legacy of the story, however, was to have put the international financial, corporate and law enforcement community on alert about what was happening, on an industrial scale, in the movement of funds out of Russia.

This was the beginning of a story about topics that are now common in the banking and broader business communities—concepts like the Suspicious Activity Report (SAR), the Know Your Client (KYC) checks, the "client onboarding process" and other processes broadly referred to as Anti-Money Laundering (AML) and Anti-Bribery and Corruption (ABC) checks and the now popular Politically Exposed Person (PEP) checks. Combined, these acronyms are designed to ensure that companies are not doing business with individuals or other companies that present an elevated level of exposure to criminal activity and corruption. To at least some degree, we have the BNY scandal to thank for these elements of regulatory rigour.

What the regulators wanted

What did regulators want? More and more, if you ask the companies they regulate. Mostly, regulators wanted to know that companies were not paying or receiving bribes, kickbacks or facilitation payments—a term for cash used to speed up otherwise routine processes—or participating in money laundering schemes. Checking for PEPs was meant to identify and exclude government or political officials with the sort of roles and influence that made them susceptible to bribery.

The US FCPA was the most feared law in the land. Prosecution over the years has fluctuated, but the act has been significantly more actively deployed in the years following 2001.[9]

Fines were levied in 2016 and 2020 that totalled in the billions of dollars. The US DoJ and the SEC are the two US agencies that enforce the FCPA.

On paper at least, the 2010 UK Bribery Act is similar to the US FCPA, but it also punishes companies that fail to prevent bribery. Transparency International, however, says the UK has dropped out of the countries actively investigating and prosecuting corruption. Of the world's forty-seven largest exporting nations, Transparency International in 2022 suggested that only two countries were actively chasing down corruption.[10]

Most regulators, including those enforcing the FCPA, also asked US companies not only to avoid corruption in their own ranks but also to ensure their business partners up and down the supply and distribution chains were also free of corruption. Sanctions law broadly mimics these requirements—US sanctions require that companies conduct enough due diligence to ensure they are not doing business with a sanctioned entity anywhere in their network of business activities.

More than anything else, regulators wanted to know that companies were taking corruption seriously. There are numerous examples of companies that, if a violation was found, were treated leniently by their regulators if they had a strong and auditable anti-corruption programme across their company. If someone went rogue and paid a bribe, it was just that—an abnormality. If you have ever had to take an online, anti-corruption training course at your company, now you know why. Companies that failed to introduce rigorous and systemic anti-corruption programmes were treated more harshly for failing to take corruption seriously.

The emphasis on US regulation here is not accidental. Lots of countries—including Russia—have anti-bribery rules, conventions or frameworks. Forty-six countries are signatories to the OECD

Anti-Bribery Convention.[11] But the US anti-corruption law has nearly global relevance and wide extraterritorial application.

Russian companies have traditionally been almost genetically opaque. They are structured primarily for tax efficiency and to shield their beneficial owners from regulatory pursuit. Tax-efficient structures are not a crime: most companies do what they can to pay as little tax as legally possible. There is a difference, though, between tax efficiency, aggressive tax minimisation and tax evasion. More transparent companies are on the front end of that range; most Russian companies were on the back end.

Russian companies' financial gymnastics around a complex legal system, and their more general allergy to paying taxes, created increasingly convoluted and opaque ownership structures, most of which ended in anonymous trusts or in shell companies in low-disclosure jurisdictions. In the case of many Russian companies, it was impossible to prove who the owner of the company—the "beneficial owner"—was. That was all by design. If the Russian government, or any government, knew who the real owners of a company was, it could (1) tax them, (2) steal their company from them or (3) force them to re-register their company openly in Russia.

The difficulty for international investors here is that if you don't precisely know who you're doing business with and can't prove it on paper, then it is impossible to be certain that the company isn't owned by, say, a politician. That sort of scenario is a red flag for the US government.

That was the private sector. The public sector—the Russian government—was even more opaque. Some Western investors were afraid to step foot inside a Russian ministry because they knew they would be asked for a bribe before they left the building.

Russian law improves, but ...

"I have to admit, it was extremely interesting how the country sobered up from being wild to being compliant," von Flemming of Russian *Forbes* and Axel Springer said. Following the 1998 financial crisis, von Flemming was on the board of the German Chamber of Commerce in Russia and was sitting at the top of its compliance committee.

"It was crystal clear that compliance was a method of survival," von Flemming said. German investors came to Russia and thought they had the system beat. "Everyone came over and said, 'Yeah, I know the governor,' and I said 'Yeah, good for you, but he could be exchanged, and you could be compromised.'"

"So the German business community started extremely early, in a German manner, to be working in a compliant way," von Flemming said. "Secondly, the German community strongly advised newcomers: 'behave.'"

But there was a catch. Having good laws is important. How they are applied is another matter entirely.

Former Moscow lawyer Tom Firestone said "[t]he legal system is ultimately an instrument, and it depends on who is wielding it and for what purposes. ... A knife can be used by a doctor to cut out cancer and can be used by a mugger to stab."

"The problem wasn't the lack of tools, it was who was going to be using those tools," he said. The laws in Russia were on the books, but they were used differently. "It all got turned around and they started threatening companies with money laundering legislation if they didn't pay protection money."

"At a certain point, the state became one with organised crime," Firestone said:

As Americans, we made the mistake over and over again. We just assumed that the Russian law enforcement system was like the US in the 1950s, before we had the RICO [Racketeer Influenced and Corrupt

Organizations] law. We assumed that if we only gave them the right laws, then they would be able to deal with the organised crime. But the problem was not the law. It was the relationship between the state and organised crime.

"The legal system in Russia has always been manipulated by the state," Firestone said. "Everything Marx said about the legal system being an instrument of the ruling class—ironically, it was, during Soviet times. In the Soviet Union it was used to repress dissidents."

Once the Soviet Union went away, "the instrument remained, but the exploiters changed slightly. And then it all just descended into gangsterism." He used the KGB, and its role as driver of the corrupt business environment, as an example.

"Once the ideology disappeared, they [the KGB] turned into a racket," Firestone said. They had the weapons, but they didn't have the ideology restraining them. So they just went for the money."

The German Chamber of Commerce, by the way, may have told its members to behave but that doesn't necessarily mean that everyone listened. Or if they were compliant on questions of the law, they lapsed elsewhere. Von Flemming said that over the course of about twenty-five years, beginning in the late 1990s (pre-dating the chamber), there were "500 to 600" cases of German businessmen photographed in compromising situations and blackmailed.

"[M]en when they were travelling to Russia, you remember, they were giving up their brain at passport control," von Flemming said. "The biggest danger for German investment is the Russian ladies." Lest anyone get the wrong impression, von Flemming expressed her keen appreciation for Russian women in the business community, many of whom were her mentors and whom she described as the "backbone of the Russian economy."

The investment decision

For many companies, the boom years of the early 2000s made the investment decision a bit of a no-brainer. That did not, however, mean that the decision was always unanimous. Debate often raged inside companies about when, where and, crucially, how, to do business in Russia.

Some companies were determined to keep Russia at a safe distance and make it an export market: make things, ship them to Russia and forget about them once they leave the factory. That business model required a minimal presence in Russia—a representative office was usually enough for answering the phone and meeting with customers.

Other companies wanted a strategic stake in Russia's future: they saw themselves as long-term investors with a significant in-country presence. The difference between those two companies depended, of course, on the sector, among other things. Not every sector can work solely as an export business.

Several factors played determining roles in the decision about how to invest in Russia. Among them was the investor's country of origin. International companies in modern Russia came from all over the world. Each of them brought with them a few important factors that determined their attitudes toward Russia. One was the amount of Cold War baggage a country was carrying, and here the champion was, of course, the United States. And even though the US had a high-profile and successful presence in Russia—there were the Golden Arches, the Boeing aircraft, the Hollywood films and the Jeeps on the highways—the relationship suffered from decades of mistrust.

Geography played a second determinant role. Europe wins the contest there. Both FDI and trade in goods between the EU and Russia was a significant multiple of that between Russia and the US.[12] Companies trade the most with the countries closest to them, full stop.

The regulatory environment in a company's home jurisdiction played a less visible, but critical role in the investment decision. Here again, the US wins the contest. Strict anti-corruption and anti-money laundering laws, and strict stock exchange regulators, made US companies jittery. Less robust home-country regulation or enforcement acted as accelerants to investment in Russia. Compliance executives argue that European companies felt more relaxed in Russia than US companies did because European regulators were less strict.

Public companies had more to worry about than private companies. On top of everything else, public companies were regulated by a stock exchange and subject to much higher disclosure standards. Private companies worked under lighter scrutiny.

"For companies, risk appetite was more of a function of whether they were publicly traded in the US," Firestone said, preferring that metric to a company's national origin. "A German company traded in the US has the SEC to worry about. A US company that is not publicly traded does not care about the SEC."

At the risk of invoking stereotypes, nationality also had a role in risk appetite.

German companies had voracious appetites for risk, perhaps as a result of their familiarity with the Russian market. So did the Italians and the French. The Brits were somewhere in the middle, and at the bottom of the scale were the Americans and the Japanese.

"There is a lot of geography to it," the IFC's Crabtree said:

> The Germans had much stronger commercial ties, and they were more accustomed to [Russia]. For the Americans, it was always remote, and it involved much more logistical challenges for these guys to come out. They had other markets—they had Latin America to deal with, so they just didn't have the experience.

"Japanese companies were the most risk averse in my view," Prior said:

> I actually spoke to a Japanese client about this. And his realistic view was that as a Japanese businessperson in Russia you are very visible, you're very conspicuous. There's nothing you can do to hide it, and you are very exposed if anyone wants to pay attention to you and start threatening you.

Wharton's Nichols adds yet another variable into the risk equation. "Shareholders in the US impose an incredibly short time horizon, whereas investors in Western European firms don't," he said. "You can make a bit of a longer play if you're a German firm than when you're an American firm."

Andrew Glass's perspective from the commodity trading industry was close to that of oil executives—in the energy sector and in the agricultural sector, Russia is almost impossible to ignore.

"We grew up exporting grain out of the prairies back to Europe," Glass said. "So throughout the history of the company it's had a very healthy appetite for risk in the markets":

> And I've always found it a bit astonishing, really. A company based in flyover country has expanded around the world very quickly. In the '50s, '60s, '70s, it went everywhere, set up offices, and took on more and more trading risk. And that's how we got into Russia. It's a type of appetite for risk that was very strong. [Being] a private company also allows you to avoid the cycle of reporting and the outcomes of that risk.

Glass said that having "early mover advantage" worked strongly to his company's benefit:

> So we established this base, which always gave us, I felt, quite an advantage over the local bureaucrats, because the minute you go for your operating permit, your construction permit, that's when they all appear and want their payoff. And because we had this really well-embedded, really well-established base, I felt it was probably

easier for us than for some other companies. So there's a very early mover advantage.

Glass reflected for a moment.

"It was incredibly gutsy at the time," he said, but then tempered his observation with nuance.

The food sector, in the broadest sense, is politically sensitive in Russia. But not necessarily every facet of the sector: "Russian customers were happy to have Western products. So they weren't a particularly political sector. And someone who was buying and putting cash into the farm economy—I mean, you'd have to be a pretty naïve Russian bureaucrat to want to frustrate that. Some tried, by the way."

"We still had the problems. There were the nearly 250 signatures required to start up a food refinery," Glass said, giving a rough approximation from memory of the number of times he needed a government official to sign a piece of paper.

In the run-up to local elections, a vice governor from the regional administration approached Glass's factory in search of campaign funds for upcoming elections. If the company didn't contribute, this individual threatened to cut off the company's water supply and prosecute it on a spurious wastewater violation. Glass said the rules governing water quality in Russia were vague enough to present ample money-making opportunities for inspectors.

The inspector forgot one small thing. The home to Glass's company was built in the Soviet period as a "company town." The agricultural enterprise at its heart was connected to the apartments built for the workers in the Soviet period. Shutting the water to the plant would have meant shutting down the water to the workers, too. Which they did. In November. In Russia. Local officials intervened on Glass's behalf.

"They very quickly turned it back on, and they went away," Glass said.

Jitter management

On top of their online anti-corruption training programmes, companies deployed a complex, and not inexpensive, array of anti-bribery defence mechanisms. Having a smart general counsel who was well connected in DC or Brussels helped, as did having access to external lawyers with on-the-ground experience. Risk consultancies would produce reams of due diligence reports and volumes of background checks on Russian partners. The work ranged from expensive, hand-crafted, in-depth reports to two-pagers produced by automated programmes. Some reports got read, others didn't. The most important thing was being able to turn to a regulator, hold up the report and say, "See, we did our best."

The companies that wanted to fill their servers with due diligence reports had a high tolerance for risk and a rather perfunctory solution for minimising it: do what the law requires and no more. The companies that dug deeper for more meaningful information sometimes found themselves enriched by the experience and were able to narrow the information gap between themselves and their Russian partners. Other times, in-depth due diligence pushed foreign executives into increasingly opaque pools of grey, making them regret their decision to dig deep.

Careful what you ask for

This is where things got interesting. Due diligence providers came under pressure to whitewash their reports. Reports got tossed in the bin. Some were shoved into filing cabinets, the deeper the better. Others went off like bombs inside the companies that ordered them. Someone's body usually got thrown on top to dampen the shock wave. Sometimes it was the due diligence consultant; sometimes it was the client.

Business intelligence and due diligence were at their worst when they raised more questions than they answered. And in Russia, the task became more challenging with time. If you have become the owner of a company privatised in the suitcases-of-cash period of the 1990s, was income generated by your company "criminal in origin"? Describing income as such could trigger a money laundering investigation.

At the bottom of it all was a fairly easy maxim: don't pay bribes and don't accept criminal funds. The reality is far more complex. There are degrees of corrupt relationships, and the lines between them are blurry. Brown envelopes stuffed with cash? Bad. European factory visits for Russian customers with a room at a luxury hotel? Harder to say, despite increasing government guidance and case precedent.

Competitive pressures weighed like a boulder on the scales of justice. If you were bidding for work against a company that was willing to pay a bribe to win, resisting the temptation to do the same could be extremely difficult. Year-end bonuses were on the line. International companies participating in tenders in Russia often knew who was paying to win. There were companies doing business in Russia that had entire departments devoted to making corrupt payments and disguising them beyond detection. In other cases, companies declined even to participate in competitive tenders if they knew a bribe-paying company was involved.

Many American companies tended to think there was some sort of magic bullet to identifying and eradicating corruption from their transactions in Russia.

"If only we could find out who was paying bribes and fire them," some companies mused.

"If only we could find an honest government official, we'd be in the clear," others assured themselves.

"If only we could determine who really owned the company we are doing business with, we'd be fine," the saying went.

The truth is that it was often impossible to establish and maintain that level of comfort in Russia. Yes, there were honest government officials. Sure, you could vet all your employees—local and expat—and try to block the bad apples. And then someone's financial circumstances would change, and they'd become vulnerable to taking a bribe. Corruption was amorphous and peripatetic.

Just say no

Executives at foreign banks said it was easy for them to avoid corrupt deals. That doesn't mean they weren't asked.

"'Give me a loan, I won't forget you,' that's how it was usually pitched," Roman Zilber, formerly of Raiffeisen, said.

Saying no involved a combination of art and science. For Zilber and his bank, the quick answers were relatively blunt.

"We don't do this," was the most frequent answer. "Even if we wanted to, we couldn't," sounded a bit more polite.

For international banks, this meant explaining there was something called a credit committee—usually located far, far away—with a panel of nameless and faceless people who took lending decisions independently of what was happening in Moscow. They were the bad guys who said no to loan applications, not the nice people in Moscow.

More to the point, perhaps, there were 4,000 banks in Russia at one point, and only twenty foreign banks among them, Zilber said. Anyone who wanted to coax a loan out of a bank and send a kickback when the money hit their account could go to any number of more "flexible" Russian banks.

Von Flemming recalls getting a cheque for USD 10,000 for her birthday from the biggest advertiser at Russian *Forbes*. The advertiser represented a network of luxury boutiques; she was told to take the money and go shopping.

"I looked at this cheque and I thought, 'How do you behave now?'" von Flemming said. "And I wrote a handwritten letter thanking them for this wonderful gift, handing it back, and I wrote: 'You understand, we have corporate rules, and you have to admit, you do not have my sizes, because I'm too big. And thank you.' And they took it."

The battle was relentless and expensive. Companies would sometimes ask themselves why they were pouring all this time, money and effort into fighting a malaise that would never really go away.

Melling said that working in Russia involved a great deal of compromise.

"How do you build a small island of compliance in a sea of nonsense?" he asked.

Some said that all the compliance work in Russia made the islands grow larger with time.

"I tried to instil in my team's head a sound practice of law," Stubbs said:

> You have to never lie. Never violate the law. Never tell your client to violate the law. I mean, you could have that little impact in your own pond, where you create integrity within your own team. I think that then these people go out into a new job. Look at the EBRD—many of the former EBRD bankers or lawyers have left and remained within the Russian community and have had a positive impact.

The use of the island metaphor, however, is apt, and it reinforces the idea that the Western business environment floated in or on the Russian business environment but never really joined it.

Intestinal fortitude

All the legal advice, all the due diligence and all the compliance training was a complete waste of money if a company couldn't come to its own view on how much risk it was prepared to tolerate. It was the rare exception for a company in its entirety to look at a market, a transaction or a relationship and be able to say "this is not for us."

If your organisation didn't have a company-wide, coast-to-coast, deep-in-the-gut feel for when enough risk was enough, it was almost impossible to build one. Most companies were either too decentralised, too dispersed geographically or too diverse by product or service to have a uniform sense of risk. Globalisation, in fact, made this incredibly difficult. If you're doing business in Finland and Nigeria, how do you arrive at a shared internal concept of risk?

Most companies, in fact, not only lacked a common vocabulary of risk but frequently harboured entirely antagonistic views on risk inside the same building. Business development and sales executives, for example, are born to discount risk. Their bonuses depend on getting deals done. Their colleagues in the legal department, however, were designed to do the opposite. For them, existential risk lurked around every corner, and in their view, companies were always one mistake away from a fatal error. Many chief legal officers saw themselves more as chief risk officers.

Taking a new transaction to the general counsel's office for approval was sort of like visiting the dentist—something to be put off to the last minute. And that's how it worked sometimes. To avoid the scrutiny of the Department of No, as legal and compliance were often called, business development teams often took their deals to approval committees at the last minute. Only when a deal became too big to kill was it time to show it to the lawyers. This is an exaggeration, but not by a lot. Some compliance officers told tales of not being allowed to discuss transactions in emails—a massive red flag they could do nothing about without risking their careers.

It could get nasty. In companies that used the dreaded 360-degree employee evaluation process, heaven help the compliance officer being reviewed by someone from sales. Compliance officers who put tricky deals under the microscope risked getting poor reviews from their peers in business development. Compliance officers who waved deals through got rave reviews.

Other companies allowed their compliance departments to swell like a puffer fish. This did not mean they were more effective—it just meant they were bigger. Aggressive regulators would go after companies that had smaller compliance departments, knowing they might be easier to haul into court.

Not every company was host to civil war between business development and compliance. Companies with a more evolved posture fused their growth and risk functions to manage risk more comprehensively in more dangerous markets. Rather than leaving the risk function out of the loop until it was too late for them to block a deal, these companies included the risk function in everything they did.

The consultants (and their invoices)

The due diligence business is a species that evolved over time. In the early days, a lot of companies investing in Russia wanted to pierce the country's opacity but were afraid to come to the consultancies that could do it. Some of these consultancies had reputations for hiring ex-intelligence officers; the ways they obtained information inside Russia were themselves opaque.

Jules Kroll fathered the due diligence and corporate investigations business in 1972 and popularised it over the following decades through his high-profile investigations into high-flying perpetrators of financial crime. Kroll's operations grew to include a significant business intelligence operation that in the early days elicited comparisons with mythical trench-coat-and-fedora-wearing spies.[13]

In Russia, there was a certain aura of intrigue around the profession, as many of its practitioners relied on connections to former or current intelligence officers there. The Russian government hired Kroll in the 1990s to unearth billions of dollars secreted overseas by the Communist Party of the Soviet Union as the country fell apart. It was a headline-grabbing case that helped cement Kroll's reputation and launched the due diligence business in Russia, but the government project was doomed from the start.

"The fact that they hired us at a press conference should have told us they weren't serious," the late Tommy Helsby of Kroll said. "They got their I.M.F. loan, which was the only real point, I suppose. We found good stuff, but it turned out they didn't want it. And then they didn't pay the balance of our bill." In 2006, the Russian parliament and the state prosecutor both announced that they were investigating Kroll for allegedly operating without a licence. The investigation was believed to be triggered in response to Kroll's involvement in a sensitive transaction touching on government interests.[14]

The government assignment provided Kroll with access to, and cooperation from, Russia's security services. "That was the kind of feedstock of your business intelligence projects. The questions asked by the client would be, 'Am I going to lose my business? Am I going to get extorted? Am I going to lose control? Is it dangerous?'" Prior said. "Those questions would be channelled to ex-KGB people now operating in the private sector who in turn worked with their contacts in the Lubyanka."[15]

The KGB at the time was undergoing convulsive change in the wake of the collapse of the Soviet Union. And while a role in state security in the Soviet Union was among the country's most elite and prestigious positions, it was no match for the cash on offer in the private sector in Russia. It was good for business all around.

The information that emerged from this supply chain carried many of the hallmarks of intrusive state-sponsored intelligence gathering that was not useful to business and included personal information that in today's environment would be a violation of privacy laws. Prior described having to explain to his sources that the personal details of Russian businesspeople were of less interest to his clients than whether they were involved in organised crime.

The business of business intelligence matured rapidly. Some risk consultancies suffered major reputational breakdowns when their methodology failed them and their clients. More than anything else, globalisation's drive into opaque emerging markets meant there was enormous money to be made in the due diligence business, and everyone got into the game. Law firms were offering business intelligence reports. The Big Four accounting firms were opening business intelligence departments. And the boutique and specialist firms cleaned up their acts to compete with the majors.

The other Hermitage

No book about international business in Russia would be complete without mention of Bill Browder, the founder of Hermitage Capital, once one of the biggest investors in Russia. This section will be brief; Browder has written his own books on his experiences in Russia.

In the early days, Browder—whose grandfather was the head of the Communist Party in the US and whose American father married a Russian wife in the Soviet Union[16]—was on the winning side of the Russian investment boom. He had a multi-billion-dollar portfolio of investments in Russian companies—a large stake in Gazprom most prominently—and used the portfolio as a platform to campaign for better corporate governance in Russian companies.[17]

In 2007, Browder and his company became the targets of a massive fraud at the hands of Russian tax and law enforcement officials who allegedly swindled him of a nine-figure sum by deploying all the best tactics of an elaborate Russian fraud— theft of the company seal used to authenticate documents, forged signatures, counterfeit corporate resolutions and a great deal of skulduggery.[18]

The worst of it came when Browder's accountant, Sergei Magnitsky, was arrested after launching an investigation into the fraud. Magnitsky died in deplorable conditions—allegedly after having been beaten—in a Russian jail. In Magnitsky's memory, Browder campaigned around the world for sanctions against corrupt Russian officials and human rights violators. The US, the UK and the EU, among others, have passed laws along these lines bearing Magnitsky's name. In response to the US round of Magnitsky sanctions, Putin banned US citizens from adopting Russian children.[19]

Browder provokes Putin almost like no other—the mere mention of Browder's name can cause Putin's face to visibly darken; the Russian president utters Browder's name only rarely.[20] Law enforcement officials in Russia requested Interpol issue an international arrest warrant against Browder; that warrant is the name of Browder's first book, *Red Notice*.

Eastern money flows west

When Roman Abramovich bought England's legendary Chelsea football team, the country quivered in delight at the billions he had to spend on the sport but then gasped to think where the money came from.

When Russians started parking their money outside Russia, or even more so, when Russian businesses started investing their money outside Russia, compliance got very interesting. The use of highly complex legal and financial architecture rooted in low-disclosure jurisdictions twinned with entry into more open markets was a massive challenge to international institutions.

"The outward stuff has a lot of the corrupting influences," O'Toole said.

London offered Russian clients a complete and complex assortment of firms—lawyers, accountants, bankers, auction houses, estate agents and public relations companies, to name a few—willing to structure Russian businesses in such a way as to protect them from excessive scrutiny. In the sprawling granite office buildings of the City of London and in the precision-built towers of Canary Wharf, executives arriving from Russia would be welcomed into the walnut walls and marble floors of cutting-edge business society.

For Russian executives, this was one of the greatest signals they had arrived. Being able to push a silent button in a conference room and have a pot of tea arrive moments later in the hands of a uniformed butler was the cherry on the cake of legitimacy. After a decade of being told not to pick their noses in public—a phrase Russians liked to use to describe how the West treated them back in the 1990s—Russians were being called "sir" and "madam" by Cambridge graduates in Ferragamo ties.

London's elite legal and financial stormtroopers had the regulatory and watchdog community beat.

If you go to work for PwC, said Jeff Kaye, a former trustee at the UK chapter of Transparency International, your salary immediately begins to outstrip what you might earn in the public sector and sooner or later will climb into six figures. "You go to HMRC [the UK revenue agency], you might never get there, even if you reach the top. So who's going to get the better people?"

London's professional services sector's love for Russian clients went through its own evolution. Lawyers, too, ordered due diligence reports from external consultants, wanting to surface red flags as part of their client-onboarding processes. Professional services firms are not meant to facilitate corruption and money laundering in the way they accept and work for clients, whether from Russia or anywhere else.

But after a brief period of taking reports, sometimes in considerable volume, from external consultants, many banks and professional services firms followed a familiar pattern: they took the process in-house. The move was in one sense easy to understand. Working with external providers was expensive and time-consuming. But more importantly, working with external consultants took away a certain amount of control over how firms brought in new Russian clients. Due diligence providers could be imprecise in their language. Loose use of the phrase "money laundering" in a background check would set off the sprinklers in most banks and law firms; reports alleging the presence of criminal funds in a potential client were meant to force a regulatory disclosure that could torpedo client acquisition. There could be mismatches in risk appetites—external consultants could raise the alarm on issues that a law firm might consider less material.

Law firms also worked under the widely accepted principle that everyone, even individuals and companies with questionable reputations, is entitled to legal representation. And this drove the final element in client acceptance—if one law firm said no to a potential client, there would always be one who said yes. Here, too, competitive pressures were enormous.

Not every London lawyer was a midwife to sharp practices, of course. The professional services sector in London and beyond was also involved in cleaning up a lot of Russian business, at least to the extent that the owners wanted things to be clean. Russian companies needed to be scrubbed and buffed in advance of listings on global stock exchanges. They needed to respond to regulatory activity in Russia and around the world. They needed advice as takeover targets or as the aggressors. Lawyers in London and New York are among the strongest advisors in the world on these and many other related fields.

Gradually and then suddenly, London was *Londongrad*, the title of a book by Mark Hollingsworth and Stewart Lansley. The book tells the story of how Russian money bought everything from football teams to Mayfair mansions and how Britain welcomed the cash with open arms. To a certain degree, the influx of Russian cash changed the texture of the city. In some cases for the better: bold-face Russian surnames adorn the façades of museums and academic institutions. This largesse, by the way, was also seen as reputation laundering. In other cases, the presence was less welcome. Political contributions from Russia–UK dual citizens almost always sparked scandal.

"Once money is washed, you don't know where it's from," Kaye said. He added that the UK not-for-profit sector—the NGOs who took up against the influence of Russian money on the British economy—came late to the topic of money laundering. Corruption was always part of the discussion; money laundering only latterly.

And then it was sort of too late.

"That was a huge mistake, this placid acceptance of a Russian oligarchic presence in the UK," Prior said. "It's clear that over a period of time the permissive attitude to Russian oligarchs and their wealth permeated the British establishment and eventually compromised some of its institutions and individuals. When such vast wealth is on display, greed tends to override propriety and the national interest."

13

YOU CAN'T GO HOME AGAIN

God bless those businessmen wanting to get back in. I don't see that being an easy proposition in the long term.[1]

We haven't done a 360, we're going somewhere else. To the extent that I have a little bit of hope that I will live long enough to see a better Russia than we have today, that's one of the embers in the darkening pile that used to be a campfire.[2]

Kakuyu stranu prosrali. We fucked this country up.[3]

Trying to get back in

After being locked out of European airspace in February, Melling went back to Moscow later in the year. Getting into Russia was almost as difficult as getting out.

"I went back in August [2022]. I flew in from Dubai, and I spent just over four hours [on arrival] in Domodedovo Airport," he said. "They went through my phone, saw the photographs on my phone, went through my laptop—they had no right to do that, but it didn't matter." The search, and the arrivals paperwork associated with the search, took about an hour. "But then they just let you sit there for another couple of hours."

Lots of expats and Russian émigrés have been back and forth to Russia since the start of the war. Leaving in a hurry was messy, and tidying up requires an enormous amount of paperwork, not to mention looking after ageing relatives or sorting out household affairs.

The level of harassment on arrivals at Moscow's international airports was heaviest at the outset of the war and amped up against passport holders from countries most vigorously supporting Ukraine. Melling is a UK citizen. Even so, he was one of the lucky ones. He got an unusually candid explanation from one of the border guards.

"Ultimately, I went to the passport room with a Russian guy who said, 'Paul, you understand we had to do these things. We're being told to do these things,'" Melling recalled.

The airport was just the beginning of a re-introduction to Melling's Moscow. Once he was in the centre of town, the changes continued. The most popular news shows on state-controlled television have become pumping stations for some of the most vile anti-Western propaganda imaginable.

"When I got into town, it was not like the Moscow I remember at all," he said. "And the TV was horrendous: 'Let's drop a bomb on the UK,' sort of stuff," he said. He is now a senior partner in Melling, Voitishkin & Partners in Moscow, the former Baker McKenzie office in the capital.

When can we really go back?

Before the war was a year old, companies started asking when they could go back into Russia. For these companies, the return to the market was a simple calculation: once the sanctions are lifted and they can legally do business in Russia, they will.

This attitude tended to be among companies that had a robust appetite for risk—their sole red line, more or less, was the letter of the law. Some of these queries arose when it looked like the war might be violent, but short. The longer the war, and the more public opinion learns about the Russian army's actions in Ukraine, the higher the reputational risk of returning to Russia, wherever the other red lines may lie.

"This country is now largely irrelevant in the global economic picture," Evgenev, formerly of Alvarez & Marsal, said. "And it's becoming less relevant by the minute."[4]

Still more companies are thinking that they will only go back to a different Russia, a post-Putin Russia that has reversed, or wants to reverse, the damage done by the war.

Almost all of these options will be slow to materialise.

"This is probably the end of the era of American business in Russia," Courtney said. "You just don't come back as Ford and expect to regain the market share that's been lost to Chinese brands."

Courtney referenced the "buy-back" clauses some companies inserted into their exits, but it really is anyone's guess whether those will work in the future. At some point, business, and its customers, move on. American companies, he said, are losing market share to Chinese, Indian and even Russian businesses. He pointed again to McDonald's, now in the hands of a local businessman in Russia and renamed "Vkusno—i Tochka," or "Tasty—and That's It."

"[A]fter a few years, who really gives a damn whether it's got McDonald's name on it, as long as the taste is the same and the price is still good?" Courtney said.

"It's just a generational transfer of wealth from American shareholders to these others," he added. "There's no visible way for them to come back in a way and reach the level where they were with market share and brand visibility and loyalty and that sort of thing."

Courtney hopes that at some point, Russia is led by a Kremlin administration that will again foster international investment. But he doesn't see US companies banging down the door to Russia as they did when the market first opened. Some companies may establish a small presence. More nimble companies may come back, but perhaps bring folding office furniture.

Stubbs, the lawyer formerly based in Moscow, concurs.

"It's a developmental case of a country which has effectively been an emerging market and is still an emerging market," he said. "In fact, it's a submerging market. Is that a word? It will take a long time for it—if it ever does—to join the league of advanced economies, and it may never do that."

Rodzianko, formerly of the American Chamber of Commerce, sees things differently.

"It's a horrible bloodletting, and I hope to God it ends soon. I don't really understand why it goes on for so long," he said:

> But back to business: Russia isn't going anywhere. The US isn't going anywhere. Europe isn't going anywhere. And in order to thrive and survive, they have to trade with each other and work with each other. And so my hope is that at some point, some sort of modus vivendi is re-established, and there is some sort of continuing link through business with Russia and the US.

Gunitsky puts it more directly and perhaps best summarises current attempts to make forecasts.

"I have no idea how it is going to shake out, it's all speculation," Gunitsky said.

Don't hold your breath

There is a lot left to play out before any company that has left can even think about going back to Russia. "Any company," broadly speaking, means most of the companies in Russia that were from G20 nations. Beyond that, most of the rest of the world, including an enormous array of countries loosely grouped into a category called the "global south," doesn't really see Russia as a problem, or at least, as its problem.

"There are two elements of withdrawal from Russia by Western European and American companies—leave aside the Indians and the Chinese, who haven't, or frankly everybody else. This is not global opprobrium, this is a Western one," said Rawi Abdelal, the former director of Harvard's Davis Center and the Herbert F. Johnson Professor of International Management at the Harvard Business School: "One is the organisation of the sanctions regime, and then the other is societal pressures for self-sanctioning. And I think they have different internal logics and dynamics."[5]

The self-sanctioning will stop before the actual sanctioning, Abdelal said. The likely trigger for the end of self-sanctioning—people who are staying out of Russia because it looks bad, rather than because the law tells them to—will be when the Putin regime ends, likely with his death.

Abdelal thinks the next guy—and it will almost certainly be a man—could be worse, and he is far from alone in that thought. He thinks the "next-next" guy might be more Western-leaning.

"When there's the next guy and the next guy, and the war is over, I think the self-sanctioning will end," Abdelal said. "I don't think this is permanent reputational damage, [or that] your stakeholders will not let you do business in Russia ever again."

Abdelal gives self-sanctioning a lifespan of about ten years or so, depending on Putin's lifespan. The sanctions imposed by the EU, the UK, the US and other members of the G7 are here to stay. The history of sanctions shows that they are easy to impose and nearly impossible to lift.

"Remember Jackson–Vanik?" Abdelal asked. "The United States was sanctioning the Soviet Union for a decade after the Soviet Union ceased to exist."

There are two types of sanctions in US legislation. Some sanctions are imposed by executive order from the White House. Others are written into law by Congress. Abdelal can't find a reason why any future president, or any future legislature, will relent. A possible Trump-like presidency might disrupt some of the assumptions about the immediate future, but even the US president has a circumscribed range of motion on sanctions.

Sanctions on Russia inflict only limited pain on the US economy; the EU is the more important issue due to the more severe impact of sanctions on European commerce. And while the EU might therefore be tempted to lift sanctions on Russia earlier than the US, European companies don't like to provoke the US by contradicting US sanctions.

Beyond that, US companies will also howl that any lack of coordination between the EU and the US in sanctions relief could prejudice the US companies that want to get back into Russia but can't. Finally, the US could weaponise its sanctions by saying that any company using the US dollar—not just US companies—could be liable to penalties. In either case, the future of sanctions on Russia could likely involve a divergence of views between the US and the EU. The EU, Abdelal predicts, won't be happy if that's the case.

"And they're going to be even more irritated by it year by year, even more than they are now," he said. "I totally get it—like, how annoying is it to have your foreign policy decided for you by some of the antics in Washington."

Gunitsky is philosophical about Russia's future. He's managing his expectations, you might say.

"The economy was prepared for isolation. [Putin's] in it for the long haul," Gunitsky said. "As long as he's in power, he will try to continue."

For the time being, Russia's economy is confounding expectations. The war has created significant distortions, but most Russians are not feeling worse off. Some of the billionaires and millionaires might be, but the average Russian is feeling slightly better off than before the war started. Unemployment is low. Wages are up. Soldiers' families, including those of soldiers killed in battle, receive generous, government-sponsored social payments. The Central Bank is wrestling with inflation, but Russia's middle class again has money in its pockets and places to spend it. Some Western goods are coming across the border from third-party countries and companies in sanctions workarounds. Other Western goods have been replaced by Chinese goods.

In February 2024, "[t]he IMF revised its own GDP growth forecast for Russia to 2.6 per cent this year, a 1.5 percentage point rise over what it had predicted last October," the *Financial Times* reported. One-third of the Russian budget is being spent on the war, but the country still generates "colossal" revenues from energy exports, even if they are down from pre-war peaks.[6]

None of this, of course, is sustainable. Governments can only spend their way out of crises for so long. And, as the *FT* piece above suggested, Russia's economy runs the risk of becoming addicted to weapons manufacturing in the same way it is addicted to oil and gas. Now there are two ways the bottom can fall out of the Russian economy.

The way we were

The roll call of the dismantling of international business in Russia—and the fate of some of its own leading brands—is as gilt-edged as its list of market entrants once was.

Yandex, Russia's leading tech company, was sold to a group of Russian investors including some of its senior managers. Yandex was, technically speaking, a Dutch entity registered to a parent company in the Netherlands and traded on New York's NASDAQ. But Yandex has always been referred to as "Russia's Google"—it was a renowned, national champion in the tech sector. Yandex founder Arkady Volozh had been under EU sanctions for charges that Yandex was "complicit" with the war.[7]

In August of 2023, Volozh took a public stance against the war,[8] and negotiations with the state commission for the sale of Yandex reportedly turned hostile and the terms of the deal changed; the value of the transaction reportedly dropped by USD 180 million.[9] The company was sold for a fraction of its price. Since his resignation from the company and its subsequent sale, Volozh has been removed from the EU's sanctions list.[10]

Renault gradually took control of AvtoVAZ over the years and sold its stake in the company for 1 rouble in 2022. The year before the sale, Renault's assets in Russia had been valued in excess of USD 2 billion. Renault embedded the possibility of a return to Russia into the sales contract.[11]

In November of 2022, Novo Nordisk announced it would stop deliveries of Ozempic to Russia. In December of 2023, the Russian government granted a licence for an analogue to the Danish drug without the company's permission.[12]

Russian *Vogue* stopped printing in March 2022.[13] Michaela Stark, a London-based artist and couturier, was the magazine's last cover model.[14]

Coca-Cola left Russia. The company that owned and bottled Coca-Cola in Russia renamed itself and began selling a Coke substitute called "Dobry Cola," or "Kind Cola," now the most popular soft drink in Russia. Coca-Cola can still be found on Russian shelves via import from third countries. In 2023, Russian economic news website The Bell said Coke was coming into Russia from "the UAE, Iran, Turkey, Azerbaijan and many other countries."[15]

On 12 February 2024, Siemens announced a voluntary liquidation. Interfax reported that the company "acknowledged it was impossible to continue importing goods into Russia." The company in Russia had become loss-making; it had "almost no assets" on its balance sheet.[16]

Siemens' final years in Russia were marked by a 2022 conflict over a Gazprom gas turbine that had been sent to Siemens Canada for repairs. Siemens was meant to block the return of the repaired turbine in keeping with sanctions on Russia. Withholding the turbine was, however, threatening gas supplies from Russia to Germany via the Nord Stream 1 pipeline, already shut as part of the energy war between Russia and Europe. Clearance was given to return the pipeline, and it headed to Russia via Germany in August of 2022.[17] This was before Nord Stream 1 and its twin Nord Stream 2, not yet in service, were damaged in September 2022 explosions that permanently debilitated that supply route.[18]

GE announced in March 2022 that it was suspending its business in Russia.[19] Elements of its healthcare business would remain and are allowed under humanitarian provisions. GE also stopped servicing the gas turbines it had installed at Russian power plants. GE no longer services the engines bolted to the wings of Russian aircraft.

"Krispy Kreme is now Krunchy Dream; its doughnuts come in a similar flat box with familiar flavors," *The New York Times* writes. "Starbucks has been reborn as Stars Coffee. Its mermaid is now a Russian swan princess."[20]

In March 2022, the German Eastern Business Association, which represents German companies with interests in Eastern Europe, said the companies remaining in Russia are in sectors "in which further economic activity is not only lawful but legitimate," association chairman Oliver Hermes told Reuters. German companies at the time reportedly employed 280,000 workers in Russia. Like a lot of other businesses in Russia, Hermes said he did not want German companies to lose assets, nor did he want to see German companies surrender market share to non-sanctioning countries. "We therefore firmly reject blanket condemnation of companies that are still active on the Russian market," Hermes told Reuters that March.[21]

On 2 May 2022, Hermes resigned from his role.[22]

BP is more or less stuck in Russia. The company took a USD 24.4 billion write-down on its Russia business in February 2022, but the company has yet to sell its stake in Rosneft. Until that stake is sold, the company is technically receiving dividends "placed by Moscow in an escrow account," according to the *Financial Times*. BP told the *FT* that it has "no expectations" it will receive any dividends in the future and that it has not received any dividends to date.[23]

Exile in Amsterdam

Sauer moved the staff of *The Moscow Times* to the Netherlands and publishes online from Amsterdam (the newspaper went fully electronic after closing its print edition in 2017). The paper is constantly dodging cyberattacks on its website, but the site, now also available in Russian, has more than a million unique viewers a month, Sauer said.

The move was forced when the organisation and its staff were labelled "foreign agents," a term used to discredit organisations and their employees for taking foreign funding.

Russia has since 2012 required organisations engaged in political activity and receiving foreign funding to register as such. The regulation subjected Russian civil society organisations and the people who worked for them to increasing pressure and provoked substantial international outcry.[24] Russia's foreign agent laws incrementally tightened with time and forced many of Russia's pro-democracy organisations, among others, to close. Most notably, the Russian government used the foreign agents law to shutter Memorial, one of Russia's oldest and most prominent human rights groups and one of the winners of the

2022 Nobel Peace Prize.[25] Being designated a foreign agent is the modern equivalent of being labelled an "enemy of the state."

More to the point, Russia made it illegal to call the war in Ukraine a "war"—which *The Moscow Times* does and did from the very beginning of the full-scale invasion. Violating the linguistic diktat carries a fifteen-year prison sentence:

> So basically, I assembled the team. And I said, guys, under the name of *The Moscow Times* we cannot follow these rules. It beats the whole idea of why I started *The Moscow Times* and honest media. So either we stop and call it quits ... or we go into exile.

Sauer was another among the business community in Russia who was much more than an expat. He landed in Russia in 1989 and made Moscow his home. He raised a family there.

When the full-scale invasion started, he said he left with one suitcase.

"We struggle so much in our heads with this dilemma. Our best friends are Russians. We have had a great time all these years in Russia," he said. Sauer is visibly distressed talking about it. "So now, I'm one of those people who is in the middle of the tunnel. And we don't see any light at the end of the tunnel."

Where did it all go wrong?

Just as American companies once looked in vain for the magic key that would unpick their most complex corruption concerns, there is no one answer that could ever explain how the people and the companies who invested billions of dollars, pounds and euros into Russia wound up where they are today. The money was never the full story, either. There was the elation of completing a complex deal. There were the celebrations after a promotion or a move to a bigger and better job. There were also sleepless nights, gruelling deadlines, marriages, divorces and the delirious exhaustion that made the money almost feel like an afterthought.

Companies made assumptions about Russia based on how they thought a market would behave, only to discover that politics drove the Russian market more than market forces did. Or they made assumptions about how Russian companies work but didn't want to explore those assumptions too vigorously.

Companies that took the time to look at the politics saw mirages or saw what they wanted to see. They ignored evidence that clashed with their ideological convictions or their sales targets. Companies that got too close to understanding the real levers of power inside Russian companies, or inside the Russian government, retreated to apply burn ointment.

But companies thought, either out of opportunism or ambition, or hope or hubris, that they could remake a collapsed construct into an economic, political and social image of our Western selves.

Russia is the only market of this sort of magnitude that opened and closed in the space of a generation. Could it have been different? Most certainly yes, but not in the way you might be thinking. It could have been worse. Russia could have descended into conflict—militarily and commercially—faster than it already has.

But could it have been what the international business community wanted, or hoped, it to be? Probably not. Set aside everything that happened: the teetering, drunken first president who presided over the birth of a brutal business culture as the state withered. Then, the ruthless, controlling second president who dismantled that dystopia in favour of a strong, statist structure that managed to be both rigid yet hollow.

None of the three presidents who have ruled Russia since 1991 laid even the first brick in durable, transparent, public-facing institutions of statecraft, despite a spate of successful reforms.

Perhaps this is the place to make at least brief mention of Dmitry Medvedev, whose jagged political odyssey initially held the promise of liberalisation before ultimately disappointing and descending into rabid anti-Westernism. Medvedev, a native of Leningrad like Putin, was Kremlin chief of staff and then first deputy prime minister during Putin's first two, four-year terms as president. In 2008, when Putin's mandate ended—prior to amendments lengthening the term of office and the number of terms a president could serve—Medvedev ran for president and publicly promised to make Putin his prime minister.

Medvedev entered office with a reputation as a pro-Western liberal, but the promise those labels held never materialised. At the end of his first term, he and Putin agreed to trade roles—Medvedev declined to run for re-election in 2012, and Putin replaced him and made him his prime minister. This series of political sleights of hand—in Russian, they were called the *rokirovka*, for the chess move when the king and the rook trade places—triggered the central Moscow protests mentioned earlier. Medvedev is now deputy chairman of the Russian Security Council and a foaming, anti-Western hawk.

Civil society developed in Russia despite, not thanks to, the state. The zombified ministries of the 1990s awoke to find themselves captured by oligarchs, gangsters or both. For a decade, the commercial tail wagged the political dog. In Russia's second decade, the ministries served not the state, but the man at its top. Under these circumstances, a transparent economy and a competitive political system able to serve the public and private sectors could never have taken root.

This view is deeply dependent on the power of hindsight. Worse still, it's highly utopian. Statecraft is perfect precisely nowhere. And even in the few places where it might come close, it's under threat. But it's just too hard to see how this could have worked in Russia, under almost any circumstances.

"It's really a shame. I feel bad for the country," Gunitsky said. "There was no reason it couldn't become a normal, regional power; not necessarily a democracy, but a hybrid regime that has corrupt oligarchs and they do what they do. But to take it to this next level where you basically destroy the standing of a country ..."

Crabtree, formerly of the IFC, agrees:

> I'm not really sure they had a chance of this whole thing working, given the foundation of this thing. The Soviet Union was so corrupt, and they were faced with changing a system, the corruption and then the collapse of that country all at once, really. The odds were very much against success.[26]

That explains the first ten years and sets the stage for the second ten.

"You can sort of understand why, when Putin comes along—someone who was born and raised and flowered under the Soviet system—and has a long-term project of trying to restore what he saw as the best of the Soviet system," Baker McKenzie's Melling said. "And the best of the Soviet system was control over the population via a strong leader, and control over your neighbours and the superiority that brings, and a certainty as to your political narrative. All those things."

Beyond the political processes and the political actors, something deeper beneath Russia's past may have miscarried its future.

"I think the problem with our ultimately not meeting our expectations—where we are now—has a lot to do with there never having been a reconciliation in this country between the common Original Sin," EY's Ostling said. "We could go back to the Red Terror, we could go back to [historian of Stalinism] Robert Conquest, we could go back to all these people who wrote about the dissonance between the aspirations of communism and the reality of how it was implemented."

So there was the busted ideology. But there was no autopsy of its demise.

South Africa had a Truth and Reconciliation Commission. In Eastern Europe, the Czech Republic, Germany and Hungary, for example, had lustration processes that exposed and then processed—on a national level—the impact of dictatorship, the traumas of their state security systems and the distortion of decades of repression. But Russia never did. Perestroika and glasnost were periods of great turmoil, openness, recognition and, to a certain degree, rehabilitation, but they were incomplete. Certain archives were never opened. Certain agencies—the KGB first among them—were never publicly dissected. A process began, but it never ran to completion.

Stubbs takes his view on the dysfunction of the Russian body politic and economy back to the social, political and economic pathology embedded in the Soviet experience. Sure, the market took off, but "they never addressed the traumas, the sociological traumas of the Soviet period, or dealt with the collapse of their empire," he said. "And so we're seeing a shitstorm—pardon my French—of unresolved empire issues, continuing pathologies from a brutal socialist period."

Evgenev, the former Alvarez & Marsal executive now in Dubai, goes all the way to Russia's imperial past to explain what's happening now:

> What we see right now, in my view, is a disintegration of the Russian Empire in slow motion. It started in 1917, and it's continuing in a fashion similar to the one the Ottoman Empire went through, the Austro-Hungarian Empire ran through, the British Empire went through, and the French Empire went through. ... Russia is a late bloomer, I would say. The first chunk was cut off in 1917. The next one was cut in 1991. And what we're seeing now is the next act of this *Danse Macabre*.

Lots of international companies remain in Russia. Companies from non-sanctioning countries will grow their businesses in Russia. But for the foreseeable future, Russia is no longer a genuinely global destination, and Moscow is no longer a buzzing world capital. Of note, no one is lamenting the end of the clubbing and the caviar. That was always a bonus, never the main attraction. Instead, the end of so much Western commerce in Russia is the end of one of the greatest experiments in global trade.

Sure, you can still make money in Russia, but for now you can't make money on Russia's future. And that's what everyone was doing in the early years—betting on the future.

"We wasted all this money on educating the children of influential Russians," Melling said, "and they either just stayed and never went home at all. And if they went home, within five years they were a member of the [Putin-supporting] United Russia party. It was depressing."

Among the expats and the long-term foreign residents, there are feelings of personal disappointment, economic loss, opportunities missed and an acute sense of the end of things. Few expats have stayed in Moscow long enough to observe its thirty-year evolution as a place to do business. There were, however, a few Russians who were paid to do exactly that. Alexander Gubsky, formerly of *Vedomosti* and *The Moscow Times*' sister publication, *Kapital*, is a graduate of Moscow State University's journalism department. The department is still in one of the "old campus" buildings in the centre of town, across the street from the Kremlin's Trinity Gates. He summed up the sentiment of the business community in one word.

"Resentment," he said. "Over these thirty years, I've spoken with a lot of successful European businessmen, and they all said the same thing: 'Russia and Europe should be together. And if we were together, we would be the strongest economic continent on Earth.'" He spoke to big business, small business, people who sold things, people who invested in funds. They all said the same thing. "People believed this and invested in Russia with that in mind."

Lessons learned, or not

"Back in the early days, Russia was a pretty good bet, a really good bet," Wharton's Nichols said. "Back then, I was discouraged that more US companies weren't going in."

"And I talk to all these executives who say, 'Yeah, doing business in a country that has an authoritarian regime or a dictatorship or autocracy is inherently unpredictable, and we can't assess them using business models, right?'" he said. "You are at the mercy of a mercurial person who has their own thing going on."

"And that's a really good lesson. That's a great lesson," Nichols continued. "But back in the day, everyone turned to President Putin and said, 'Now we've got political stability, and we have a great economic foundation, and a better political foundation, so charge away.'"

"It wasn't like, 'You should be aware of the Russkies,'" he said, purposefully using a Cold War term. "It looked good back then."

Until it didn't.

"It stopped looking good, and some companies weren't paying attention, and that's really not good," Nichols said.

For Cescotti, formerly of Germany's GEA, the lessons learned have been painful, but not the lessons he expected.

"I am totally disillusioned by the values of many companies," Cescotti said. "It's just about KPIs [key performance indicators] and money, essentially it is about greed and purely opportunistic. Usually the advertised values just 'beautify' the essence of everyday business—greed."

One of the more remarkable outcomes of Russia's renewed isolation from the West is that, while it has turned its back on the people who brought capitalism to Russia's shores, it hasn't turned its back on capitalism.

"Russia's not going to turn away from capitalism," Gubsky said. "This is Putin's dream—to rule like Stalin and live like Abramovich."

It has only been since the full-scale invasion of Ukraine that the market in Russia is so deeply distorted and the role of the state so exaggerated that it would be even more difficult now to call the country capitalist.

Following the full-scale invasion of Ukraine, EBRD president Odile Renaud-Basso, in an interview with *The Banker* magazine in April 2023, spoke haltingly about the bank's mission in Russia.

"We really hoped that investing, developing the private sector in Russia would help the country to deeply transform," she said, acknowledging the bank's remit to encourage political and economic transition. "And it wasn't the case."[27]

The landmark moments

Everyone has their own views on the warning signals, whether they were visible at the time and whether anything could be done about them anyway. Perhaps not surprisingly, some of them get multiple mentions.

Putin's reaction to the sinking of the *Kursk* submarine in 2000, the first year of his presidency, stands out. The nuclear submarine suffered an internal explosion and sank to the bottom of the Barents Sea, killing all 118 crew on board. Putin was on vacation at the time and did not make a statement about the incident, nor return to Moscow, for more than a week. He was hammered in the media, particularly on television's Channel One, privately owned by oligarch Boris Berezovsky. Putin reportedly froze with panic immediately following the disaster and sought to blame the tragedy on a state apparatus weakened during the 1990s. Not long after the *Kursk* disaster, Putin nationalised Channel One.[28]

Russia-watchers talk about the "Munich Speech," Putin's address to the Munich Security Conference in 2007. For more than fifty years, this annual gathering has been one of the most important platforms for geopolitical and security policy discussions. In his speech to the conference, Putin said that the US dominance of the global security system meant that no one could feel safe, and that a US-led liberal order was of no interest to Russia.

Commentators at the time and in retrospect say that this was the moment when Putin told the world "Who he is."[29] This is the number one instance on Ostling's list of red flags. He and many other observers spotted this concern contemporaneously. Ostling further recalls when Putin disparaged the Mechel steel company at an international forum in 2008. His criticisms of Mechel's pricing policy briefly wiped USD 6 billion off Mechel's value on the New York Stock Exchange.[30]

It's miles away from where Ostling thought this would all wind up.

"I had all the hope in the world," he said of Russia. "I thought they could be the 51st state," he said, using an expression to show unusual closeness with the US.

Before Abdullaev went into consulting, he was a political journalist and a newspaper editor.

"I've seen this arc," he said of the last thirty years. To Ostling's metrics, he would add the Putin and Medvedev swap and the 2004 Beslan incident. That siege against a hostage-taking incident at an elementary school triggered the loss of more than 300 people, almost 200 of whom were children. Most of the deaths came when Russian troops stormed the school in a horrendously botched attempt to liberate them.

Putin reacted to Beslan by tightening media censorship and eliminating gubernatorial elections, neither of which seem very much like counter-terrorism responses. If you add the subsequent invasions of Georgia and Ukraine, the promise of Putin's first term, which Abdullaev thought was at least partially justified, went only in one direction: "Tightening the screws."

Harvard's Vacroux, in fact, left Russia after the Beslan incident. When Putin went on national TV to express regret for the losses of Russian troops suffered in Beslan, Vacroux packed her bags a few weeks later.

"If that's what he's upset about, I'm done," Vacroux said. She moved to Washington, DC and finished her PhD dissertation on corruption in the Russian pharmaceutical industry.

Nothing lasts forever

Baring Vostok's Nielsen puts it all much more simply.

"What do business take away from this? And what lesson should they learn?" she asked. "And I think it's an age-old, totally cliché, totally universal lesson, which is there's a ton of money to be made in chaos. There's a ton of money to be made when things are transitioning."

Nielsen was in Russia for years. She was not there to make a fast buck.

"The biggest mistake in the world is to think that that's going to last forever. So yeah, get in. Yeah, make that money. And yeah, get out," she said. "And the people who are stupid are the people who didn't get out, who thought that was always going to be the case and I don't care whether it's Russia or South Africa or Indonesia. There's always money to be made in transition. But it's always temporary."

14

NOW WHAT?

People will put capital where the risk adjusted return will be attractive. Full stop.[1]

The thing with history is that it doesn't have to make sense. That's what you learn if you study history.[2]

Darkness at Davos

The mood was dark at Davos. Geopolitics loomed large over the 2024 Swiss mountain gathering, where the world's political and business leaders meet annually to measure and steer the global zeitgeist. That task was looking challenging. Two regional wars gripped the world; global shipping was under threat from one of them. The electoral cycle this year would bring more than a billion people to the ballot box; the outcomes of some of these elections held the potential for seismic disruption. The *Financial Times* summed it up in a headline: "Geopolitical Risks Overshadow Economic Optimism in Davos."[3]

In a speech at the conference, European Commission President Ursula von der Leyen called the current times a period of "conflict and confrontation, of fragmentation and fear." She continued: "There is no doubt we face the greatest risk to the global order in the postwar era."[4] The gloom came despite economic news that should have been more uplifting: forecasts of a recession in the US and an economic downturn in China were not materialising.

The erosion of the global order, our decades-old geopolitical comfort zone, is one of the more unsettling developments since the collapse of the Soviet Union. The nuclear-tipped US–Soviet standoff was one of the more predictable and oddly stabilising features of the Cold War. It was tense: enormous atomic arsenals were pointed at each other and ready to fly at a moment's notice. But once you got used to it, you could get a lot of work done.

Now, there's nothing to get used to.

Globalisation is reaching the end of its elasticity. The universe can only expand so much until it starts to contract again. We are meant to either be de-coupling from China or at least de-risking our relationship with China. Governments that once told their biggest companies to invest in Russia are now telling those same companies to friend-shore or near-shore, shrink their supply chains and route them around geopolitical tensions the way airline pilots fly around thunderstorms. Borders were meant to be a thing of the past. They have come roaring back in heavy, dark lines.

Crises and conflicts large and small come one after the other. Technological development and climate change drive transformation gradually (the adoption of AI and rising sea levels) and at lightning speed (cyberattacks and severe weather events). China's arrival as a major power attracts and repels companies in almost equal measure. Migration patterns are changing, and the movement of populations is accelerating. Generational and demographic change are moving large cohorts out of or into economic and political power, while the US seems gripped by gerontocracy. Democracy is in retreat around the world; authoritarian governments are on the rise.

Columbia University's Adam Tooze calls this "the polycrisis," a term first used in the 1990s but now more popularly associated with Tooze's writings.[5] Global warming creates a shortage of water. Water shortages trigger migration. Migration triggers political instability. Instability triggers conflict over scarce resources, including water. You get the idea.

Every generation puts itself at the centre of a "never before" or "worse than ever" spectrum of threats. There is, in part, an explanation for this. A phenomenon known as "recency bias" makes us think that events in the recent past are more severe than those in the distant past. But if you feel like the current moment is quantitively and qualitatively different from any other crisis-ridden moment before it, you are probably right, recency bias aside. Disruption in the twenty-first century is broader, deeper and travels further and faster than it did in the past.

Patricia Cohen, the global economic correspondent for *The New York Times*, summed it up pretty well in an article headlined "Why It Seems Everything We Knew about the Global Economy Is No Longer True," in which she discusses the dismantling of all the assumptions about how the world works that have been in place since the collapse of the Berlin Wall. Her piece cites, among other things, a report from the World Bank.

"Nearly all the economic forces that powered progress and prosperity over the last three decades are fading," the article says, quoting the World Bank. "The result could be a lost decade in the making—not just for some countries or regions as has occurred in the past—but for the whole world."[6]

One of the assumptions investors and political leaders have long made was that capitalism, or at the very least a market economy, was a feature more or less associated with liberal democracies. As globalisation gained pace and then accelerated following the fall of the Berlin Wall, that assumption came unstuck. There were plenty of authoritarian regimes and unreformed socialist or communist countries suddenly open for business.

"Market systems turned out to be politically promiscuous; they could share a bed with any number of political regimes, from Nordic democracies to Singaporean meritocracies," Michael Ignatieff, the Canadian politician, academic and former president and rector of the Central European University, wrote. "In Xi Jinping's China and Vladimir Putin's Russia, Western liberal democracy faces a competitor [Francis] Fukuyama did not anticipate: states that are capitalist in economics, authoritarian in politics, and nationalist in ideology."[7]

Gunitsky, of the University of Toronto, backs him up: "We think that capitalism and democracy have to go together—that they're natural partners. But it's just a post-1945 phenomenon that we think that way. There are lots of ways that businesses can survive in a non-democratic society, and they have. You might prefer stability over electoral turnover."[8]

Destination unknown

The problem with the current period of disruption to our geopolitical assumptions is that it defies easy categorisation. Are we in a transition period on the way to a new global order? If we are, what will it be, and how long before we get there? Do China and the US reach an accommodation on trade, technology and security and let us all get on with things? That would likely be a best-case scenario. Or, is this period of transition itself the new permanent state of affairs, where the US retreats from its role as the global sheriff, no single state actor takes its place and we are left with ongoing, rudderless turmoil?

We have been here before. Abdelal at the Harvard Business School reminds us that the world was once governed by a UKcentric system. We are now—perhaps—in the end phase of the US-centric system. Abdelal does not believe the leader of the next phase has emerged yet.

"We're not on the verge of a Sino-centric system," he said. "There are lots of questions about the trajectory of Chinese growth."

If history is cyclical, we will at some point reach some sort of new equilibrium, enjoy the stability it affords for a while and then wait until some new disruptor emerges to upset the status quo. If history is linear, then disruption remains a more permanent feature as we all lurch forward in a direction that becomes difficult to forecast.

"The war in Ukraine, much like the war in Israel and Gaza, and a number of other regional wars, are manifestations of a disintegrating world order," Abdelal said. "And insofar as the ongoing disintegration of the global order requires every company in the world to have a point of view about geopolitical risks, then yes, this is a new era."

Abdelal caught himself and made a telling correction.

"Well, this is an era that resembles basically all of the other eras that existed, except for 1945 to 2010," he said.

In other words, prolonged periods of peace and growth are the exception, rather than the rule, in geopolitics. The relatively peaceful, prosperous period following the Second World War is, however, our only recent point of reference. This is when today's world grew up, professionally and otherwise. The executives running companies today have never had to navigate a period of constant, intense conflict.

Nokian Tires once manufactured 80 per cent of its tires in Russia; Russian consumers bought 20 per cent of the tires Nokian made. After the full-scale invasion of Ukraine, the company left Russia and began constructing a new factory in Romania. As Nokian looked for a place to site its new factory, it had a list of all the usual investment criteria, but, as *The New York Times* reported, the new site had to be in a country with two other "make or break" criteria: it had to be in the European Union and NATO.

"Geopolitical risk 'was the starting point,'" *The New York Times* said, quoting Jukka Moisio, CEO and president of Nokian. Even Hungary, which ticked the two most important boxes, was ruled out because of the politics of its leader, Viktor Orbán.[9]

Stop chasing swans

After years of languishing in the "nice to know" category, geopolitics and political risk are finally at or near the top of most international companies' agendas, up to and including at board level. Too many companies have been burned in too many markets for these issues to go unexamined any longer. Understanding the way countries and companies interact is now in the "have to know" category. This new level of awareness is a positive development, but it is only the beginning of managing risk better. Now that companies know they need to talk about geopolitics, they need to understand how to do it well.

In the past, companies dealt with risk in a highly unproductive manner. They made a fetish of former US Defense Secretary Donald Rumsfeld's phraseology and wasted their time pondering the "unknown unknowns."

Then came Nassim Nicholas Taleb and his concept of "black swans." This framework was a bit more elegantly and elaborately presented than Rumsfeld's linguistic cocktail, so companies spent time and money looking for precisely where a meteor might fall from outer space and hit them in the bottom line. Predicting black swans is an oxymoron—by their very nature, black swans are meant to be unpredictable. Perhaps also not the best use of an executive's time.

More recently, the risk vocabulary has alighted on a more productive place. Smart companies are now trying to grasp "emerging risks." These are a category of potential events, trends or issues close enough to be known to us. But they are still far enough away to be slightly out of focus, and unpredictable. Ruling in or ruling out these emerging risks is still difficult to do, so companies monitor them. Some will increase in importance; others will recede from relevance. But they are topics that bear regular monitoring.

The very exercise of naming, categorising and prioritising these risks for a company is time extremely well spent. Among other things, it helps create a shared vocabulary of risk, something most companies sorely lack.

And much like Gustafson and Yergin wrote scenarios for Russia in 2010, companies are once again devising scenarios along longer and longer timelines to create a view, or views, of the future and see how, or whether, their company fits against those scenarios. The point here is not to forecast—it is to build institutional resilience in the face of several scenarios. Plus which, the next consultant who tells a client that a regional conflict is a "low likelihood event" will be sent packing.

Listen to governments (with one ear)

Governments encouraged their private sectors to invest in Russia, and companies not only listened but believed. Even if there was a significant peace dividend to be harvested from a more democratic and market-oriented Russia, companies should learn to listen to government pronouncements on emerging markets more critically. The US made the same mistake with China that it did with Russia—as China developed, America thought that with enough time and enough money, China's system would converge with the United States'.

"The Russian example of 1991–1992—you had the US government encouraging US firms to pile into Russia: 'Let's get in there,' and most of them were just running with it and it ended up going badly," said Cameron Mitchell, former head of geopolitical risk for HSBC in London.

That has not prevented the same thing from happening with the United States' views on China, Mitchell said. US engagement with China was based on "convergence theory," or the assumption that "engage China and their political system will liberalise the way their economy has. The US government was encouraging everyone to pile into China, and now they're saying, 'Get out of the Chinese market.'"

Companies should challenge the assumptions governments make when they are promoting a country. Geopolitical interests do not always align with commercial interests. They could, but they don't. The internal geopolitical risk function is there "to warn [companies] against whatever the government of the day is saying, because it may change on a dime because of the geopolitical risk reality out there," Mitchell said.

Where is the stage? Who are the actors?

The question returns to the role and position of the company in geopolitics.

"When the firm meets the sovereign in a struggle, the sovereign always wins," Abdelal said on the interaction of company and state. "If the sovereign means it, if we want to destroy Microsoft, we can destroy Microsoft. If we want to destroy Apple, we can destroy Apple."

Shareholders in Microsoft and Apple, worry not. Or don't worry too much. There are only a small handful of nation-states that wield that sort of power. And it's not certain that any of them want to destroy Microsoft or Apple if for no other reason than most governments run on Microsoft. When the Russian government forced its officials in sensitive roles to relinquish their iPhones in a security-conscious burst of anti-Western spite, they turned in their work iPhones but were allowed to keep the ones they had for personal use.[10]

As for companies, some can influence geopolitics; others can't.

"There are lots of firms that exert influence on the world without directly shaping the geopolitics of the world," Abdelal said. "And there are lots of firms that exert influence on the world while simultaneously reshaping the geopolitics of the world."

If you're a company with significant geopolitical weight, CEOs and boards beware.

"Corporate strategy produces geopolitical outcomes," Abdelal said. "Building Nord Stream 2 [a gas pipeline from Russia to Germany under the Baltic Sea] was a geopolitical outcome. It began to disintermediate Ukraine. It created fissures in the European Union."

It might be interesting to measure which group is larger: countries that can meaningfully influence companies, or companies that can meaningfully influence countries. Perhaps that's the subject of a different book.

Bye. For now

This book started with a question about what companies were thinking when they invested in Russia over the past thirty years.

It ends with a series of questions. Was that thinking clear-headed? Did that thinking hold up? Did it withstand the routine and the extraordinary pressures visited on companies and their executives in Russia over the decades? Companies, executives, regulators and political leaders—within and across their groups—will always answer these questions differently.

It remains to be seen whether they ask them again.

In June 2024, Coca-Cola and Starbucks applied to extend their trademarks in Russia.[11]

ACKNOWLEDGEMENTS

Trying to describe a generation of international commerce in Russia is something no one should do alone. I most assuredly did not.

I would in the very first instance like to thank all the individuals quoted in this book for being so generous with their time and their insights. Sincere and deep thanks to Rawi Abdelal, Nabi Abdullaev, Tom Adshead, Oksana Antonenko, Patti Baral, Vladimir Borodin, Maxim Boycko, William Burke-White, Michael Calvey, Roger Canton, Oliver Cescotti, Robert Courtney, Eric Crabtree, Alexei Evgenev, Tom Firestone, Laurie Fry, Tony Gambrill, Andrew Glass, Nigel Gould-Davies, David Grant, Alexander Gubsky, Seva Gunitsky, Hugh Hallard, Robyn Holt, Harry Itameri, Jeff Kaye, Elizabeth Krasnoff, Stuart Lawson, Hassan Malik, Heidi McCormack, Paul Melling, Cameron Mitchell, Paul Moxness, Philip Nichols, Holly Nielsen, Nicolas Ollivant, Mitchell Orenstein, Paul Ostling, Brian O'Toole, Richard Prior, William Reichert, Alexis Rodzianko, Robert Sasson, Derk Sauer, Anton Shingarev, Robert Starr, Timothy Stubbs, Bernie Sucher, Joshua Tulgan, Alexandra Vacroux, Regina von Flemming, Sergey Vorobyev, Christine Wootliff and Roman Zilber.

The same thanks are due to a small number of contributors who asked that their names not be used, or whose comments may not appear in the final draft but whose input was essential. All these people have made this book far richer than it could be otherwise. Speaking with each of them was a pleasure and a privilege.

I am delighted to thank Dr Ben Noble for supporting this book from its inception. He has been a patient, engaging and insightful guide through the research, the writing and the crafting of this book. The same is the case for Michael Dwyer at Hurst Publishers, whose family of authors I feel incredibly fortunate to join. Michael's initial expressions of confidence in a kernel of an idea were at once reassuring and enormously energising. A very big thank you to the entire team at Hurst, including Alice Clarke, Daisy Leitch, Raminta Uselytė and the Hurst graphic design department. My thanks also to Tim Page for copyediting and Ross Jamieson for proofreading.

I would like to thank a few family members for doing what family does best: providing unconditional love and support in bottomless quantities. My sister Judy Hecker, brother-in-law Matt Furman and my late mom and dad have always been the deepest seams of support in all my endeavours. In the 1980s, my dad approved of my education in Soviet studies by declaring that "The Soviet Union will always be around. People who understand it will always be useful." He more or less got it right; Russia's rapid re-Sovietisation has made his words once again so terribly relevant. My two nephews, Malcolm and Ethan Furman, inspire me with their voracious intellectual appetite and equally boundless aptitude. These people, together with the invincible and unshakeable Gloria Hecker and my beautiful, eclectic stepfamily, are the bedrock and the springboard beneath me.

I am humbled by the encouragement of my friends and allies. All of them have provided logistical, technical, moral, editorial and food-and-beverage support, sometimes all at the same time. They opened their address books, their homes and their refrigerators without hesitation, and I am hugely grateful to all of them, including Zaira Abdullaeva, Mustapha Backili, Inna Bazhanova, Gergo Bagladi, James Greenshields, Brook Horowitz, Larissa Kouznetsova, Nuno da Silva, Martin Stone and Gary Duffield, and Ben Wootliff. William Flemming, Ian Garner, Rosie Hawes, Max Hess, Kay Hope, Alena Ledeneva, Owen Matthews, David Munns and Boris Starling have been hugely generous with their time and insights. A big thank you, too, to Michael Denison.

On top of their generous supplies of sparkling hospitality, I'd like to thank Mike Yule and particularly Georgina Godwin for single-handedly providing the subtle, yet deeply supportive nudge that got this entire enterprise off the ground. Never has a seemingly impromptu remark been so transformative. The entire Monocle Radio team, especially on-air boosters Emma Nelson and Andrew Mueller, has been brilliantly supportive. A very big thank you also to Nadia Manuelli.

Outside the UK, I am hugely indebted to Jay Croft, Katherine Docampo, Gerhard Eisenacher, Sasha Gubsky, Chris Marlin, Kaj Moeller, Lisa Osofsky, Robert Otto, Daniel Satinsky, Oliver Scholz, Bathyr Shikhmuradov and Konstantin Shmondrik, and Dafne Ter-Sakarian and Graham Fowles. Alison Taylor served double duty as friend and book-world guru.

The extended C28 family of Rich Harris, Andy Pasternak and Lori Kisch, and Marc and Abby Posner, are the sort people everyone should have in their life, in generous measures. I am outrageously fortunate to have had them in mine for more than forty years.

My early Moscow days with Abi Wright and Greg Johnson, whom I met while queueing to get into a bar on Bolshaya Nikitskaya Ulitsa in 1994, launched a never-ending series of

Russia discussion sessions and created foundational friendships that have only grown more central and important with time. How lucky also to have Stuart Macphee in the gang.

Having Harvard's Davis Center as a source of inspiration is a great privilege. My periodic trips back there, to top up on the latest and some of the best thinking on Russia from a group of engaging and welcoming individuals, have been enormously motivating. Thank you also to the University of Pennsylvania for accepting a late application to the Russian and Soviet Studies major. What a pleasure to cite in this book the great Alfred Rieber, one of my professors at Penn. I blame Penn's Masha Lekic and Cynthia Martin for making me love the Russian language, and credit Harvard's Anna Bobrova for testing that love and making it durable.

I would like to thank Control Risks, which was my professional home for more than two decades, for paying me to combine my vocation and avocation. Drawing a salary for being a Russia geek was like winning the lottery. A sign of a good professional home is the number of people you feel you want to thank after all these years. A few, for the sake of brevity: CEO Nick Allan and CMO Hannah Kitt have been enthusiastically supportive of this project. Claudine Fry has been enthusiastically supportive of me, while also shouldering all the work I dodged while on book leave. For years, Jonathan Wood generously covered all the gaps in my knowledge, without making me feel they were there. Richard Fenning, whose role morphed so easily from former CEO to friend, has been an inspiration.

Nabi Abdullaev and Tim Stanley (now a Control Risks alumnus), who both succeeded me as head of Control Risks' Moscow office, have provided invaluable insights and advice, as did James Owen and alumnus and friend Toby Latta, my predecessor in Moscow and the clairvoyant who hired me. Thank you also to Adam Strangfeld. Control Risks' Moscow office, which opened in 1993, is now closed. I want to pay tribute to Viktoria Denisenko and Elena Karsonova, who were there for me as colleagues when I first arrived in Moscow and have been there as friends ever since. I also want to express my admiration of everyone from Control Risks' Moscow team who uprooted their lives and relocated to London or other offices, showing great courage and resilience in the process.

Several of the people above read early versions of the manuscript, including the eagle-eyed Eve O'Sullivan. They offered wise counsel and rigorously deleted errors. I am indebted to all of them. Any remaining mistakes, of course, are entirely my own.

Robust surges of intellectual horsepower came from research assistants Bella Rafailova and Alexander Finiarel, whose ability to dig deep, analyse and deliver was of great support. I owe them, and Katherine Ray Akwa, enormous thanks. A very big thank you to Kathrine Schutz and data whiz Daniil Surikov.

Tom Adshead, one of the first individuals I spoke to for this book, suggested that everyone else I wanted to interview would, like him, gladly agree to talk. His remark surprised and encouraged me, but I wondered why he was so sure in that view. He responded by saying that for almost everyone, the years they worked and lived in Russia were full of all sorts of excitement, and who doesn't like telling a good story? Almost every expat who worked in Russia encountered at least one defining personal or professional experience while they were there. Some got married or started families. Some travelled to places or met people they will never forget.

For many, he said, their time in Russia was quite simply among the best years of their lives.

As it was for me.

London, June 2024

NOTES

LIST OF INDIVIDUALS

1. ESG is an acronym that represents Environmental, Social and Governance and is meant to describe the new parameters for how businesses examine their impact on the world around them.
2. In 2024–5, Vacroux is on leave from Harvard for a one-year posting at the Kyiv School of Economics as its vice president for strategic engagement.

1.   THE PHONE RINGS

1. Here and elsewhere, Tom Firestone, author interview, London–Washington, DC, 5 May 2023.
2. Here and elsewhere, William Reichert, author interview, London–Dubai, 11 July 2023.
3. Here and elsewhere, author interview, London, 6 July 2023.
4. Luke Harding et al., "Macron Claims Putin Gave Him Personal Assurances on Ukraine," *The Guardian*, 8 Feb. 2022, https://www.theguardian.com/world/2022/feb/08/macron-zelenskiy-ukraine-talks-moscow-denies-deal-to-de-escalate
5. Dan Sabagh, "US and UK Intelligence Warnings Vindicated by Russian Invasion," *The Guardian*, 24 Feb. 2022, https://www.theguardian.com/us-news/2022/feb/24/us-uk-intelligence-russian-invasion-ukraine

6. Max Seddon, Christopher Miller and Felicia Schwartz, "How Putin Blundered into Ukraine—then Doubled Down," *Financial Times*, 23 Feb. 2023, https://www.ft.com/content/80002564-33e8-48fb-b734-44810afb7a49

7. Here and elsewhere, author interview, Cambridge, MA, 30 Oct. 2023.

8. Daniel Yergin and Thane Gustafson, *Russia 2010 and What It Means for the World* (New York: Random House, 1994), 112.

9. Yergin and Gustafson, *Russia 2010*, 14.

10. Yergin and Gustafson, *Russia 2010*, 131.

11. Yergin and Gustafson, *Russia 2010*, 14.

12. Yergin and Gustafson, *Russia 2010*, 15.

13. Yergin and Gustafson, *Russia 2010*, 16.

14. This is a topic discussed in Gwendolyn Sasse's *The Crimea Question: Identity Transition and Conflict* (Cambridge, MA: Harvard University Press, 2007).

15. Yergin and Gustafson, *Russia 2010*, 132.

16. Yergin and Gustafson, *Russia 2010*, 16.

17. Here and elsewhere, author interview, Tel Aviv, 25 June 2023.

18. Thomas Friedman, "Foreign Affairs Big Mac I," *The New York Times*, 8 Dec. 1996, https://www.nytimes.com/1996/12/08/opinion/foreign-affairs-big-mac-i.html

19. Author interview, London, 11 May 2023.

20. Michael Schwirtz, Maria Varenikova and Rick Gladstone, "Putin Calls Ukrainian Statehood a Fiction: History Suggests Otherwise," *The New York Times*, 21 Feb. 2022, https://www.nytimes.com/2022/02/21/world/europe/putin-ukraine.html

21. Isaac Chotiner, "Why John Mearsheimer Blames the US for the Crisis in Ukraine," *The New Yorker*, 1 Mar. 2022, https://www.newyorker.com/news/q-and-a/why-john-mearsheimer-blames-the-us-for-the-crisis-in-ukraine

22. Here and elsewhere, author interview, Boca Raton–Delray Beach, FL, 11 Jan. 2024.

23. Here and elsewhere, author interview, London–Dubai, 5 Oct. 2023.

24. Anastasia Stognei and Max Seddon, "Trapped or Nationalised: Walls Close in on Western Businesses in Russia," *Financial Times*,

21 July 2023, https://www.ft.com/content/c6108c1a-97dc-4469-aeb3-8b81ab52aaa9

25. "Duma razreshila Putinu natsionalizirovat' inostranniye kompanii" [The Duma has allowed Putin to nationalise foreign companies], *The Moscow Times*, Russian Service, 8 Dec. 2023, https://www.moscowtimes.ru/2023/12/08/duma-razreshila-putinu-natsionalizirovat-inostrannie-kompanii-ssha-hotyat-ubedit-rossiyu-poiti-namir-sukrainoi-kkontsu-2024-goda-vlasti-dopustyat--loyalnih-blogerov-kgoskontraktam-sinu-baidena-grozyat-17-let-tyurmi-zauklonenie-otuplati-nalogov-a115597

26. "Number of Russian Billionaires Jumps in 2023 Despite Sanctions—Forbes," *The Moscow Times*, 20 Apr. 2023, https://www.themoscowtimes.com/2023/04/20/billionaires-a80889

27. Here, author interview, London–Berlin, 23 Mar. 2024.

28. Stognei and Seddon, "Trapped or Nationalised."

29. Andrew Roth et al., "Putin Signals Escalation as He Puts Nuclear Force on High Alert," *The Guardian*, 28 Feb. 2022, https://www.theguardian.com/world/2022/feb/27/vladimir-putin-puts-russia-nuclear-deterrence-forces-on-high-alert-ukraine

30. Contents of a private conversation with the author.

31. Contents of a private conversation with the author.

32. Contents of a private conversation with the author.

33. "Russian Parliament Examines Plan to Seize Dissidents' Assets," Reuters, 22 Jan. 2024, https://www.reuters.com/world/europe/russian-parliament-examines-plan-seize-dissidents-assets-2024-01-22

34. "'Party Like a Russian' Turns Toxic at Putin's Flagship Forum," Bloomberg, 12 June 2022, https://www.bloomberg.com/news/articles/2022-06-12/-party-like-a-russian-turns-toxic-at-putin-s-flagship-forum

35. "Over 1,000 Companies Have Curtailed Operations in Russia—but Some Remain," Yale School of Management, Chief Executive Leadership Institute, 28 Jan. 2024, https://som.yale.edu/story/2022/over-1000-companies-have-curtailed-operations-russia-some-remain

36. "Stop Doing Business with Russia," Leave-Russia.org/KSE Institute, 29 May 2024, https://leave-russia.org/staying-companies

37. "McDonald's to Exit from Russia," corporate.mcdonalds.com, 16 May 2022, https://leave-russia.org/staying-companies

38. Kara Swisher and Jeffrey Sonnenfeld, "The Corporations Passing—and Failing—the Ukraine Morality Test: The Yale Professor Jeffrey Sonnenfeld Makes the Case for Full Corporate Withdrawal from Russia," *The New York Times*, 24 Mar. 2022, https://www.nytimes.com/2022/03/24/opinion/sway-kara-swisher-jeffrey-sonnenfeld.html

39. Garry Kasparov (@Kasparov63), "Companies that were doing business in Russia decided it was worth the risk and were happy supporting a police state when the profits were good. Staying after ...," Twitter/X, 15:01, 17 July 2023, https://x.com/Kasparov63/status/1680940684398788608

40. Andy Dolan, "Italian Fashion House under Pressure to Condemn Vladimir Putin over £10,500 Coat," Mail Online, 23 Mar. 2022, https://www.dailymail.co.uk/news/article-10641965/Italian-fashion-house-pressure-condemn-Vladimir-Putin-10-500-coat.html

41. Nick Wadhams, "Russia Is Now the World's Most-Sanctioned Nation," Bloomberg, 7 Mar. 2022, https://www.bloomberg.com/news/articles/2022-03-07/russia-surges-past-iran-to-become-worlds-most-sanctioned-nation

42. "World Economic Outlook Update: Inflation Peaking amid Low Growth," International Monetary Fund, Jan. 2023, https://www.imf.org/en/Publications/WEO/Issues/2023/01/31/world-economic-outlook-update-january-2023

43. Robin Brooks, "German exports of cars and parts ...," Twitter/X, 17:33, 2 Dec. 2023, https://twitter.com/robin_j_brooks/status/1731003784027939181?s=20

44. Denis Kasyanchuk, "Russia's Big Sanctions Workaround," The Bell, 6 Oct. 2023, https://en.thebell.io/russias-big-sanctions-workaround

45. Kasyanchuk, "Russia's Big Sanctions Workaround."

46. "Proizvoditeli bytovoi tekhniki nachali blokirovat' parallel'nyi import v RF" [Appliance manufacturers have started to block parallel import into the RF], *Kommersant*, 15 Mar. 2024, https://www.kommersant.ru/doc/6564526; "I chainik ne proskochit" [A kettle won't make it through], *Kommersant*, 15 Mar. 2024, https://www.kommersant.ru/doc/6564261

47. Denis Kasyanchuk, "How Russia Uses China to Get Round Sanctions," The Bell, 20 Feb. 2024, https://en.thebell.io/how-russia-uses-china-to-get-round-sanctions

48. Bryan Harris, "Brazil's Imports of Russian Oil Products Soar," *Financial Times*, 30 Jan. 2024, https://www.ft.com/content/7ebb679e-099e-49ac-a750a46538dee

49. "The Russian Economy Is in Good Shape—If You Cherry Pick Data," The Bell, 8 Dec. 2023, https://en.thebell.io/the-russian-economy-is-in-good-shape-if-you-cherry-pick-data/

50. Burger King is still in Russia, despite a pledge to leave. Burger King's presence in Russia is complex; the company says it is trying to leave. The Yale group says that Burger King's intricate, multi-party franchise agreement in Russia is a "convenient smokescreen." Michael Race, "Ukraine War: Burger King Still Open in Russia Despite Pledge to Exit," BBC News, 3 Oct. 2023, https://www.bbc.co.uk/news/business-66739104

51. Ernst & Young rebranded as EY in 2013.

52. Here and elsewhere, author interview, New York City, 25 July 2023.

53. "Russia Probes U.S. Chocolate Giant Mars for Funding Ukraine Army," *The Moscow Times*, 7 July 2023, https://www.themoscowtimes.com/2023/07/07/russia-probes-us-chocolate-giant-mars-for-funding-ukraine-army-a81764

54. Sam Jones, "Raiffeisen Generated Almost Half Its Profits This Year from Russia," *Financial Times*, 3 Nov. 2023, https://www.ft.com/content/0df0617c-bb98-4185-b57c-422c8d34d52f

55. "European Banks Are Making Heady Profits in Russia," *The Economist*, 6 June 2024, updated 10 June 2024, https://www.economist.com/finance-and-economics/2024/06/06/european-banks-are-making-heady-profits-in-russia

56. Stognei and Seddon, "Trapped or Nationalised."

57. Madeleine Speed, "Mondelez Chief Says Investors Do Not 'Morally Care' if Group Stays in Russia," *Financial Times*, 22 Feb. 2024, https://www.ft.com/content/10621358-55f2-4152-90a4-4cb4fea5116a

58. Speed, "Mondelez Chief Says Investors Do Not 'Morally Care.'"

59. Nikolai Petrov, "Putin Is Using De-privatization to Create a New Generation of Loyal Oligarchs," Chatham House, 4 Oct.

2023, https://www.chathamhouse.org/2023/10/putin-using-de-privatization-create-new-generation-loyal-oligarchs

60. Jared Gans, "US Businesses Were Largest Tax Contributors to Russia among International Companies in 2022: Report," The Hill, 8 July 2023, https://thehill.com/policy/international/4086790-us-businesses-were-largest-tax-contributors-to-russia-among-international-companies-in-2022-report

61. "The Russian Economy Is in Good Shape—If You Cherry Pick Data," The Bell, 8 Dec. 2023, https://en.thebell.io/the-russian-economy-is-in-good-shape-if-you-cherry-pick-data

62. Anastasia Stognei et al., "Russia Seizes Subsidiaries of Finland's Fortum and Germany's Uniper," Financial Times, 26 Apr. 2023, https://www.ft.com/content/aa7ffb41-bcb9-4983-a312-1473fa0513b8

63. Madeleine Speed, Courtney Weaver and Max Seddon, "'Blood in the Water': How Carlsberg Lost Its Russian Business," Financial Times, 10 Nov. 2023, https://www.ft.com/content/af2fa231-881e-4241-9b37-ab772bf376a2

64. Polina Ivanova and Adrienne Klasa, "Moscow Seizes Russian Subsidiaries of Danone and Carlsberg's Baltika," Financial Times, 16 July 2023, https://www.ft.com/content/95530b86-dd98-4f26-b115-3f6e8cca6ce5

65. "Update from Danone on Its EDP Business in Russia," Danone, 22 Mar. 2024, https://www.danone.com/media/press-releases-list/danone-update-edp-business-russia.html

66. Courtney Weaver and Adrienne Klasa, "Danone Plans to Sell Russian Operations to Chechnya-Linked Businessman," Financial Times, 21 Feb. 2024, https://www.ft.com/content/6c1c5fe0-5a98-4d67-acfb-caf482e109cf

67. "Carlsberg Group Terminates License Agreements in Russia," Carlsberg Group, 3 Oct. 2023, https://www.carlsberggroup.com/newsroom/carlsberg-group-terminates-license-agreements-in-russia

68. Michael Race, "Carlsberg Cuts Ties with 'Stolen' Russian Business," BBC, 31 Oct. 2023, https://www.bbc.co.uk/news/articles/cgxkx9g2kn4o

69. Madeleine Speed and Courtney Weaver, "Ex-Carlsberg Executives Detained in Russia over Fraud Claims," Financial Times, 16 Nov

2023, https://www.ft.com/content/145f2310-7222-4df9-9976-f268ed1f1eb2

70. Speed, Weaver and Seddon, "'Blood in the Water.'"

71. Anastasia Stognei, Silvia Sciorilli Borrelli and Joshua Franklin, "Russia Court Seizes €700mn Assets from UniCredit, Deutsche Bank and Commerzbank," *Financial Times*, 18 May 2024, https://www.ft.com/content/481d418e-9366-4152-8ec5-92b81d020991

72. Peggy Hollinger, Eri Sugiura and Oliver Telling, "European Companies Suffer €100 Billion Hit from Russia Operations," *Financial Times*, 6 Aug. 2023, https://www.ft.com/content/c4ea72b4-4b02-4ee9-b34c-0fac4a4033f5

73. Hollinger, Sugiura and Telling, "European Companies Suffer €100 Billion Hit."

74. Margarita Sobol, "Only Nine of the World's 100 Most Valuable Brands Are Staying in Russia," *Vedomosti*, 25 Nov. 2023, https://www.vedomosti.ru/business/articles/2023/11/24/1007629-11-dorogih-brendov

75. Courtney Weaver and Madeleine Speed, "Western Businesses Backtrack on Their Russia Exit Plans," *Financial Times*, 28 May 2024, https://www.ft.com/content/88b047e9-8cad-426a-b649-265ff6582db0

76. Here and elsewhere, author interview, London–Dubai, 16 Nov. 2023.

2. LOOKING BACK, WAS IT EVER THUS?

1. Here and elsewhere, unless otherwise noted, author interview, London, 11 Aug. 2023.

2. Walther Kirchner, "Western Businessmen in Russia: Practices and Problems," *The Business History Review* 38, no. 3 (1964): 325.

3. M.E. Falkus, *The Industrialisation of Russia, 1700–1914*, 2nd edn, ed. M.W. Finn, Studies in Economic and Social History (London: Macmillan Press, 1977 [1970]), [44].

4. Falkus, *Industrialisation of Russia*, 63, 70.

5. *Manchester Examiner and Times*, 22 Dec. 1849, citing information from *The Globe* of Wednesday, 19 Dec. 1849.

6. Jeffry A. Frieden, *Global Capitalism, Its Fall and Rise in the Twentieth Century and Its Stumbles in the Twenty-First* (New York: W.W. Norton & Company, 2020), 19.

7. Falkus, *Industrialisation of Russia*, 76.

8. Falkus, *Industrialisation of Russia*, 70–1.

9. Falkus, *Industrialisation of Russia*, 70–1.

10. Alexandre Tarsaidze, "American Pioneers in Russian Railroad Building," *The Russian Review* 9, no. 4 (1950): 286–7.

11. "United States Relations with Russia: Establishment of Relations to World War Two," Historical Background, Office of the Historian, Washington, DC, United States Department of State Archive, https://2001-2009.state.gov/r/pa/ho/pubs/fs/85739.htm

12. George L. Vose, *A Sketch of the Life and Works of George W. Whistler, Civil Engineer* (Boston: Lee and Shepard, 1887), 33.

13. Vose, *Sketch of the Life and Works of George W. Whistler*, 29–42.

14. Vose, *Sketch of the Life and Works of George W. Whistler*, 39.

15. Vose, *Sketch of the Life and Works of George W. Whistler*, 40.

16. Tarsaidze, "American Pioneers," 294.

17. Alfred J. Rieber, *Merchants and Entrepreneurs in Imperial Russia* (Chapel Hill: University of North Carolina Press, 1982), 146.

18. Alexandra Swetzer, "Foreign Investment and Economic Development in Tsarist Russia," in *Foreign Investment in Russia and Other Soviet Successor States*, ed. Patrick Artisien-Maksimenko and Yuri Adjubei (Houndmills: Macmillan Press, 1996), 25.

19. Walther Kirchner, "The Industrialization of Russia and the Siemens Firm 1853–1890," *Jahrbücher für Geschichte Osteuropas* 22, no. 3 (1974): 323.

20. Kirchner, "Industrialization of Russia," 323.

21. Kirchner, "Industrialization of Russia," 324.

22. Kirchner, "Industrialization of Russia," 325.

23. Kirchner, "Industrialization of Russia," 332.

24. Rieber, *Merchants and Entrepreneurs*, 247.

25. Kirchner, "Industrialization of Russia," 327.

26. Kirchner, "Western Businessmen in Russia," 316. Please note here that Kirchner, writing in 1964, is (1) using historical names and spellings for some Russian cities (Caffa is Feodosia, on the Crimean Peninsula) and (2) labelling as Russian cities that were in the Ukrainian lands of the Russian Empire.

27. Kirchner, "Western Businessmen in Russia," 317.

28. Kirchner, "Western Businessmen in Russia," 327.

29. Oliver Cescotti, author interview, London–Berlin, 1 June 2023.

30. Kirchner, "Western Businessmen in Russia," 319.

31. Kirchner, "Industrialization of Russia," 333.

32. Walther Kirchner, "Siemens and AEG and the Electrification of Russia, 1890–1914," *Jahrbücher für Geschichte Osteuropas* 30, no. 3 (1982): 401. The quote is believed to be from the 1890s.

33. Kirchner, "Industrialization of Russia," 333.

34. John P. McKay, *Pioneers for Profit: Foreign Entrepreneurship and Russian Industrialization, 1885–1913* (Chicago: University of Chicago Press, 1970), 291, 292.

35. Kirchner, "Industrialization of Russia," 333.

36. Kirchner, "Western Businessmen in Russia," 325.

37. Kirchner, "Industrialization of Russia," 335.

38. McKay, *Pioneers for Profit*, 269.

39. Kirchner, "Industrialization of Russia," 337.

40. Kirchner, "Industrialization of Russia," 337.

41. McKay, *Pioneers for Profit*, 273.

42. Kirchner, "Industrialization of Russia," 336.

43. Kirchner, "Industrialization of Russia," 338.

44. Kirchner, "Industrialization of Russia," 351.

45. Kirchner, "Siemens and AEG and the Electrification of Russia," 407.

46. Falkus, *Industrialisation of Russia*, 66.

47. Falkus, *Industrialisation of Russia*, 70.

48. Olga Crisp, *Studies in the Russian Economy before 1914* (London: Macmillan Press, 1976), 159.

49. Crisp, *Studies in the Russian Economy*, 40.

50. Currency conversions calculated using Markus A. Denzel, *Handbook of World Exchange Rates, 1590–1914* (Farnham: Ashgate, 2010), 371.

51. Kirchner, "Siemens and AEG and the Electrification of Russia," 421.

52. Kirchner, "Siemens and AEG and the Electrification of Russia," 424.

53. Peter Gatrell, "Industrial Expansion in Tsarist Russia, 1908–14," *The Economic History Review* 35, no. 1 (1982): [99, 101].

54. Swetzer, "Foreign Investment," 38.

55. Crisp, *Studies in the Russian Economy*, 159.

56. Thomas Jones, "British Business in Russia, 1892–1914" (PhD diss., University College London, 2017), 110, https://discovery.ucl.ac.uk/id/eprint/1559904/1/Final%20Thesis%201606.pdf

57. Crisp, *Studies in the Russian Economy*, 161–2.

58. Crisp, *Studies in the Russian Economy*, 165–6.

59. Martin Lutz and Ewald Blocker, "Siemens in Russia," Siemens, n.d., https://www.siemens.com/global/en/company/about/history/stories/siemens-russia.html

60. Hassan Malik, *Bankers and Bolsheviks* (Princeton: Princeton University Press, 2018), 10.

61. Peter Gatrell, *The Tsarist Economy 1850–1917* (New York: St Martin's Press, 1986), 222.

62. Gatrell, *Tsarist Economy*, 222–3.

63. Malik, *Bankers and Bolsheviks*, 27–8.

64. Malik, *Bankers and Bolsheviks*, 31.

65. Malik, *Bankers and Bolsheviks*, 10.

66. Vincent Bignon and Marc Flandreau, "The Economics of Badmouthing: Libel Law and the Underworld of the Financial Press in France before World War I," *The Journal of Economic History* 71, no. 3 (2011): 616–53. With thanks to Hassan Malik for the introduction. "Arthur Raffalovich Obituary," *The New York Times*, 13 Jan. 1922, 12.

67. Olga Crisp, "The Russian Liberals and the 1906 Anglo-French Loan to Russia," *The Slavonic and East European Review* 39, no. 93 (1961): 499, citing Stephen Gwynn, ed., *The Letters and Friendships of Sir Cecil Spring Rice* (Boston: Houghton Mifflin Co., 1929).

68. Crisp, "Russian Liberals and the 1906 Anglo-French Loan," 500–1.

69. Malik, *Bankers and Bolsheviks*, 61.

70. Malik, *Bankers and Bolsheviks*, 77.

71. Malik, *Bankers and Bolsheviks*, 86.

72. Malik, *Bankers and Bolsheviks*, 97–8.

73. Malik, *Bankers and Bolsheviks*, 98.

74. Malik, *Bankers and Bolsheviks*, 98.

75. Malik, *Bankers and Bolsheviks*, 129.

76. Malik, *Bankers and Bolsheviks*, 130.

77. Malik, *Bankers and Bolsheviks*, 133.

78. Malik, *Bankers and Bolsheviks*, 135–7, quote sourced from the Russian State Historical Archive 624/1/5/202.

79. Malik, *Bankers and Bolsheviks*, 138.

80. Hassan Malik, author interview, London, 11 Aug. 2023.

81. Malik, *Bankers and Bolsheviks*, 145.

82. Malik, *Bankers and Bolsheviks*, 148, citing HSBC archives.

83. Malik, *Bankers and Bolsheviks*, 146.

84. Malik, *Bankers and Bolsheviks*, 156–7.

85. Malik, *Bankers and Bolsheviks*, 203.

86. Malik, *Bankers and Bolsheviks*, 214.

87. "200 Years Citi: ZAO Citibank Annual Report 2011," Citigroup, n.d., https://www.citigroup.com/rcs/citigpa/akpublic/storage/public/russia_2011_english.pdf

88. "Russia," n.d., Citigroup, https://www.citigroup.com/global/about-us/global-presence/russia; Joanne Levine, "Cautiously, Citibank Opens Office," *The Moscow Times*, 2 Oct. 1992, https://www.themoscowtimes.com/archive/cautiously-citibank-opens-office

3. THE "UNBREAKABLE UNION"

1. Paul Melling.

2. John Slater, "Foreign Direct Investment in the Transition to a Market Economy," in Artisien-Maksimenko and Adjubei, *Foreign Investment in Russia*, 6.

3. Marshall Goldman, *Détente and Dollars* (New York: Basic Books, 1975), 18–19.

4. A. Egupets, "Ot Krymskoi Voiny do konflikta na Ukraine, 170-letnyaya istoriya rossiiskogo biznesa Siemens" [From the Crimean War to the conflict in Ukraine: 170-year history of Russian business Siemens], *Kommersant*, 21 May 2022, https://www.kommersant.ru/doc/5348654; Lutz and Blocker, "Siemens in Russia."

5. Michael Kaser, "American Credits for Soviet Development," *British Journal of International Studies* 3, no. 2 (1977): 137, http://www.jstor.org/stable/20096798

6. Reuters, "Soviet Gets Loan from Eximbank," *The New York Times*,

21 Mar. 1973, https://www.nytimes.com/1973/03/21/archives/soviet-gets-loan-from-eximbank-pact-provides-202million-to-buy-us.html

7.   Associated Press, "180-Million Loan to Soviet Union Is Made by US," *The New York Times*, 22 May 1974, https://www.nytimes.com/1974/05/22/archives/180million-loan-to-soviet-union-is-made-by-us-biggest-credit-yet.html

8.   Kaser, "American Credits for Soviet Development," 137–50.

9.   Kaser, "American Credits for Soviet Development," quoting Peter G. Peterson, *A Foreign Economic Perspective* (Washington, DC: United States Government Publishing Office, 1971), 28.

10. Kaser, "American Credits for Soviet Development," quoting "US–Soviet Commercial Relations: The Interplay of Economics, Technology Transfer and Diplomacy," prepared for the Subcommittee on National Security Policy and Scientific Development of the Committee on Foreign Affairs, US House of Representatives, 10 June 1973 (Washington, DC: United States Government Publishing Office, 1973), 58.

11. Maria A. Blackwood, Cathleen D. Cimino-Isaacs and Liana Wong, "The Jackson–Vanik Amendment and Permanent Normal Trade Relations," Congressional Research Service, 20 Dec. 2023, https://crsreports.congress.gov/product/pdf/IF/IF12556

12. Elena Kudryashova, "Samyi-samyi port Pivdenny: Ot Khammera do nashikh dnei" [The very best port Pivdenniy: from Hammer to our times], Ukrainian Shipping Magazine, 11 June 2021, https://usm.media/samyj-samyj-port-pivdennyj-ot-hammera-do-nashih-dnej

13. Edward Jay Epstein, *Dossier: The Secret History of Armand Hammer*, 1st edn (New York: Random House, 1996), 167.

14. Epstein, *Dossier*, 267–76.

15. Kaser, "American Credits for Soviet Development," 143.

16. Rebecca Reich, "Preserving the Voice of Tolstoy for All Time," *The Moscow Times*, 11 Sept. 2003, https://www.themoscowtimes.com/archive/preserving-the-voice-of-tolstoy-for-all-time

17. "Dnieper Dam Began Operation (1932)," Today in Conservation, n.d., https://todayinconservation.com/2020/02/october-10-dnieper-dam-began-operation-1932

18. Olena Goncharova and Martin Fornusek, "Zaporizhzhia's Dnipro

Hydroelectric Power Plant Hit amid Russian Attack on Energy Infrastructure," The Kyiv Independent, 22 Mar. 2024, https://kyivindependent.com/russia-launches-large-scale-missile-drone-attack-against-ukraine

19. Wladimir Naleszkiewicz, "Technical Assistance of the American Enterprises to the Growth of the Soviet Union, 1929–1933," *The Russian Review* 25, no. 1 (1966): 68, https://doi.org/10.2307/126832

20. Theodore Shabad, "GE and Soviet Sign Pact for Technology Exchange," *The New York Times*, 13 Jan. 1973, https://www.nytimes.com/1973/01/13/archives/ge-and-soviet-sign-pact-for-technology-exchange-agreement-includes.html

21. Adam Burns, "Little Joe Locomotives," American-Rails.com, last updated 30 Nov. 2023, https://www.american-rails.com/joes.html

22. Shabad, "GE and Soviet Sign Pact."

23. Mikhail Kozyrev, "Sumerechnaya Zona" [The Twilight Zone], *Forbes*, 2 Dec. 2004, https://www.forbes.ru/forbes/issue/2004-12/21881-sumerechnaya-zona

24. Kozyrev, "Sumerechnaya Zona."

25. "GE and Rosneft Announce Joint Venture to Modernize Russia's Oil and Gas Infrastructure," GE, 21 June 2013, https://www.ge.com/news/press-releases/ge-and-rosneft-announce-joint-venture-modernize-russias-oil-and-gas-infrastructure

26. Company material provided to author.

27. Slater, "Foreign Direct Investment," 11–12.

28. Kirill Tuchapsky and Ramil Magasumov, "A Few Home Truths ...," in *Trading with Uncertainty: Foreign Investment Trends in the Soviet Union*, ed. Mark Meredith (Chur, CH: Worldwide Information, 1991), 24.

29. Jeffrey M. Hertzfeld, "Joint Ventures: Saving the Soviets from Perestroika," *Harvard Business Review* (January–February 1991), https://hbr.org/1991/01/joint-ventures-saving-the-soviets-from-perestroika

30. Swetzer, "Foreign Investment," 38.

31. Lorraine Watkins-Mathis and Malcolm R. Hill, "A Retrospective Study of Joint Ventures in Eastern Europe and the Former USSR," *Journal of East–West Business* 1, no. 2 (1994): 66.

32. "Illuminated Sign for Aeroflot," *Financial Times*, 6 May 1965, 13.

33. Christopher S. Wren, "Britain Offering Soviets $2-Billion in Trade Credits," *The New York Times*, 18 Feb. 1975, https://www.nytimes.com/1975/02/18/archives/britain-offering-soviet-2billion-in-trade-credits-wilson-ending.html

34. Kaser, "American Credits for Soviet Development," 142.

35. Ludmilla Gricenko Wells, "'Brad's Drink' in the Soviet Union," 1991, https://ojs.library.carleton.ca/index.php/pcharm/article/view/2021/1836

36. John-Thor Dahlburg, "Pepsico to Swap Cola for Soviet Vodka and Ships," *Los Angeles Times*, 10 Apr. 1990, https://www.latimes.com/archives/la-xpm-1990-04-10-mn-1040-story.html

37. Flora Lewis, "Foreign Affairs: Soviets Buy American," *The New York Times*, 10 May 1989, https://www.nytimes.com/1989/05/10/opinion/foreign-affairs-soviets-buy-american.html

38. Dahlburg, "Pepsico to Swap Cola."

39. Dahlburg, "Pepsico to Swap Cola."

40. Dahlburg, "Pepsico to Swap Cola."

41. Clare Fitzgerald, "Pepsi Once Had the 6th Largest Navy in the World," War History Online, 30 Sept. 2021, https://www.warhistoryonline.com/cold-war/pepsi-once-had-the-6th-largest-navy-in-the-world.html

42. Lewis, "Foreign Affairs."

43. Here and elsewhere, author interview, London, 6 July 2023.

44. Hertzfeld, "Joint Ventures."

45. Michael Dobbs, "Moscow Plays Ketch-Up," *The Washington Post*, 1 Feb. 1990, republished on 8 Mar 2022, https://www.washingtonpost.com/history/2022/03/08/soviet-union-mcdonalds-moscow

46. Dobbs, "Moscow Plays Ketch-Up."

47. Dobbs, "Moscow Plays Ketch-Up."

48. Dobbs, "Moscow Plays Ketch-Up."

49. Geoffrey D. Swindler, "Joint Ventures in the Soviet Union: Problems Emerge," *Seattle University Law Review* 13, no. 165 (1989): 170–2.

50. Swindler, "Joint Ventures in the Soviet Union," 184.

51. Vesa Turtiainen, "Identifying and Evaluating the Right Business Opportunity," in Meredith, *Trading with Uncertainty*, 15.

52. Turtiainen, "Identifying and Evaluating."
53. An acquaintance whose privacy the author is maintaining.
54. Jack Redden, "Freedom Came with a Phone Call," United Press International, 19 Dec. 1986, https://www.upi.com/Archives/1986/12/19/Freedom-came-with-a-phone-call/9238535352400
55. Rene Gatling, *Investing in Eastern Europe and the USSR: Financial Strategies and Practices for Successful Operations* (London: Economist Publications, 1991), 109.
56. Gatling, *Investing in Eastern Europe and the USSR*, 101.
57. Gatling, *Investing in Eastern Europe and the USSR*, 101–5.
58. Gatling, *Investing in Eastern Europe and the USSR*, 109.
59. Gatling, *Investing in Eastern Europe and the USSR*, 110.
60. Gatling, *Investing in Eastern Europe and the USSR*, 117.
61. Carl H. McMillan, "Foreign Investment in Russia: Soviet Legacies and Post-Soviet Prospects," in Artisien-Maksimenko and Adjubei, *Foreign Investment in Russia*, 47.
62. McMillan, "Foreign Investment in Russia," 54.
63. McMillan, "Foreign Investment in Russia," 55.
64. John M. Berry, "The Road to Moscow: Companies Eager to Get Rolling," *The Washington Post*, 29 Nov. 1989, https://www.washingtonpost.com/archive/business/1989/11/29/the-road-to-moscow-companies-eager-to-get-rolling/2d90bc38-a546-40a6-90bc-5ffbf25adb16
65. McMillan, "Foreign Investment in Russia," 59.
66. McMillan, "Foreign Investment in Russia," 60.
67. McMillan, "Foreign Investment in Russia," 61–2.
68. Lorraine Watkins-Mathys, "The Role of Joint Ventures in East–West Trade up to 1990" (PhD diss., Loughborough University, 1992), 303, https://hdl.handle.net/2134/10492
69. Watkins-Mathys, "Role of Joint Ventures in East–West Trade," 308.
70. Watkins-Mathys, "Role of Joint Ventures in East–West Trade," 318–19.
71. McMillan, "Foreign Investment in Russia," 51.
72. Here and elsewhere, author interview, London–Washington, DC, 11 Sept. 2023.
73. Here and elsewhere, author interview, London, 18 July 2023.

74. Here and elsewhere, author interview, New York–Miami, 17 June 2023.

75. Oliver Cescotti, 1 June 2023.

4.   A BORDERLESS WORLD ARISES

1.   Here and elsewhere, Mitchell Orenstein, author interview, London–Philadelphia, 23 May 2023.

2.   Here and elsewhere, Cameron Mitchell, author interview, London–Singapore, 24 May 2023.

3.   "When Did Globalisation Start?," *The Economist*, 23 Sept. 2013, https://www.economist.com/free-exchange/2013/09/23/when-did-globalisation-start

4.   Nigel Gould-Davies, *Tectonic Politics: Global Political Risk in an Age of Transformation* (Washington, DC: Brookings Institution, 2019), 15, citing data from the World Bank (https://data.worldbank.org/indicator/NE.TRD.GNFS.ZS) and UNCTAD (http://unctadstat.unctad.org/wds/TableViewer/tableView.aspx).

5.   Gould-Davies, *Tectonic Politics*, 15–16.

6.   "Global Foreign Direct Investment Flows over the Last 30 Years," UNCTAD, 5 May 2023, https://unctad.org/data-visualization/global-foreign-direct-investment-flows-over-last-30-years

7.   Gould-Davies, *Tectonic Politics*, 66.

8.   Frieden, *Global Capitalism*, 391.

9.   Orenstein, author interview.

10. Frieden, *Global Capitalism*, 411–12.

11. Frieden, *Global Capitalism*, 423–4.

12. Frieden, *Global Capitalism*, 432.

13. Matt Taibbi, "Hockey Team Gets U.S. Link," *The Moscow Times*, 1 July 1993, https://www.themoscowtimes.com/archive/hockey-team-gets-u-s-link

14. David McClintick, "How Harvard Lost Russia," Institutional Investor, 12 Jan. 2006, https://www.institutionalinvestor.com/article/2btfpiwkwid6fq6qrokcg/home/how-harvard-lost-russia

15. Martin Gilman, "Russia Overtakes Portugal—and Spain Is Next," *The Moscow Times*, 8 Oct. 2012, https://www.themoscowtimes.

com/2012/10/08/russia-overtakes-portugal-and-spain-is-next-a18420

16. Larisa Vostryakova, "Working on the Other Side," *The Moscow Times*, 5 Dec. 1995, https://www.themoscowtimes.com/archive/working-on-the-other-side

17. "Why Nobody Wanted to Eat Lunch with Putin at G20," Money Clip, Bloomberg TV, 17 Nov. 2014, https://www.bloomberg.com/news/videos/2014-11-17/why-nobody-wanted-to-eat-lunch-with-putin-at-g20

18. "IFC, the First Six Decades: Leading the Way in Private Sector Development; A History," IFC, Washington, DC, 1 Jan. 2016, https://documents1.worldbank.org/curated/en/668851478627391927/pdf/109806-WP-IFC-History-Book-Web-Version-OUO-9.pdf

19. Here and elsewhere, unless noted, author interview, New York–Philadelphia, 15 Aug. 2023.

20. Dani Rodrik, *The Globalisation Paradox* (New York: W.W. Norton & Company, 2011).

21. Neil Buckley, "Putin's 'Managed Democracy,'" *Financial Times*, 26 June 2006, https://www.ft.com/content/39682de4-053d-11db-9b9e-0000779e2340

22. Alexander Golts, "Putin's Power Vertical Stretches Back to Kursk," *The Moscow Times*, 16 Aug. 2010, https://www.themoscowtimes.com/2010/08/16/putins-power-vertical-stretches-back-to-kursk-a674

23. The acronym initially referred to four countries known as the "BRIC countries," sometimes shortened to "the BRICs" with a lower-case, plural "s." This is not to be confused with the updated acronym BRICS, with an upper-case "S" to indicate that the acronym now includes South Africa. The group has more recently grown again.

24. "With GS Research Report, 'BRICs' Are Born," Goldman Sachs, n.d., https://www.goldmansachs.com/our-firm/history/moments/2001-brics.html

25. Stephen Grenville, "Twenty Years of BRICS," Lowy Institute, 3 Dec. 2021, https://www.lowyinstitute.org/the-interpreter/twenty-years-brics

26. Jason Corcoran and Denis Maternovsky, "Goldman Finding Third

Time a Charm as Blankfein Courts Kremlin," Bloomberg, 24 May 2011, https://www.bloomberg.com/news/articles/2011-05-23/goldman-finding-third-time-in-russia-a-charm-as-blankfein-courts-kremlin

27. Jim O'Neill, "The 'Next Eleven' and the World Economy," Project Syndicate, 18 Apr. 2018, https://www.project-syndicate.org/commentary/n-11-global-economy-by-jim-o-neill-2018-04

5.   THE WALLS COULDN'T TALK, BUT THEY COULD LISTEN

1.   Here and elsewhere, Hugh Hallard, author interview, London–Bucharest, 19 Sept. 2023.

2.   Here and elsewhere, Elizabeth Krasnoff, author interview, London–Los Angeles, 1 Dec. 2023.

3.   The *Star Wars* bar scene depicted an intergalactic canteen frequented by shady, underworld characters from an assortment of alien civilisations, fed by potent bar drinks and sporadic bursts of violence.

4.   Paul Moxness, author interview, London–Kelowna, BC, 8 June 2023.

5.   Martin Gilman, *No Precedent, No Plan: Inside Russia's 1998 Default* (Cambridge, MA: MIT Press, 2010), 19

6.   Elena Slobodyan, "Chto takoe 'nozhki Busha?'" [What are Bush's legs?], *Argumenty i Fakty*, 16 July 2019, https://aif.ru/food/products/chto_takoe_nozhki_busha

7.   Here and elsewhere, author interview, London, 12 Sept. 2023.

8.   Charles Hecker, "Resurrected Escalators Raise Sprits at Airport," *The Moscow Times*, 2 Mar. 1996, https://www.themoscowtimes.com/archive/resurrected-escalators-raise-spirits-at-airport

9.   Charles Hecker, "Police Raid Startles Hotel Staff, Guests," *The Moscow Times*, 6 Dec. 1995, https://www.themoscowtimes.com/archive/police-raid-startles-hotel-staff-guests

10. Alessandra Stanley, "An American's Bizarre Sit-In in Moscow," *The New York Times*, 6 May 1995, https://www.nytimes.com/1995/05/06/business/international-business-an-american-s-bizarre-sit-in-in-moscow.html

11. Erin Arvedlund and Maria Atanasov, "Murder in Moscow," CNN

Money, reprinted from *Fortune* magazine, 3 Mar. 1997, https://money.cnn.com/magazines/fortune/fortune_archive/1997/03/03/222753

12. Nick Allen, "Tatum Shot Dead by 11 Bullets," *The Moscow Times*, 5 Nov. 1996, https://www.themoscowtimes.com/archive/tatum-shot-dead-by-11-bullets

13. Arvedlund and Atanasov, "Murder in Moscow."

14. Rachel Katz, "EBRD Consultant Killed in Hotel Shooting," *The Moscow Times*, 28 Feb. 1996, https://www.themoscowtimes.com/archive/ebrd-consultant-killed-in-hotel-shooting

15. Valeria Korchagina, "Forbes Editor Klebnikov Shot Dead," *The Moscow Times*, 12 July 2004, https://www.themoscowtimes.com/archive/forbes-editor-klebnikov-shot-dead

16. At the time she was living in Moscow, Krasnoff's surname was Szatmari.

17. Mark Galeotti, *The Vory: Russia's Super Mafia* (New Haven: Yale University Press, 2019), 11.

18. Galeotti, *The Vory*, 12–13.

19. Galeotti, *The Vory*, 36.

20. Galeotti, *The Vory*, 81.

21. Galeotti, *The Vory*, 111, citing Associated Press, 7 June 1994.

22. Private conversation described to author.

23. Michael Specter, "U.S. Business and the Russian Mob," *The New York Times*, 8 July 1994, https://www.nytimes.com/1994/07/08/business/us-business-and-the-russian-mob.html

24. Galeotti, *The Vory*, 181–2.

6. JOINT ADVENTURES

1. Paul Ostling, author interview, London–New Canaan, CT, 20 Sept. 2023.

2. Oliver Cescotti, 1 June 2023.

3. Ostling, author interview, 20 Sept. 2023.

4. Sander Thoenes, "Moscow: A Costly Place for Business," *The Moscow Times*, 1 Oct. 1993, https://www.themoscowtimes.com/archive/moscow-a-costly-place-for-business

5. Private conversation with author.

6. Ben Laurance et al., "Maxwell's Body Found in Sea," *The Guardian*, 6 Nov. 1991, https://www.theguardian.com/fromthearchive/story/0,,1078193,00.html&q=Maxwell%27s_body_found_in_sea

7. Ron Berger et al., "Developing International Business Relationships in a Russian Context," *Management International Review* 57, no. 3 (2017): 441–71, at 463.

8. Tom Wilson, "Oligarchs, Power and Profits: The History of BP in Russia," *Financial Times*, 24 Mar. 2022, https://www.ft.com/content/e9238fa2-65a2-4753-a845-ce8129f93a0c

9. "Twice Burned, BP Not Shy," *The Moscow Times*, 16 Jan. 2011, https://www.themoscowtimes.com/2011/01/16/twice-burned-bp-not-shy-a4246; "Too Much Trouble," *The Economist*, 8 Jan. 1998, https://www.economist.com/finance-and-economics/1998/01/08/too-much-trouble

10. Sabrina Tavernise, "BP Prevails in Struggle for Company in Russia," *The New York Times*, 2 Aug. 2001, https://www.nytimes.com/2001/08/02/business/bp-prevails-in-struggle-for-company-in-russia.html; Catherine Belton, "Russian Roulette: How BP Is Falling Out with Its Partners at TNK," *Financial Times*, 4 June 2008, https://www.ft.com/content/7dba991e-3277-11dd-9b87-0000779fd2ac

11. Paul Starobin, "A Slick Move in Russia's Oil Patch?," Bloomberg, 29 May 2001, https://www.bloomberg.com/news/articles/2001-05-29/a-slick-move-in-russias-oil-patch. Parentheses removed from quote.

12. Tavernise, "BP Prevails."

13. Tavernise, "BP Prevails."

14. Anna Raff, "BP Buys Sidanco Stake for $375M," *The Moscow Times*, 17 Apr. 2002, https://www.themoscowtimes.com/archive/bp-buys-sidanco-stake-for-375m

15. Catherine Belton, "BP Strikes Record $6.75Bln TNK Deal," *The Moscow Times*, 12 Feb. 2003, https://www.themoscowtimes.com/archive/bp-strikes-record-675bln-tnk-deal.

16. Wilson, "Oligarchs, Power and Profits."

17. Belton, "BP Strikes Record $6.75Bln TNK Deal."

18. Belton, "Russian Roulette."

19. Wilson, "Oligarchs, Power and Profits."

20. Luke Harding, "Oil: 'Harassed' Head of BP Venture Exits Moscow," *The Guardian*, https://www.theguardian.com/business/2008/jul/25/bp.oil

21. Lex: European Companies, BP/AAR/Rosneft, "Latest Spat Suggests One or Both Sides May Be Looking to Exit TBK-BNP," *Financial Times*, 27 January 2011, https://www.ft.com/content/68f1d938-29fb-11e0-997c-00144feab49a

22. Courtney Weaver, "TNK-BP: Another Game of Chicken," *Financial Times*, 1 June 2012, https://www.ft.com/content/880a2022-ae2a-3b83-b0de-439638a696aa

23. Wilson, "Oligarchs, Power and Profits."

24. Wilson, "Oligarchs, Power and Profits."

25. Howard Amos, "Russian Tycoon Fridman Should Make U.K. Feel Nervous," *The Moscow Times*, https://www.themoscowtimes.com/2015/03/10/russian-tycoon-fridman-should-make-uk-feel-nervous-a44604

26. Guy Chazan, "Telecoms Case Shows Fridman's Taste for Combat," *Financial Times*, 5 Mar. 2015, https://www.ft.com/content/e291cdc6-c325-11e4-ac3d-00144feab7de

27. Reuters, "Armed Men Escort Marshal into Telenor Office," *The Moscow Times*, 17 Sept. 2012, https://www.themoscowtimes.com/archive/armed-men-escort-marshal-into-telenor-office

28. Courtney Weaver, "Telenor and Alfa Closer to Pooling Resources," *Financial Times*, 17 Apr. 2010, https://www.ft.com/content/050f8d28-4961-11df-8e4f-00144feab49a

29. Arkady Ostrovsky and Rupini Bergstrom, "Alfa Jumps In with Turkcell Bid," *Financial Times*, 31 Mar. 2005, https://www.ft.com/content/bc2928c6-a20d-11d9-8483-00000e2511c8

30. Andrew Hurst, "Alfa Group May Be Losing Its Touch, Skeptics Say," *The Moscow Times*, 12 Sept. 2005, https://www.themoscowtimes.com/archive/alfa-group-may-be-losing-its-touch-skeptics-say

31. "Wal-Mart to Close Moscow Office, Sees No Deals," Reuters, 13 Dec. 2010, https://www.reuters.com/article/us-walmart-idUSTRE6BC26B20101213

32. Jonathan Birchall, "Walmart to Close Moscow Office," *Financial*

Times, 13 Dec. 2010, https://www.ft.com/content/06c7a670-06e7-11e0-8c29-00144feabdc0

33. Javier Espinoza, Henry Foy and Max Seddon, "EU Court Rules in Favour of Russian Oligarch Fridman and Aven in Blow to Sanctions Regime," *Financial Times*, 10 Apr. 2024, https://www.ft.com/content/5cc41a3d-1fa9-497b-8681-086b0c1e3b20

34. James Henderson and Alastair Ferguson, *International Partnership in Russia: Conclusions from the Oil and Gas Industry* (Houndmills: Palgrave Macmillan, 2014), 55.

35. Henderson and Ferguson, *International Partnership in Russia*, 55.

36. Henderson and Ferguson, *International Partnership in Russia*, 191.

37. Henderson and Ferguson, *International Partnership in Russia*, 213.

38. Henderson and Ferguson, *International Partnership in Russia*, 217.

39. Henderson and Ferguson, *International Partnership in Russia*, 224.

40. "Russia's Unlikely Communist," *The Economist*, 30 Sept. 1999, https://www.economist.com/business/1999/09/30/russias-unlikely-communist

41. Michele A. Berdy, "Derk Sauer on Journalism, Russia and Being a Black Sheep," *The Moscow Times*, 9 Oct. 2017, https://www.themoscowtimes.com/2015/03/10/russian-tycoon-fridman-should-make-uk-feel-nervous-a44604

42. Simon Kuper, "Tales from a Traitor: An Encounter with Cold War Spy George Blake," *Financial Times*, 29 Jan. 2021, https://www.ft.com/content/945d7119-0b51-4129-80c1-42bab678006d

43. Alex S. Jones, "Russian-Language Edition of The Times Begins Today," *The New York Times*, 28 Apr. 1992, https://www.nytimes.com/1992/04/28/business/the-media-business-russian-language-edition-of-the-times-begins-today.html

44. Carey Scott, "New York Times Quits the Russian Scene," *The Moscow Times*, 17 Feb. 1994, https://www.themoscowtimes.com/archive/new-york-times-quits-the-russian-scene

45. "Foreign Media Law Makes Putin Less Glamorous," *The Moscow Times*, 25 Sept. 2014, https://www.themoscowtimes.com/2014/09/25/foreign-media-law-makes-putin-less-glamorous-a39796

46. Alec Luhn, "Russia Tightens Limit on Foreign Ownership of

Media," *The Guardian*, 26 Sept. 2014, https://www.theguardian.com/world/2014/sep/26/russia-limit-foreign-ownership-media

47.　Baturina sued Russian *Forbes* over the cover headline accompanying a profile of her inside the December 2006 magazine. The quote on the cover initially read "I am guaranteed protection," which Baturina said made it look like she relied on her powerful husband to safeguard her business interests. The full quote inside the story was: "As an investor, I am guaranteed protection of my rights." The cover quote was changed to say, "As an investor, I am guaranteed protection." The issue was delayed on newsstands while the disagreement was discussed between the parties.

48.　Here and elsewhere, author interview, 22 Feb 2024, London-Sydney.

49.　Here and elsewhere, author interview, London, 18 Dec. 2023 and 16 Feb. 2024.

50.　John Reed, "GM Considers Adding Capacity in Russia," *Financial Times*, 11 Sept. 2007, https://www.ft.com/content/c09b65d8-6086-11dc-8ec0-0000779fd2ac

51.　John Reed, "US Carmakers Step Up Russian Drive," *Financial Times*, 11 Dec. 2007, https://www.ft.com/content/b410fedc-a75c-11dc-a25a-0000779fd2ac

52.　Bill Vlasic and Nick Bunkley, "Obama Is Upbeat for GM's Future," *The New York Times*, 1 June 2009, https://www.nytimes.com/2009/06/02/business/02auto.html

53.　"GM Retreats from Russian Market, Closes Plant and Winds Down Opel Brand," *The Moscow Times*, 18 Mar. 2015, https://www.themoscowtimes.com/2015/03/18/gm-retreats-from-russian-market-closes-plant-and-winds-down-opel-brand-a44876;　Andy Sharman, "General Motors to Halt Opel Drive into Russia," *Financial Times*, 18 Mar. 2015, https://www.ft.com/content/0c5ea948-cd6d-11e4-9144-00144feab7de

54.　Gleb Stolyarov and Alexander Marrow, "General Motors Pulls Out of Russian Car Assembly Business with Avotvaz Deal," Reuters, 9 Dec. 2019, https://www.reuters.com/article/us-gm-russia-avtovaz-idUSKBN1YD12Z

55.　The FCPA is a wide-ranging piece of US legislation that makes it illegal "to make payments to foreign government officials to assist in obtaining or retaining business." The FCPA further requires business to keep accurate "books and records" of their financial transactions and to "devise and maintain an adequate system of internal accounting controls." The law applies to US and foreign individuals and companies where there is a link with the US via, for example, a listing on a US stock exchange. See "Foreign Corrupt Practices Act," US DoJ, updated 26 Sept. 2023, https://www.justice.gov/criminal/criminal-fraud/foreign-corrupt-practices-act SEC Enforcement Actions: FCPA cases, updated 22 Apr 2024, sec.gov, https://www.sec.gov/enforce/sec-enforcement-actions-fcpa-cases

56. SEC Charges Networking and Cybersecurity Solutions Company with Violations of the FCPA, Administrative Proceeding, File No. 3-19397, 29 Aug 2019, sec.gov, https://www.sec.gov/enforcement-litigation/administrative-proceedings/34-86812-s

57. "Teva Pharmaceutical Paying $519 Million to Settle FCPA Charges," 22 Dec 2016, sec.gov, https://www.sec.gov/newsroom/press-releases/2016-277

58. AstraZeneca Charged with FCPA Violations, Administrative Proceeding, File No. 3-17517, 30 Aug 2016, sec.gov, https://www.sec.gov/files/litigation/admin/2016/34-78730-s.pdf

59. SEC Charges Engineer and Former Employer with Bribe Scheme in Russia," 3 March 2016, sec.gov, https://www.sec.gov/files/litigation/admin/2016/34-77288-s.pdf

60. SEC Charges California-Based Bio-Rad Laboratories with FCPA Violations," 3 Nov 2014, sec.gov, https://www.sec.gov/newsroom/press-releases/2014-245

61. SEC Charges Eli Lilly and Company with FCPA Violations," 8 May 2013, sec.gov, https://www.sec.gov/newsroom/press-releases/2012-2012-273htm

62. "Siemens Aktiengesellschaft," US SEC, Litigation Releases, 15 Dec. 2008, https://www.sec.gov/litigation/litreleases/lr-20829#:

63. Galeotti, *The Vory*, 210.

64. Noah Buckley, "Corruption and Power in Post-Communist Russia," Foreign Policy Research Institute, Apr. 2018, https://www.fpri.org/wp-content/uploads/2018/04/Buckley.pdf

65. "Former Minister Ulyukayev Handed 8 Years in Rosneft Bribery Case,"

The Moscow Times, 15 Dec. 2017, https://www.themoscowtimes.com/2017/12/15/former-minister-ulyukayev-handed-8-years-in-rosneft-bribery-case-a59957

66. Oliver Cescotti.

67. Oliver Cescotti.

7.   INSECURITIES

1. Bernie Sucher.

2. Alexandra Vacroux.

3. Patricia Kranz, "Boris Jordan: The Man Who Made Moscow's Market," Bloomberg, 22 May 1995, https://www.bloomberg.com/news/articles/1995-05-21/boris-jordan-the-man-who-made-moscows-market

4. J. Millar, "Stephen Jennings—Billion-Dollar Visions," Unfiltered, 2016, https://unfiltered.tv/public/stephen-jennings (url no longer active).

5. McClintick, "How Harvard Lost Russia."

6. John-Thor Dahlburg, "Vouchers Giving Russians a Small Piece of the Action: Privatization; Certificates Worth 10,000 Rubles Are Distributed to Buy Shares of State Property, or Be Sold," *Los Angeles Times*, 2 Oct. 1992, https://www.latimes.com/archives/la-xpm-1992-10-02-mn-334-story.html

7. Dahlburg, "Vouchers Giving Russians a Small Piece of the Action."

8. Joanne Levin, "Russia: The Land of Opportunity," *The Moscow Times*, 22 Oct. 1992, https://www.themoscowtimes.com/archive/russia-the-land-of-opportunity

9. Here and elsewhere, author interview, London, 12 Sept. 2023.

10. Maxim Boycko, Andrei Shleifer and Robert Vishny, *Privatizing Russia* (Cambridge, MA: MIT Press, 1995), 5.

11. Here and elsewhere, author interview, London–British Columbia, 17 Nov. 2023. Baral's surname at the time was Kostuchuk.

12. Erik Ipsen, *International Herald Tribune*, "When Privatizing Firms, Russians Do It by the Book," *The New York Times*, 12 Mar. 1993, https://www.nytimes.com/1993/03/12/business/worldbusiness/IHT-when-privatizing-firms-russians-do-it-by-the-book.html

13. Author interview, Cambridge, MA, 24 Oct. 2023.

14. Patricia Kranz, "The Most Powerful Man in Russia: At 36, Capitalist Vladimir Potanin Rules the Country's Economy; Here's How He Does It," Bloomberg, 24 Nov. 1997, https://www.bloomberg.com/news/articles/1997-11-23/the-most-powerful-man-in-russia

15. Jonas Bernstein, "Loans for the Sharks?," *The Moscow Times*, 19 Dec. 1995, https://www.themoscowtimes.com/archive/loans-for-the-sharks

16. United States GAO, "Foreign Assistance: International Efforts to Aid Russia's Transition Have Had Mixed Results," 1 Nov. 2000, 95, https://www.gao.gov/assets/gao-01-8.pdf

17. Matt Taibbi and Mark Ames, "The Journal's Russia Scandal," *The Nation*, 4 Oct. 1999, https://www.thenation.com/article/archive/journals-russia-scandal

18. Yegor Gaidar and Leon Aron, "The Russian Economy after Yukos," American Enterprise Institute, the Russian Economy: Strategic Trends, Problems, and Opportunities, 30 Jan. 2004, via Gaidar Institute for Economic Policy, https://www.iep.ru/en/publications/publication/2149.html

19. James Flanigan, "President Rides Russia's Wave of Privatisation," *Los Angeles Times*, 6 Oct. 1993, https://www.latimes.com/archives/la-xpm-1993-10-06-fi-42783-story.html

20. David Hoffmann, "Banditry Threatens the New Russia," *The Washington Post*, 11 May 1997, https://www.washingtonpost.com/archive/politics/1997/05/12/banditry-threatens-the-new-russia/e46ef158-bd84-4ca9-870f-612817fe5854

21. "Traitors: Part I; The Beginning," Anti-Corruption Fund, n.d., https://predateli.navalny.com/en

22. "'A Distortion of History': Russian Political Actors and Historians on Team Navalny's New Film about Yeltsin's Role in Putin's Rise to Power," Meduza, 23 Apr. 2024, https://meduza.io/en/feature/2024/04/23/a-distortion-of-history

23. "Commanding Heights: Boris Jordan," PBS, 3 Oct. 2000, https://www.pbs.org/wgbh/commandingheights/shared/minitext/int_borisjordan.html

24. PBS, "Commanding Heights: Boris Jordan."

25. Ruben Vardanyan, "Where Dreams Lead To," Personal Blog, 2020, http://rubenvardanyan.info/ru/pages/where-dreams-take-you

26. Author interview, New York–Miami, 17 June 2023.

27. Stanislav V. Shekshnia, "Troika Dialog's Founder Ruben Vardanian on Building Russia's First Investment Bank," *The Academy of Management Executive* 15, no. 4, Themes: Business Strategies and Employee Development (Nov. 2001): 16–23.

28. PBS, "Commanding Heights: Boris Jordan."

29. Boycko, Shleifer and Vishny, *Privatizing Russia*, 78–9, 92.

30. Boycko, Shleifer and Vishny, *Privatizing Russia*, 78–9, 92.

31. "'Bolshevik' po-frantsuzskii."

32. "Mikhail Fridman: Prioritet reputatsii nad dengami eshche ne vozobladal" [Reputation's priority over money has yet to prevail], *Vedomosti*, 3 June 2001, https://www.vedomosti.ru/newspaper/articles/2001/07/03/mihail-fridman-prioritet-reputacii-nad-dengamiesche-ne-vozobladal

33. Nikolai Grishin, "Dnevnik Nablyudenij: RAZGON PARAVOZA Kraft Foods poluchila control nad krupneishim v Rossii proizvoditelem pechenya—fabrikoi 'Bolshevik,' Nichego khoroshego rossiiskie distribyutori ot novogo igroka ne zhdut" [Observation diary: THE LOCOMOTIVE ACCELERATES; Kraft Foods has gained control over Russia's largest biscuit manufacturer—the 'Bolshevik' factory, Russian distributors expect nothing good from the new player], *Kommersant Sekret Firmy*, 10 Dec. 2007, https://www.kommersant.ru/doc/858997

34. "After Landlord Quarrels, BeeLine Is Moving to the Bolshevik Factory—CNews," CNews, 22 Dec. 2017, https://www.cnews.ru/news/top/2017-12-22_posle_ssory_s_arendodatelem_bilajn_pereezzhaet

35. Boycko, Shleifer and Vishny, *Privatizing Russia*, 108–9.

36. Boycko, Shleifer and Vishny, *Privatizing Russia*, 108–9.

37. Ed Crooks, "Gazprom Looks to Fuel Growth," *Financial Times*, 9 Dec. 2008, https://www.ft.com/content/f7dbb648-c61e-11dd-a741-000077b07658

38. Boycko, Shleifer and Vishny, *Privatizing Russia*, 117.

39. PBS, "Commanding Heights: Boris Jordan."

40. Shekshnia, "Troika Dialog's Founder Ruben Vardanian on Building Russia's First Investment Bank," 16–23.

41. PBS, "Commanding Heights: Boris Jordan."

42. Bernie Sucher, "Stephen Jennings' Exit Is a Big Loss for Russia," *The Moscow Times*, 25 Nov. 2012, https://www.themoscowtimes.com/2012/11/25/stephen-jennings-exit-is-a-big-loss-for-russia- a19666

43. James Flanigan, "President Rides Russia's Wave of Privatization," *Los Angeles Times*, 6 Oct. 1993, https://www.latimes.com/archives/la-xpm-1993-10-06-fi-42783-story.html

44. Boycko, Shleifer and Vishny, *Privatizing Russia*, 2.

45. Carey Goldberg, "US Says 2 Russia Advisers Misused Positions for Gain," *The New York Times*, 27 Sept. 2000, https://www.nytimes.com/2000/09/27/us/us-says-2-russia-advisers-misused-positions-for-gain.html

46. "Moscow 'Tsar' Quits CSFB," *The Independent*, 5 May 1995, https://www.independent.co.uk/news/business/moscow-tsar-quits-csfb-1618370.html

47. Stefan Wagstyl, "Jennings Sells Out of Renaissance Capital," *Financial Times*, 14 Nov. 2012, https://www.ft.com/content/bdb3bd6a-e38d-31af-bde7-d4925cc3e893

48. Michael R. Gordon, "Two Financiers to Form No. 1 Investment Bank in Russia," *The New York Times*, 10 July 1997, https://www.nytimes.com/1997/07/10/business/two-financiers-to-form-no-1-investment-bank-in-russia.html

49. Denis Maternovsky and Jason Corcoran, "Sberbank to Buy Troika in State Push into Investment Banking," Bloomberg, 11 Mar. 2011, https://www.bloomberg.com/news/articles/2011-03-11/sberbank-to-acquire-troika-for-1-billion-in-push-into-investment-banking

50. "Deutsche Bank Buys into UFG," RFE/RL Business Watch, 11 Nov. 2003, https://www.rferl.org/a/1341591.html

51. "Deutsche Bank Buys UFG," *Financial News*, 6 Dec. 2005, https://www.fnlondon.com/articles/deutsche-bank-buys-ufg-20051206

52. Carter Dougherty, "Dresdner Action Foreshadows Gazprombank IPO in 2006," *The New York Times*, 7 Dec. 2005, https://www.nytimes.com/2005/12/07/business/worldbusiness/dresdner-action-foreshadows-gazprombank-ipo-in-2006.html

8.   APPLES AND ORANGES

1. Mitchell Orenstein.

2. US GAO, "Foreign Assistance," 9.

3. Howard Amos, "Mercedes Pays to Topple Logo," *The Moscow Times*, 2 Nov. 2011, https://www.themoscowtimes.com/2011/11/02/mercedes-pays-to-topple-logo-a10585

4. Here and elsewhere, unless noted, author interview, London, 27 Mar. 2024.

5. Martin Gilman, *No Precedent, No Plan*, 15.

6. James Owen, Rosie Hawes and Charles Hecker, "Grey Practices in the Russian Business Environment," Control Risks, 2010.

7. This is paraphrasing remarks made at a conference by the late Patricia Cloherty, a pioneering private equity investor in Russia. See her obituary at https://www.nytimes.com/2022/10/05/business/dealbook/patricia-cloherty-dead.html

8. Maxim Boycko and Robert J. Shiller, "Popular Attitudes toward Markets and Democracy: Russia and United States Compared 25 Years Later," *American Economic Review* 106, no. 5 (2016): 224–9.

9. Author interview, Tel Aviv, 25 June 2023.

10. Julie Brooks, "Experience: I Was Shot by a Sniper," *The Guardian*, 8 Oct. 2021, https://www.theguardian.com/lifeandstyle/2021/oct/08/experience-i-was-shot-by-a-sniper

11. "U.S.–Russia Summits, 1992–2000," US Department of State, July 2000, https://1997-2001.state.gov/regions/nis/chron_summits_russia_us.html

12. German Chancellor Helmut Kohl, in a speech to the Bundestag on 25 Mar. 1993, https://dserver.bundestag.de

13. UK Prime Minister John Major, 27 Mar. 1992, in a speech in Wales, https://johnmajorarchive.org.uk/1992/03/27/press-release-prime-ministers-comments-on-foreign-policy-27-march-1992/

14. French President Jacques Chirac, 26 Sept. 1997, in a speech in Moscow, https://www.elysee.fr

15. US Deputy Secretary of State Strobe Talbott, 19 Sept. 1997, in an address at Stanford University https://1997-2001.state.gov

16. Here and elsewhere, author interview, London–Toronto, 21 June 2023.

17. Here, and elsewhere, author interview London–Raleigh, NC, 15 June 2023.

18. Nick Sargen, "What the End of the 'Peace Dividend' Will Mean for

Americans," *Forbes*, 3 Mar. 2022, https://www.forbes.com/sites/nicksargen/2022/03/03/what-the-end-of-the-peace-dividend-will-mean-for-americans

19. Author interview, 9 July 2023.

20. David Shimer, "Election Meddling in Russia: When Boris Yeltsin Asked Bill Clinton for Help," *The Washington Post*, 26 June 2020, https://www.washingtonpost.com/history/2020/06/26/russian-election-interference-meddling

21. Boycko, Shleifer and Vishny, *Privatizing Russia*, 151–2.

22. US GAO, "Foreign Assistance," 6.

23. US GAO, "Foreign Assistance," 173.

24. US GAO, "Foreign Assistance," 91.

25. 102nd Congress (1991–2), S.2353 Freedom Support Act, US Congress, https://www.congress.gov/bill/102nd-congress/senate-bill/2532/text

26. US GAO, "Foreign Assistance," 34.

27. US GAO, "Foreign Assistance," 182.

28. US GAO, "Foreign Assistance," 59.

29. Celestine Bohlen, "The World: Westward Ho; An Empire Tries to Become a Normal Nation," *The New York Times*, 19 May 2002, https://www.nytimes.com/2002/05/19/weekinreview/the-world-westward-ho-an-empire-tries-to-become-a-normal-nation.html

30. "Basic Documents of the EBRD," EBRD, Sept. 2013, https://www.ebrd.com/news/publications/institutional-documents/basic-documents-of-the-ebrd.html

31. US GAO, "Foreign Assistance."

32. Erik Berglof in Peter Sanfey, Franklin Steves and Utku Teksoz, "Life in Transition: A Survey of People's Experiences and Attitudes," EBRD, 2016, 5, https://www.ebrd.com/news/publications/special-reports/life-in-transition-survey-i.html

33. Charles Clover, "US Lawyer Expelled from Russia over Fresh Spy Allegations," *Financial Times*, 20 May 2013, https://www.ft.com/content/45a2ac28-c143-11e2-b93b-00144feab7de

34. Here and elsewhere, author interview, London, 17 July 2023.

35. Here and elsewhere, author interview, London, 31 May 2023.

36. Here and elsewhere, author interview, London, 23 Feb 2024.

37. "Russia: Landmark Debt Restructuring Deal Signed," RFE/RL, https://www.rferl.org/a/1086755.html

38. "Russia: Landmark Debt Restructuring Deal Signed."

39. Gilman, *No Precedent, No Plan*, 31.

40. Gilman, *No Precedent, No Plan*, 96.

41. Chrystia Freeland, *Sale of the Century* (New York: Crown, 2000), 234.

42. Gilman, *No Precedent, No Plan*, 30–1.

43. David Sanger, "Next 'Asian' Crisis?," *The New York Times*, 28 May 1998, https://www.nytimes.com/1998/05/28/world/next-asian-crisis.html

44. Dmitry Zaks, "Yeltsin Puts Off Showdown with Ministers," *The Moscow Times*, 2 Dec. 1997, https://www.themoscowtimes.com/archive/yeltsin-puts-off-showdown-with-ministers

45. Daniel Williams, "New Ruble Has Russians Counting Their Kopecks," *The Washington Post*, 3 Jan. 1998, https://www.washingtonpost.com/archive/politics/1998/01/03/new-ruble-has-russians-counting-their-kopecks/84d93cb0-937b-4c93-8a8b-4edcdd6b82e0

46. Andrew McChesney, "Kinder Surprise Goes Russian," *The Moscow Times*, 4 Sept. 2012, https://www.themoscowtimes.com/2012/09/04/kinder-surprise-goes-russian-a17530

47. Gilman, *No Precedent, No Plan*, 167.

48. Gilman, *No Precedent, No Plan*, 180.

49. Here and elsewhere, author interview, Tel Aviv, 25 June 2023.

50. John Thornhill, "Communists Attack Yeltsin and Foreign Investors: Zyuganov Demands President's Resignation over Monetary Policy U-turn," *Financial Times*, 19 Aug. 1998.

51. Andrew Higgins, Betsy McKay and Mark Whitehouse, "Going for Broke: U-turn on Ruble Puts Mother Russia on a Dangerous Road; Currency Drop and Default May Hurt Russians Most and Threaten Stability—'Worst Nightmare' Happens," *The Wall Street Journal*, 18 Aug. 1998.

52. Timothy L. O'Brien, "Russia to Pump Huge Ruble Reserve into Bank," *The New York Times*, 19 Sept. 1998, https://www.nytimes.com/1998/09/19/world/russia-to-pump-huge-ruble-reserve-into-banks.html

53. Timothy L. O'Brien, "Moscow Madness from the Inside: Investment Bank That Rode Boom Now Faces Bust," *The New York Times*, 11 Sept 1998, https://www.nytimes.com/1998/09/11/business/international-business-moscow-madness-inside-investment-bank-that-rode-boom-now.html

54. "Russia: G7 Asked to Lend a Further $10bn," *The Financial News*, 7 Sept. 1998.

55. "Russia: G7 Asked to Lend a Further $10bn."

56. Celestine Bohlen, "As Ruble Crashes, Hangover Hurts a Lot," *The New York Times*, 9 Sept. 1998.

57. Bohlen, "As Ruble Crashes, Hangover Hurts a Lot."

58. Bohlen, "As Ruble Crashes, Hangover Hurts a Lot."

59. "Firms Shed More Staff in Europe to Adjust to Emerging Markets Slump," Dow Jones Online News, 15 Oct. 1998.

60. Timothy L. O'Brien, "Russian Derivatives May Burn Investors," *The New York Times*, 27 Aug. 1998.

61. Steven Mufson and David Hoffman, "Russian Crash Shows Risks of Globalization," *The Washington Post*, 8 Nov. 1998, https://www.washingtonpost.com/archive/politics/1998/11/08/russian-crash-shows-risks-of-globalization/74f16b3b-eba5-459f-a62c-c49bf17d2e8e

62. Mark Whitehouse et al., "Bear Tracks: In a Financial Gamble, Russia Lets Ruble Fall, Stalls Debt Repayment—Other Markets Face Pressure from Move, but so Far Their Reaction Is Modest—Blow to a Weary Citizenry," *The Wall Street Journal*, 18 Aug. 1998.

9. THE VALERIAN DAYS

1. William Reichert.

2. A relatively well-known expat saying that is largely true.

3. An IPO, or initial public offering, is the process that describes how a private company makes shares available for the public to purchase on a stock exchange.

4. Ashley Seager, "Russia Pays Off Its Soviet Era Debts to the West," *The Guardian*, 22 Aug. 2006, https://www.theguardian.com/business/2006/aug/22/russia

5. Frieden, *Global Capitalism*, 492–3.

6. Richard Maslen, "BA Upgrades Moscow Route with 747-400

Introduction," *Aviation Week*, 15 Sept. 2011, https://aviationweek. com/air-transport/airports-networks/ba-upgrades-moscow-route-747-400-introduction

7. Catherine Belton and Peter Thal Larsen, "Lehman Joins Bank Bonanza in Russia," *Financial Times*, 8 Mar. 2007, https://www. ft.com/content/8dff4a92-cdc2-11db-839d-000b5df10621

8. Paul J. Davies, "Russian Loans Prove Flavour of Season," *Financial Times*, 26 Sept. 2005, https://www.ft.com/content/2dddfba0-2ea8-11da-9aed-00000e2511c8

9. Agis Salpukas, "British Airways and Aeroflot Discuss Starting an Airline," *The New York Times*, 13 Oct. 1990, https:// timesmachine.nytimes.com/timesmachine/1990/10/13/131290. html?pageNumber=33; "British Airways, Soviets Talk of 'Air Russia,'" *Los Angeles Times*, 12 Oct. 1990, https://www.latimes.com/archives/ la-xpm-1990-10-12-fi-2416-story.html

10. Ian Cobain and Dan Milmo, "Radioactive Material Found on BA Planes," *The Guardian*, 30 Nov. 2006, https://www.theguardian. com/business/2006/nov/30/theairlineindustry.britishairways1

11. AK Lufthansa, "Yubilei aviakompanii 'Lyuftganza' 30 let poletov v Rossiyu" [Lufthansa's anniversary: Thirty years of flights to Russia], AviaPort, 5 Feb. 2002, https://www.aviaport.ru/news/22381

12. "AA Pulls Moscow Link," *Aviation News*, 23 Sept. 2009, https:// aviationweek.com/air-transport/airports-networks/aa-pulls-moscow-link

13. Emma Haslett, "Delta Airlines Suspends Its Service to Moscow as Dollar Strengthens," *City A.M.*, 15 Apr. 2015, https://www.cityam. com/delta-airlines-suspends-its-service-moscow-dollar-strengthens

14. Gwyn Topham, "EasyJet Launches Cheap Flights from London to Moscow," *The Guardian*, 18 Mar. 2013, https://www.theguardian. com/business/2013/mar/18/easyjet-cheap-flights-london-moscow

15. "Budget Airline EasyJet Cancels London–Moscow Flights," *The Moscow Times*, 13 Sept. 2015, https://www.themoscowtimes. com/2015/09/13/budget-airline-easyjet-cancels-london-moscow-flights-a49509

16. Isabel Gorst, "Russia's Wealthy Turn to Drink," *Financial Times*,

21 Mar. 2012, https://www.ft.com/content/fe2a3cae-1f5e-361a-8f38-176de659261d

17. Clifford G. Gaddy and Barry W. Ickes, "Russia after the Global Financial Crisis," Brookings Institution, 10 May 2010, 286, https://www.brookings.edu/wp-content/uploads/2016/06/05_russia_financial_crisis_gaddy.pdf

18. Alexander Churov, "Bentley v 2019 godu uvelichila prodazhi v Rossii na 9%" [Bentley increased sales in Russia by 9 per cent in 2019], Autostat Analytic Agency, 14 Jan. 2020, https://m.autostat.ru/news/amp/42457

19. Alastair Gee, "Donatella's Jaunt to Russia," *Women's Wear Daily*, 29 Nov. 2007, https://wwd.com/feature/donatella-s-jaunt-to-russia-475175-2052870

20. Jeanne Whalen, "Gucci Unveils City Boutique," *The Moscow Times*, 11 Dec. 1997, https://www.themoscowtimes.com/archive/gucci-unveils-city-boutique

21. "Christian Dior Opens," *The Moscow Times*, 19 Dec. 1998, https://www.themoscowtimes.com/archive/christian-dior-opens

22. Yulia Savelyeva, "Fendi Fashion Takes the Bolshoi," *The Moscow Times*, 6 Nov. 1999, https://www.themoscowtimes.com/archive/fendi-fashion-takes-the-bolshoi

23. Savelyeva, "Fendi Fashion Takes the Bolshoi."

24. Gaddy and Ickes, "Russia after the Global Financial Crisis," 287.

25. "Moscow, the Hottest Market in Banking, Pays Twice as Much as New York," *International Herald Tribune*, 14 May 2007, https://www.nytimes.com/2007/05/14/business/worldbusiness/14iht-russbankers.1.5697946.html

26. "Handbags Fly Off Ralph Lauren Shelves," *The Moscow Times*, 21 May 2007, https://www.themoscowtimes.com/archive/handbags-fly-off-ralph-lauren-shelves

27. "Supreme Luxury Forum 2007," Eventica, https://www.eventica.co.uk/supreme-luxury-forum-2007

28. Catherine Blanchard, "Brooks Brothers Opens in Moscow," *Women's Wear Daily*, 16 Apr. 2013, https://wwd.com/business-news/retail/brooks-brothers-opens-in-moscow-6896447

29. "Gucci to Operate Independently in Russia," *The Moscow Times*, 31

July 2013, https://www.themoscowtimes.com/2013/07/31/gucci-to-operate-independently-in-russia-a26328

30. "M&S Enters Russian Market," *The Grocer*, 9 June 2005, https://www.thegrocer.co.uk/marks-and-spencer/mands-enters-russian-market/102560.article

31. Colin McMahon, "Russians Flock to IKEA as Store Battles Moscow," *Chicago Tribune*, 16 May 2000, https://www.chicagotribune.com/2000/05/16/russians-flock-to-ikea-as-store-battles-moscow

32. Andrew Osborn, "In Fear of His Life: Ikea's Man in Moscow Tells of Threats and Bribes," *The Independent*, 15 Dec. 2004, https://www.independent.co.uk/news/world/europe/in-fear-of-his-life-ikea-s-man-in-moscow-tells-of-threats-and-bribes-688373.html

33. Andrew E. Kramer, "Ikea Fires 2 Officials in Russia Bribe Case," *The New York Times*, 15 Feb. 2010, https://www.nytimes.com/2010/02/16/business/global/16ikea.html

34. Gaddy and Ickes, "Russia after the Global Financial Crisis," 284–5.

35. Gaddy and Ickes, "Russia after the Global Financial Crisis," 286.

36. Pekka Sutela, "Russia's Response to the Global Financial Crisis," Carnegie Endowment for International Peace, Policy Outlook, 3, https://carnegieendowment.org/files/russia_crisis.pdf

37. Andrew E. Kramer, "A $50 Billion Bailout in Russia Favors the Rich and Connected," *The New York Times*, 30 Oct. 2008, https://www.nytimes.com/2008/10/31/business/worldbusiness/31oligarch.html

38. Kramer, "$50 Billion Bailout in Russia Favors the Rich."

39. Andrew E. Kramer, "New Anxiety Grips Russia's Economy," *The New York Times*, 30 Oct. 2008, https://www.nytimes.com/2008/10/31/business/worldbusiness/31ruble.html

40. Kramer, "New Anxiety Grips Russia's Economy."

41. Jason Bush, "The Financial Crisis Deepens in Russia," Bloomberg Businessweek, 4 Dec. 2008, https://www.bloomberg.com/news/articles/2008-12-03/the-financial-crisis-deepens-in-russia

42. Sutela, "Russia's Response," 5.

43. "Global Foreign Direct Investment Flows over the Last 30 Years," UNCTAD, 5 May 2023, https://unctad.org/data-visualization/global-foreign-direct-investment-flows-over-last-30-years

44. Bush, "Financial Crisis Deepens."

45. Rebecca R. Ruiz and Michael Schwirtz, "Russian Insider Says State-Run Doping Fueled Olympic Gold," *The New York Times*, 12 May 2016, https://www.nytimes.com/2016/05/13/sports/russia-doping-sochi-olympics-2014.html

46. Tariq Panja and Kevin Draper, "U.S. Says FIFA Officials Were Bribed to Award World Cups to Russia and Qatar," *The New York Times*, 6 Apr. 2020, https://www.nytimes.com/2020/04/06/sports/soccer/qatar-and-russia-bribery-world-cup-fifa.html

47. Heather Timmons, "From Russia to London, for Stock Listing," *The New York Times*, 20 Jan. 2006, https://www.nytimes.com/2006/01/20/business/worldbusiness/from-russia-to-london-for-stock-listing.html

48. Timmons, "From Russia to London."

49. Here and elsewhere, author interview, London, 14 Nov. 2023.

10. TIME OUT

1. Jonathan Glancey, "Basic Instincts," *The Guardian*, 29 July 2000, https://www.theguardian.com/travel/2000/jul/29/russia.moscow. Copyright Guardian News & Media Ltd 2024. Used with kind permission.

2. "How to Blow Through $40,000 in One Night," ABC News, 15 Apr. 2008, https://abcnews.go.com/Travel/BusinessTravel/story?id=4658291&page=1

3. "Aeroflot History, 1990–1999," Aeroflot, https://www.aeroflot.ru/gb-en/about/aeroflot_today/aeroflot_history/1990_1999

4. "Tol'ko dlya uzkogo kluba," *Kommersant*, 15 Oct. 2007, https://www.kommersant.ru/doc/813912

5. Sophia Kishkovsky, "Letter from Moscow: Where the High Rollers Dine," *The New York Times*, 25 May 2006, https://www.nytimes.com/2006/05/25/travel/25webletter.html

6. John Kenyon, "Hedonistic Hungry Duck Closes Doors," *The Moscow Times*, 20 Mar. 1999, https://www.themoscowtimes.com/archive/hedonistic-hungry-duck-closes-doors

7. James Verini, "Lost Exile: The Unlikely Life and Sudden Death of The Exile, Russia's Angriest Newspaper," *Vanity Fair*, Feb. 2010, https://www.vanityfair.com/culture/2010/02/exile-201002

8. Propaganda announced it was closing permanently in July 2024.

9. "Moscow Has Hot Clubs—but It's a Cold Wait if You're Not on the List," *The New York Times*, 23 Nov. 2007, https://www.nytimes.com/2007/11/22/style/22iht-rsoc.1.8438441.html

10. Mark Cina, "How Much Can a Top-Name Artist Make For Private Shows?," *Billboard*, 3 Mar. 2011, https://www.billboard.com/music/music-news/how-much-can-a-top-name-artist-make-for-private-shows-1179008

11. Anatoly Zhelty, "Svad'ba Veka 2.0," Gazeta.ru, 28 Mar. 2016, https://www.gazeta.ru/social/2016/03/28/8146817.shtml

12. Jessica Mairs, "Zaha Hadid's Only House Finally Completes in Russian Forest," Dezeen, 12 Apr. 2018, https://www.dezeen.com/2018/04/12/zaha-hadid-architecture-vladislav-doronin-capital-hill-residence-moscow-russia

13. "Mean Salary in Rubles and Dollars in Moscow 2000–2022," Goldomania.ru, goldomania.ru/finance/srednyaya_zarplata_moskva.html; "Average Salary in Russia by Year from 1999 to 2024," fincan.ru/articles/49_srednjaja-zarplata-v-rossii-po-godam/

14. Andrew E. Kramer and David M. Herszenhorn, "Boosted by Putin, Russia's Middle Class Turns on Him," *The New York Times*, 11 Dec. 2011, https://www.nytimes.com/2011/12/12/world/europe/huge-moscow-rally-suggests-a-shift-in-public-mood.html; Miriam Elder, "Vladimir Putin's Return to Presidency Preceded by Violent Protests in Moscow," *The Guardian*, 6 May 2012, https://www.theguardian.com/world/2012/may/06/vladimir-putin-presidency-violent-protests-moscow

15. "In Photos: Moscow Metro Inaugurates 'World's Longest' Circle Line," *The Moscow Times*, 2 Mar. 2023, https://www.themoscowtimes.com/2023/03/02/in-photos-moscow-metro-inaugurates-worlds-longest-circle-line-a80376

11. "WHO'S THE BOSS?"

1. Former US government official who requested anonymity, author interview, 9 July 2023.

2. Alexis Rodzianko.

3. Matthew Bodner, "Russia's 8 Most Memorable Davos Moments,"

The Moscow Times, 22 Jan. 2014, https://www.themoscowtimes. com/2014/01/22/russias-8-most-memorable-davos-moments-a31309

4. Matthew Weaver, "Boris Yeltsin's Magic Moments," *The Guardian*, 23 Apr. 2007, https://www.theguardian.com/news/blog/2007/apr/ 23/borisyeltsins

5. Taylor Branch, *The Clinton Tapes: Wrestling History in the White House* (New York: Simon & Schuster, 2009), 198.

6. "Putin Tells German Parliament 'Evil Must Be Punished,' 2001-09-25," Voice of America, 27 Oct. 2009, https://www.voanews.com/a/a-13-a-2001-09-25-32-putin-66398312/548955.html

7. Michael McFaul, "U.S.–Russia Relations after September 11, 2001," Testimony, 24 Oct. 2001, Carnegie Endowment for International Peace, https://carnegieendowment.org/2001/10/24/u.s.-russia-relations-after-september-11-2001-pub-840

8. "Ballot-Stuffing Caught on Camera at Russian Polls," RFE/RL, 19 Mar. 2018, https://www.rferl.org/a/russia-election-violations/ 29109634.html

9. Guy Faulconbridge and Andrew Osborn, "Putin Wins Russia Election in Landslide with No Serious Opposition," Reuters, 18 Mar. 2024, https://www.reuters.com/world/europe/russias-presidential-vote-starts-final-day-with-accusations-kyiv-sabotage-2024-03-17

10. Kristen Ghodsee and Mitchell Orenstein, *Taking Stock of Shock* (Oxford: Oxford University Press, 2021), 56.

11. "How the State Share in Russia's Economy Exceeded 50%: Infographic," RBC.ru, 11 May 2023, https://www.rbc.ru/ economics/11/05/2023/645b94f89a794700cb727aa5

12. Here and elsewhere, author interview, London, 30 Nov. 2023.

13. Gaidar and Aron, "Russian Economy after Yukos."

14. Henderson and Ferguson, *International Partnership in Russia*, 62.

15. Kate Blackwood, "Middle Class Actually Enables Autocrats in post-Soviet Countries," *Cornell Chronicle*, 7 Dec. 2020, https://news. cornell.edu/stories/2020/12/middle-class-actually-enables-autocrats-post-soviet-countries

16. Sabrina Tavernise, "Putin, Exerting His Authority, Meets with Russia's Tycoons," *The New York Times*, 29 July 2000, https://

www.nytimes.com/2000/07/29/world/putin-exerting-his-authority-meets-with-russia-s-tycoons.html

17. Former US government official who requested anonymity, author interview, 9 July 2023.

18. Carl Mortished, "Growing Power of the Oligarchs Defies Putin," *The Times*, 10 Apr. 2004, https://www.thetimes.co.uk/article/growing-power-of-the-oligarchs-defies-putin-39qlc0jd5mk

19. See, in particular, coverage from *Financial Times*, *The Economist* and Richard Sakwa's well-received *Putin and the Oligarch* (London: I.B. Tauris, 2014).

20. Diana Yousef-Martinek, Rafael Minder and Rahim Rabimov, "Yukos Oil: A Corporate Governance Success Story?," Chazen Web Journal of International Business (Fall 2003), Columbia Business School, SSRN: https://ssrn.com/abstract=637741

21. S.V. Stepashin, ed. *Analiz protsessov privatizatsii gosudarstvennoy sobstvennosti v Rossiyskoy Federatsii za period 1993–2003 gody (ekspertno-analiticheskoye meropriyatie)* [Analysis of the processes of state property privatisation in the Russian Federation for the period 1993–2003 (expert-analytical activity)] (Moscow: Olita, 2004), https://www.susu.ru/sites/default/files/dissertation/analiz-processov-privatizatsii.pdf

22. "On the Approval of the List of Strategic Enterprises and Strategic Joint Stock Companies," Presidential Decree no. 1009, 2004, https://ivo.garant.ru/#/document/76803596/paragraph/142617951:0

23. S. Bazylchik, "Suvorinskii elevator ne prodaetsya" [The Surovikin elevator is not being sold], *Kommersant*, 1 Sept. 2004, https://www.kommersant.ru/doc/501924; A. Chervakov, "Mekhanikam stalo ne do kosmosa" [Mechanics aren't interested in space], *Kommersant*, 25 Sept. 2004, https://www.kommersant.ru/doc/508320

24. "Kompanii" [Companies], *Kommersant Company's Secret*, no. 42, 8 Nov. 2004, 1010, https://www.kommersant.ru/doc/860084

25. Konstantin Smirnov, "Investnetmest" [Noplacetoinvest], *Kommersant*, 31 Oct. 2005, https://www.kommersant.ru/doc/622328

26. I. Rybalchenko, "Investory zhdut strategicheskikh zakonov" [Investors are waiting for strategic laws], *Kommersant*, 23 Sept. 2005, https://www.kommersant.ru/doc/611462

27. R. Yambayeva and E. Kiseleva, "Vrag u zavodskykh vorot" [The enemy at the factory gates], *Kommersant*, 9 February 2005, https://www.kommersant.ru/doc/545890

28. "Siemens' Machines Bid Nixed," *The Moscow Times*, 13 Sept. 2007, https://www.themoscowtimes.com/archive/siemens-machines-bid-nixed

29. Federal law of 29 Apr. 2008, N 57-FZ, "On the Procedure for Foreign Investments in Economic Companies of Strategic Importance for Ensuring the Country's Defense and State Security (with Changes and Additions)," GARANT, base.garant.ru/12160212

30. Harry G. Broadman, "U.S. Foreign Investment Policy Gets a Tougher but More Transparent CFIUS," *Forbes*, 4 Jan. 2019, updated 11 Jan. 2021, https://www.forbes.com/sites/harrybroadman/2019/01/04/u-s-foreign-investment-policy-gets-a-tougher-but-more-transparent-cfius/?sh=394ee8d71fe6

31. Document provided to the author.

32. Mikhail Khodorkovsky (@khodorkovsky_en), Twitter/X, 15:24, 8 July 2023, https://twitter.com/khodorkovsky_en/status/ 1677685171 124928513

33. "Global Foreign Direct Investment Flows over the Last 30 Years," UNCTAD, 5 May 2023, https://unctad.org/data-visualization/global-foreign-direct-investment-flows-over-last-30-years

34. "Russia's Most Admired Executives," *Institutional Investor*, 13 Oct. 2004, https://www.institutionalinvestor.com/article/2btgjlni4ewiins7ac9a8/home/russias-most-admired-executives

35. "Russia's Most Admired Executives."

36. Valeriy Kodachigov and Ekaterina Kinyakina, "Apple Pay v Rossii b'et rekordi" [Apple Pay in Russia breaks records], *Vedomosti*, 15 Dec. 2020, https://www.vedomosti.ru/technology/articles/2020/12/14/850949-apple-pay

37. Here and elsewhere, author interview, London–Tampa, 22 Dec. 2023.

38. Peter Hobson, "Why Expats Are Still Fleeing Russia," *The Moscow Times*, 28 Dec. 2015, https://www.themoscowtimes.com/2015/12/28/why-expats-are-still-fleeing-russia-a51334

39. "Global Foreign Direct Investment Flows over the Last 30 Years," UNCTAD, 5 May 2023, https://unctad.org/data-visualization/global-foreign-direct-investment-flows-over-last-30-years

40. Max Seddon, "Baring Vostok Appoints New Leadership Team after Founder's Arrest," *Financial Times*, 18 Feb. 2019, https://www.ft.com/content/b1bc24ae-334b-11e9-bd3a-8b2a211d90d5

41. Max Seddon, "Calvey's Arrest Sends Chill through Russia's Foreign Investors," *Financial Times*, 19 Feb. 2019, https://www.ft.com/content/fc2f021a-32ae-11e9-bd3a-8b2a211d90d5

42. The Editorial Board, "Russia's Investment Image Suffers Yet Another Blow," *Financial Times*, 4 Mar. 2019, https://www.ft.com/content/1e593a18-3c3c-11e9-b72b-2c7f526ca5d0

43. Max Seddon, "Kremlin Says Michael Calvey May Be Released from House Arrest," *Financial Times*, 3 June 2019, https://www.ft.com/content/24afc82c-85e9-11e9-a028-86cea8523dc2

44. Max Seddon, "Calvey Fraud Case Casts Pall over Putin's St Petersburg Summit," *Financial Times*, 6 June 2019, https://www.ft.com/content/a3d01b84-8797-11e9-a028-86cea8523dc2

45. Max Seddon and Henry Foy, "US Investor Michael Calvey's Hopes of Release Fade in Russian Dispute," *Financial Times*, 24 Sept. 2020, https://www.ft.com/content/4f9e0995-26ba-45af-8f29-f426517e9a30

46. "Vostok Investments Acquires Baring Vostok's 28% Stake in Russian Marketplace Ozon," Interfax, 15 Apr. 2024, https://interfax.com/newsroom/top-stories/101364/

47. "Russia Overview," EBRD, n.d., https://www.ebrd.com/where-we-are/russia/overview.html#

48. Roula Khalaf, "GCHQ's Jeremy Fleming: 'Xi Doesn't Want to See Putin Humiliated,'" *Financial Times*, 26 May 2023, https://www.ft.com/content/7979924f-dfa3-4da2-adda-23c1dceda41c

49. Tony Blair, "Tony Blair Doesn't Regret Trying to Bring Putin into the World Order," Times Radio, 15 June 2023, https://www.youtube.com/watch?v=D5pslYUGI78

12. THAT TIME COMPLIANCE WAS SEXY

1. Paul Melling.

2. Philip Nichols.

3. Author interview, Brighton, UK, 30 May 2023.

4. Author interview, London, 19 May 2023.

5. Timothy L. O'Brien with Raymond Bonner, "Banker and Husband Tell of Role in Laundering Case," *The New York Times*, 17 Feb. 2000, https://www.nytimes.com/2000/02/17/world/banker-and-husband-tell-of-role-in-laundering-case.html

6. Raymond Bonner and Timothy L. O'Brien, "Activity at Bank Raises Suspicion of Russian Mob Tie," *The New York Times*, 19 Aug. 1999, https://www.nytimes.com/1999/08/19/world/activity-at-bank-raises-suspicions-of-russia-mob-tie.html; Eric Schmitt, "Bank's Head Admits 'Lapse' in Money Laundering Case," *The New York Times*, 23 Sept. 1999, https://www.nytimes.com/1999/09/23/world/bank-s-head-admits-lapse-in-money-laundering-case.html

7. O'Brien with Bonner, "Banker and Husband Tell of Role in Laundering Case."

8. Timothy L. O'Brien, "Bank Settles U.S. Inquiry into Money Laundering," *The New York Times*, 9 Nov. 2005, https://www.nytimes.com/2005/11/09/business/bank-settles-us-inquiry-into-money-laundering.html

9. "Foreign Corrupt Practices Clearinghouse: A Collaboration with Sullivan & Cromwell LLP," Stanford Law School, n.d., https://fcpa.stanford.edu/statistics-analytics.html

10. "Report Finds Just Two of World's 47 Biggest Exporters Actively Enforce against Cross-Border Bribery," Transparency International UK, 11 October 2022, https://www.transparency.org.uk/uk-foreign-bribery-enforcement-exporting-corruption

11. "Convention on Combating Bribery of Foreign Public Officials in International Business Transactions," OECD, 21 Nov. 1997, https://www.oecd.org/corruption/oecdantibriberyconvention.htm

12. "Russia: Trade Flows Value between Russia and the European Union (EU) from 2007–2021," n.d., Statista, https://www.statista.com/statistics/1099626/russia-value-of-trade-in-goods-with-eu; "Trade in Goods with Russia," United States Census Bureau, n.d., https://www.census.gov/foreign-trade/balance/c4621.html; "Statistika vneshnogo sektora | Bank Rossii" [Foreign sector statistics | The Bank of Russia], Cbr.ru, n.d., http://cbr.ru/statistics/macro_itm/svs

13. William Finnegan, "The Secret Keeper: Jules Kroll and the World of Corporate Intelligence," *The New Yorker*, 12 Oct. 2009, https://www.newyorker.com/magazine/2009/10/19/the-secret-keeper

14. Louise Armitstead, "Watching the Kroll Detectives in Russia," *The Times*, 4 June 2006, https://www.thetimes.com/article/watching-the-kroll-detectives-in-russia-6x6vc2hfnnh

15. Author interview, London, 18 July 2023.

16. Daniel Ben-Ami, "Crusade against the Kremlin," *Financial Times*, 20 Sept. 2013, https://www.ft.com/content/b39168d8-2024-11e3-9a9a-00144feab7de

17. Stephen Schurr and Neil Buckley, "A Breed Apart with Influential Allies," *Financial Times*, 27 Apr. 2006, https://www.ft.com/content/e48aee24-d620-11da-8b3a-0000779e2340

18. Neil Buckley and Catherine Belton, "Hermitage in Russian Fraud Claim," *Financial Times*, 3 Apr. 2008, https://www.ft.com/content/da0bbffe-01b7-11dd-a323-000077b07658

19. Ben-Ami, "Crusade against the Kremlin."

20. Natasha Bertrand, "Putin's Big Tell?," *The Atlantic*, 18 July 2018, https://www.theatlantic.com/politics/archive/2018/07/putins-big-tell/565460

13. YOU CAN'T GO HOME AGAIN

1. Here and elsewhere, Seva Gunitsky, author interview, London–Toronto, 21 June 2023.

2. Bernie Sucher.

3. This phrase was often used to express regret at the fall of the Soviet Union. In this case, Gunitsky is talking about Russia.

4. Alexei Evgenev.

5. Here and elsewhere, author interview, Cambridge, MA, 30 Oct. 2023.

6. Anastasia Stognei and Max Seddon, "The Surprising Resilience of the Russian Economy," *Financial Times*, 2 Feb. 2024, https://www.ft.com/content/d304a182-997d-4dae-98a1-aa7c691526db

7. Mariko Oi, "Yandex: Owner of 'Russia's Google' Pulls Out of Home Country," BBC News, 6 Feb. 2024, https://www.bbc.co.uk/news/business-68213191#

8. "Yandex Founder Slams Russia's 'Barbaric' War in Ukraine," BBC News, 10 Aug. 2023, https://www.bbc.co.uk/news/world-europe-66341619

9. "Antivoenniye zayavleniya mogut stoit' Arkadiyu Volozhu pochti 180 mln" [Anti-war pronouncements could cost Arkady Volozh 180 mln], *The Moscow Times*, Russian Service, 6 Oct. 2023, https://www.moscowtimes.ru/2023/10/06/antivoennie-zayavleniya-mogut-stoit-arkadiyu-volozhu-pochti-180mln-a109114

10. Henry Foy and Max Seddon, "Russian Billionaire Pleads for EU Sanctions Relief after Decrying War," *Financial Times*, 27 Aug. 2023, https://www.ft.com/content/24c47ec1-dc7f-48a9-960e-7ad89cda8e1a

11. "Renault Sells Russia's Avtovaz Stake, but Leaves Room for Return," Reuters, 16 May 2022, https://www.reuters.com/markets/deals/renault-sells-its-stake-russias-avtovaz-option-buy-it-back-2022-05-16

12. "Vlasti razreshili rossiiskim kompaniyam vypuskat' piratskuyu versiyu populyarnogo preparata dlya pokhudeniya" [The authorities have allowed Russian companies to produce a pirated version of a popular weight-loss drug], *The Moscow Times*, Russian Service, 29 Dec. 2023, https://www.moscowtimes.ru/2023/12/29/vlasti-razreshili-rossiiskim-kompaniyam-vipuskat-piratskuyu-versiyu-populyarnogo-preparata-dlya-pohudeniya-a117505

13. Fleur Britten, "Vogue Russia Closes as Condé Nast Stops Publishing after 'Rise in Censorship,'" *The Guardian*, 20 Apr. 2022, https://www.theguardian.com/fashion/2022/apr/20/vogue-russia-closes-as-conde-nast-stops-publishing-after-rise-in-censorship

14. Maximilian, "Michaela Start Covers Vogue Russia March 2022 by Lea Colombo," Fashionotography, 25 Mar. 2022, https://www.fashionotography.com/michaela-stark-vogue-russia-march-2022

15. "The Bell Weekly: How Coca-Cola Quit Russia, but Stayed on the Country's Shelves," The Bell, 18 July 2023, https://en.thebell.io/the-bell-weekly-9

16. "Krupneishii nemetskii postavshchik tekhniki zakryvaet biznes v Rossii" [Germany's largest technology supplier is closing its business in Russia], *The Moscow Times*, Russian Service, 12 Feb. 2024,

https://www.moscowtimes.ru/2024/02/12/krupneishii-nemetskii-postavshchik-tehniki-zakrivaet-biznes-v-rossii-a121357

17. Tatyana Dyatel, "Turbina dvinulas' po naznachiyu" [The turbine is headed for its destination], *Kommersant*, 18 Aug. 2022, https://www.kommersant.ru/doc/5468944

18. Melissa Eddy and Victoria Kim, "Leaks in Undersea Gas Pipelines from Russia to Germany after Blasts Raise Suspicions of Sabotage," *The New York Times*, 27 Sept. 2022, https://www.nytimes.com/2022/09/27/world/europe/germany-nord-stream-pipelines-leak.html

19. "GE Suspends Its Operations in Russia," Reuters, 8 Mar. 2022, https://www.reuters.com/business/ge-suspends-its-operations-russia-2022-03-08

20. Paul Sonne and Rebecca Ruiz, "How Putin Turned a Western Boycott into a Bonanza," *The New York Times*, 17 Dec. 2023, https://www.nytimes.com/interactive/2023/12/17/world/putin-companies-economy-boycott-elites-benefit-ukraine-war.html

21. "German Eastern Business Lobby Defends Continued Activities in Russia," Reuters, 22 Mar. 2022, https://www.reuters.com/business/german-eastern-business-lobby-defends-continued-activities-russia-2022-03-22

22. Laurenz Gehrke, "Head of Germany's Russophile Business Lobby Group Resigns," Politico, 4 May 2022, https://www.politico.eu/article/head-germany-russophile-business-lobby-group-resign-oliver-hermes

23. Max Seddon and Henry Foy, "Russia Offers to Swap Frozen Assets with the West," *Financial Times*, 23 Aug. 2023, https://www.ft.com/content/a5598c9d-99f5-45c3-98eb-2f797f2cc85b

24. Katherin Machalek, "Factsheet: Russia's NGO Laws," Freedom House, https://freedomhouse.org/sites/default/files/Fact%20Sheet_0.pdf

25. "Russia: New Restrictions for 'Foreign Agents,'" Human Rights Watch, 1 Dec. 2022, https://www.hrw.org/news/2022/12/01/russia-new-restrictions-foreign-agents

26. Eric Crabtree, author interview, London, 11 Sept. 2023.

27. "The EBRD on Ukraine and Leaving Russia," The Banker, 25 Apr. 2023, https://www.thebanker.com/The-EBRD-on-Ukraine-and-leaving-Russia-1682380800

28. Matthew Luxmoore, "The Kursk Catastrophe, a Lesson for Putin, Is Fading from Russia's Attention 20 Years Later," RFE/RL, 11 Aug. 2020, https://www.rferl.org/a/the-kursk-catastrophe-a-lesson-for-putin-is-fading-from-russian-attention-20-years-later/30778500.html

29. Daniel Fried and Kurt Volker, "The Speech in Which Putin Told Us Who He Was," Politico, 18 Feb. 2022, https://www.politico.com/news/magazine/2022/02/18/putin-speech-wake-up-call-post-cold-war-order-liberal-2007-00009918

30. Andrew E. Kramer, "Putin's Criticism Puts a $6 Billion Hole in a Company," *The New York Times*, 26 July 2008, https://www.nytimes.com/2008/07/26/business/26steel.html

14. NOW WHAT?

1. Rawi Abdelal.

2. Seva Gunitsky.

3. Sam Fleming, "Geopolitical Risks Overshadow Economic Optimism in Davos," *Financial Times*, 17 Jan. 2024, https://www.ft.com/content/d6efc1f0-a1fc-42fb-b9b6-22728b3b6fe5

4. Fleming, "Geopolitical Risks Overshadow Economic Optimism."

5. Jonathan Derbyshire, "Year in a Word: Polycrisis," *Financial Times*, 1 Jan. 2023, https://www.ft.com/content/f6c4f63c-aa71-46f0-a0a7-c2a4c4a3c0f1

6. Patricia Cohen, "Why It Seems Everything We Knew about the Global Economy Is No Longer True," *The New York Times*, 18 June 2023, https://www.nytimes.com/2023/06/18/business/economy/global-economy-us-china.html

7. Michael Ignatieff, "Doubling Down on Democracy," *The Atlantic*, 15 Oct. 2014, https://www.theatlantic.com/magazine/archive/2014/10/doubling-down-on-democracy/379340

8. Seva Gunitsky.

9. Patricia Cohen, "The Ukraine War Changed This Company Forever," *The New York Times*, 5 July 2023, https://www.nytimes.com/2023/07/05/business/economy/nokian-tyres-finland-romania.html. Moisio in March 2024 announced his intent to retire from Nokian.

10. Anastasia Stognei, "Thousands of Russian Officials to Give Up iPhones over US Spying Fears," *Financial Times*, 16 July 2023, https://www.ft.com/content/6567e7f2-c5fb-4da4-bd95-bf7ceef54038

11. "Coca-Cola, Starbucks File to Extend Trademarks in Russia, Newspaper Reports," Reuters, citing *Vedomosti*, 14 June 2024, https://www.reuters.com/business/retail-consumer/coca-cola-starbucks-file-extend-trademarks-russia-newspaper-reports-2024-06-14

INDEX

INDEX